T0295711

Leveraged

Leveraged

The New Economics of Debt
and Financial Fragility

EDITED BY
MORITZ SCHULARICK

The University of Chicago Press
Chicago and London

The University of Chicago Press, Chicago 60637
The University of Chicago Press, Ltd., London
© 2022 by The University of Chicago
All rights reserved. No part of this book may be used or reproduced in any manner
whatsoever without written permission, except in the case of brief quotations in critical
articles and reviews. For more information, contact the University of Chicago Press,
1427 E. 60th St., Chicago, IL 60637.
Published 2022
Printed in the United States of America

31 30 29 28 27 26 25 24 23 22   1 2 3 4 5

ISBN-13: 978-0-226-81693-7 (cloth)
ISBN-13: 978-0-226-81694-4 (e-book)
DOI: https://doi.org/10.7208/chicago/9780226816944.001.0001

Library of Congress Cataloging-in-Publication Data

Names: Schularick, Moritz, 1975– editor.
Title: Leveraged : the new economics of debt and financial fragility /
    edited by Moritz Schularick.
Other titles: New economics of debt and financial fragility
Description: Chicago ; London : The University of Chicago Press, 2022. |
    Includes bibliographical references and index.
Identifiers: LCCN 2022012491 | ISBN 9780226816937 (cloth) |
    ISBN 9780226816944 (ebook)
Subjects: LCSH: Finance. | Capital market. | Debt. | Risk. | Financial crises. |
    BISAC: BUSINESS & ECONOMICS / Economics / Macroeconomics |
    BUSINESS & ECONOMICS / Economic Conditions
Classification: LCC HG173 .L4835 2022 | DDC 332—dc23/eng/20220511
LC record available at https://lccn.loc.gov/2022012491

♾ This paper meets the requirements of ANSI/NISO Z39.48-1992 (Permanence of Paper).

Contents

Foreword

In June 2019, the Private Debt Initiative of the Institute for New Economic Thinking (INET) convened an extraordinary group of economists for a conference on expanding the boundaries of economic thinking on credit cycles, private sector debt, and financial stability. Since they were from among a new generation of economists whose thinking was shaped strongly by the 2008 financial crisis, the conference was titled, appropriately, "NextGen."

This book presents the new economic thinking discussed at this groundbreaking conference. It offers a synthesis of the new ideas that have emerged over the past decade along with an examination of questions that have yet to be addressed. I hope you will find the work presented on these pages as challenging and rewarding as those of us in attendance at the conference did.

Private debt and credit cycles have not received their due in economic scholarship, which helps explain why mainstream economists missed the mountainous ascent of U.S. debt that led to the 2008 crisis. Though public debt has drawn much more academic attention than private debt, there is far more private debt than government debt across the world, and it is more directly linked to economic outcomes and financial crises. In 2020, the fragility of an economy with high private debts became apparent again. Only extraordinary policy intervention could stabilize an ever more fragile macroeconomy.

INET's private debt team led by Matthew Sware was instrumental for the success of the conference. Thanks also go to Chad Zimmerman and Christine Schwab at the University of Chicago Press for their guidance, and to Zach Gajewski for help with editing. Special thanks go to Rob Johnson and INET, an organization founded in the wake of the 2008 financial crisis in large part because of mainstream economists' failure to anticipate that crisis. INET stands out in its commitment to developing and sharing the ideas that can repair our broken economy and create a more equal, prosperous, and just society.

Richard Vague, INET board member
May 2022

The New Economics of Debt and Financial Fragility

MORITZ SCHULARICK

Nobel Prize–winning economist James Tobin once called debt "the Achilles heel of capitalism." Though written in the late eighties, it was a prescient statement that has continued to resonate. When the COVID-19 pandemic struck in 2020, global debt stood at record highs. In advanced economies, households and companies were so deep in debt, levels were roughly equal in value to three years of economic output. Companies around the world had used a decade of low interest rates after the 2008 crisis to leverage up and boost their returns on equity. In the pandemic, these debts turned into a massive risk, threatening not only the survival of businesses but also the integrity of the financial system.

In an effort to stem the further spread of the COVID-19 virus, mass shutdowns began, spooking financial markets. Concerns over how many of these debts would be repaid, which companies would be able to withstand this new crisis, and how big the damage would be for lenders, especially banks, quickly came into focus. Within a week in March 2020, equity markets lost one third of their value, the prices of corporate bonds fell dramatically, bank share prices collapsed, and even the market for U.S. government debt—usually one of the most liquid financial markets in the world—froze.

The policy response followed a now well-known playbook, the same used during the Great Recession. Talk of "bailouts" was back in the news. Policy makers rushed to contain the financial fallout with emergency lending, asset purchases, and liquidity injections. Central banks' balance sheets provided the backstop for the financial system and were expanded at unprecedented speed.

Moritz Schularick is professor of economics at Sciences Po and the University of Bonn, and a fellow at the Institute for New Economic Thinking.

Some of the lessons of the last crisis were learned. With the banking sector having more capital than it had in 2008, it was able to withstand the first shock caused by the pandemic. Yet without the actions taken by governments, another financial crisis was a real possibility.

And herein lies the problem. Clearly, 2008 and 2020 represent different types of crisis. The first came from a credit-fueled bubble in the housing market, the second was triggered by a virus. But both exposed the fragility of a system built on high leverage and debt. Though the 2008 crisis taught us a lot about banks, the Great Recession should have been a wake-up call to how fragile the entire financial system has become, due, in a large part, to our leveraged existence. The more leveraged we are, the harder it becomes to withstand repeated shocks to the economy. As these shocks continue to occur—no matter where they come from—their effects could become increasingly worse unless we take the time now to concentrate on the issues that have made our system vulnerable in the first place. Instead of maintaining a shoddy roof guaranteed to spring a new leak even though an old hole is patched, it is time to go beyond short-term fixes and consider building a stronger, more resilient roof.

With higher leverage, it has become ever more difficult to stabilize the economy. The legacy of the COVID-19 recession will be even more debt, and the overhang could cloud the economic outlook for years to come. In the future, the economy will be even more fragile. Echoing the proverbial hair of the dog that bit us, we are drinking to get over the hangover, but the more booze we glug down, the more severe our long-term drinking problem becomes.

When financial liberalization started in the late 1970s and early 1980s, on both sides of the Atlantic, this outcome was not what the cheerleaders of free financial markets then envisaged. On the contrary, freeing up and deregulating the financial sector came with the promise of more opportunity, higher growth, and better risk-sharing through more complete markets. Put simply, the prevailing school of thought said that bigger was better—and it looks like it was wrong.

Deeper and larger financial markets have not made our economies safer or more stable. Instead, we have seen growing financial fragility. The past forty years have witnessed a dramatic rise in the frequency of financial crises and more correlated risk-taking, with increasing economic and political damage. Policy interventions by governments and central banks have grown bolder and more frequent as well; central banks' balance sheets are already bigger than annual GDP in many countries. The invisible hand of the market has needed an outsized helping hand to assist it.

Whether the promise of higher growth has been fulfilled remains an open question; it is difficult to know what would have happened otherwise. But on first inspection, growth has slowed down—not accelerated—in the United States and elsewhere since the 1980s. What we know for sure is that with financial sectors and outstanding debt many times larger than the real economy, we now live in an age of latent financial fragility, kept together by government backstops that have come to play a crucial role in stabilizing an inherently fragile credit system. Paraphrasing the words of Hyman Minsky, we have gotten used to stabilizing an ever more unstable economy.

An Unstable, Fragile System

Today, we must consider if, at the heart of our economies, there stands a sector that has grown tremendously in size but whose benefits are hard to pin down and whose workings are hard to explain with standard economic models. If so—how big would we want such a sector to be and how many safeguards would we want to put in place? How many bets on the future do we want this sector to make?

This book brings together a new generation of economists, from different fields of the discipline, to address these questions. Among them are scholars working in the areas of macroeconomics, banking and finance, asset pricing, and financial history. What unites them is that the financial instability experienced in 2008 was a watershed event for their economic thinking that has only been reinforced by the pandemic. Their academic careers began around the time of the financial crash and the crisis shaped their research agendas for the following decade. For them, as for many others, the crisis demonstrated the shortcomings of mainstream economics' treatment of financial markets, credit cycles, and asset prices. Fresh economic thinking was clearly needed.

Questioning established wisdom in economics curricula, the researchers in this volume have made groundbreaking contributions to the discipline and are now working at the world's leading academic institutions. They form the core of a renaissance of thinkers shaping research agendas. Their work may well become the new canon. The Institute for New Economic Thinking's Private Debt Initiative brought them together to take stock of what we have learned about the causes and costs of financial fragility and how we can apply this knowledge to today's circumstances, and to those in the future.

These new voices come with a new message that, though nuanced and varied, forms the intellectual core of this book: financial instability is endemic to modern economies, and the origins of this instability reach deeper than the dry, technical debates about banking regulation, countercyclical capital buffers, or living wills for financial institutions.

They argue that the growth of debt has to do with structural processes, such as shifts in the income distribution, that can bring about changes in the supply of credit, triggering waves of lending and borrowing. Such credit booms are often linked to asset price booms—with stock and house prices going through the roof—and waves of optimism that influence the expectations of bankers and households alike. Overoptimism, neglected crash risks, and "bad beliefs" about risk and returns more generally have all emerged as important explanations of recurring credit booms that can pose grave financial stability risks.

This argument marks a clear break with past economic orthodoxy. Until recently, most economists agreed that high debt may increase vulnerability to bad events. For example, financial stability reports produced by central banks are typically full of discussions of potential vulnerabilities to changes in interest rates, inflation, or economic growth. But economists have hardly discussed financial markets themselves as the *source* of instability. Today, we are not so sure anymore about the inherent stability of financial markets. New economic thinking suggests that the financial sector itself could, in fact, be the source of instability, a result of overoptimism and neglected tail risks in good times and possibly overly bearish expectations in bad times. New approaches assembled in this book aim to understand precisely the risks stemming from animal spirits governing risk-taking in financial markets.

Many contributions put the repeating patterns of financial boom and bust, originating in excessive private borrowing, at the heart of crisis dynamics: Why do credit booms happen if they predictably increase the risk of financial crises? Why do markets, time and again, convince themselves that "this time is different"—as Carmen Reinhart and Kenneth Rogoff (2009) put it—and repeat the same old mistakes? Why are boom and bust phases in lending and risk appetite so frequent and often hard—and sometimes even impossible—to square with basic financial logic? Arguably, no other subfield in the discipline of economics is so full of puzzles and phenomena that are often difficult to explain from the point of view of rational human behavior.

At the same time, the authors here embrace a much more refined view of the benefits of financial liberalization and the blessings of "more finance" a.k.a. "financial deepening." They dispense with the certainty of simple assumptions and instead point to repeated boom and bust patterns that often seem to cause substantial damage to the economy. This new economic thinking is empirically oriented, open to insights from economic history and behavioral economics.

The original insights about the deeper causes of financial instability assembled in this book have important implications for economic policy. Without a better understanding of the true drivers of financial instability, the reforms introduced during the previous crises may never make the next crisis any less likely. As long as we do not understand the deeper causes, our current financial system is not much safer than it was in the early 2000s, and policy makers will continue to fly blind. Without taking new thinking into account, other important lessons of 2008 will remain unlearned.

Where We've Been and Where We're Going

The structure of the book is meant to encourage debate and critique. Contributions are followed by responses from other scholars of equal reputation and standing. These responses may make important additional points that support the arguments laid out in the main contribution. Yet sometimes they may also underscore open issues, put the finger on a missing link in the argument, or highlight evidence pointing in other directions.

This book intentionally preserves the spirit of critical comment and plurality of opinion that has slowly permeated economics in the last decade. Above all, every contributor shares a vision of economics that is question-driven, not method-driven, allowing for a fruitful conversation arising from different angles and perspectives on important questions.

The topics discussed here are broken up into four thematic parts, covering the dramatic increase of financialization and its real economic effects, the actors behind excessive risk-taking, the mispricing of risks, and the origins and consequences of past financial crises. To better understand the scope of the work and the issues the authors tackle, both individually and collectively, let's take a closer look at each theme.

The Rise of Finance

Until the 2008 crisis, most macroeconomists believed the financial position of a household could be sufficiently described by a single number: net wealth. It did not matter whether a household had, say, $100,000 in cash versus assets of $1.1 million and debt of $1 million. As the net wealth number was the same, both were assumed to be identical for all practical purposes. Today, there is a consensus among financial economists that balance-sheet positions and leverage make a big difference for real economic outcomes, particularly if asset prices, such as house values, fluctuate excessively. We now understand the aggregate demand effects of changes in borrowing constraints (Eggertsson and Krugman 2012; Mian and Sufi 2011, 2014a) and the importance of debt overhang for slow recoveries from financial crises (Jordà, Schularick, and Taylor 2013).

Before the 2008 crisis, if economists worried about debt, they mistakenly worried about public debt, not private debt. Spain's public debt, for example, reached 35% of GDP in 2007, and the budget was solidly in surplus. The situation looked even better in Ireland. Two years later, both countries' financial systems had imploded, their unemployment was up sharply, and Madrid and Dublin were forced to seek bailouts from the EU. There was next to nothing in key indicators of public debt that hinted at the imminent catastrophe. Private sector borrowing, however, would have sounded the alarm—it was the epicenter of the crisis, and private credit growth, real estate lending in particular, would have given the correct early warning signal. Throughout history, financial stability risks in advanced economies have almost exclusively come from private sector debt growth, not from the public sector (Jordà, Schularick, and Taylor 2016b). Public debt increases after a crisis, not before one, as governments step in to stabilize a weak postcrisis economy (Reinhart and Rogoff 2009; Laeven and Valencia 2012; Schularick 2012).

Since much of precrisis macroeconomics had put theory ahead of empirical data, the discipline missed the extraordinary buildup of private debt in the second half of the twentieth century. It was not until long-run data were finally compiled that the extent to which private debt had grown faster than incomes in industrial countries became clear. The break with the past has been particularly evident since the 1970s, when private debt began to skyrocket. Today, the indebtedness of households in the United States and elsewhere is a much-debated phenomenon. The numbers are eye-catching—between 1950 and the 2008 financial crisis, American household debt has grown fourfold relative to income. In 2010, the household debt-to-income ratio peaked at 120%, up from 30% on the eve of World War II.

From an accounting perspective, the sharp increase of credit-to-GDP ratios in advanced economies in the twentieth century has been first and foremost a result of the rapid growth of loans secured on real estate, that is, mortgage and hypothecary lending. The share of mortgage loans in banks' total lending portfolios has roughly doubled over the course of the past century, from about 30% in 1900 to about 60% today. To a large extent, the core business model of banks in advanced economies now resembles a real estate fund: banks are borrowing short-term from the public in the form of deposits and in capital markets to invest into long-term assets linked to real estate, placing the majority of their eggs into one basket. This "Great Mortgaging" has been driven by the rapid growth of mortgage lending to households. The intermediation of household savings for productive investment in the business sector—the standard textbook role of the financial sector—constitutes only a minor share of the business of banking today, even though it was a central part of that business in the nineteenth and early twentieth centuries.

The deeper drivers of the process of increasing private debt remain much debated. Rising income inequality is frequently invoked as a significant factor. Raghuram Rajan's influential book *Fault Lines* (2010) popularized the view that growing income inequality and indebtedness were two sides of the same coin. The idea is that households with stagnant incomes increasingly relied on debt to finance consumption, be it out of sheer necessity to "get by" or to "keep up with the Joneses," whose incomes were growing nicely.

This link between rising inequality and household borrowing features prominently in post-2008 research. In their important work, Mian and Sufi (2009) demonstrated that household borrowing in low-income regions of the United States increased strongly before the 2008 crisis, followed by substantial employment losses during the Great Recession. Kumhof, Rancière, and Winant (2015) have exposed the connection between inequality, debt accumulation, and financial instability. Economic historians have also shown that both major financial and economic crises in the twentieth and twenty-first centuries—the Great Depression and the Great Recession—were preceded by a sharp rise of income inequality and growing household indebtedness. Krippner (2012) has linked the debt buildup to growing socioeconomic pressures. In a similar spirit, historian Hyman (2012) tied the growth of household debt in America to widening income disparities.

A recent paper by Mian, Straub, and Sufi (2020) lays out a potential mechanism that ties inequality and increasing debt together. They argue that rising income concentration at the top brought about a "savings glut of the rich" that supplied the funds for increased borrowing by nonrich households. For every borrower, there must be a lender, and wealthy Americans provided the savings for the borrowing of the less fortunate. In his intervention in this book, Atif Mian discusses, in greater detail, the link between rising income and wealth inequality, excessive borrowing, and financial instability. He argues that the credit supply shock from the "savings glut of the rich" has predominantly financed the demand-side of the real economy. This increasing reliance on "credit as demand" raises serious policy and equity questions he exposes and examines. In her response, Karen Dynan concurs, but she is somewhat less concerned with the immediate risks for the U.S. economy, as recent credit growth largely came from the corporate and government sector.

In his intervention, Emil Verner addresses the question whether credit booms are beneficial for the real economy. A large literature in the 1990s supported the view that financial deepening—making markets larger and more complete—was unequivocally beneficial for economic development. This view now looks somewhat naive. Verner argues that credit supply expansions can finance either an expansion in demand *or* an increase in the economy's productive capacity. Key patterns in the data indicate that private debt booms often boost demand instead of productive capacity. His conclusion is that debt booms and developmental credit deepening should be seen as "fundamentally different phenomena that operate through different channels." In his response, Holger Mueller highlights that the policy implications of these findings might well be more complex. For example, how would economies evolve in the absence of credit booms? Mueller believes it is possible that a world without such periodic bursts of excessive risk-taking might still develop more slowly and exhibit lower rates of growth.

Excessive Risk-Taking

Evidence shows that crises and severe economic downturns can be predicted by buoyant conditions in credit markets, measured either by increases in the quantity of credit (Schularick and Taylor 2012, Mian et al. 2017) or by low expected returns on credit assets (Krishnamurty and Muir 2019). But why do economic agents borrow and lend so much if it predictably leads to a financially fragile economy? What explains the excessive risk-taking observed before crises? The interventions in the second part of the book present the important inroads that have been made in the past decade in answering these questions and in understanding the deeper causes of recurring excessive risk-taking.

The central debate here concerns the role of incentives and institutions versus beliefs as the driver of excessive risk-taking. Incentives are often referred to as financial actors having "skin in the game." In this line of thinking, low levels of equity play a central role in generating credit booms. Bankers have an incentive to take excessive risks because the payouts from their bets are asymmetrical. Heads they win, tails someone else loses. Financial regulation post-2008 has emphasized this incentive aspect, but various authors in this book make a strong case that misguided incentives might have less to do with excessive risk-taking than is commonly held. The true reasons for risk-taking could lie elsewhere, hence the risks for financial stability. Regulators, in other words, might be barking up the wrong tree.

In his intervention, Rüdiger Fahlenbrach looks at the incentives of bank CEOs before the 2008 crisis, studying a classic question in risk-taking literature: Are bank CEOs to blame for the recurrent bouts of excessive risk-taking we face in modern economies? He does not find much support for the idea that bad financial incentives have been a first-order contributing factor to excessive bank risk-taking. Instead, the evidence suggests that most bank executives believed that the risks they took were good for shareholders. Bank CEOs often lost substantial amounts of money when their stock packages became worthless, and in light of the considerable sums involved—sometimes hundreds of millions of dollars—it is difficult to argue that a lack of skin in the game explains why these CEOs pushed their banks to take risks that led to bankruptcy. Fahlenbrach concludes that all actors—households, banks, rating agencies, investors, and policy makers alike—failed to see the risks and believed in the upside potential of the U.S. housing market. By implication, regulating incentive structures alone might do little to mitigate socially excessive risk-taking.

In his response, Samuel Hanson agrees in principle, but he adds qualifications with regard to the interdependence of "bad beliefs" and "bad incentives" as explanations for excessive risk-taking during credit booms. Overoptimistic beliefs may well lead to problematic incentive structures on the bank level that aggravate the effects. On the other hand, monetary incentives may induce people to find ways to rationalize economic phenomena or "dance as long as the music is playing," although they are aware of the risks.

Stefania Albanesi provides an important new perspective on the 2008 crisis itself. Based on meticulous data work, she demonstrates that real estate investors—borrowers with two or more first mortgages—played a prominent role in the 2007–2009 crisis, accounting for close to 50% of foreclosures at some point. This narrative is very different from the one prominent in the media, as Fernando Ferreira points out in his response. In fact, poor and minority "subprime borrowers" did not play a central role in the housing crisis and subsequent Great Recession. In terms of credit volumes, the 2008 crisis was mostly a middle-class affair. The narrative that places the blame on "subprime borrowers" has its origin in media coverage that, early on in the events, singled out certain parts of the population.

While many authors agree that incentives play a role for excessive risk-taking in credit booms, they are not the only factor. Imagine a market where actors have the right incentives because everyone is playing with their own money and has maximum skin in the game. Should we expect this market to be stable, and therefore avoid bubbles, excessive volatility, and spectacular crashes? A good part of the literature on incentive-driven financial stability would likely answer "yes." As soon as people are not playing with others' money, we would think the many puzzling phenomena we observe in credit markets would disappear. But if we look at a real-world market that fulfills these criteria of substantial incentives and low leverage—the equity market—we still encounter bubbles, manias, and crashes. Incentives, in short, are not the whole story.

In their intervention, Òscar Jordà et al. look at the risk-taking and incentives issue from a macroeconomic angle, ultimately coming to very similar conclusions. The authors ask if higher capital ratios—more bankers' skin in the game—make financial systems safer. To address this question, they study financial crises in seventeen countries since 1870 and ask if changes in capital ratios are associated with risks of financial instability. The answer is resoundingly negative. They point out, however, that while capital apparently does very little to restrain endogenous risk-taking in financial markets, it helps absorb exogenous shocks and provides for speedier recoveries from crises. Anna Kovner's thoughtful response stresses it will always be problematic to disprove microeconomic theories with macroeconomic time series; it is possible that changes in capital on an aggregate level do not reduce tail risk in aggregate, but higher bank capital may still lead to lower risk at individual banks and make the system more resilient to shocks.

Mispricing Risks

If "bad" incentives are only half the story, and "bad" beliefs the other half, what exactly do we know about the repeated mistakes that economic agents make, and how frequent they are? To what extent do "bad beliefs" permeate financial markets and lead to boom-bust cycles? In their intervention, Alessia di Stefani and Kaspar Zimmermann review the evidence for misguided beliefs and assumptions—particularly related to borrowers' and lenders' overoptimism—as the driver of credit booms. Using survey data and bank balance-sheet information, they document how expectations of different economic agents can be systematically biased and how this bias often takes the form of extrapolating past fundamentals, consistently leading to similar results as those of the past. A consequence is that sentiment indicators are reliable predictors of reversals—so when sentiment is irrationally exuberant, we can be assured disappointment is lurking around the corner. Di Stefani and Zimmermann conclude that waves of optimism and neglect of crash-risk play an important role for credit booms and crisis dynamics.

Yueran Ma provides an informed and comprehensive discussion of the recent literature on the nexus of deviations from perfectly rational forecasts and credit cycles. She identifies a common theme in the data: economic agents overextrapolate recent events. When things are good, people expect them to get even better; in bad times, there is no light at the end of the tunnel and economic agents remain too cautious for too long. Put differently, when good things happen, they feed extrapolation and overoptimism and, if connected to the credit system, can lead to excessive credit growth. When the overoptimistic expectations disappoint and don't pan out as hoped, excessive lending eventually turns into losses, the moment of truth comes, and financial panic sets in.

It is important to note that these recent advances in the understanding of behavioral credit cycles are reminiscent of older approaches associated with Hyman Minsky and Charles Kindleberger, but the new implications for economic policy today are profound. If periodic mispricings of risk caused by expectational errors is an inherent feature of unfettered financial markets, then market discipline—an underlying principle of financial regulation—has to be reconsidered. It's possible that when market discipline is needed most— that is, in times of financial exuberance and excessive risk-taking—this discipline fails systematically.

In her contribution, Juliane Begenau proposes to advance beyond slow-moving balance-sheet indicators and measure banks' risk exposure in real time. To do this, she invites us to think of a bank's balance sheet as a portfolio of bonds of different maturities. The bank balance sheet's risk can then be measured in exactly the same way as the bond portfolio's risk. In a standard asset pricing framework, the return can be expressed as a combination of different factors. The opacity of a typical bank balance sheet then gives way to a combination of measurable risk factors that can be hedged. Nina Boyarchenko discusses the assumptions underlying this novel approach with regard to the nettability of the asset, the liability side of banks' balance sheets, and the absence of limits to arbitrage. Possibly her most important criticism is that banks are often the marginal intermediaries in asset markets, so their leverage constraints influence prices. Risk premia and expected asset returns may be determined by the relative health of the very financial intermediary whose risk exposure we are trying to measure. Banks partly set the prices for the risks they face.

In his chapter, Tyler Muir studies the price of risk and asks if it is systematically too low during credit booms. He shows that credit booms typically occur when risk is low in asset markets even though the fact that a credit boom is underway means that future risks are high. Put differently, risk premiums fall in credit booms while the quantity of risk appears to rise. This situation suggests a low, possibly too low, price of risk in markets. An important insight from Muir's intervention is that risk aversion in the economy appears very low in credit booms. This insight is fundamentally consistent with the idea that low risk in the past (e.g., low volatility of asset returns) leads agents to view the world as safe, causing them to be overoptimistic about risk going forward and inducing them to underprice risk and take on excessive leverage in a credit boom.

Reconsidering the Origins and Consequences of Crises

Financial history is back in vogue since the 2008 financial crisis. On the one hand, researchers turned to the past to better understand the events that unfolded. On the other hand, the 2008 crisis opened up new windows on past crises as researchers began to look for commonalities and dissimilarities, and they are now again being explored in light of the economic effects of the COVID-19 pandemic. By now, it is well understood that financial crises are not black swan events but regular occurrences in industrial and developing economies, whether the result of poor financial foresight or an internationally debilitating virus.

Matthew Baron and Daniel Dieckelmann make this point by proposing a new quantitative approach for reconstructing and analyzing the global history of banking crises. Importantly, this new quantitative chronology points to the overlooked phenomenon of "quiet crises," situations characterized by large declines in bank stock prices that are somehow missed in narrative chronologies of financial instability. The effects of such quiet episodes of financial distress are also severe. In his response, Mark Carlson underlines the importance of quantitative measures of banking distress and, at the same time, points out that the responsiveness of bank equity to economic distress will shift over time as banks' role in financial intermediation changes.

In Natacha Postel-Vinay's chapter, she argues that, in some respects, the U.S. Great Depression can also be seen as a credit boom gone bust, similar to the 2008 crisis. The response by Eugene White, however, raises questions over whether the asset price bubbles on top of the real economic boom of the 1920s were credit supply–driven, as was the real-estate lending boom of the 2000s, or ultimately caused by exuberant home buyers. This question remains open, but it is part of a reassessment of the Great Depression that is currently underway.

In the final intervention, taking a systematic historical view, Karsten Müller looks at the sectoral allocation of credit and what it tells us about financial stability risks. He finds that growth in housing debt, on both the household and corporate sides, is a frequent precursor of financial instability. This idea meshes nicely with the focus of recent literature on expansions of the nontradable service sector, expansions that often precede crises, and it helps explain the fact that credit booms often forecast lower rather than higher growth going forward (as Emil Verner's intervention shows). In her response, Orsola Costantini points to the complex political economy of intervening in the credit allocation to specific sectors. Capital allocation and financial regulation, she asserts, cannot be separated from the political economy.

New Economic Thinking

A new economics of debt, credit, and crisis is taking shape. The work in this book marks a new point of departure for research in financial economics, providing the much-needed first nail in the roof to move forward and build a research agenda for the future. This new economics goes to places that were off-limits to neoclassical finance. The old mainstream was too often content with looking for answers in places where assumptions would lead it.

The story of an old man who lost his key in the street comes to mind. If he looks for the key only underneath the streetlamps where the street is well lit, he will never peer into the darkness; it may not even occur to him that he could have lost the key in a place where the light does not shine.

This is the essence of what the new thinking on debt and crisis assembled in this volume aims to accomplish: the authors shed new light in places that were dark before and that have been bypassed by previous research. These places might well be where the key to understanding the financial fragility of contemporary economies was lost, but unless they are examined thoroughly, as they are here, it will never be found.

REFERENCES

Eggertsson, Gauti B., and Paul Krugman. 2012. Debt, Deleveraging, and the Liquidity Trap: A Fisher-Minsky-Koo Approach. Quarterly Journal of Economics 127 (3): 1469–1513.

Hyman, Louis. 2011. Debtor Nation. Princeton, NJ: Princeton University Press.

Jordà, Òscar, Moritz Schularick, and Alan M. Taylor. 2013. When Credit Bites Back. Journal of Money, Credit and Banking 45 (s2): 3–28.

———. 2015a. Betting the House. Journal of International Economics 96: S2–S18.

———. 2015b. Leveraged Bubbles. Journal of Monetary Economics 76: S1–S20.

———. 2016a. The Great Mortgaging: Housing Finance, Crises and Business Cycles. Economic Policy 31 (85): 107–52.

———. 2016b. Sovereigns versus Banks: Credit, Crises, and Consequences. Journal of the European Economic Association 14: 45–79.

Kindleberger, Charles P. 1978. Manias, Panics, and Crashes: A History of Financial Crises. New York: Basic Books.

Krippner, Greta. 2012. Capitalizing on Crisis: The Political Origins of the Rise of Finance. Cambridge, MA: Harvard University Press.

Krishnamurthy, Arvind, and Tyler Muir. 2017. How Credit Cycles across a Financial Crisis. Working paper.

Kumhof, Michael, Romain Rancière, and Pablo Winant. 2015. Inequality, Leverage, and Crises. American Economic Review 105 (3): 1217–45.

Laeven, Luc, and Fabian Valencia. 2012. Systemic Banking Crises Database; An Update. IMF Working Papers 12/163.

Mian, Atif, Ludwig Straub, and Amir Sufi. 2020. Indebted Demand. NBER Working Paper 26940.

Mian, Atif, and Amir Sufi. 2009. The Consequences of Mortgage Credit Expansion: Evidence from the U.S. Mortgage Default Crisis. Quarterly Journal of Economics 124: 1449–96.

———. 2011. House Prices, Home Equity-Based Borrowing, and the US Household Leverage Crisis. American Economic Review 101 (5): 2132–56.

———. 2014a. House of Debt: How They (and You) Caused the Great Recession and How We Can Prevent It from Happening Again. Chicago: University of Chicago Press.

———. 2014b. What Explains the 2007–2009 Drop in Employment? Econometrica 82 (6): 2197–2223.

Mian, Atif, Amir Sufi, and Emil Verner. 2017. Household Debt and Business Cycles Worldwide. Quarterly Journal of Economics 132 (4): 1755–1817.

———. 2020. How Does Credit Supply Expansion Affect the Real Economy? The Productive Capacity and Household Demand Channels. Journal of Finance 75 (2): 949–94.

Minsky, Hyman P. 1986. Stabilizing an Unstable Economy. New Haven, CT: Yale University Press.

Rajan, Raghuram. 2010. Fault Lines: How Hidden Fractures Still Threaten the World Economy. Princeton, NJ: Princeton University Press.

Reinhart, Carmen, and Kenneth Rogoff. 2009. This Time Is Different: Eight Centuries of Financial Folly. Princeton, NJ: Princeton University Press.

Schularick, Moritz. 2012. Public Debt and Financial Crises in the Twentieth Century. European Review of History 19 (6): 881–97.

Schularick, Moritz, and Alan M. Taylor. 2012. Credit Booms Gone Bust: Monetary Policy, Leverage Cycles, and Financial Crises, 1870–2008. American Economic Review 102 (2): 1029–61.

PART ONE

Finance Unbound:
The Rise of Finance and the Economy

1

How to Think about Finance

ATIF MIAN

The left panel of figure 1.1 shows that total credit in the United States remained relatively flat at around 140% of GDP in the postwar years until 1980.
Since 1980, however, credit has gone up at a rapid pace, reaching a historic
high of 258% of GDP in the most recent numbers available for 2016. Even
the Great Recession did not put much of a dent in the growth of credit, with
total credit rising from 232% in 2007 to 258% in 2016. The phenomenal
rise in credit is in fact a global phenomenon, as the work of Òscar Jordà,
Moritz Schularick, and Alan Taylor has carefully documented. The recently
released global debt database from the International Monetary Fund (IMF)
that covers both advanced and emerging economies also shows a big increase
in global credit to GDP, from around 150% between 1960 and 1980 to over
250% in 2016.

The right panel of figure 1.1 splits total credit into nonfinancial firm credit
and credit going to households plus government. The figure shows that most
of the increase in credit since 1980 has been driven by credit going to households and the government. Credit going to the corporate sector plays a relatively minor role in explaining the big rise in total credit. In particular, 82%
of the increase in total credit as a share of GDP since 1980 is driven by credit
going to households and the government. The big increase in total credit,

Atif Mian is the John H. Laporte Jr. Class of 1967 Professor of Economics, Public
Policy, and Finance at Princeton University and director of the Julis-Rabinowitz Cen-
ter for Public Policy and Finance at the Princeton School of Public and International
Affairs.

especially credit going to households and government, is not unique to the United States. Jordà et al. (2016) show that there has been a large increase in private bank credit in all advanced countries since 1980. The authors further show that the increase in credit is dominated by mortgage credit going to the household sector.

The large increase in credit has been accompanied by a persistent decline in the price of credit as long-term interest rates have fallen to historic lows. For example, the average ten-year real interest rate has declined from a high of 6% in 1983 to zero in recent years (IMF WEO 2014). The fall in the price of credit even as the quantity of credit exploded suggests that the expansion in the financial sector is driven by an increase in the "supply" of credit. What is behind this structural shift in finance?

The United States, and the global economy, experienced a couple of major structural shifts around 1980. First, share of income going to the top 1% of earners went up significantly. The richest 1% of Americans captured 11% of total income in 1980 and 20% in 2014 (Piketty and Saez 2003). The rise in top-income share occurred in many other countries as well (see, e.g., Alvaredo et al. 2018). Second, the collapse of the Bretton Woods system in 1971 ushered in the era of global capital flows. A number of countries started running large current account deficits or surpluses post 1980. High savings by oil-rich countries and high-growth Asian economies have also contributed to the global rise in credit through cross-border flows that have accelerated since 1980. The United States had close to a balanced current account in 1980 but has been consistently running current account deficits of over 2% of GDP since then.

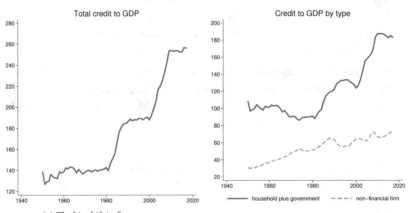

FIGURE 1.1 The big shift in finance

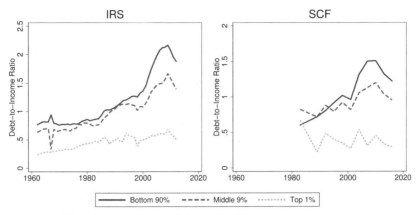

FIGURE 1.2 Debt-to-income ratio across the income distribution

Top Incomes and Debt at the Bottom

The rise in top income share contributes to the expansion of the size of the financial sector. High-income earners save a large share of their income, creating a larger "financial surplus" within the economy that is then channeled back through the financial sector. The financial sector deploys these larger gross savings back into the economy through credit creation. There is a close association between the rise in top-income share of the top 1% and the rise in household leverage for the rest of the population, suggesting that increased gross savings from the top 1% were partly absorbed by increased borrowing by the remaining household sector.

Figure 1.2 shows the evolution of debt to income for the top 1%, middle 9%, and remaining bottom 90% in both Internal Revenue Service and Survey of Consumer Finance (SCF) data sets. The rise in household credit is concentrated in the bottom 99% and not the top 1%, while income gains since the 1980s have largely gone to the top 1%. Mian and Sufi (2018b) show the same pattern holds when using individual-level credit bureau data.

What Has the Increased Credit Supply Financed?

The increasing financial surpluses, or savings gluts, have expanded the total supply of credit to the economy, lowering long-term interest rates in the process. What has the increased supply of credit financed?

The textbook model of finance says that credit is used to finance real investment: savers deposit their surplus funds in the banking sector which then lends these funds to firms for investment. In other words, credit is used to finance production, or the supply side of the economy. However, evidence suggests that a relatively small fraction of the increase in credit has gone toward funding production. For example, despite the large increase in credit creation, rate of investment has not gone up. The average U.S. gross investment rate was 22.5% from 1947 through 1979 and 21.8% from 1980 onward.

Other evidence is also at odds with the idea that the additional credit has gone into increasing productive capital. Overall growth is not any higher post-1980. Moreover, there is strong evidence that productivity growth has slowed down significantly over the last decade and a half. If additional credit has not gone into financing production as much, then the other possibility is that credit has increasingly been used to fund demand. There is indeed robust evidence to support this view.

I have already shown that most of the increase in credit since 1980 has been used to fund government fiscal deficits, or household financial deficits, especially households outside of the top 1%. The concentrated growth in government and household debt suggests that aggregate demand is increasingly reliant on credit creation for support.

Credit and Growth

The reliance on credit creation for supporting aggregate demand is a natural consequence of a higher share of income being saved due to increased inequality (see, e.g., Kumhof et al. 2015). Equilibrium condition for the real economy implies that as a larger fraction of the output is saved, the increased savings must be channeled back to the real economy either as investment or consumer demand. In the absence of such a channel, the real economy will be forced to contract—or not grow as fast—in order to equate supply and demand. This phenomenon is sometimes referred to as the "liquidity trap" or "savings trap" in the literature (e.g., Eggertsson and Krugman 2012).

Theoretically, as long as certain sectors within the economy such as the government or households below the top 1% are willing to run larger deficits, the real economy can continue to grow at full capacity. However, as the economy continues to rely on credit creation for supporting demand, it becomes increasingly more difficult to do so. The reason is that as household and government credit builds up, interest rates need to fall in order to keep the debt service requirement manageable. The reduction in interest rate also tends to raise asset prices, especially housing values, which enables households to borrow more easily. But the dependence on ever-lower interest rates to support a larger stock of debt cannot go on forever.

At some point it becomes difficult for interest rates to drop any further without adding costs of their own. First, there is the natural zero lower bound constraint on nominal interest rates. Second, and perhaps more importantly, very low interest rates introduce other problems that are damaging for the overall economy. For example, at very low interest rates asset markets are more prone to bubbles. It becomes increasingly difficult to fund pension plans and insurance funds with long-dated liabilities. The combination of high debt and increased likelihood of bubbles makes the financial sector more fragile. Low interest rates can also inhibit productivity growth due to greater misallocation of capital (Gopinath et al. 2016) or increased market concentration (Liu et al. 2019).

Long-Run Policy Implications

The remarkable growth in credit and the accompanying fall in long-term interest rates since 1980 represents the most important shift in finance in the modern era. The discussion above highlights why this shift is not sustainable, at least not without major harm to economic growth. A reliance on continuous credit creation to generate demand eventually slows down economic growth through liquidity-trap scenarios and other ill effects of very low interest rates.

What can be done to reduce the dependence on credit and create more space for economic growth as a result? As I mentioned, the root causes of secular credit growth lie in large financial surpluses in the economy that are then channeled through the financial system. A reversal of excessive credit dependence requires that financial surpluses be brought down to healthier levels. There are three types of structural changes in the economy that can help reduce the dependence on credit creation for aggregate demand.

First, more equitable growth will reduce the excessive savings that are accumulated by the top 1%. As explained above, there is a direct relationship between highly skewed economic growth and a bloated financial sector that results in broader economic malaise. Second, estate taxes and wealth tax (e.g., as proposed by Piketty [2014]), especially on "money-like" instruments, can be useful in restraining excessive surpluses. Some of the revenue raised from wealth and estate taxes can be used to lower income taxes for lower income brackets that have a high propensity to spend. Third, high intergenerational mobility helps to reduce the adverse effects of financial surpluses as accumulated surpluses naturally get liquidated across generations. Thus policies that strengthen public education and provide more equitable opportunities to the entire population help reduce dependence on credit creation.

Cyclical and More Immediate Policy Implications

I next turn my attention to more immediate steps that can be taken to reduce the cyclical costs of problems emanating from financial markets. The
most striking empirical regularity connecting credit and business cycles in
recent decades is that a large run-up in credit, especially household credit,
tends to be followed by an increase in unemployment. The 2008 global crisis, as shown in figure 1.3, was one manifestation of this broader trend. U.S.
states that had a larger increase in household leverage between 2002 and 2007
ended up experiencing a much more severe recession. Remarkably, we find
exactly the same relationship across countries.

In Mian and Sufi (2018a), we explain how recurrent business cycle contractions, such as the one in figure 1.3, are the result of a "credit-driven
household demand channel." The basic idea is that expansion in the supply of
credit fuels a boom in credit and asset prices that boosts household aggregate
demand. However, the expanding credit boom also sows the seeds of its own
destruction and ultimately results in a macroeconomic slowdown.

How should policy be tailored to address such credit-induced boom-bust
cycles? I discuss steps regarding macroprudential policy, tax policy, banking
regulation, GSE (government-sponsored entity) reforms, and bankruptcy law
that help reduce the likelihood and adverse consequences of credit-induced
boom-bust cycles. On the macroprudential front, the most important policy
focus should be to facilitate better risk-sharing between creditors and borrowers. Credit creates problems for the macroeconomy in the event of a downturn
due to differences across creditors and debtors in their marginal propensity to

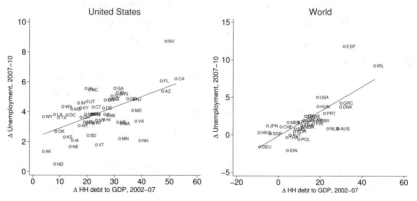

FIGURE 1.3 Credit growth and recessions
Source: U.S. data, Mian and Sufi (2010); world data, Mian, Sufi, and Verner (2017).

spend. A downturn naturally hurts borrowers disproportionately more since they are leveraged. Borrowers are also more sensitive to shocks as they tend to have much higher propensity to respond to shocks. The combination of these two forces implies that for any given macro shock, headwinds faced by the macroeconomy are stronger the more levered the economy is. Moreover, households may not fully internalize the possibility of such headwinds when deciding how much leverage to undertake. This results in economies getting "over-leveraged" with deeper and more frequent recessions.

More Equitable Risk-Sharing

A natural solution to minimizing the disruptions caused by credit is to promote "state-contingent contracting" that allows a more equitable sharing of downside risk between creditor and debtor in the event of a macro downturn. The creditor will naturally be compensated for sharing downside risk upfront. State-contingent contracting does not suffer from the usual moral hazard problem in risk-sharing contracts, because the risk-sharing is contingent upon a macro state of nature over which the borrower has no direct control.

There are multiple examples of state-contingent contracts that have been proposed in the past. For example, sovereign debt repayment can be linked to GDP as proposed by Robert Shiller. Student debt repayment can link to the earning potential of a graduating student's cohort and major. We proposed a state-contingent "shared responsibility mortgage" (SRM) in our book House of Debt (Mian and Sufi 2014). SRM works by reducing monthly mortgage payments in the event of a local downturn in the housing market without altering the amortization schedule—effectively providing both cash-flow and principal relief for borrowers.

The promotion of state-contingent contracts will have multiple advantages at the macro level. First, it will significantly reduce real macroeconomic volatility through the introduction of automatic stabilizers as debtors and creditors share risk more efficiently. Economic volatility is especially harmful for lower income households with more fragile economic conditions. Second, it will raise total welfare by avoiding long periods when the economy operates below capacity due to the aftereffects of debt overhang. In this way an economy with state-contingent contracting is both more resilient and stronger. Empirical evidence coming out of the Great Recession shows that better risk-sharing between debtors and creditors would have significantly reduced the extent and scale of the recession. Di Maggio et al. (2017) show that lower interest rates post-2008 were not passed through to many constrained households which were therefore unable to refinance, thus putting a real drag on aggregate demand. Ganong and Noel (2017) show that reduction in mortgage payments under a government program significantly increased spending and lowered defaults. More than four million homes were foreclosed over a short period during the Great Recession. Mian et al. (2015) show these fire sales put further downward pressure on house prices, thus worsening an already bad situation. State-contingent mortgages would have helped reduce the number of homes going into foreclosure.

Tax Advantages to Debt

A natural question that arises is that if state-contingent contracts are so beneficial, why do we not see more of them around us? There are three main reasons for this. First, the argument in favor of state-contingent contracting is based on the negative macro externalities inherent in standard debt contracts. Private agents, for both rational and behavioral reasons, are not likely to internalize these externalities. There is thus a rationale for promoting state-contingent contracting as part of macroprudential policies. Second, as Admati et al. (2018) point out, shareholders have an incentive to ratchet leverage up since some of the benefits of reducing leverage accrue to creditors and not shareholders. Third, there are a number of institutional features in the United States and abroad that hinder the adoption of state-contingent contracting. I discuss specific policy steps that remove such obstacles and encourage adoption of state-contingent contracts.

The U.S. tax system offers an interest expense deduction that reduces the effective cost of debt financing for homeowners. The tax subsidy is naturally capitalized in people's housing decisions and the value of the housing market. The tax subsidy distorts the financial system by encouraging leverage that is harmful from a macroprudential perspective. Removing the tax subsidy is not feasible politically, and doing so may also depress the housing market. Therefore, we proposed in Mian and Sufi (2014) that the subsidy be moved over toward state-contingent contracts like the SRM that have nice macroprudential characteristics. The current system not only subsidizes the housing sector but does so in a way that is harmful from a prudential perspective.

Bank capitalization rules under the Basel system are also structured to discourage banks from holding state-contingent securities in their portfolios. For example, suppose a bank issues a traditional mortgage of $100,000 with an 80% loan-to-value ratio. How much capital does the bank need to issue this mortgage? The typical capitalization requirement is 8%, implying the bank needs $8,000 of capital. However, Basel rules would give this mortgage a "risk weight" of 0.3, meaning that the bank only needs to cover 0.3 times the 8%, or $2,400 in capital.

Now imagine the bank issued the same mortgage as an SRM. The risk weight would increase substantially, probably close to 1. As a result, the bank would need to have $8,000 in capital, instead of the $2,400, to issue the mortgage as an SRM. The higher capital requirement for state-contingent contracts is unfortunate and somewhat ironic from a societal viewpoint.

The banking system is designed to discourage banks from holding state-contingent contracts that would be more beneficial from a macro perspective. The premise behind banking regulations such as Basel III is that losses must be minimized for the banking sector, or creditors at large. The banking system is therefore encouraged to originate the "safest" of assets from the creditors' perspective and pass on all risk to debtors. However, as I have already explained, doing so leads to much worse outcomes in the event of a cyclical downturn. The current structure of banking regulation does not split risk between creditors and debtors in a socially beneficial manner.

The adoption of a new "standard" in financial markets often requires the government to step in and define new rules. For example, there is now an active and liquid market for inflation-indexed treasuries or TIPS. But that market was created by the U.S. government itself under the Clinton administration. Similarly, the thirty-year fixed rate mortgage became the standard mortgage in the United States after the government actively encouraged it. Today GSEs are by far the largest players in the mortgage origination business. The explicit government support enjoyed by "conforming" mortgages supported by the GSEs means that it is more difficult for the private sector to introduce new solutions like state-contingent mortgages.

 Given the existing large role of government in mortgage origination and the societal benefits associated with state-contingent contracts such as SRMs, the government could include state-contingent mortgages in its definition of "conforming." The government could also help in defining states of the world, such as official local house price indexes, to promote state-contingent mortgages. State-contingent contracting is an example of ex ante macroprudential intervention. If properly implemented, it has the virtue of endogenously reducing economic volatility and crises, and hence the need for ex post intervention in the first place. However, to the extent ex post intervention is needed, efficient bankruptcy laws help in dealing with debt overhang. The United States has better bankruptcy laws compared to the rest of the advanced world, especially for households. However, there are certain areas, such as student loans, where bankruptcy laws need to be amended to enable restructuring of odious student debt.

Conclusion

The broader message to take away is that risk-sharing between creditors and debtors is an important principle to promote. Macroprudential and regulatory policies should be designed to favor risk-sharing. Unfortunately, the current tax and regulatory system is designed to do the opposite. The present regulatory regime is "bank-centric," with an exclusive focus on minimizing default probability for banks. This is short-sighted and does not take into account the true cost for the real economy when the financial system passes risk squarely on to debtors. The banking sector should be better capitalized, as argued forcefully by Admati and Hellwig (2013), with a capital structure that is more suited to absorbing losses without going into bankruptcy.

REFERENCES

Admati, Anat, and Martin F. Hellwig. 2013. The Bankers' New Clothes: What's Wrong with Banking and What to Do about It. Princeton, NJ: Princeton University Press.

Admati, Anat R., Peter M. Demarzo, Martin F. Hellwig, and Paul Pfleiderer. 2018. The Leverage Ratchet Effect. Journal of Finance 73 (1): 145–98.

Agarwal, Sumit, Gene Amromin, Itzhak Ben-David, Souphala Chomsisengphet, Tomasz Piskorski, and Amit Seru. 2017. Policy Intervention in Debt Renegotiation: Evidence from the Home Affordable Modification Program. Journal of Political Economy 125 (3): 654–712.

Aladangady, Aditya. 2014. Homeowner Balance Sheets and Monetary Policy. FEDS Working Paper, Federal Reserve Board.

Alvaredo, Facundo, Lucas Chancel, Thomas Piketty, Emmanuel Saez, and Gabriel Zucman. 2018. World Inequality Report. Working paper.

Baker, Scott R. 2018. Debt and the Response to Household Income Shocks: Validation and Application of Linked Financial Account Data. Journal of Political Economy 126 (4): 1504–57.

Chomsisengphet, Souphala, Neale Mahoney, and Johannes Stroebel. 2018. Do Banks Pass Through Credit Expansions to Consumers Who Want to Borrow? Evidence from Credit Cards. Quarterly Journal of Economics 133 (1): 129–90.

Cloyne, James, Clodomiro Ferreira, and Paolo Surico. 2020. Monetary Policy When Households Have Debt: New Evidence on the Transmission Mechanism. Review of Economic Studies 87 (1): 102–29.

Di Maggio, Marco, Amir Kermani, Benjamin J. Keys, Tomasz Piskorski, Ramcharan Rodney, Amit Seru, and Vincent Yao. 2017. Interest Rate Pass-Through: Mortgage Rates, Household Consumption, and Voluntary Deleveraging. American Economic Review 107 (11): 3550–88.

Eggertsson, Gauti B., and Paul Krugman. 2012. Debt, Deleveraging, and the Liquidity Trap: A Fisher-Minsky-Koo Approach. Quarterly Journal of Economics 127 (3): 1469–1513.

Ganong, Peter, and Pascal Noel. 2017. Consumer Spending during Unemployment: Positive and Normative Implications. Working paper.

Gopinath, Gita, Sebnem Kalemli-Ozcan, Loukas Karabarbounis, and Carolina Villegas-Sanchez. 2016. Capital Allocation and Productivity in South Europe. NBER Working Paper 21453.

Jordà, Òscar, Moritz Schularick, and Alan M. Taylor. 2014. Betting the House. Federal Reserve Bank of San Francisco Working Paper 2014-28.

———. 2016. The Great Mortgaging: Housing Finance, Crises and Business Cycles. Economic Policy 31 (85): 107–52.

Kumhof, Michael, Romain Rancière, and Pablo Winant. 2015. Inequality, Leverage, and Crises. American Economic Review 105 (3): 1217–45.

Liu, Ernest, Atif Mian, and Amir Sufi. 2019. Low Interest Rates, Market Power and Productivity Growth. NBER Working Paper 25505.

Mian, Atif, and Amir Sufi. 2010. Household Leverage and the Recession of 2007–09. IMF Economic Review 58 (1): 74–117.

———. 2014. House of Debt: How They (and You) Caused the Great Recession and How We Can Prevent It from Happening Again. Chicago: University of Chicago Press.

———. 2018a. Finance and Business Cycles: The Credit-driven Household Demand Channel. Journal of Economic Perspectives 32 (3): 31–58.

———. 2018b. Inequality, Credit Creation and Aggregate Demand. Working paper.

Mian, Atif, Amir Sufi, and Francesco Trebbi. 2015. Foreclosures, House Prices, and the Real Economy. Journal of Finance 70 (6): 2587–2634.

Mian, Atif, Amir Sufi, and Emil Verner. 2017. Household Debt and Business Cycles Worldwide. Quarterly Journal of Economics 132 (4): 1755–1817.

Piketty, Thomas. 2014. Capital in the Twenty-First Century. Cambridge, MA: Harvard University Press.

Piketty, Thomas, and Emmanuel Saez. 2003. Income Inequality in the United States, 1913–1998. Quarterly Journal of Economics 118 (1): 1–41.

Comment by Karen Dynan

Atif Mian continues to offer up thought-provoking observations and arguments regarding the use of credit. A central focus of his latest research is the striking increase in credit in the United States and globally in recent decades. He argues that a key cause of this increase is a buildup in financial surpluses, which has come hand in hand with a drop in real interest rates. Mian outlines various costs and risks associated with these trends and suggests policies that can help mitigate the harm.

These general themes touch on some of the most important macroeconomic challenges that we are currently confronting. They echo the concerns put forward by the recent literature on secular stagnation. The financial surpluses that Mian describes reflect the supply of loanable funds having outpaced the demand for these funds in recent decades, leading to a substantial decline in the equilibrium price of these funds—the neutral real interest rate.

Karen Dynan is professor of the practice in the Department of Economics at Harvard University and a nonresident senior fellow at the Peterson Institute of International Economics.

Indeed, Summers and Rachel (2019) estimate a decline in the real neutral rate of 3 to 4 percentage points since 1980.

Collectively, these developments have spurred a number of concerns. Some have argued that large financial surpluses and low interest rates have left us in a situation where the economy may not be able to reach full employment without consumers taking on large and perhaps unsustainable amounts of debt. The risks to both borrowers and the broader economy from high debt and leverage have been a running theme in Mian's work. Another concern is that low neutral interest rates may make the financial system more prone to bubbles and other types of financial instability. Low rates, particularly if unexpected, can also create problems for insurance and pension providers because the resulting low returns on their portfolios may leave them struggling to make promised payments. Yet another important worry is that low interest rates limit the ability of central banks to respond to economic downturns because their traditional lever for boosting aggregate demand—the "policy" rate—cannot fall below zero. While central banks have used quantitative easing and other measures in recent years to get around this "zero-lower-bound" problem, these unconventional monetary tools are less well understood, come with potential risks, and face their own limitations when it comes to influencing aggregate demand.

A key issue raised by Mian's research is how worried we should be about debt and leverage at the current time. There is fairly wide consensus that the U.S. economy has reached full employment and yet households do *not* appear to be overextended at this time. Household debt relative to after-tax income remains at levels seen prior to the precrisis credit boom, and the share of after-tax income committed to household debt service payments is at the low end of the range since 1980. Bankruptcy rates and delinquency rates on most types of household credit remain very low.

What then explains the current high level of U.S. credit cited by Mian? Figure 1C.1 reproduces his chart showing the ratio of total nonfinancial domestic U.S. credit to GDP, and figure 1C.2 breaks credit down into its major components (with shorter vertical and horizontal ranges so one can clearly see the recent patterns). Figure 1C.1 shows that overall credit relative to GDP climbed sharply during the early 2000s, reaching a high level just prior to the financial crisis and remaining at that level since then. Figure 1C.2 shows that the current high level is explained by high levels of government debt, which nearly doubled during the period of great economic weakness that occurred during the recession years that followed.

Figures 1C.1 and 1C.2 raise the question of how worried we should be about the current level of government debt. The traditional view is that high levels of government borrowing can be quite costly for an economy because

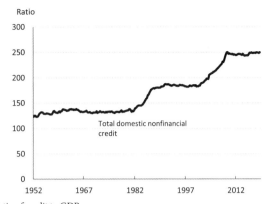

FIGURE 1C.1 Ratio of credit to GDP
Source: Financial Accounts of the United States.

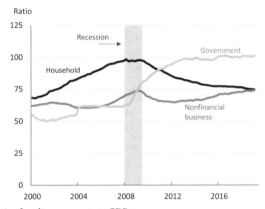

FIGURE 1C.2 Ratio of credit components to GDP
Source: Financial Accounts of the United States.

they soak up funds that could otherwise be used for productive investment. In addition, the need to make interest payments on large amounts of accumulated debt can exacerbate the challenge of reducing debt. However, a recent literature has pointed out that these costs have fallen because of the long-term downtrend in real interest rates previously discussed (Elmendorf and Sheiner 2017; Blanchard 2019). Moreover, as argued by Summers and Rachel (2019), higher government debt in the United States and other countries has likely kept real interest rates considerably higher than they otherwise would be, implying that the zero-lower-bound problems and financial instability risks posed by low interest rates might be far worse if government debt had not risen.[1]

While I am not as pessimistic as Mian about where household debt and leverage are now, I agree that some households face risks related to their use of credit (particularly if the economy were to weaken) and that the group of at-risk borrowers could become much larger if we experience another household credit boom. State-contingent debt contracts such as the "shared responsibility mortgage" proposed by Mian and Sufi (2014) could help home-owners avoid foreclosure in an economic downturn, keeping the macroeconomy stronger. They would also reduce the need for politically charged and administratively complicated ad hoc homeowner rescue programs like those used in the last mortgage crisis. But there are complications associated with such proposals. For example, lenders would need to be compensated for tak-ing on more risk and the higher resulting mortgage rates could substantially reduce demand for such products. Of course, the government could limit the rise in rates by subsidizing the product but doing so would use funds that might be deployed in some other way that helped households. All in all, these types of contracts seem worth exploring but more research needs to be done to pin down their likely costs and benefits.

Dokko and Dynan (2018) highlight a number of complementary ideas for better protecting households and the broader economy from the risks of credit use. For example, another mortgage innovation potentially worth promoting is the "Wealth-Building Home Loan" developed by Oliner, Peter, and Pinto (2020), which allows homeowners to accumulate equity faster than with a traditional mortgage and, in turn, reduces the odds that they will en-counter the hardships associated with falling underwater. Macroprudential regulators need to be willing to deploy countercyclical capital buffers in credit booms, which would lean against the inclination of financial institutions to make riskier loans and reduce the likelihood of bubbles. We should also make sure that any future reform of the housing finance system includes a mecha-nism for the government to sustain the flow of mortgage credits in downturns to prevent home prices from overcorrecting and pushing more households than necessary into negative equity. Finally, we should preserve strong con-sumer financial protection to steer households away from products that cause them to take on excessive risk.

---

1. This line of thinking does not let the U.S. government off the hook from fixing the sharp further rise in debt scheduled to occur under current policy; there remains widespread consen-sus that debt cannot rise indefinitely relative to GDP without causing problems.

REFERENCES

Blanchard, Olivier. 2019. Public Debt and Low Interest Rates. American Economic Association 2019 Presidential Address. Available at https://www.aeaweb.org/aea/2019conference/pro gram/pdf/14020_paper_etZgfbDr.pdf.

Dokko, Jane, and Karen Dynan. 2018. Ten Years since the Financial Crisis: Some Lessons for Reducing Risks to Households. Working paper. Available at https://www.stlouisfed.org /~/media/files/pdfs/hfs/assets/2018/tipping-points/dokko_dynan_tipping_points_paper _2018_11.pdf?la=en.

Elmendorf, Douglas W., and Louise M. Sheiner. 2017. Federal Budget Policy with an Aging Population and Persistently Low Interest Rates. Journal of Economic Perspectives 31 (3): 175–94.

Mian, Atif, and Amir Sufi. 2014. House of Debt: How They (and You) Caused the Great Recession and How We Can Prevent It from Happening Again. Chicago: University of Chicago Press.

Oliner, Stephen D., Tobias Peter, and Edward J. Pinto. 2020. The Wealth-Building Home Loan. Regional Science and Urban Economics 80(C).

Rachel, Lukasz, and Lawrence H. Summers. 2019. On Secular Stagnation in the Industrialized World. Brookings Papers on Economic Activity 50 (1): 1–76.

2

Reconsidering the Costs and Benefits of Debt Booms for the Economy

EMIL VERNER

Private debt booms are episodes of rapid expansion in credit to households and firms. These booms have been playing an increasingly prominent role in economic fluctuations over the past few decades. A rapid expansion in debt can reflect structural improvements in the financial sector's ability to inter- mediate funds toward productive investment or an acceleration in productiv- ity growth. Thus, private debt booms may be part of the road to financial and economic development through the beneficial effects of credit deepening.

However, debt booms have also been followed by growth slowdowns and severe financial crises. Debt booms can generate distortions in the economy, fuel asset price booms and busts, increase banks' vulnerability to losses, and saddle the private sector with debt overhang that depresses consumption and investment. Instead of facilitating economic development, debt booms may be periods of excessive lending that increase financial fragility and sow the seeds of a future economic crash.

Ten years after the trough of the Great Recession, it is useful to revisit a crucial set of questions about debt booms. How should policy makers, market participants, and economic theory view private debt booms? Do the ben- efits of potential credit deepening outweigh the costs of potentially higher financial fragility? And what are the key channels through which debt booms propagate to the real economy?

In this chapter, I revisit the connection between private debt booms and the real economy using recently assembled unbalanced panel data covering

Emil Verner is the Class of 1957 Career Development Professor and assistant profes- sor of finance at the Sloan School of Management, Massachusetts Institute of Technology.

143 countries over the past six decades. Along the way, I review the rapidly growing literature on the connection between debt booms, growth, and crises. Across countries, the level of private debt-to-GDP, a proxy for financial development, is strongly positively associated with real income per capita. Moreover, expanding credit depth over the past forty years is strongly correlated with real GDP growth over the same period. Thus, long-run economic growth goes hand in hand with credit deepening.

In sharp contrast to gradual financial development over the long run, private debt booms are associated with short-term real GDP booms followed by future growth slowdowns. The future growth slowdown implies that private debt booms are not, on average, followed by a higher future level of real GDP. Taken at face value, the data suggest that real GDP may actually be lower in the long run following a debt boom, relative to a counterfactual without a boom. Not only do private debt booms generate boom-bust cycles, but the busts overwhelm the booms.

Debt booms are unlikely to represent episodes of credit deepening. Examining how debt booms propagate to the real economy provides insights into why debt booms are not beneficial for growth. In particular, the evidence shows that debt booms affect the real economy through completely different channels than those that drive beneficial credit deepening.

To understand how debt booms propagate to the real economy, we first need to understand what drives the expansion in lending during debt booms. Debt booms coincide with declines in credit spreads and an increase in credit availability to riskier borrowers. This indicates that these booms are driven by an expansion in credit supply, not by increased demand for credit due to fundamental productivity improvements. That is, debt booms are driven by an increased willingness to lend on the part of financial intermediaries.

The credit supply expansion can finance either an expansion in demand or an increase in the economy's productive capacity. Key patterns in the data indicate that private debt booms largely boost demand instead of productive capacity. In particular, debt booms coincide with an expansion in nontradable employment relative to tradable employment and with real exchange rate appreciation. Debt booms also finance surging imports but are associated with a slowdown in exports. In addition, debt booms fuel unsustainable house price booms, which create additional distortions by reallocating resources toward the less productive construction sector.

Once the credit cycle that drives the expansion in debt reverses, the economy slows due to a combination of factors resulting from the imbalances generated in the boom. Banking sector losses lead to a sharp contraction in credit supply that depresses consumption and investment. The overhang of debt accumulated in the boom itself depresses demand and leads to asset fire sales. House price declines reinforce the decline in demand by depressing borrowers' net worth. Real exchange rate overvaluation combined with nominal rigidities generate sustained output losses when demand falls in the bust. The bust is further exacerbated by real rigidities, which slow reallocation from the bloated nontradable sector to the tradable sector.

Therefore, while credit deepening may contribute to economic development, this is unlikely to happen through rapid debt booms. Such booms are instead often episodes when credit expands for reasons unrelated to economic fundamentals, and where the expansion generates distortions and vulnerabilities that often end in crisis. In short, credit booms are not the way toward financial development-led growth, and we should view debt booms and credit deepening as fundamentally different phenomena that operate through different channels.

Credit Deepening: The Potential Benefits of a Debt Boom

Why might a debt boom be a good sign for economic growth? The potential benefits of a private debt boom come from credit deepening. Theory and a large body of empirical evidence suggest that a better-functioning financial system contributes to and facilitates higher GDP growth. Credit depth measures, such as private debt-to-GDP, may proxy for such financial development (King and Levine 1993; Levine 2004). Private debt booms may thus simply be periods of accelerating credit deepening.

Figure 2.1 presents the striking positive correlation between credit depth and real income per capita across countries. The data on real GDP and population are from the World Bank's World Development Indicators database. Private debt-to-GDP is from the Bank for International Settlements (BIS) Long Series on Credit to the Private Sector and the International Monetary Fund's Global Debt Database.[1] The complete sample is listed in table 2A.1.

The figure shows that countries that are more economically developed have higher private debt-to-GDP ratios. Each observation represents the level of real GDP per capita and the level of credit to GDP in 2015 for each country in the sample. The dashed line captures the estimated nonparametric relation between private debt-to-GDP and real GDP per capita. This is the country-level income-debt curve.

1. In all the analysis in this chapter, I drop countries that do not have at least twenty years of GDP and private debt data, as well as countries with a population lower than half a million.

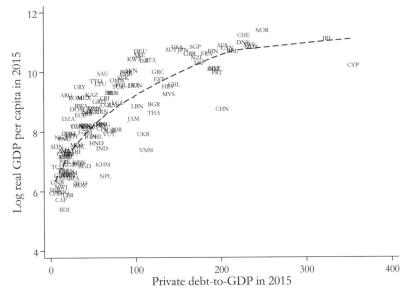

FIGURE 2.1 Higher income countries have higher credit depth

Note: This figure presents a country-level scatterplot of private debt-to-GDP against log real GDP per capita. Both variables are measured in 2015. Private debt-to-GDP is from the BIS Long Series on Credit to the Private Sector and the IMF's Global Debt Database. Real GDP per capita is from the World Bank's World Development Indicators.

The positive relation in figure 2.1 implies that moving from a level of private debt-to-GDP of 100% to 170% (a 1 standard deviation increase) is associated with an increase in income per capita from $10,000 to $27,000, a 170% difference. This strong positive relation has intrigued empirical researchers since a version of it was first documented by Goldsmith (1969).

Interestingly, the relation in figure 2.1 is also concave. The positive relation flattens out once debt-to-GDP exceeds about 200%. This suggests that any potential benefits of expanding private debt-to-GDP may be lower in more advanced economies. Differences in credit depth across advanced economies partly reflect different institutional features. For example, countries with funded pension systems tend to have higher household debt levels, as households borrow against illiquid pension wealth (Scharfstein 2018).

Income per capita and credit depth are not only strongly correlated in levels. Long-run economic development also goes hand in hand with financial development. Figure 2.2 reveals that countries that have seen stronger economic growth over the past forty years have also seen stronger financial development in terms of credit market depth. This implies that the correlation

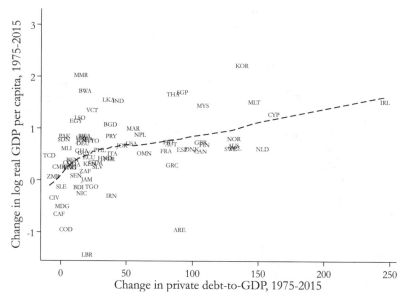

FIGURE 2.2 Economic development goes hand in hand with credit market development
Note: This figure presents a country-level scatterplot of the change in private debt-to-GDP from 1975 to 2015 against the change in log real GDP per capita over the same period.

in figure 2.1 is not solely driven by historical fixed differences across countries that determine both real income and credit depth.

Figures 2.1 and 2.2 suggest that credit depth, and financial development more generally, play an active role in increasing real output. A large "finance-growth" literature over the past three decades argues that better functioning credit and financial markets boost output (see Levine 2004 for an overview). Convincing causal evidence is difficult to come by, but some studies have found that open and better functioning financial markets increase real GDP growth.

Greater access to credit can increase output through several channels, all of which ultimately boost the productive capacity of the economy. Expanding credit can increase access to finance for constrained firms and, at the same time, lower the cost of capital, leading to an increase in investment. Expanding credit may be part of financial deepening that leads to a more efficient allocation of savings to investment (Greenwood and Jovanovic 1990) and a better allocation of capital across firms (Larrain and Stumpner 2017). Greater access to credit may also increase firm entry and product market competition (Varela 2018). Rising debt may also result from "efficient bubbles," where bubbles in the price of capital relax financing constraints for productive entrepreneurs, again leading to more productive investment (Martin and Ventura 2012). Moreover, credit can allow firms to expand demand for skilled labor (Fonseca and Van Doornik 2018). Credit booms may also be driven by improving institutions such as property rights and creditor protections.

Figures 2.1 and 2.2, of course, do not prove that credit deepening causes higher income per capita. Causality certainly also runs from income per capita to credit depth. Higher productivity growth increases the demand for credit from businesses who can take advantage of new investment opportunities. Rising debt, to a large extent, may follow real economic progress. However, even when credit follows real economic improvements, access to credit reinforces the benefits of productivity advances by allowing firms to invest. Moreover, access to credit allows households to reap the welfare benefits of expected future income growth by borrowing to smooth consumption. Indeed, most of the increase in global private debt over the past four decades has been driven by household loans, both in advanced and emerging economies (Jordà, Schularick, and Taylor 2014; Müller 2018a).

Private Debt Booms and Real GDP

DEBT BOOMS PREDICT LOWER FUTURE REAL GDP

Are private debt booms a reflection of credit deepening? That is, are these booms part of the path up the income-debt curve in figure 2.1? Or are debt booms periods of excessive lending that do not result in higher real GDP and may even lead to growth slowdowns?

To examine the relation between private debt booms and real GDP, I start by identifying private debt boom events at the country level as periods when private debt-to-GDP, d_{it}^P, is high relative to its previous trend.[2] I then construct a dummy variable, DebtBoom$_{it}$, that equals 1 in the first year of each

---

2. Specifically, following the approach suggested by Hamilton (2018), I estimate the time series regression

$$d_{it+h}^P = \alpha + \sum_{j=0}^{4} \beta_j d_{it-j}^P + u_{it+h}$$

separately for each country i in the sample, setting $h = 4$. Denoting the predicted value from this regression as $\hat{d}_{it}^P$, the Hamilton-filtered value of debt-to-GDP is then $\tilde{d}_{it}^P = d_{it}^P - \hat{d}_{it}^P$.

I identify debt booms as periods when the Hamilton-filtered debt-to-GDP exceeds 1.64 times its country-specific standard deviation, i.e., when $\tilde{d}_{it}^P \geq 1.64 \cdot \sigma_i(\tilde{d}^P)$. The threshold value of 1.64 is chosen based on the 95th percentile of the standard normal distribution, but the results are robust to using other reasonable thresholds.

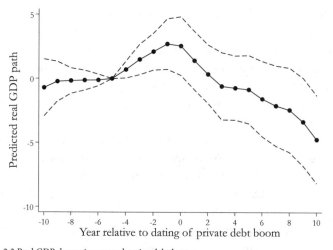

FIGURE 2.3 Real GDP dynamics around major debt booms
Note: This figure presents the estimated response of real GDP to a debt boom. Dashed lines represent
95% confidence intervals.

debt boom event. In a recent study, Richter, Schularick, and Wachtel (2021)
use a similar approach to identify debt booms.

To trace the predicted dynamics of real GDP around a debt boom, I estimate a sequence of regressions on the full country-year panel from $t - 5$ to
$t + 15$.[3]

Figure 2.3 presents the estimated dynamics of real GDP around a private
debt boom event. Note that $t = 0$ marks when the boom is identified, which is
often the peak of the boom. However, since debt booms typically last three to
four years, the boom generally starts between $t = -3$ and $t = -4$. For example,
for the United States in the 2000s, the boom is identified in 2005.

The figure shows that during the debt boom, GDP growth accelerates, and
real GDP rises above its trend. However, starting in the year after the boom is
identified, real GDP declines sharply by 3% over the subsequent three years.
Debt booms thus predict lower subsequent real GDP growth. This evidence

---

3. The regression equation is

$$y_{it-5+h} - y_{it-5} = \alpha_i^h + \beta^h \text{DebtBoom}_{it} + \varepsilon_{it+h}.$$

Log real GDP, y_{it}, is benchmarked to five years before when the debt boom is identified to allow
for a potentially positive impact of the debt boom on contemporaneous GDP. Standard errors
are dually clustered on country and year. The sequence of estimated coefficients $\{\hat{\beta}^h\}$ presents
the average path of real GDP around a private debt boom event, relative to periods without a
debt boom.

is consistent with the patterns documented by Mian, Sufi, and Verner (2017) for household debt expansions.

In addition to the negative growth impact, figure 2.3 also suggests that debt booms predict a lower long-run level of output. From three years after the boom is identified, real output is below its previous trend, and output continues to decline for several years after. Ten years after the debt boom, real GDP is 5% lower than its previous trend, and the difference is statistically significant. That is, figure 2.3 not only suggests that debt booms predict lower future real GDP growth. It also suggests that debt booms lead to a persistently lower level of future output.

In general, estimating the impact of debt booms on the long-run level of output is challenging, as the uncertainty rises with the forecast horizon. The large sample I use here helps increase the power for estimating longer-run impacts. However, even with this sample, there is substantial uncertainty in the longer-run estimates. At a minimum, the data show that debt booms certainly do not predict higher output, and there is suggestive evidence that these booms predict a lower level of output.

The suggestive negative impact of debt booms on the subsequent level of output connects the dots between several existing pieces of evidence. Debt booms have been shown to predict lower growth and financial crises (Schularick and Taylor 2012; Mian, Sufi, and Verner 2017). Financial crises, in turn, result in highly persistent or even permanent output losses (Cerra and Saxena 2008; Baron, Verner, and Xiong 2021). The negative relation between debt booms and subsequent output suggests that increased financial crisis risk is not offset by growth booms following debt booms that do not end in a financial crisis.

At this point, it is important to emphasize an important caveat. Debt booms are not exogenous events. These booms could merely coincide with periods of lower productivity growth, real exchange rate overvaluation, or other contractionary forces. However, most economic models would suggest that debt booms should follow or anticipate stronger economic growth. For example, an expected future productivity shock would lead to a positive relation between credit expansion today and future output growth.[4]

Therefore, while caution is warranted in interpreting debt booms as causally lowering future output (that is, interpreting that debt booms themselves have "costs"), the fact that debt booms do not seem to be positively related

---

4. If agents anticipate a growth slowdown or a credit crunch, they may borrow to hoard liquidity. Surveys of professional forecasters and the behavior of stock prices around credit booms, however, suggest that crashes are not anticipated by market participants.

to future output raises important questions. In particular, the idea that debt booms are part of beneficial credit deepening is soundly rejected by the data. Credit booms cannot explain the positive relation between economic development and credit depth. Financial development may cause higher income, but it does not operate through debt booms.

Earlier studies examining the impact of increases in debt-to-GDP on subsequent growth using country-level panel data find a positive relation (e.g., Levine, Loayza, and Beck 2000; Loayza and Rancière 2006). What explains the sharp difference with the evidence I present here? The earlier panel studies connecting finance and growth typically average data over nonoverlapping periods, generally of five years, and estimate dynamic panel models on these averaged data. These models are intended to capture the impact of financial development on steady-state growth. The averaging procedure, therefore, filters away many of the very rapid expansions in credit that constitute credit booms. This is consistent with my thesis. Credit booms, rapid expansions in credit, are associated with lower growth. More gradual expansions in credit are more benign and may represent beneficial financial deepening.

ROBUSTNESS

The results in figure 2.3 are robust to alternative approaches to trace the impact of debt booms. In particular, the fact that debt booms predict lower subsequent growth is not sensitive to how debt booms are identified. Figure 2.4 examines the correlation with growth from $t - 3$ to $t - 2, t - 1, \ldots$, and $t + 7$.[5] I choose a private debt expansion of three years based on the evidence in Mian, Sufi, and Verner (2017) that debt expansions typically last for three to four years. Figure 2.4 shows that private debt expansions are associated with real GDP expansions in the short run, but a strong reversal in the medium run that translates into a lower subsequent level of output.

Figure 2.5 presents the impulse response of real GDP to private debt-to-GDP innovations estimated using Jordà (2005) local projections.[6] Figure 2.5 again suggests that innovations in debt lead to slower growth in the medium

---

5. Formally, it presents estimates of β^h from

$$(1)\ y_{t-3+h} - y_{t-3} = \beta^h \Delta_3 d_t^P + \alpha_i + \varepsilon_{it+h}, h = 1,\ldots,10.$$

That is, I fix the right-hand side to be private credit expansions from year $t - 3$ to t and examine the correlation with growth from $t - 3$ to $t - 2, t - 2, \ldots$, and $t + 7$.

6. Specifically, the figure plots the estimates of β_0^h from the following specification:

$$(2)\ y_{it+h} = \alpha_i + \sum_{j=0}^{5}\beta_j^h d_{it-j}^P + \sum_{j=0}^{5}\delta_j^h y_{it-j} + \varepsilon_{it+h}, h = 1,\ldots,10.$$

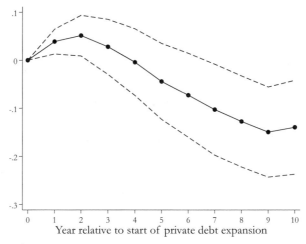

FIGURE 2.4 Real GDP dynamics around private debt expansions
Note: This figure presents the dynamics of real GDP around private debt expansions, estimated using equation (1). Dashed lines represent 95% confidence intervals computed using standard errors that are two-way clustered on country and year.

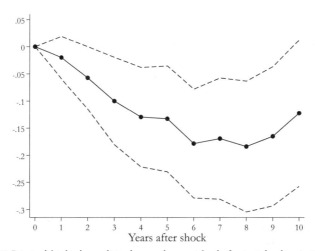

FIGURE 2.5 Private debt shocks predict a lower subsequent level of output: local projection impulse response
Note: This figure presents the response of real GDP to a private debt-to-GDP shock estimated using Jordà (2005) local projections given by equation (2). Dashed lines represent 95% confidence intervals computed using standard errors that are two-way clustered on country and year.

run. The local projection impulse response also suggests that debt expansions lead to a lower subsequent level of output.

Why Are Debt Booms Associated with Lower Future Output?

Private debt booms predict lower medium-run growth and perhaps even a lower long-run level of output. Here I outline the key systematic patterns in the data that help understand the destructive impact of private debt booms. Understanding the potential mechanisms also reinforces the hypothesis that debt booms play a causal role in depressing future output, as opposed to merely being a passive reflection of real economic dynamics.

CREDIT SUPPLY EXPANSION

Private debt booms often start with an increased willingness of the financial sector to lend, that is, with an increase in credit supply. Credit supply expansion can be driven by a variety of factors. Financial innovation such as securitization may increase the flow of savings toward private credit such as mortgage loans. Banking market liberalization can also drive an expansion in credit supply by increasing competition in the lending market, as, for example, the experience of the Nordic countries during the 1980s demonstrated.

Credit supply can also expand due to an increase in saving, either domestically or from abroad. For many open economies with free capital mobility, credit expansion is often driven by increased global liquidity, which lowers borrowing costs and fuels capital inflows. Increased global liquidity and lower global borrowing costs can, in turn, be driven by loose monetary policy in leading economies (Miranda-Agrippino and Rey 2015). Credit supply may also rise because of overoptimism that leads lenders to overextrapolate recent low defaults or neglect downside risk (Minsky 1986; Bordalo, Gennaioli, and Shleifer 2018). Regardless of the underlying source, the expansion in credit supply explains why credit expands rapidly without merely following faster productivity growth.

Figure 2.6 provides evidence of the role of credit supply at the country level. It shows that during private debt booms, credit spreads decline and fall below their trend level. Specifically, it plots the average of the Hamilton-filtered private debt-to-GDP and corporate credit spread around the debt boom events identified above. Credit spreads are measured as the difference between corporate bond yields and the long-term treasury bond yield. This evidence is consistent with Krishnamurthy and Muir (2017), who find that credit spreads tend to be low before financial crises, and Mian, Sufi, and

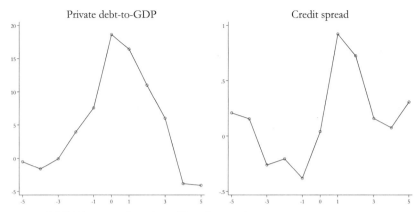

FIGURE 2.6 Debt booms are driven by credit supply expansion
Note: This figure shows the average path of private debt-to-GDP and credit to GDP around private debt boom episodes. Both series are in percentage point deviations from the Hamilton-filtered trend, as described in the text. The credit spread variable is from a variety of sources combined by Baron, Verner, and Xiong (2021).

Verner (2017), who show that mortgage spreads are low during household credit booms.

In addition to declining spreads, credit supply expansion can also lead to a decline in lending standards and an increase in lending to riskier borrowers. Greenwood and Hanson (2013) document that credit expansions coincide with an increase in the share of bond issuance by risky firms, i.e., the high yield share, which López-Salido, Stein, and Zakrajšek (2017) argue captures periods of elevated credit market "sentiment." Building on Greenwood and Hanson (2013), Kirti (2018) presents evidence for a broad sample of countries showing that the high yield share increases during credit expansions. The evidence of declining lending standards provides further support for the view that debt booms are driven by credit supply expansions.

DISTORTIONARY DEMAND BOOMS

The expansion in credit supply can affect the economy in two ways. First, it can boost productive capacity by allowing constrained firms to increase investment or by improving the allocation of capital across firms. The productive capacity channel is the channel through which credit supply expansion may lead to higher long-run income. Second, it can boost demand by increasing household access to disposable funds. Credit expansion that only operates through demand is unlikely to represent growth-enhancing credit deepening.

Mian, Sufi, and Verner (2020) present a simple framework to diagnose whether debt booms operate through the demand channel. They show that credit expansions that operate through demand lead to an expansion in nontradable relative to tradable employment and real exchange rate appreciation. The logic is the following. A credit expansion operating through demand will boost demand for both nontradable and tradable goods. Tradable goods can be imported, but nontradable goods must be produced locally. This requires an increase in production of nontradable goods, leading to a reallocation of employment to the nontradable sector. Rising demand also increases the price of nontradables relative to tradables, reflecting the shortage of nontradable goods. The rise in the relative price of nontradables fuels a real exchange rate appreciation.

In contrast, Mian, Sufi, and Verner (2020) show that credit expansions that operate by expanding the economy's productive capacity do not lead to a reallocation toward nontradables. This is true even if the credit expansion has a differential effect on the nontradable or tradable sector's access to credit. Moreover, credit expansions that operate through supply also lead to expanding exports, as the economy becomes more productive.

Figure 2.7 presents evidence that private debt booms fuel demand booms. Nontradable relative to tradable employment expands during debt booms and then collapses in the busts. Nontradable to tradable output shows similar dynamics. The reallocation toward nontradable sectors, including construction, is especially difficult to square with the productivity-enhancing effects of debt booms. These sectors have generally seen slower productivity growth than tradable sectors such as manufacturing (Borio et al. 2016).

Figure 2.7 also shows that debt booms lead to an appreciation of the real exchange rate and the relative price of nontradables. The reallocation toward nontradables coincides with expanding imports, but falling exports, as the tradable sector loses competitiveness. Overall, debt booms appear to operate primarily by boosting demand rather than productive capacity. In the process, these booms create distortions that will exacerbate the subsequent bust.

CREDIT SUPPLY REVERSAL AND BANKING SECTOR TROUBLES

Figure 2.6 shows that the expansion in credit supply eventually reverses with a spike in credit spreads and a sharp slowdown in lending. The reversal starts in year 0 of the peak and accelerates in year 1 after the peak of the debt boom. Understanding what precipitates the reversal and its exact timing is one of the least well understood aspects of private debt booms. Professional economic forecasters seldom predict turning points, including recessions. Bordalo,

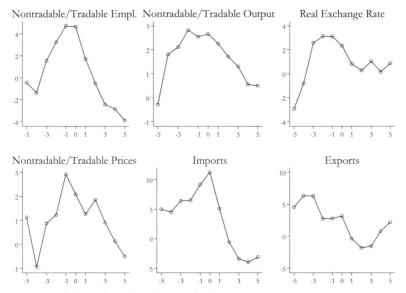

F I G U R E 2.7 Debt booms boost demand, not productive capacity

Note: This figure shows the average path of nontradable relative to tradable employment, output, and prices; the real exchange rate; imports; and exports around private debt boom events identified as described in the text. All series are in percentage point deviations from the Hamilton-filtered trend. Nontradable and tradable employment, output, and prices are from a variety of sources combined by Mian, Sufi, and Verner (2020). The real exchange rate is from the BIS. Imports and exports are from the World Bank's World Development Indicators.

Gennaioli, and Shleifer (2018) present a theory of "diagnostic expectations," in which a sequence of negative shocks leads to a sharp reversal from optimism to pessimism, leading to a contraction in credit supply that marks the start of the bust phase of the cycle. These negative shocks are often unexpected losses on loans. For example, in the model of Greenwood, Hanson, and Jin (2019), unexpected defaults lead to an excessive cutback in access to credit, as investors overextrapolate recent losses.

Figure 2.8 shows that the bank equity total-returns index peaks and begins declining two years before (year $t = -2$) the peak of the debt boom. In contrast, nonfinancial equities peak with the peak of the credit boom ($t = 0$). This is consistent with Baron, Verner, and Xiong (2021), who find that bank stocks tend to detect banking crises before nonfinancial equities and credit spreads. Bank equity is a levered portfolio of loans to households and businesses. The decline in bank equity represents losses on these loans that create banking sector distress. The banking sector distress, whether in the form of a full-blown banking crisis or more quiet banking undercapitalization,

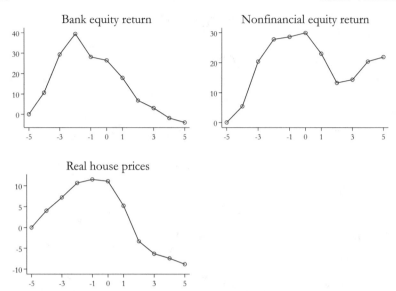

FIGURE 2.8 Bank equity, nonfinancial equity, and house prices
Note: This figure shows the average cumulative bank equity returns, nonfinancial equity returns, and real house prices around private debt boom events. All series are in log (times 100) deviations from the Hamilton-filtered trend and benchmarked to period $t = -5$, i.e., five years before the peak of the debt boom. Bank and nonfinancial equity returns are from Baron, Verner, and Xiong (2021). Real house prices are from the BIS's residential property prices database, deflated by the consumer price index.

translates into a contraction in credit supply that depresses new lending and raises the cost of credit for households and firms. The fall in credit supply directly depresses consumption, investment, and output (e.g., Chodorow-Reich 2014; Huber 2018).

DEBT OVERHANG, HOUSING BUSTS, AND OVERVALUATION

The contraction in credit supply interacts with several distortions created in the boom phase to produce a sharp slowdown in output. First, the overhang of debt itself from the credit boom acts as an important contractionary force. Elevated debt depresses demand and leads to asset fire sales for distressed borrowers. Drehmann, Juselius, and Korinek (2018) show that real GDP growth slows following debt booms precisely when funds start to flow from borrowers back to lenders due to higher debt service requirements.

Verner and Gyöngyösi (2020) provide direct evidence of the contraction role of higher household debt burdens following a debt boom. They compare borrowers and cities with greater exposure to foreign currency debt relative to domestic currency debt during a currency crisis in Hungary. Cities that experienced larger increases in real debt burdens through foreign currency debt exposure experience a collapse in spending, local employment, and house prices. The rise in foreign currency debt burdens has negative spillover effects on nearby borrowers with only domestic currency debt. This evidence highlights that the negative consequences of debt booms can be especially severe when the boom is financed with risky contracts such as foreign currency loans denominated in funding currencies.

Second, private debt booms fuel unsustainable asset price booms, including house price booms, that then reverse in the bust. During the boom, the expansion in debt is reinforced by rising asset prices that increase collateralized borrowing (Mian and Sufi 2011). The boom in house prices also reinforces the reallocation of employment toward the nontradable sector through the increase in construction activity. Figure 2.8 shows the boom and bust and house prices around private debt booms. Mian and Sufi (2014) estimate how the interaction of high household debt and house price declines depressed local demand and employment across U.S. regions in the Great Recession.

Third, the real appreciation created by the demand boom sows the seeds of a more severe slowdown. When the credit supply expansion reverses, the economy is left with higher wages and prices. The fall in demand translates into higher unemployment and lower output because of downward rigidity in wages (Schmitt-Grohé and Uribe 2016). Moreover, the economy is left with a bloated nontradable sector and an uncompetitive tradable sector that is difficult to reverse because of real frictions that make it difficult for workers to transition from nontradable to tradable sector jobs.

Overvaluation may also have long-term negative effects. Sustained overvaluation may reduce the long-term competitiveness of the tradable sector (Krugman 1987; Rodrik and Subramanian 2009). As tradable industries lose market share internationally, they also fail to adopt new technologies and improve productivity through learning-by-doing. Overvaluation and the reallocation toward nontradables can also reduce human capital formation. For example, Charles, Hurst, and Notowidigdo (2015) show that the 2000s housing boom in the United States led many individuals to forgo a college education and instead work in the construction sector. Many of these jobs were based on temporarily elevated demand and disappeared when the boom reversed.

THE ROLE OF HOUSEHOLD DEBT AND HOUSING

Household debt booms are particularly likely to lead to lower output growth and increased risk of a financial crisis (Jordà, Schularick, and Taylor 2014;

Mian, Sufi, and Verner 2017). House price booms have been suggested as one of the best signals for detecting whether a debt boom will end in a financial crisis (Richter, Schularick, and Wachtel 2021). The patterns highlighted above help explain why. Household debt booms are particularly likely to finance demand and real estate booms. While expanding household borrowing can improve welfare by allowing households to smooth consumption, household debt booms are less likely to finance improvements in productive capacity. However, while household debt is important to monitor, bank and firm leverage also matter. The negative consequences of debt busts on the real economy are even more powerful when bank and firm balance sheets are also highly levered (Giroud and Mueller 2016).

How Do We Deal with Debt Booms?

Private debt booms predict growth slowdowns and an increased risk of a banking crisis. Moreover, as I show, the data suggest that debt booms even predict a lower future real GDP in the long term. The evidence is mounting that the costs of private debt booms are severe, and these costs likely outweigh the benefits.

What, if anything, should policy do about credit booms? On this question, theory is ahead of practice and empirical evidence. Recent theoretical models with macroeconomic and financial frictions show that debt booms can be socially inefficient (e.g., Lorenzoni 2008; Farhi and Werning 2016; Korinek and Simsek 2016). However, excessive borrowing occurs in equilibrium because borrowers and lenders do not internalize the negative equilibrium consequences of high debt in a crisis. These models imply that it can be optimal for regulators to limit private borrowing during credit booms.

Surely this means there is a major role for macroprudential policy. Not so fast. Macroprudential policies have a role in limiting the most excessive debt booms. However, macroprudential policy cannot be expected to avoid all crises, and these policies have several practical challenges.

The first challenge is that we still have a limited understanding of how macroprudential policies work, and these policies can have unintended consequences. For example, prudential policies targeting one sector, such as housing markets, can increase risk-taking by financial intermediaries in other segments, such as corporate lending, as demonstrated by Acharya et al. (2020). Macroprudential policy may also shift intermediation toward unregulated institutions in the "shadow banking" sector without reducing systemic risk.

The second challenge is that policy makers may also be engulfed by the same overoptimistic expectations that spur a risky credit expansion. In many cases, we cannot rely on policy makers being smarter than the market. This challenge applies especially to time-varying macroprudential instruments that aim to time the cycle. Even if policy makers can recognize a buildup of risk, a third challenge is that politicians may not have an incentive to curb credit booms that boost short-run growth. Müller (2018b), for example, shows that macroprudential policy displays an electoral cycle, with policy being loosened prior to elections.

The fourth and perhaps most critical challenge facing macroprudential policy is that assessing its success is close to impossible. How do we know when crises are averted? If macroprudential policies can avert crises for a sustained period, their benefits may be difficult to judge, while their costs in the form of restricted access to credit will be clear. In contrast, for monetary policy, it is much easier to know whether inflation is close to a 2% target. Altogether, these challenges imply that simple macroprudential tools have a role in curbing the worst excesses of debt booms, but macroprudential policy cannot be expected to avoid all crises. A central task of future research is to improve our understanding of whether and how macroprudential tools work.

Appendix

TABLE 2A.1 Sample

Country	Years	Country	Years
Afghanistan	2006–2016	Central African Rep.	1960–2016
Algeria	1995–2016	Chad	1960–2016
Argentina	1984–2016	Chile	1983–2016
Australia	1960–2016	China	1985–2016
Austria	1960–2016	Colombia	1996–2016
Azerbaijan	1992–2016	Comoros	1982–2016
Bahrain	1980–2015	Congo	1960–2016
Bangladesh	1974–2016	Costa Rica	1996–2016
Belgium	1970–2016	Cote d'Ivoire	1960–2016
Benin	1960–2016	Croatia	1995–2016
Bhutan	1983–2016	Cyprus	1975–2016
Botswana	1972–2016	Czech Rep.	1993–2016
Brazil	1996–2016	Dem. Rep. of the Congo	1963–2016
Bulgaria	1991–2016	Denmark	1966–2016
Burkina Faso	1960–2016	Djibouti	1990–2015
Burundi	1964–2016	Dominica	1977–2016
Cambodia	1993–2016	Dominican Rep.	1991–2016
Cameroon	1960–2016	Ecuador	1960–2016
Canada	1960–2016	Egypt	1960–2016
Cape Verde	1980–2016	El Salvador	1965–2016

(continued)

Country	Years	Country	Years
Eritrea	1995–2011	Morocco	1966–2016
Estonia	1995–2016	Mozambique	1988–2016
Ethiopia	1981–2008	Myanmar	1960–2016
FS Micronesia	1995–2016	Nepal	1960–2016
Finland	1970–2016	Netherlands	1961–2016
France	1969–2016	New Zealand	1977–2016
Gambia	1966–2014	Nicaragua	1960–2016
Georgia	1995–2016	Niger	1960–2016
Germany	1970–2016	Nigeria	1960–2016
Ghana	1960–2016	Norway	1960–2016
Greece	1970–2016	Oman	1972–2015
Grenada	1977–2016	Pakistan	1960–2016
Guatemala	1960–2016	Papua New Guinea	1973–2016
Guinea	1989–2016	Paraguay	1960–2016
Guinea–Bissau	1990–2016	Peru	1960–2016
Guyana	1960–2016	Philippines	1960–2016
Haiti	1996–2016	Poland	1992–2016
Honduras	1960–2016	Portugal	1960–2016
Hungary	1991–2016	Qatar	2000–2016
India	1960–2016	Rep. of Korea	1962–2016
Indonesia	1976–2016	Rep. of Moldova	1995–2016
Iran	1961–2016	Romania	1996–2016
Ireland	1971–2016	Russian Federation	1995–2016
Israel	1990–2016	Rwanda	1964–2016
Italy	1960–2016	Saint Lucia	1977–2016
Jamaica	1966–2016	St. Vincent	1975–2016
Japan	1964–2016	Samoa	1982–2016
Jordan	1975–2016	Sao Tome and Principe	2000–2016
Kazakhstan	1995–2016	Saudi Arabia	1993–2016
Kenya	1961–2016	Senegal	1960–2016
Kuwait	1965–2016	Serbia	1997–2016
Kyrgyzstan	1995–2016	Sierra Leone	1960–2016
Lao People's Dem. Rep.	1989–2010	Singapore	1970–2016
Latvia	1995–2016	Slovakia	1995–2016
Lebanon	1988–2016	Slovenia	1995–2016
Lesotho	1973–2016	Solomon Islands	1990–2016
Liberia	1974–2015	South Africa	1965–2016
Lithuania	1995–2016	Spain	1970–2016
Madagascar	1962–2016	Sri Lanka	1961–2016
Malawi	1965–2016	Sudan	1960–2016
Malaysia	1964–2016	Sweden	1961–2016
Maldives	2001–2016	Switzerland	1980–2016
Mali	1967–2016	Tanzania	1988–2016
Malta	1970–2016	Thailand	1970–2016
Mauritania	1962–2012	Togo	1960–2016
Mexico	1980–2016	Tonga	1981–2016
Mongolia	1991–2016	Trinidad and Tobago	1960–2016

TABLE 2A.1 (continued)

Country	Years	Country	Years
Turkey	1986–2016	Vanuatu	1979–2016
USA	1960–2016	Venezuela	1960–2014
Uganda	1982–2016	Viet Nam	1992–2016
Ukraine	1995–2016	Yemen	1990–2013
United Arab Emirates	1975–2016	Zambia	1965–2016
United Kingdom	1963–2016	Zimbabwe	1979–2005
Uruguay	1960–2016		

Note: This table presents the countries and years used in the country-level analysis. The range of years represents the intersection of the years available for the key variables, which is the sample used in the analysis.

REFERENCES

Acharya, Viral V., Katharina Bergant, Matteo Crosignani, Tim Eisert, and Fergal McCann. 2020. The Anatomy of the Transmission of Macroprudential Policies. NBER Working Paper 27292.

Baron, Matthew, Emil Verner, and Wei Xiong. 2021. Banking Crises without Panics. Quarterly Journal of Economics 136 (1): 51–113.

Bordalo, Pedro, Nicola Gennaioli, and Andrei Shleifer. 2018. Diagnostic Expectations and Credit Cycles. Journal of Finance 73 (1): 199–227.

Borio, Claudio, Enisse Kharroubi, Christian Upper, and Fabrizio Zampolli. 2016. Labour Reallocation and Productivity Dynamics: Financial Causes, Real Consequences. BIS Working Paper 534.

Cerra, Valerie, and Sweta Chaman Saxena. 2008. Growth Dynamics: The Myth of Economic Recovery. American Economic Review 98 (1): 439–57.

Charles, Kerwin Kofi, Erik Hurst, and Matthew J. Notowidigdo. 2015. Housing Booms and Busts, Labor Market Opportunities, and College Attendance. NBER Working Paper 21587.

Chodorow-Reich, Gabriel. 2014. The Employment Effects of Credit Market Disruptions: Firm-level Evidence from the 2008–9 Financial Crisis. Quarterly Journal of Economics 129 (1): 1–59.

Drehmann, Mathias, Mikael Juselius, and Anton Korinek. 2018. Going with the Flows: New Borrowing, Debt Service and the Transmission of Credit Booms. NBER Working Paper 24549.

Farhi, Emmanuel, and Iván Werning. 2016. A Theory of Macroprudential Policies in the Presence of Nominal Rigidities. Econometrica 84 (5): 1645–1704.

Fonseca, Julia, and Bernardus Van Doornik. 2018. Financial Development, Labor Markets, and Aggregate Productivity: Evidence from Brazil. Working paper.

Giroud, Xavier, and Holger M. Mueller. 2016. Firm Leverage, Consumer Demand, and Employment Losses during the Great Recession. Quarterly Journal of Economics 132 (1): 271–316.

Goldsmith, Raymond W. 1969. Financial Structure and Development. New Haven, CT: Yale University Press.

Greenwood, Jeremy, and Boyan Jovanovic. 1990. Financial Development, Growth, and the Distribution of Income. Journal of Political Economy 98 (5): 1076–1107.

Greenwood, Robin, and Samuel G. Hanson. 2013. Issuer Quality and Corporate Bond Returns. Review of Financial Studies 26 (6): 1483–1525.

Greenwood, Robin, Samuel G. Hanson, and Lawrence J. Jin. 2019. Reflexivity in Credit Markets. NBER Working Paper 25747.

Hamilton, James D. 2018. Why You Should Never Use the Hodrick-Prescott Filter. Review of Economics and Statistics 100 (5): 831–43.

Huber, Kilian. 2018. Disentangling the Effects of a Banking Crisis: Evidence from German Firms and Counties. American Economic Review 108 (3): 868–98.

Jordà, Òscar. 2005. Estimation and Inference of Impulse Responses by Local Projections. American Economic Review 95 (1): 161–82.

Jordà, Òscar, Moritz Schularick, and Alan M. Taylor. 2014. The Great Mortgaging: Housing Finance, Crises, and Business Cycles. NBER Working Paper 20501.

King, Robert G., and Ross Levine. 1993. Finance and Growth: Schumpeter Might Be Right. Quarterly Journal of Economics 108 (3): 717–37.

Kirti, Divya. 2018. Lending Standards and Output Growth. IMF Working Paper 2018/023.

Korinek, Anton, and Alp Simsek. 2016. Liquidity Trap and Excessive Leverage. American Economic Review 106 (3): 699–738.

Krishnamurthy, Arvind, and Tyler Muir. 2017. How Credit Cycles across a Financial Crisis. NBER Working Paper 23850.

Krugman, Paul. 1987. The Narrow Moving Band, the Dutch Disease, and the Competitive Consequences of Mrs. Thatcher: Notes on Trade in the Presence of Dynamic Scale Economies. Journal of Development Economics 27 (1–2): 41–55.

Larrain, Mauricio, and Sebastian Stumpner. 2017. Capital Account Liberalization and Aggregate Productivity: The Role of Firm Capital Allocation. Journal of Finance 72 (4): 1825–58.

Levine, Ross. 2004. Finance and Growth: Theory and Evidence. NBER Working Paper 10766.

Levine, Ross, Norman Loayza, and Thorsten Beck. 2000. Financial Intermediation and Growth: Causality and Causes. Journal of Monetary Economics 46: 31–77.

Loayza, Norman, and Romain Rancière. 2006. Financial Development, Financial Fragility, and Growth. Journal of Money, Credit and Banking 38 (4): 1051–76.

López-Salido, David, Jeremy C. Stein, and Egon Zakrajšek. 2017. Credit-market Sentiment and the Business Cycle. Quarterly Journal of Economics 132 (3): 1373–1426.

Lorenzoni, Guido. 2008. Inefficient Credit Booms. Review of Economic Studies 75 (3): 809–33.

Martin, Alberto, and Jaume Ventura. 2012. Economic Growth with Bubbles. American Economic Review 102 (6): 3033–58.

Mian, Atif, and Amir Sufi. 2011. House Prices, Home Equity-Based Borrowing, and the US Household Leverage Crisis. American Economic Review 101 (5): 2132–56.

———. 2014. What Explains the 2007–2009 Drop in Employment? Econometrica 82 (6): 2197–2223.

Mian, Atif, Amir Sufi, and Emil Verner. 2017. Household Debt and Business Cycles Worldwide. Quarterly Journal of Economics 132 (4): 1755–1817.

———. 2020. How Does Credit Supply Expansion Affect the Real Economy? The Productive Capacity and Household Demand Channels. Journal of Finance 75 (2): 949–94.

Minsky, Hyman P. 1986. Stabilizing an Unstable Economy. Vol. 1. New York: McGraw-Hill.

Miranda-Agrippino, Silvia, and Hélène Rey. 2015. US Monetary Policy and the Global Financial Cycle. NBER Working Paper 21722.

Müller, Karsten. 2018a. Credit Markets around the World, 1910–2014. Available at https://ssrn .com/abstract=3259636.

———. 2018b. Electoral Cycles in Prudential Regulation. Available at https://ssrn.com/abstract =3159086.

Richter, Björn, Moritz Schularick, and Paul Wachtel. 2021. When to Lean Against the Wind. Journal of Money, Credit and Banking 53 (1): 5–39.

Rodrik, Dani, and Arvind Subramanian. 2009. Why Did Financial Globalization Disappoint? IMF staff papers, 56 (1): 112–38.

Scharfstein, David S. 2018. Presidential Address: Pension Policy and the Financial System. Journal of Finance 73 (4): 1463–1512.

Schmitt-Grohé, Stephanie, and Martín Uribe. 2016. Downward Nominal Wage Rigidity, Currency Pegs, and Involuntary Unemployment. Journal of Political Economy 124 (5): 1466–1514.

Schularick, Moritz, and Alan M. Taylor. 2012. Credit Booms Gone Bust: Monetary Policy, Leverage Cycles, and Financial Crises, 1870–2008. American Economic Review 102 (2): 1029–61.

Varela, Liliana. 2018. Reallocation, Competition, and Productivity: Evidence from a Financial Liberalization Episode. Review of Economic Studies 85 (2): 1279–1313.

Verner, Emil, and Győző Gyöngyösi. 2020. Household Debt Revaluation and the Real Economy: Evidence from a Foreign Currency Debt Crisis. American Economic Review 110 (9): 2667–702.

Comment by Holger Mueller

I would like to commend Emil Verner for writing an interesting and thought-provoking chapter. The central thesis of his chapter is that credit booms—rapid expansions in private credit to GDP—are associated with lower long-run growth. In line with prior literature, Emil distinguishes between credit booms and credit deepening—gradual expansions in private credit that may be beneficial for long-run growth. My discussion consists of three parts. First, I briefly review the empirical evidence on which Emil's thesis is based. Second, I ask what is the counterfactual in the absence of a credit boom—is it the same growth path, just without the boom-bust cycle, or a different growth path altogether? Third, I discuss policy implications: in particular, how can policy makers distinguish "good" from "bad" credit booms, and what tools do they have available to curb credit booms or alleviate their adverse long-run effects?

EMPIRICAL EVIDENCE

Emil's thesis is based on a number of figures depicting the dynamics of real GDP around a credit boom. In these figures, real GDP first rises above its previous trend and then declines. Importantly, several years after the credit boom, the level of real GDP appears to fall below its initial value. I write "appears" because measuring the long-run impact of credit booms is characterized by

Holger Mueller is the Nomura Professor of Finance at the Leonard N. Stern School of Business, New York University.

significant uncertainty and large confidence bands, something Emil is well aware of. Accordingly, he is careful to interpret these figures as suggesting that, in the long run, the costs of credit booms may outweigh their benefits.

WHAT IS THE COUNTERFACTUAL?

Suppose we take the evidence that credit booms are associated with lower long-run output at face value. The question is whether the economy would be better off without a credit boom? The answer is that it depends on the counterfactual which, by definition, is unobserved. If we believe that the economy would have continued along its previous growth path, that is, along its pre-existing trend, then the answer is probably yes. However, there is an intriguing alternative hypothesis, advanced by Rancière, Tornell, and Westermann (2008), stating that the choice might not be between the same growth path with and without credit booms but instead between a slow but steady growth path without credit booms and a higher growth path with credit booms but occasional "boom-bust cycles." Thus, although credit booms can be potentially avoided by choosing a slow but steady growth path, the price to be paid is lower long-run growth. Put differently, while long-run output might indeed be lower after a credit boom than before, an economy without credit booms (and occasional "boom-bust cycles") might exhibit yet *even lower* long-run output.

To illustrate, Rancière, Tornell, and Westermann provide the examples of India and Thailand. Between 1980 and the early 2000s, India exhibited slow but steady GDP growth, whereas Thailand experienced high growth, credit booms, and financial crises. Despite these crises, however, Thailand's overall GDP growth during this period was much higher than India's (162% versus 114%). Thus, in the long run, India's economy, which exhibited steady growth without credit booms, was less successful than Thailand's.

To explain these differences, the authors develop a theory in which systemic risk-taking reduces firms' cost of capital and relaxes borrowing constraints. This leads to more investment but also occasional financial crises. Importantly, under certain conditions, the benefits of systemic risk outweigh the costs, and long-run growth in a risky economy with financial crises is higher than in a safe economy without financial crises. As the authors make clear, "this finding *does not* imply that financial crises are good for growth. It suggests, however, that high growth paths are associated with the undertaking of systemic risk and with the occurrence of *occasional* crises" (Rancière, Tornell, and Westermann 2008, 360; emphasis in original).

Finally, the authors test their theory using the skewness of credit growth as an indicator of systemic financial risk. Unlike variance, negative skewness isolates the effects of large, infrequent, and abrupt credit busts that are commonly associated with financial crises. Using a large sample of countries over a forty-year period, they find that countries with higher systemic financial risk indeed experience higher long-run GDP growth, confirming the main prediction from their theory model.

POLICY IMPLICATIONS

The choices outlined above have different policy implications. Under the Rancière-Tornell-Westermann "trade-off view," the policy choice is between a financially liberalized economy that encourages risk-taking and an economy that does not encourage risk-taking. By contrast, under the views expressed in Emil's chapter, the policy goal ought to be to prevent credit booms or at least mitigate their negative consequences. Given that Emil's chapter does not primarily focus on policy, I would like to briefly discuss Dell'Ariccia et al. (2016), an interesting study by researchers from the International Monetary Fund and European Central Bank that addresses this issue. The study covers 170 countries over the 1970–2010 period and identifies 176 credit booms using similar criteria as in Emil's study. In line with Emil's main hypothesis, the authors find that 32% of all credit booms are followed by a financial or banking crisis within three years and 62% are followed by below-trend real GDP growth during the six years after the end of the boom.

However, not all credit booms end badly. As the authors note, "in about 40% of the episodes, the credit-to-GDP ratio seems to shift permanently to a new, higher 'equilibrium' level. In fact, there is a positive correlation between long-term financial deepening (measured as the change in the credit-to-GDP ratio over the period 1970–2010) and the cumulated credit growth that occurred during boom episodes." Further, and consistent with the "trade-off view," "[t]here is a positive correlation between the number of years a country has undergone a credit boom and the cumulative real GDP per capita growth achieved since 1970," meaning countries with longer credit booms also tend to exhibit higher long-run GDP growth (Dell'Ariccia et al. 2016, 309).

As the authors point out, predicting whether or not a credit boom will eventually turn bad—in which case policy intervention is desirable—is very difficult, though they note that booms starting at higher levels of credit to GDP are more likely to end badly. Based on their empirical evidence, the authors conclude that monetary or fiscal policy is unlikely to be effective in taming credit booms or alleviating their negative consequences. By contrast, they argue that macroprudential policies are likely to be promising. In principle, such policies are aimed at smoothing credit cycles to prevent systemic crises and cushion against their adverse effects and include capital and liquidity requirements, credit growth ("speed") limits, and loan eligibility (e.g., debt-to-income and loan-to-value ratios) limits. In particular, while capital and liquidity requirements appear to have been less successful in curbing the incidence and duration of credit booms, they have been broadly successful in building up buffers to deal with the ensuing busts.

REFERENCES

Dell'Ariccia, Giovanni, Deniz Igan, Luc Laeven, and Hui Tong. 2016. Credit Booms and Macro-financial Stability. Economic Policy 31: 299–355.
Rancière, Romanin, Aaron Tornell, and Frank Westermann. 2008. Systemic Crises and Growth. Quarterly Journal of Economics 123: 359–406.

PART TWO

Risk-Taking:
Incentives, Investors, Institutions

3

Are Bank CEOs to Blame?

RÜDIGER FAHLENBRACH

Compensation systems—designed in an environment of cheap money, intense competition, and light regulation—too often rewarded the quick deal, the short-term gain—
without proper consideration of long-term consequences. Often, those systems encouraged the big bet—where the payoff on the upside could be huge and the downside
limited. This was the case up and down the line—from the corporate boardroom to the
mortgage broker on the street.

FINAL REPORT OF THE U.S. GOVERNMENT'S NATIONAL
COMMISSION ON THE CAUSES OF THE FINANCIAL AND
ECONOMIC CRISIS IN THE UNITED STATES

I will distinguish between two types of "excessive" risk-taking. The first type
of excessive risk-taking means that financial incentives created distortions
that led bank executives to focus on short-term results to the detriment of
long-term shareholder value. The second type of excessive risk-taking arises
because shareholders do not internalize fully systemic risk externalities. Hence,
there could be levels of risk-taking that are both optimal for shareholders and
socially excessive.

I will focus on three questions: First, did bank executives willingly and
knowingly take excessive risks vis-à-vis their shareholders? To address this
question, I will study executives' trading in their own bank's stock prior to
the crisis. Second, what do we know about the impact of broader corporate
governance mechanisms on bank risk-taking? Third, do bankers in boom
time have incentives to do less due diligence and less monitoring because
default seems remote, collateral value is high, and in particular because there
is investor appetite for a securitization of the loans banks originate?

The evidence is supportive of a particular type of excessive risk-taking,
vis-à-vis society. In addition to optimistic beliefs about lending opportunities, shareholders also held the belief that the government would bail out

Rüdiger Fahlenbrach is professor of finance at the École Polytechnique Fédérale de
Lausanne and is affiliated with the Swiss Finance Institute.

large banks during a crisis, making it optimal for shareholders to make banks more risky than was socially desirable. For example, Acharya et al. (2012) show that banks made large dividend payments before and during the financial crisis, which represented a transfer from creditors to equity holders and rendered banks more fragile. As another example, the evidence reported in this chapter shows that the originate-to-distribute mortgage model created incentives to increase risky lending while compromising loan quality.

Solutions to this type of excessive risk-taking are difficult. Two sensible solutions are to increase lockup periods for shares of bank insiders or to pay part of bankers' bonuses using debt instruments. These mechanisms would give bank executives incentives to be more cautious during boom periods, and there is some evidence that so-called inside debt mitigated risk-taking during the last crisis. A problem that these solutions cannot address is that even those bank executives who see problems in the buildup of a crisis and have money locked up in their banks may conclude that it is better for them to cater to optimistic shareholders than to swim against the tide. For example, during the last crisis, shareholders may have pushed boards to fire executives in publicly listed banks if they had reduced risky lending while their peers continued to engage in those activities. The famous quote of Chuck Prince, former CEO of Citigroup, summarizes the problem: "As long as the music is playing, you've got to get up and dance."

Financial Incentives of Bank Executives and Financial Crises

In this first section, I discuss the notion that compensation in the financial sector in the buildup of the crisis was the result of a conflict between managers and shareholders. There are three different versions of the "poor financial incentives" explanation of the crisis. The first version is that bank executives had strong incentives to focus on the short run instead of the long run, because they received large cash bonuses that only rewarded the upside and there was no opportunity to claw back some of the bonus should its attribution have been unjustified. The second version states that the performance-based equity grants executives received had short vesting periods so that while theoretically these executives had downside exposure, in reality they could undo it very quickly. A third version is that option compensation gave executives incentives to take more risks than would have been optimal for shareholders.

A useful starting point is to examine the level and structure of the compensation of chief executive officers in the financial industry in the year just

TABLE 3.1 Key compensation variables for CEOs of bank holding companies and investment banks for fiscal year 2006

	Mean	Median
Annual compensation		
Total compensation	$7,798	$2,454
Salary	$761	$748
Cash bonus	$2,138	$637
Cash bonus / salary	2.8	0.9
Dollar value of annual stock grant	$2,653	$296
Dollar value of annual option grant	$1,608	$196
Other compensation	$637	$129
Equity—total value		
Value of total equity portfolio	$87,467	$35,557
Value of shares	$61,190	$22,255
Value of exercisable options	$17,358	$5,729
Value of unexercisable options	$3,243	$929
Value of unvested restricted stock	$5,677	
Equity incentives		
Percentage ownership from shares	1.6	0.4
Percentage ownership options + shares	2.4	1.0
Dollar gain from +1% increase in share price	$1,119	$468
Dollar gain from +1% increase in volatility	$189	$53
Inside debt		
Value of inside debt (Pension + deferred comp)	$12,582	$4,168
Value of inside debt / value of total equity portfolio	25%	16%

Note: Compensation figures are in thousands of dollars.

prior to the financial crisis.[1] Table 3.1 shows means and medians of the key compensation and equity ownership variables for a sample of the largest ninety-five bank CEOs that are part of the S&P 1500 at the end of 2006.[2] The total compensation (including new option and stock grants, but excluding gains from exercising options) of sample CEOs was on average $7.8 million for 2006, and median compensation was $2.5 million. Core and Guay (2010) compare these numbers with a sample of characteristics-matched

1. The use of CEO compensation here and in the literature is mainly driven by the availability of detailed compensation data, not necessarily by the belief that bank CEOs are the most important individuals to study risk-taking during the crisis. Data on compensation plans of traders or of employees at banks' proprietary trading desks, for example, is not available.
2. See Fahlenbrach and Stulz (2011) for details on the sample construction and variable definitions.

nonfinancial firms and conclude that, if anything, bank CEOs received actually less total annual compensation than the CEOs of industrial firms.[3]

The majority of total CEO compensation stems from performance-based pay, as the average base salary of $760,000 is less than 10% of the average total compensation. Cash bonuses are large relative to cash salary. The average value of cash bonus (measured as the sum of nonincentive-based pay, bonus, and long-term incentive plan payouts) over cash salary is 2.8, with a median of 0.9. The relatively large cash bonus component is controversial and is a key part of the first version of the "poor incentives" explanation of the crisis (e.g., Bebchuk 2010; Bebchuk and Spamann 2010; or Bhagat and Bolton 2014). When executives receive high cash bonuses for success but bonuses cannot go below zero for failure, executives potentially have incentives to take risks that are not in the interests of the shareholders or of the safety and soundness of their institutions. However, Kolasinski and Yang (2018) and Fahlenbrach and Stulz (2011) both find in regression analyses that the cash bonus / salary variable is unrelated to performance and risk-taking during the financial crisis of 2007/2009.

The second version of the poor financial incentives explanation of the crisis deals with equity grants and their contribution to risk-taking incentives. Table 3.1 shows that the average bank CEO received annual stock grants totaling $2.65 million and option grants totaling $1.61 million in 2006, together considerably larger than the cash bonus.

The table shows summary statistics for key compensation variables for a sample of ninety-five CEOs of bank holding companies and investment banks for fiscal year 2006. The data are from the Compustat Execucomp database. Values are reported in thousands of dollars. Most of the variables of the table are taken directly from Execucomp. "Cash bonus" is defined as the sum of bonus and nonequity incentive awards payouts. "Percentage ownership" uses the detailed information on current and previous option grants to calculate the options' delta and multiplies the number of options held in each series by its delta when calculating the percentage ownership. "Dollar

3. The picture reverses when one looks at the twenty-five largest banks in the United States—in those, CEOs make significantly more than in comparable industrial firms.

gain from +1% increase in share price" is equal to the dollar change in the executive's stock and option portfolio value for a 1% change in the stock price. "Dollar gain from +1% increase in volatility" is equal to the dollar change in the executive's equity portfolio value for a 1% change in stock volatility and is calculated from all option series held by the CEO. Inside debt is equal to the present value from accumulated pension benefits and the fiscal year-end balance of nonqualified deferred compensation. All compensation numbers in the table are in thousands of dollars.

The annual grant of stock and stock options typically is only a small part of the overall equity incentives of CEOs, as most CEOs accumulate large equity stakes during their tenure. The mean value of the bank CEO's equity stake is $87.5 million, or more than 100 times annual salary and more than 10 times total annual compensation.[4] Twenty-one sample CEOs have equity stakes valued at more than $100 million. The top three equity positions at the end of fiscal year 2006 were held by James Cayne (Bear Stearns, $1,062 million), Richard Fuld (Lehman Brothers, $911.5 million), and Stan O'Neal (Merrill Lynch, $349 million).

Interestingly, much of the equity (both stocks and options) is fully vested and CEOs could have freely disposed of it. Table 3.1 shows that on average less than $9 million of the total equity stake valued at $87.5 million was not yet vested. These numbers will become important for the interpretation of the evidence.

Table 3.1 next presents two measures of sensitivity of the equity portfolio of the CEO to changes in the bank's stock price. The average CEO ownership from shares and delta-weighted options represents 2.4% of the outstanding shares. The second measure is the dollar gain for a 1% increase in shareholder value. The average (median) dollar gain is $1.1 million ($0.5 million) for a 1% change in bank equity value. Sample CEOs have a significant pay-for-performance sensitivity from their equity holdings.

Fahlenbrach and Stulz (2011) find that U.S. bank CEOs did not materially reduce the large equity positions they held in December 2006.[5] Adebambo, Brockman, and Yan (2017) examine the ability of corporate executives to

4. I define the total dollar value of equity of a CEO at the end of fiscal year 2006 as the sum of unrestricted and restricted shares held multiplied by the end-of-year share price plus the Black-Scholes value of exercisable and unexercisable stock options plus the fair value of unearned equity incentive plans.

5. It may have been difficult for executives to sell a large portion of their holdings after they had material insider information on upcoming bank losses. However, such restrictions should have made bank executives more cautious ex ante and make it even more surprising that they had accumulated large positions in their stock.

anticipate the 2007–2008 financial crisis by comparing trading by executives of financial firms with trading by executives of nonfinancial firms. They conclude that corporate insiders of financial firms in their sample appear to be unaware of the timing and extent of the financial crisis, as net purchases of their own shares by managers of financial firms exceed those by managers of nonfinancial firms over the entire 2006–2008 period.

Most bank executives, as shown in table 3.1, had considerable equity stakes going into the crisis that they did not sell and on which they lost a lot of money. The results seem inconsistent with the argument that managers willingly and knowingly took risks that they should not have taken. These managerial decisions can arise, for example, if managers have expectations that fail to take risks correctly into account. Neglected risks can lead to a credit boom, because lenders and market participants become too optimistic about the risks of new lending opportunities (e.g., Kindleberger 1978; Minsky 1977). Gennaioli, Shleifer, and Vishny (2012) propose a new approach to modeling financial markets that gives the neglect of low probability risks a central role in accounting for understanding boom-and-bust cycles. A critical component of these models is that market participants are assumed to neglect some risk, but its materialization sharply changes their understanding of the distribution of risks. A fascinating but understudied research question is to what extent there are interdependencies between the beliefs of shareholders and managers and the financial incentive systems in place.

OPTION COMPENSATION

The third version of the poor incentives explanation of the crisis is that option compensation gave executives incentives to take more risks than would have been optimal for shareholders.[6] Table 3.1 shows the change in the dollar value of the CEO's wealth for a 1% increase in stock return volatility (dollar equity risk sensitivity).[7] At the end of 2006, the median dollar equity risk sensitivity is $53,000.

Several authors have estimated the correlation between these equity risk incentives and performance and risk-taking before and during the financial

6. Early studies of equity incentives and bank performance such as Houston and James (1995), Adams and Mehran (2003), and John and Qian (2003) all find evidence of a lower reliance on stock option pay for CEOs of bank holding companies compared to manufacturing firms, which suggests that shareholders and directors may be concerned about the issue.

7. An increase in equity volatility of 10% is very large, given that precrisis bank equity volatility was approximately 20%.

crisis, with mixed findings. Gande and Kalpathy (2017) find, using data on U.S. Federal Reserve emergency loans provided to large financial firms, that the amount of emergency loans and total days the loans are outstanding are positively correlated with precrisis CEO risk-taking incentives. Boyallian and Ruiz-Verdú (2017), Fahlenbrach and Stulz (2011), and Kolasinski and Yang (2018) all examine the relation between equity volatility risk-taking incentives from options measured in year 2006 and some measure of bank performance during the financial crisis. None of these papers finds a significant relation between bank failure or performance and the sensitivity of the value of CEOs' stock option portfolios to the volatility of their firms' stock.

Guay's (2010) observation helps explain why there may not be much of a relation between these volatility risk measures derived from options and crisis performance. He compares incentives from increases in volatility with the incentives from a 1% increase in the stock price and notes that equity volatility sensitivity is quite low relative to the stock price sensitivity. In table 3.1, the median risk incentives for a 1% increase in volatility of $53,000 are dwarfed by the median equity incentives for a 1% increase in the stock price of $468,000.

Financial Incentives of Non-CEO Bank Employees to Take Risks

Due to the data availability in the Execucomp database, many of the papers discussed above also examine the four other highest paid bank executives, reaching broadly the same conclusions. However, those executives are often the chief financial officer, general counsel, or president and not the individuals one would really like to have more information on. There is surprisingly little evidence on individual responses to performance-based compensation by traders, division heads of the investment banking division, or rank-and-file employees at the heart of the crisis, such as securitization agents or loan officers making actual lending decisions. However, it is important to note that no individual in a bank can take unlimited risks. There are constraints on risk-taking imposed by internal risk management and external regulators. Traders, for example, operate under a system of risk limits. Researchers would not only need information on the structure of compensation but also information on how much risk individuals were allowed to carry.

Cheng, Raina, and Xiong (2014) approach the question from a very different angle. They are interested in whether Wall Street employees foresaw the crash of the U.S. housing bubble. They ask whether Wall Street employees involved in securitization systematically missed the housing bubble, despite having better information than others. Cheng, Raina, and Xiong (2014) first obtained a list of conference attendees of the 2006 American Securitization

Forum, the largest industry conference. These individuals were vice presidents, senior vice presidents, managing directors, and other nonexecutives who worked at major investment houses. They then obtained the personal home transaction history of these securitization agents from public sources. Cheng, Raina, and Xiong (2014) found little evidence of securitization agents' awareness of a housing bubble and impending crash in their own home transactions. In fact, agents increased, rather than decreased, their housing exposure during the boom period. Their overall conclusion is that their evidence is incompatible with an incentives-based view of the crisis and more compatible with a role for beliefs as in Gennaioli, Shleifer, and Vishny (2012).

Broader Corporate Governance Mechanisms and the Crisis

My overall read of the literature is that governance problems between shareholders and management did not lead to increased risk-taking. To the contrary, the evidence seems to show that the actions of better boards and the design of CEO compensation packages, especially under strong institutional ownership, reflected shareholders' preference for increasing risks. Executives received and held strong incentives to maximize long-term shareholder wealth. The goals of increasing risk were largely successful, even though the realizations of that risk during the crisis were not (see also Mehran, Morrison, and Shapiro 2012). However, serving the interests of common shareholders could induce a higher degree of risk-taking than is *socially* desirable. Accordingly, while corporate governance measures such as board quality, institutional shareholder oversight, or equity incentives eliminate risk-taking that is excessive from shareholders' points of view, they cannot prevent risk-taking that serves shareholders but is socially excessive.

The problem from society's point of view is that maximizing shareholder wealth may create systemic risk because shareholders do not internalize fully the systemic risk externalities. The primary concern here is that banks are interconnected and that their failure has large real effects when the provision of credit to the economy is no longer guaranteed during a crisis. Because of this link, governments often intervene when their financial systems are threatened. The result is privatized gains and socialized losses. If things go well, banks' owners and employees claim the profits, but if things go poorly, society subsidizes the losses. Shareholders therefore have an incentive to take more risk than they otherwise would, which increases the chance of bank failures, systemic risk, and taxpayer costs. Mehran, Morrison, and Shapiro (2012) add that the increasing complexity of bank holding companies following the deregulatory wave starting in 1999 amplified the problem, because banks had more opportunities to take risks.

Policy Implications

These observations have important policy implications. For example, proposals such as more financial expertise on the board of directors or a shareholder say on pay vote may not address the right problem. French et al. (2010) have argued that the link between the risks financial institutions take and the costs they impose on taxpayers gives society a stake in the structure of executive compensation and justifies regulating it, at least at systemically important financial firms. To reduce employees' incentives to take socially excessive risk, they suggest that systemically important financial firms hold back a significant share of each senior manager's annual compensation for several years and that employees forfeit their deferred compensation if the firm goes bankrupt or receives extraordinary government assistance. Resignation from the firm should not accelerate the payment of the deferred compensation as otherwise the incentive alignment would be weakened.[8]

A literature on executive inside debt, defined as the sum of all debt-based compensation such as defined benefit pensions and deferred compensation, explicitly discusses this additional layer of complexity in bank governance. The research question is whether making bank managers bank debt holders can align the incentives of managers to take excessive risks.[9] The literature, using sample periods in the buildup of the financial crisis, provides findings consistent with the view that debt-based compensation can reduce socially excessive risk-taking. Kolasinski and Nang (2018), Tung and Wang (2012), Bennett, Güntay, and Unal (2015), and van Bekkum (2016) all examine bank CEOs' inside debt. Because such commitments are unsecured and unfunded liabilities of the firm, executives would stand in line with other unsecured creditors in the event of default. The last two rows of table 3.1 show that the inside debt of bank CEOs at the end of 2006 was economically meaningful. The average sample CEO had $12.5 million in inside debt, and the average ratio of inside debt to the CEO's equity holdings was a meaningful 25%. A high ratio of CEO inside debt to equity could make the bank executives less

8. Comparable proposals have been made by, e.g., Bebchuk and Spamann (2010) and Bhagat and Bolton (2014).

9. Bank CEOs are often constrained to have all of their accounts with their banks. To the extent that their total deposits are in excess of the deposit insurance limits, those excess deposits add to the amount of inside debt.

prone to risk-taking that results in difficulties for their banks. The above papers indeed find that higher inside debt ratios at the beginning of the crisis are associated with fewer risks and better performance during the crisis. The results suggest that making CEOs also debt holders of the company could help solve the problem of socially excessive risk-taking.

Some financial companies have indeed experimented post crisis with pay arrangements in which they pay part of the variable compensation in debt instruments.[10] Baily et al. (2013) discuss how the contingent deferred "bonus bond" compensation at UBS could reduce the need for future bank bailouts.

Incentives to Monitor Loans during Credit Booms

A large body of work has documented reduced credit quality during credit expansions and subsequent bad economic outcomes (e.g., Baron and Xiong 2017; Jordà, Schularick, and Taylor 2013; and Reinhart and Rogoff 2009).[11] It is easy to see a role for incentives. For example, in a strong economy, bankers and shareholders may not be as concerned about default because it feels remote, and even if default happened, they could sell the collateral easily. A strong economy thus potentially reduces incentives to do due diligence or monitoring.

Baron and Xiong (2017) demonstrate in their cross-country analysis of twenty developed countries that bank shareholders did not fully recognize the risks of credit expansion. In their sample, bank credit expansion predicts increased bank equity crash risk, but, despite the elevated crash risk, also predicts lower mean bank equity returns in the subsequent one to three years. Fahlenbrach, Prilmeier, and Stulz (2018) provide within-country evidence on

10. For example, Credit Suisse describes in their 2015 annual report: "For Managing Directors and Directors in 2015, a portion of deferred variable compensation was delivered in Contingent Capital Award ('CCA'). CCAs [. . .] have rights and risks similar to those of certain contingent capital instruments issued by the Group in the market, such as the high-trigger contingent capital instruments referred to as contingent convertible instruments ('CoCos'). CCAs have loss-absorbing features such that prior to settlement, the principal amount of the CCAs would be written down to zero and cancelled if any of the following trigger events were to occur [. . .]." https://www.credit-suisse.com/media/assets/corporate/docs/about-us/investor-relations/regulatory-disclosures/pillar-3-uk-remuneration-disclosures-2015.pdf.

11. Greenwood and Hanson (2013) present evidence of deteriorating credit quality during boom times for the corporate bond market over the last century. López-Salido, Stein, and Zakrajšek (2017) show that when credit risk is aggressively priced, it tends to be followed by a subsequent widening of credit spreads. Keys et al. (2010) and Mian and Sufi (2009) provide evidence for mortgage lending and Axelson et al. (2013) for leveraged loans prior to the recent crisis.

the consequences of fast loan growth. They analyze a panel of U.S. publicly listed banks between 1972 and 2014 and find that banks that grow quickly make loans that perform worse than the loans of other banks and that neither investors nor equity analysts anticipate the poorer performance.

Any incentives explanation of the loan growth would therefore require incentives that shareholders cannot observe or interpret and that vary in the cross section of banks. While it could be that in their push for growth, bank executives set incentives that led loan officers to make riskier loans along dimensions that are not directly observable by shareholders or analysts, Fahlenbrach, Prilmeier, and Stulz (2018) caution that a loan officer incentive explanation would require that high loan growth banks were acting suboptimally for their shareholders in ways that auditors, investors, analysts, boards, and regulators would not have been able to discern and correct for forty years. Both Baron and Xiong (2017) and Fahlenbrach, Prilmeier, and Stulz (2018) favor a neglected risk explanation of their aggregate results.

Fahlenbrach, Prilmeier, and Stulz (2018) calculate loan growth using ordinary bank loans retained on the balance sheet. A large strand of the literature on the recent crisis has focused on the lowered incentives of banks due to the originate-to-distribute model and investors' appetite for those loans. Originators had substantial skin in the game by holding on to a fraction of the originated loans on their balance sheets. There is indeed evidence that the ability to securitize did not automatically drive down credit quality.

Mian and Sufi (2009) examine potential explanations for the expansion in mortgage credit to subprime zip codes from 2002 to 2005. They collect data on the flow of new mortgage loans through the Home Mortgage Disclosure Act data set from 1990 through 2007, aggregate the data at the zip code level, and match it with Equifax data on outstanding credit and defaults. Their analysis shows that denial rates for subprime zip codes disproportionately fell between 2002 and 2005. At the same time, the fraction of originated mortgages sold to non-government-sponsored entities almost doubled. The increase in the rate of securitization is much stronger in subprime zip codes compared to prime zip codes during this period, and the relative increase is driven by securitized mortgages sold to financial institutions not affiliated with the mortgage originator. Default rates increase significantly more from 2005 to 2007 in zip codes that experience an increase in the fraction of mortgages sold in private securitizations or to noncommercial bank finance companies from 2002 to 2005. Overall, their results imply that moral hazard on the part of originators was a factor contributing to the expansion in credit supply.

Rajan, Seru, and Vig (2015) use data on securitized subprime mortgages issued during 1997–2006 to analyze the failure of statistical default models to assess default risk correctly. They show that the breakdown in the quality of predictions from default models stems from using parameters estimated with data from a period during which a low proportion of loans was securitized. The models worked poorly because they relied entirely on hard information, such as borrower credit scores, but ignored the changes in the incentives of lenders to collect soft information about borrowers. Due to the significant growth in securitization in the subprime sector after 2000 that is based mostly on hard information, lenders chose to not collect soft information about borrowers anymore. Hence, among borrowers with similar reported hard information characteristics, the set that received loans changed in a fundamental way as the securitization regime changed: it become worse along the unreported soft information dimension. Models trained during a different regime consequently had difficulty in mapping characteristics to defaults.

Overall, the papers discussed above suggest that moral hazard problems led to distortions in the credit markets. In the buildup to the financial crisis, the increase in securitization, especially of subprime mortgages, gave incentives to financial institutions to originate mortgages without holding them on their books. These moral hazard problems led to significant increases in default rates. Because loan pricing did not take into account the additional risks, some of the loans were negative net present value projects.

Conclusion

Top executives at U.S. banks had large financial incentives to maximize shareholder value before the global financial crisis. Most bank executives believed that the risks they took were good for shareholders, and they were as surprised as most other market participants when the ex post realizations were poor.

I believe that the bigger agency problem during the last financial crisis was between management and shareholders on one side and the government as a stakeholder on the other. Risks that are good for shareholders are not necessarily good for society because implicit or explicit government bailout guarantees can make it optimal for shareholders to make banks more risky than is socially desirable.

The link between the risks financial institutions take and the costs they impose on taxpayers justifies regulating banks more, including their incentive compensation. Suggestions to hold back a significant share of each executive's annual compensation for several years and to forfeit their deferred compensation if the bank goes bankrupt or receives extraordinary government assistance may succeed in affecting bank executives' beliefs, making them more cautious during boom times.

REFERENCES

Adams, Renée B. 2012. Governance and the Financial Crisis. International Review of Finance 12: 7–38.

Adams, Renée B., and Hamid Mehran. 2003. Is Corporate Governance Different for Bank Holding Companies? Federal Reserve Bank New York Economic Policy Review 9: 123–42.

Adebambo, Biljana, Paul Brockman, and Xuemin Yan. 2015. Anticipating the 2007–2008 Financial Crisis: Who Knew What and When Did They Know It? Journal of Financial and Quantitative Analysis 50: 647–69.

Agarwal, Sumit, and Itzhak Ben-David. 2018. Loan Prospecting and the Loss of Soft Information. Journal of Financial Economics 129: 608–28.

Ahmed, Anwer S., Brant E. Christensen, Adam J. Olson, and Christopher G. Yust. 2019. Déjà vu: The Effect of Executives and Directors with Prior Banking Crisis Experience on Bank Outcomes around the Global Financial Crisis. Contemporary Accounting Research 36: 958–98.

Akin, Ozlem, José M. Marín, and José-Luis Pedró. 2019. Anticipating the Financial Crisis: Evidence from Insider Trading in Banks. Economic Policy 35: 213–67.

Axelson, Ulf, Tim Jenkinson, Per Strömberg, and Michael Weisbach. 2013. Borrow Cheap, Buy High? Determinants of Leverage and Pricing in Buyouts. Journal of Finance 68: 2223–67.

Baily, Martin N., John Y. Campbell, John H. Cochrane, Douglas W. Diamond, Darrell Duffie, Kenneth R. French, Anil K. Kashyap, Frederic S. Mishkin, David S. Scharfstein, Robert J. Shiller, Matthew J. Slaughter, Hyun Song Shin, and René M. Stulz. 2013. Aligning Incentives at Systemically Important Financial Institutions: A Proposal by the Squam Lake Group. Journal of Applied Corporate Finance 25: 37–40.

Baron, Matthew, and Wei Xiong. 2017. Credit Expansion and Neglected Crash Risk. Quarterly Journal of Economics 132: 713–64.

Bebchuk, Lucian A. 2010. How to Fix Bankers' Pay. Daedalus 139 (4): 52–60.

Bebchuk, Lucian A., Alma Cohen, and Holger Spamann. 2010. Wages of Failure: Executive Compensation at Bear Stearns and Lehman 2000–2008. Yale Journal on Regulation 27: 257–82.

Bebchuk, Lucian A., and Holger Spamann. 2010. Regulating Bankers' Pay. Georgetown Law Journal 98: 247–87.

Begley, Taylor A., and Amiyatosh Purnanandam. 2017. Design of Financial Securities: Empirical Evidence from Private-Label RMBS Deals. Review of Financial Studies 30: 120–61.

Beltratti, Andrea, and René M. Stulz. 2012. The Credit Crisis around the Globe: Why Did Some Banks Perform Better? Journal of Financial Economics 105: 1–17.

Benmelech, Efraim, Jennifer Dlugosz, and Victoria Ivashina. 2012. Securitization without Adverse Selection: The Case of CLOs. Journal of Financial Economics 106: 91–113.

Bennett, Rosalind, Levent Güntay, and Haluk Unal. 2015. Inside Debt, Bank Default Risk, and Performance during the Crisis. Journal of Financial Intermediation 24: 487–513.

Berger, Allen N., and Gregory F. Udell. 2004. The Institutional Memory Hypothesis and the Procyclicality of Bank Lending Behavior. Journal of Financial Intermediation 13: 458–95.

Bhagat, Sanjay, and Brian Bolton. 2014. Financial Crisis and Bank Executive Incentive Compensation. Journal of Corporate Finance 25: 313–41.

Boyallian, Patricia, and Pablo Ruiz-Verdú. 2018. Leverage, CEO Risk-Taking Incentives, and Bank Failure during the 2007–10 Financial Crisis. Review of Finance 22: 1763–1805.

Cheng, Ing-Haw, Harrison Hong, and José Scheinkman. 2015. Yesterday's Heroes: Compensation and Creative Risk-Taking. Journal of Finance 70: 839–79.

Cheng, Ing-Haw, Sahil Raina, and Wei Xiong. 2014. Wall Street and the Housing Bubble. American Economic Review 104: 2797–2829.

Chernenko, Sergey, Samuel G. Hanson, and Adi Sunderam. 2016. Who Neglects Risk? Investor Experience and the Credit Boom. Journal of Financial Economics 122: 248–69.

Cole, Shawn, Martin Kanz, and Leora Klapper. 2015. Incentivizing Calculated Risk-Taking: Evidence from an Experiment with Commercial Bank Loan Officers. Journal of Finance 70: 537–57.

Core, John E., and Wayne R. Guay. 1999. The Use of Equity Grants to Manage Optimal Equity Incentive Levels. Journal of Accounting and Economics 28: 151–84.

———. 2010. Is There a Case for Regulating Executive Pay in the Financial Services Industry? In Yasuyuki Fuchita, Richard J. Herring, and Robert E. Litan, eds., After the Crash: The Future of Finance. Washington, DC: Brookings Institution Press.

Cziraki, Peter. 2018. Trading by Bank Insiders before and during the 2007–2008 Financial Crisis. Journal of Financial Intermediation 33: 58–82.

Diamond, Douglas W., Yunzhi Hu, and Raghuram G. Rajan. 2018. Liquidity and Securitization. Working paper, University of Chicago.

Efing, Matthias, Harald Hau, Patrick Kampkötter, and Johannes Steinbrecher. 2015. Incentive Pay and Bank Risk-Taking: Evidence from Austrian, German, and Swiss Banks. Journal of International Economics 96: 123–40.

Ellul, Andrew, and Vijay Yerramilli. 2013. Stronger Risk Controls, Lower Risk: Evidence from US Bank Holding Companies. Journal of Finance 68: 1757–1803.

Erkens, David H., M. Mingyi Hung, and Pedro Matos. 2012. Corporate Governance in the 2007–2008 Financial Crisis: Evidence from Financial Institutions Worldwide. Journal of Corporate Finance 18: 389–411.

Fahlenbrach, Rüdiger, Robert Prilmeier, and René M. Stulz. 2018. Why Does Fast Loan Growth Predict Poor Performance for Banks? Review of Financial Studies 31: 1014–63.

Fahlenbrach, Rüdiger, and René M. Stulz. 2011. Bank CEO Incentives and the Credit Crisis. Journal of Financial Economics 99: 11–26.

French, Kenneth R., Martin N. Baily, John Y. Campbell, John H. Cochrane, Douglas W. Diamond, Darrell Duffie, Anil K. Kashyap, Frederic S. Mishkin, Raghuram G. Rajan, David S. Scharfstein, Robert J. Shiller, Hyun Song Shin, Matthew J. Slaughter, Jeremy C. Stein, and René M. Stulz. 2010. The Squam Lake Report: Fixing the Financial System. Princeton, NJ: Princeton University Press.

Gande, Amar, and Swaminathan Kalpathy. 2017. CEO Compensation and Risk-Taking at Financial Firms: Evidence from U.S. Federal Loan Assistance. Journal of Corporate Finance 47: 131–50.

Gennaioli, Nicola, and Andrei Shleifer. 2018. A Crisis of Beliefs: Investor Psychology and Financial Fragility. Princeton, NJ: Princeton University Press.

Gennaioli, Nicola, Andrei Shleifer, and Robert Vishny. 2012. Neglected Risks, Financial Innovation, and Financial Fragility. Journal of Financial Economics 104: 452–68.

Gopalan, Radhakrishnan, Todd Milbourn, Fenghua Song, and Anjan V. Thakor. 2014. Duration of Executive Compensation. Journal of Finance 69: 2777–2817.

Greenwood, Robin, and Samuel G. Hanson. 2013. Issuer Quality and Corporate Bond Returns. Review of Financial Studies 26: 1483–1525.

Guay, Wayne R. 2010. Excessive Risk and Executive Incentives. Columbia Business School conference presentation.

Hall, Brian J., and Jeffrey Liebman. 1998. Are CEOs Really Paid Like Bureaucrats? Quarterly Journal of Economics 113: 653–91.

Ho, Po-Hsin, Chia-Wei Huang, Chih-Yung Lin, and Ju-Fang Yen. 2016. CEO Overconfidence and Financial Crisis: Evidence from Bank Lending and Leverage. Journal of Financial Economics 120: 194–209.

Holmstrom, Bengt. 1979. Moral Hazard and Observability. Bell Journal of Economics 10: 74–91.

Holmstrom, Bengt, and Paul Milgrom. 1987. Aggregation and Linearity in the Provision of Intertemporal Incentives. Econometrica 55: 303–28.

Houston, Joel F., and Christopher James. 1995. CEO Compensation and Bank Risk: Is Compensation in Banking Structured to Promote Risk Taking? Journal of Monetary Economics 36: 405–31.

Jiang, Wei, Ashlyn Aiko Nelson, and Edward Vytlacil. 2014. Liar's Loan? Effects of Origination Channel and Information Falsification on Mortgage Delinquency. Review of Economics and Statistics 96: 1–18.

John, Kose, and Yiming Qian. 2003. Incentive Features in CEO Compensation in the Banking Industry. Federal Reserve Bank of New York Economic Policy Review 9: 109–21.

Jordà, Òscar, Moritz Schularick, and Alan M. Taylor. 2013. When Credit Bites Back. Journal of Money, Credit and Banking 45: 3–28.

Keys, Benjamin J., Tanmoy Mukherjee, Amit Seru, and Vikrant Vig. 2010. Did Securitization Lead to Lax Screening? Evidence from Subprime Loans. Quarterly Journal of Economics 125: 307–62.

Kindleberger, Charles P. 1978. Manias, Panics, and Crashes: A History of Financial Crises. New York: Basic Books.

Kolasinski, Adam C., and Nan Yang. 2018. Managerial Myopia and the Mortgage Meltdown. Journal of Financial Economics 128: 466–85.

Laeven, Luc, and Ross Levine. 2009. Bank Governance, Regulation and Risk-Taking. Journal of Financial Economics 93: 259–75.

López-Salido, David, Jeremy C. Stein, and Egon Zakrajšek. 2015. Credit-Market Sentiment and the Business Cycle. Quarterly Journal of Economics 132: 1373–1426.

Ma, Yueran. 2015. Bank CEO Optimism and the Financial Crisis. Working paper, Harvard University.

Mehran, Hamid, Alan Morrison, and Joel Shapiro. 2012. Corporate Governance and Banks: What Have We Learned from the Financial Crisis? In Mathias Dewatripont, and Xavier Freixas, eds., The Crisis Aftermath: New Regulatory Paradigms. London: Centre for Economic Policy Research.

Mian, Atif, and Amir Sufi. 2009. The Consequences of Mortgage Credit Expansion: Evidence from the U.S. Mortgage Default Crisis. Quarterly Journal of Economics 124: 1449–96.

Minsky, Hyman P. 1977. A Theory of Systemic Fragility. In E. D. Altman, and A. W. Sametz, eds., Financial Crises: Institutions and Markets in a Fragile Environment, 138–52. New York: John Wiley and Sons.

Minton, Bernadette A., Jérome P. Taillard, and Rohan Williamson. 2014. Financial Expertise of the Board, Risk Taking, and Performance: Evidence from Bank Holding Companies. Journal of Financial and Quantitative Analysis 49: 351–80.

Rajan, Uday, Amit Seru, and Vikrant Vig. 2015. The Failure of Models That Predict Failure: Distance, Incentives, and Defaults. Journal of Financial Economics 115: 237–60.

Reinhart, Carmen, and Kenneth Rogoff. 2009. This Time Is Different: Eight Centuries of Financial Folly. Princeton, NJ: Princeton University Press.

Tung, Frederick, and Xue Wang. 2012. Bank CEOs, Inside Debt Compensation, and the Global Financial Crisis. Working paper.

Van Bekkum, Sjoerd. 2016. Inside Debt and Bank Risk. Journal of Financial and Quantitative Analysis 51: 359–85.

Yu, Yang. 2018. Is This Time Different? Do Bank CEOs Learn from Crisis Experiences? Working paper, Singapore Management University.

Comment by Samuel G. Hanson

In this excellent survey, Rüdiger Fahlenbrach assesses the extent to which "bad incentives" contributed to excessive risk-taking by banks and other financial institutions in the run-up to the 2007–2009 financial crisis. He first explores the possibility that banks took excessive risks because bank CEO incentives were not aligned with shareholders. Rüdiger surveys the literature and concludes there is little evidence that bank executives knowingly took excessive risks to benefit themselves at shareholders' expense before the crisis. Specifically, he finds little evidence that CEOs with better-aligned incentives took less risk; if anything, he points to evidence that CEOs with better incentives took on more risk. He next explores the possibility that banks took excessive risks because lower-level employees—for example, loan officers or traders—had bad incentives. While far less is known here due to a lack of data, there is evidence that banks with stronger risk management practices took on less risk. The overall picture Rüdiger paints is one in which "bad incentives" played a secondary, albeit nontrivial role, in driving risk-taking during the precrisis boom.

Before beginning, I want to summarize my own views about the key drivers of the 2007–2009 financial crisis. My view is that the crisis had two root causes. First, there was a massive credit-fueled housing boom. This boom was largely driven by "bad beliefs" on the part of banks, investors, and households alike. Following a long period of tranquility, lenders neglected downside risks and made increasingly risky mortgage loans. Second, the financial system was inadequately regulated: it wasn't built to withstand a twenty-year flood let alone a hundred-year flood. Large banks had insufficient equity capital and were overly reliant on short-term wholesale funding. These problems were exacerbated by the migration of activity toward more lightly regulated markets and nonbank lenders—that is, the "shadow banking system"—and a set of market-based amplification mechanisms (e.g., fire sales) that proved

Samuel G. Hanson is the William L. White Professor of Business Administration at Harvard Business School.

stronger than previously understood. Thus, despite their modest scale, the initial losses on subprime mortgages hobbled the financial system.

Thus, it should come as little surprise that, like Rüdiger, my reading is that "bad incentives," taken in isolation, played only a secondary role in driving the 2007–2009 financial crisis. Therefore, in this discussion, I want to underscore several of Rüdiger's conclusions and draw out a few implications. However, in closing I will suggest that "bad beliefs" and "bad incentives" explanations for the crisis may be less separable and more complementary than we often assume.

Like Rüdiger, I am skeptical of the "inside job" view that bank executives knew the financial system was a "house of cards" from 2004 to 2006 and knowingly "drove the bus over the cliff" to profit in the short run at shareholders' expense.[1] For me, this view simply doesn't pass the smell test: I usually think of bank executives as overly optimistic and overconfident types (see the literature reviewed in Malmendier 2018), not as evil geniuses. And the evidence about how bank executives traded on their own accounts—see, for example, Fahlenbrach and Stulz (2011) and Chen, Raina, and Xiong (2014)—strongly suggests that executives were closer to "true believers" in the housing boom than to the evil masterminds postulated by the "inside job" view.

In fact, Fahlenbrach and Stulz (2011) find that banks whose CEOs had larger financial stakes—and, thus, were more aligned with shareholders—performed worse during the crisis as judged using both accounting and stock price returns. Why did better-governed banks perform worse? A potential resolution to this puzzle comes from the behavioral corporate finance literature, which argues that strong governance can be a double-edged sword: in an "irrationally exuberant market," there are costs to aligning executives' incentives with shareholders' perceived near-term interests (see Baker and Wurgler 2012 for a review). Specifically, incentives to "cater" to exuberant shareholders often lead executives to give shareholders what they currently want—here an expansion in low-quality lending—even if executives worry this may be contrary to shareholders' longer run interests.[2] As Citigroup's Chuck Prince explained in July 2007, "As long as the music is playing, you've got to get up and dance. We're still dancing." Furthermore, catering of this sort fuels the inevitable

---

1. For instance, the Financial Crisis Inquiry Commission (2011) argued that "alarm bells were clanging inside financial institutions" during the precrisis mortgage boom.

2. This is analogous to the idea that, despite some skepticism, many institutional equity investors decided to "ride" the 1998–2000 dot-com bubble because they worried they would have been fired by their clients if they had underweighted dot-com stocks and missed out on the historic dot-com rally (Abreu and Brunnermeier 2002; Brunnermeier and Nagel 2004; and Griffin, Harris, Shu, and Topaloglu 2011).

boom-time race-to-the-bottom among lenders: it is harder for Chuck Prince to pull Citigroup back from the riskiest lending markets—effectively, saying say "no" to his shareholders—if Merrill Lynch is making record profits by originating risky loans.[3]

Unfortunately, from a policy perspective, I suspect we may be largely stuck with this tendency to cater to shareholders in the short run. Incentive-based compensation is surely needed to combat standard agency problems. And it is hard to imagine we could eliminate executives' incentives to cater to shareholders by, say, lengthening share lockups: even if a CEO holds many re-stricted shares, a CEO who doesn't expand risky lending in some future boom will worry about being forced out by profit-hungry shareholders. To be sure, requiring longer lockup and claw-back periods as well as requiring managers to hold "inside debt" (French et al. 2010) strike me as sensible proposals for top executives and key risk-takers at large banks. However, I wouldn't put much faith in these reforms to prevent the next crisis and I would keep the rules far simpler than they have become. In sum, the insights of behavioral corporate finance make me skeptical of the idea that we can safeguard finan-cial stability simply by improving governance at financial institutions.

I want to close my discussion by discussing the interdependence between "bad beliefs" and "bad incentives" explanations for excessive risk-taking dur-ing credit booms. My hunch is that "bad incentives" and "bad beliefs" will prove to be less separable than academics often think. And I think we need more research on the two-way feedback between "bad incentives" and "bad beliefs."

First, why might bad incentives give rise to bad beliefs? A first reason stems from that fact that our desire to minimize cognitive dissonance often leads to motivated reasoning and confirmation bias. If a principal gives an agent strong incentives to take some action, the agent often comes to think that the action is good, regardless of what the agent used to think. Structured finance products during the precrisis boom strike me as a leading example. Faced with strong incentives to believe that these products were of the very highest credit quality, rating agencies, investment banks, and institutional in-vestors alike all came to believe this was indeed the case.

The idea that good incentives promote good beliefs suggests that the ben-efits of having strong internal risk management practices may accrue, not simply because they help solve classic agency problems within banking or-

----

3. Anecdotally, such a desire to "keep up with the Joneses" seems to have driven some of the most extreme risk-taking in subprime mortgages and collateralized debt obligations (CDOs) by large banks in 2005–2007.

ganizations, but also because they promote sensible beliefs about risk versus return among bank employees. Indeed, my view is that having a good "banking culture"—an explanation practitioners often invoke when explaining why certain banks were able to successfully navigate the hazardous precrisis boom—refers to a favorable situation when good incentives promote good beliefs, and vice versa. In good banking cultures, employees are rewarded for expressing skepticism that one can sustainably earn outsized returns without bearing significant risk. By contrast, in bad banking cultures, employees who believe in a "free lunch" are rewarded. The persistence of bad banking cultures is one plausible reason why Fahlenbrach, Prilmeier, and Stulz (2012) find that banks who did poorly in the 1998 crisis also did poorly in 2008.

Second, why might bad beliefs lead to bad incentives? For starters, if in 2006 a bank executive believed that "this time is different" and the mortgage boom would continue indefinitely, it would make sense for that executive to set up bad incentive schemes for bank employees—for example, taking power away from internal risk managers and compensating loan officers based on origination volume as in Cole, Kanz, and Klapper (2015) and Agarwal and Ben-David (2018). Going further, there is accumulating evidence that past firsthand experiences shape risk-taking in credit booms: people and organizations who were burned in a past bust, take less risk in later booms (Berger and Udell 2004; Bouwman and Malmendier 2015; and Chernenko, Hanson, Sunderam 2017). Arguably, this is because bad past experiences lead to good current beliefs, which then lead managers to erect better incentive structures and risk management practices.

The important role of firsthand experiences and organizational memory suggests the process generating credit booms and financial crises may be highly path dependent, leading to some interesting policy implications. Specifically, this insight leads to the concern that overly aggressive stabilization policies—for example, a "central bank put" where central banks always ease monetary policy in response to financial market turbulence—may be counterproductive. By smoothing out the normal bumps in the road, these policies may encourage overoptimistic thinking and, hence, bad incentive structures that generate excessive risk-taking and financial crises. The natural prescription here is similar to that recommended by standard moral hazard views: policy makers need to let market participants suffer the consequences of the moderate mistakes they make every few years. However, unlike the standard moral hazard view, the goal is not to dissuade hyperrational bankers from maximizing the put value of mispriced government debt guarantees. Instead, the goal is to promote sensible beliefs about risk versus return and, hence, promote strong risk-management practices at financial institutions.

REFERENCES

Abreu, Dilip, and Markus Brunnermeier. 2002. Synchronization Risk and Delayed Arbitrage. Journal of Financial Economics 66 (2): 341–60.

Agarwal, Sumit, and Itzhak Ben-David. 2018. Loan Prospecting and the Loss of Soft Information. Journal of Financial Economics 129: 608–28.

Baker, Malcolm, and Jeffrey Wurgler. 2012. Behavioral Corporate Finance: A Current Survey. In George M. Constantinides, Milton Harris, and Rene Stulz, eds., Handbook of the Economics of Finance, vol. 2. Handbooks in Economics. New York: Elsevier.

Berger, Allen, and Gregory Udell. 2004. The Institutional Memory Hypothesis and the Procyclicality of Bank Lending Behavior. Journal of Financial Intermediation 13: 458–95.

Bouwman, Christa, and Ulrike Malmendier. 2015. Does a Bank's History Affect Its Risk-Taking? American Economic Review 105 (5): 321–25.

Brunnermeier, Markus, and Stefan Nagel. 2004. Hedge Funds and the Technology Bubble. Journal of Finance 59 (5): 2013–40.

Cheng, Ing-Haw, Sahil Raina, and Wei Xiong. 2014. Wall Street and the Housing Bubble. American Economic Review 104: 2797–2829.

Chernenko, Sergey, Samuel Hanson, and Adi Sunderam. 2016. Who Neglects Risk? Investor Experience and the Credit Boom. Journal of Financial Economics 122 (2): 248–69.

Cole, Shawn, Martin Kanz, and Leora Klapper. 2015. Incentivizing Calculated Risk-Taking: Evidence from an Experiment with Commercial Bank Loan Officers. Journal of Finance 70: 537–57.

Fahlenbrach, Rüdiger, Robert Prilmeier, and René Stulz. 2012. This Time Is the Same: Using Bank Performance in 1998 to Explain Bank Performance during the Recent Financial Crisis. Journal of Finance 67: 2139–85.

Fahlenbrach, Rüdiger, and René Stulz. 2011. Bank CEO Incentives and the Credit Crisis. Journal of Financial Economics 99: 11–26.

Financial Crisis Inquiry Commission. 2011. The Financial Crisis Inquiry Report. Washington, DC: US Government Printing Office.

French, Kenneth, Martin Baily, John Campbell, John Cochrane, Douglas Diamond, Darrell Duffie, Anil Kashyap, Frederic Mishkin, Raghuram Rajan, David Scharfstein, Robert Shiller, Hyun Song Shin, Matthew Slaughter, Jeremy Stein, and René Stulz. 2010. The Squam Lake Report: Fixing the Financial System. Princeton, NJ: Princeton University Press.

Griffin, John, Jeffrey Harris, Tao Shu, and Selim Topaloglu. 2011. Who Drove and Burst the Tech Bubble? Journal of Finance 66 (4): 1251–90.

4

A New Narrative of Investors, Subprime Lending, and the 2008 Crisis

STEFANIA ALBANESI

This chapter argues that real estate investors played a dominant role in the 2007–2009 foreclosure crisis and that economists and policy makers interested in understanding this crisis and devising strategies to prevent similar episodes in the future should play close attention to these borrowers. Real estate investors have mostly been overlooked, since they are hard to identify in the data and it is difficult to incorporate real estate investment in equilibrium models of the housing market.[1] Albanesi, DeGiorgi, and Nosal (2017) were the first to show that investors led the spike in mortgage defaults that started in late 2006, particularly among high credit score borrowers.

There are a number of reasons to expect higher default rates for investors relative to noninvestors. First, mortgages for non-owner-occupied properties must meet stricter credit standards to qualify for GSE (government-sponsored entity) insurance, which makes it more likely for real estate investors to contract more expensive nonstandard mortgages. Second, if investors are motivated by the prospect of capital gains, they are more likely to default if the value of the mortgage is higher than the value of the property, especially with no recourse.[2] Finally, the monetary and psychological costs of default for resident owners are typically quite substantial, including moving

Stefania Albanesi is professor of economics at the University of Pittsburgh.

1. Kindermann and Kohls (2016) examine a housing model with investors to study the European rental market. Albanesi (2018) develops a general equilibrium housing model with investors to provide a quantitative analysis of their role in housing markets and examine the resulting policy implications.

2. Ghent and Kudlyak (2011) show that foreclosure rates were 30% higher in nonrecourse states during the crisis.

and storage costs and longer commute times. Real estate investors are not subject to these costs.

This chapter provides a novel and comprehensive empirical analysis of real estate investors using individual and geographically aggregated data. I identify investors as borrowers who hold two or more first mortgages. Since each first mortgage is associated with a separate property, a borrower with two or more first mortgages cannot by definition legally reside in more than one of them. The additional properties could be held for investment purposes or as vacation homes. I document characteristics of investors, the dynamics of investor activity, and analyze in detail their default behavior in comparison to noninvestors. Despite their higher income and higher credit scores, investors display much higher default rates than noninvestors, and this gap grew dramatically during the 2007–2009 crisis. During the 2004–2006 intensification of investor activity, investor income and credit scores remained stable; however, there was a surge of younger investors, specifically twenty- to thirty-nine-year-olds. I show that investors mostly constitute a "class," as the probability of acquiring additional mortgages is much higher for borrowers with two, three, or more than it is for borrowers with only one. Though investor activity slowed during and after the 2007–2009 crisis, borrowers with three or more first mortgages tended to retain that number of properties, despite their higher default rates. Investors appear to be highly leveraged compared to noninvestors. Their mean per mortgage balance is substantially higher and they are more likely to hold second mortgages and home equity lines of credit. Additionally, despite their higher income, they display much higher mortgage payment to income ratios compared to noninvestors. I also show that investors' first mortgages have a higher balance to initial credit ratio, consistent with the notion that they are more leveraged.

I also study investors' default behavior in detail. I show that investors display mortgage delinquency at more than twice the rate of noninvestors during the 2007–2009 crisis, though they display foreclosure rates at more than eight times the rate of noninvestors. Investors experiencing a mortgage delinquency are more likely to subsequently experience foreclosure relative to noninvestors and less likely to cure the delinquency. I also find that investors do not default on all their first mortgages, and on average they default on the mortgage with the smallest balance. This suggests that investors may experience less financial distress than noninvestors. To explore this hypothesis, I measure the prevalence of strategic default among investors and noninvestors. Strategic default is defined in the industry as a straight roll from no delinquency to severe delinquency on a first mortgage, with no concurrent delinquencies on non–real estate trades. A distressed default instead happens if a severe mortgage delinquency occurs in concurrence with other non–real estate delinquencies. I find that the share of strategic defaults is three to five times higher for investors compared to noninvestors, peaking at 35% at the height of the crisis. By contrast, the share of distressed defaults in 2007–2009 is approximately 60% for noninvestors and below 50% for investors.

I end this analysis by exploring the geography of investor activity. A natural question is whether urban locations were particularly attractive from a housing market perspective and whether this led to both an increase in investor activity and a more pronounced housing cycle. There are several factors that suggest urban areas may have been particularly attractive. Gentrification likely contributed to a growth in housing values in cities.[3] At the same time, the rise of the service sector and the growth in professional occupations have determined a greater concentration of employment opportunities in urban areas.[4] Technological change leading to job polarization (see Acemoglu and Autor 2011) may have been accelerated in urban areas, since the high costs of living increase firms' incentive to replace routine workers with automated technologies (Eeckhout, Hedtrich, and Pinheiro 2019). These factors may have contributed to the rise of superstar cities, as argued in Gyourko, Mayer, and Sinai (2013), with a high concentration of wealthy households and very high housing values. Based on this evidence, we will explore the role of location for investor activity and the evolution of the housing and mortgage markets. Urban locations also have higher income and a higher share of young households, as shown in Albanesi, DeGiorgi, and Nosal (2017), which would make them attractive for investors.

I found a substantial geographical dispersion in investor activity. Investor activity is higher in metropolitan areas with high population density and high population in 2000, and it is positively related to the 2000–2010 growth in population. Areas with a high fraction of borrowers with a first mortgage also display high investor activity and a stronger increase in investor activity during the 2004–2006 boom, consistent with their higher levels of income per capita. The magnitude of the rise in default rates is positively correlated with the magnitude of the rise in house prices during the boom and the magnitude

3. Guerrieri, Hartley, and Hurst (2013) develop a model of gentrification, and Couture and Handbury (2017) show that cities experienced a higher concentration of young college graduates starting in the late 1990s. Ferreira and Gyourko (2011) show that local income was the only potential demand shifter for the housing market in metropolitan areas and that it had an economically and statistically significant change around the time that local housing booms began.

4. Rossi-Hansberg et al. (2009) show that information technology allowed separation of production and management operations, leading to a concentration of management positions in the city center.

of their decline during the crisis. The largest fluctuations in housing values also occurred in areas with high population density and strong population growth in 2000–2010.

I show that investors played a disproportionate role in the 2007–2009 housing and mortgage crisis and that their borrowing and default behavior differed from other mortgage borrowers. The fact that it is real estate investors that drove the foreclosure crisis leads to policy implications that are very different from those enacted based on the notion that the crisis was driven by subprime borrowers. Investors have high income and exhibit strategic default behavior, suggesting that alleviating their debt burden may be suboptimal and lead to moral hazard. Moreover, understanding investor activity is not only important from a historical perspective. Investor demand is currently causing an affordability crisis in housing markets for many American cities, and the higher default risk associated with investor mortgages increases systemic risk. The following analysis provides insights to mitigate and correct these outcomes.

Evidence from Individual Data

There are a number of reasons that would lead investor mortgages to display higher default rates than mortgages for owner-occupied properties. First, defaulting on an investment property does not incur the typical psychological and monetary costs associated with foreclosure, such as loss of community, moving expenses, and longer commuting time, among others. Additionally, GSE-sponsored investor mortgages carry a premium in interest rates and fees over owner-occupied mortgages,[5] and therefore investors are more likely to seek funding from nonconventional lenders and use alternative products, such as Alt-A mortgages or adjustable rate mortgages, which are typically more expensive.[6] Finally, investors motivated by prospective capital gains have an incentive to maximize leverage, especially in states in which

5. The schedule of price adjustments by mortgage type for GSE-sponsored mortgages is available at https://www.fanniemae.com/content/pricing/llpa-matrix.pdf.

6. Keys et al. (2012) document the sizable increase of Alt-A mortgages, which have low standards for income documentation and would be particularly appropriate for real estate investors who have variable and hard-to-document income. Further, Foote and Willen (2016) also discuss the role of alternative mortgage products and the fact that their structure may increase the risk of default. However, Elul, Tilson, and Payne (2019) present evidence of substantial misrepresentation of home purchases as primary residences, for the purpose of qualifying for GSE-sponsored mortgages.

foreclosure is nonrecourse as losses are limited. This strategy also increases default risk.

I examine investor activity using data from the Experian credit bureau. The data is quarterly, starting in 2004Q1 and ending in 2015Q4 and comprises over 200 variables for an anonymized panel of one million households. The panel is nationally representative, with attributes on all consumer debt except for payday loans. Information includes the number of trades for each type of loan, the outstanding balance and available credit, the monthly payment, and whether any of the accounts are delinquent. All balances are adjusted for joint accounts to avoid double counting. The Vantage Score 3.0, a credit score produced by the Experian credit bureau, is considered as well as an estimate of individual and household labor income based on IRS data.

I follow Haughwout et al. (2011) and define investors as borrowers who hold two or more first mortgages. Figure 4.1 presents basic statistics on investor activity. As can be seen in the top panel of figure 4.1, the fraction of investors (measured on the left axis) was just above 9% in 2004Q1, and it rose rapidly, reaching a peak of 12% in 2007Q4. It then declined to 10% by mid-2010, where it stabilized.

The investor share of first mortgage balances (measured on the right axis) was close to 20% in 2004Q1, and it rose to a peak of 28% in 2007Q4, after which it declined to 23% in 2011Q2, where it stabilized for the remaining period. The fact that the investor share of first mortgage balances is higher than their share in the population of first mortgage holders stems not only from the fact that investors have multiple first mortgages but also from the fact that the average balance for each first mortgage is higher. This can be seen in figure 4.2, which plots the average first mortgage balance per mortgage by number of first mortgages. Borrowers with only one first mortgage start with an average first mortgage balance of $125,000 in 2004Q1, slightly below the average first mortgage balance for borrowers with two and three or more first mortgages, at $131,000 and $139,000, respectively. Between 2004 and the end of 2008 the growth in average balances is much larger for investors, with peaks of $186,000 and $209,000 for borrowers with two and three or more first mortgages, respectively, in 2009Q1, when this variable reaches only $162,000 for noninvestors. Mortgage balances stabilize at the peak for the remaining sample period for borrowers with one or two first mortgages, while they decline rapidly for those with three or more first mortgages, reaching $185,000 by the end of 2012.

The investor delinquency and foreclosure shares, shown in the middle panel of figure 4.1, are substantially higher than investor share in the population. The investor share of 90+ day mortgage delinquencies (left axis) starts

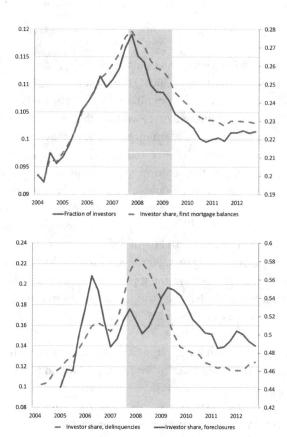

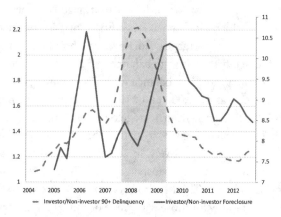

FIGURE 4.1 Statistics for borrowers with two or more first mortgages (investors), three-quarter moving averages

Source: Author's calculations based on Experian data.

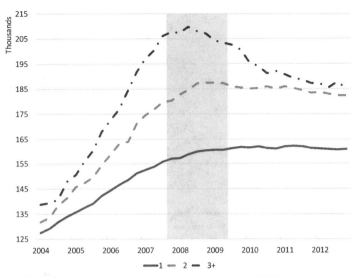

FIGURE 4.2 Mean first mortgage balance by number of first mortgages (USD)
Source: Author's calculations based on Experian data.

at 10% in 2004Q1 and rises to 22% by 2007Q4. It then drops to 12% by mid-2011, where it stabilizes. The investor share of foreclosures (right axis) is even higher: starting at 44% in 2005Q1, it first rises to 56% in 2006Q2, dropping to 49% in 2007Q1. It then starts rising again, reaching 55% in 2009Q2, after which it falls to 49% by 2011Q2, and remains mostly stable thereafter. The double peak in the investor share of foreclosures reflects a difference in timing in the rise in foreclosures for investors and noninvestors. Specifically, the pattern is consistent with investor foreclosure rates starting to rise in mid-2005, while noninvestor foreclosure rates start rising in late 2006. The second peak is consistent with noninvestor foreclosures declining at a more rapid pace than investor foreclosures. The bottom panel of figure 4.1 plots the investor/noninvestor ratios of 90+ day delinquencies and foreclosures. For delinquencies (left axis), the ratio is just above 1 in 2004Q2 and rises to 2.2 in 2008Q2, when it starts declining, stabilizing at 1.2 in mid-2011. The investor/noninvestor ratio of new foreclosures (right axis) in the last four quarters starts at 7 but rises well over 10 when the investor share of foreclosures peaks.

The high investor shares of delinquencies and foreclosures suggest that default rates are much higher for investors. This can be clearly seen in figure 4.3, which plots the 90+ day delinquency rate (top panel) and the foreclosure rate (bottom panel) by number of first mortgages. Here borrowers with only two first mortgages are distinguished from those with three or more. For borrowers with two first mortgages, their second property is likely to be a vacation

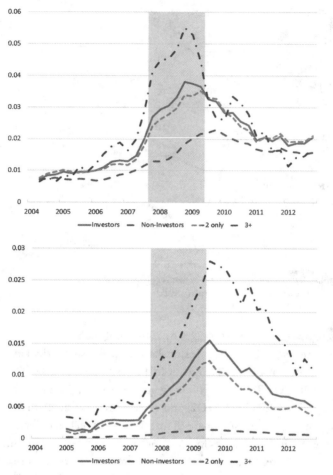

FIGURE 4.3 Fraction with a new 90+ day mortgage delinquency in the last quarter (*top panel*). Fraction with a new foreclosure in the last four quarters (*bottom panel*). Three-quarter moving averages by number of first mortgages.

Source: Author's calculations based on Experian data.

home, whereas borrowers with three or more first mortgages will have at least one investment property. The delinquency rates are very similar by number of first mortgages at the beginning of the sample, averaging around 1%. Starting in 2006Q1, they start rising rapidly for investors, particularly for those with three or more first mortgages. For investors, the peak in the delinquency rate is reached in 2009Q1 at 5.5% for those with three or more first mortgages, and in 2009Q2 at 3.5% for those with only two. The peak delinquency rate for noninvestors, which occurs in 2009Q4, is 2.2%. Another notable difference between investors and noninvestors is the pace of decline in the delinquency rate, which is very rapid for investors. For borrowers with three or more first mortgages, the delinquency rate drops by more than half by 2009Q4, and then further declines to 1% by 2012Q1, which is close to precrisis values. For borrowers with two first mortgages, the delinquency rate declines more slowly. It stabilizes at 2% by 2010Q4, which is more than twice the precrisis rate. By contrast, for noninvestors the mortgage delinquency rate declines by only 0.5 percentage points relative to the peak by the end of the sample.

The pattern is similar but highly accentuated for foreclosures. Even before the start of the crisis, the foreclosure rate is orders of magnitude larger for investors relative to noninvestors as previously noted. For those with three or more first mortgages, the foreclosure rate rises from 0.5% in 2006Q1 to a peak of 2.8% in 2009Q3, after which it declines very rapidly for the rest of the sample period, reaching 1% by mid-2012. For borrowers with two first mortgages, the foreclosure rate rises from 0.25% to 1.5% over the same period and declines to 0.4% by the end of the sample. By contrast, for noninvestors, the rise in the foreclosure rate is barely detectable, and starts well into 2008.

To provide more comprehensive evidence on investor activity, I also studied individual investor characteristics, such as age, income, and the pattern of acquisition of investor mortgages.

Investors by Age, Income, and Credit Score

We now examine investor activity by age, income, and credit score. The findings are displayed in figure 4.4. The top panel displays the fraction of borrowers with two or more first mortgages, among those with at least one, by ten-year age brackets, for twenty- to eighty-year-olds. The fraction of investors is increasing in age up to sixty-nine-year-olds throughout the sample period. The fraction of investors for borrowers over 70 is approximately 8% throughout the sample. Borrowers in the fifty- to sixty-nine-year-old age bracket also display a relatively stable but higher fraction of investors. Among these borrowers, investors comprise 11% of all those with a first mortgage in 2004Q1. This fraction rises to a peak of 13% at the beginning of 2008, then declines to preboom values by the end of the sample. For younger borrowers, the fraction of investors is lower but displays a very marked rise during the boom, and then a similarly large decline. This pattern is most evident for twenty- to twenty-nine-year-olds, for whom the fraction of investors rises from 5% in 2004Q1 to a peak of 9% by early 2008, and then drops very rapidly to 4% by early 2010, when it stabilizes. A similar pattern applies to the thirty- to thirty-nine-year-olds, for whom the fraction of investors starts at 8%, rises to 11% by the start of the Great Recession, and then declines, though less rapidly, to

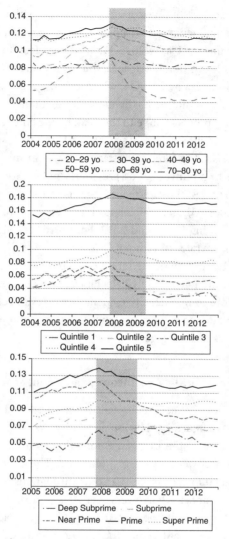

FIGURE 4.4 Fraction with two or more first mortgages among borrowers with at least one first mortgage, by age (*top panel*), by household income (*center panel*), and by four-quarter lagged credit score category (*bottom panel*)
Source: Author's calculations based on Experian data.

8% by the end of 2010. The forty- to forty-nine-year-old group displays a pattern which is an average of those of the adjacent younger and older groups.

I next examine investor activity based on household income quintile, reported in the middle panel of figure 4.4. The fraction of investors is increasing in income. Borrowers in the top quintile begin with a 15% fraction of investors. This fraction rises to a peak of 19% by the end of 2007, after which it declines slowly, stabilizing at around 17% by the end of 2009. The fraction of borrowers in the fourth quintile of the income distribution is about half of that in the top quintile, with a similar pattern of modest rise during the boom and return to preboom levels by mid-2010. The bottom three quintiles of the income distribution display very similar behavior in the prerecession period, with the fraction of investors rising by about 3 percentage points from an initial level of around 5%. For borrowers in the third quintile, the fraction of investors declines to preboom values by 2010. For borrowers in the two bottom quintiles, the decline in the fraction of investors during and after the 2007–2009 recession is more substantial, and the fraction of investors stabilizes about 1 percentage point below the level at the beginning of the sample by mid-2009.

Finally, I consider investor activity by four-quarter lagged credit score, reported in the bottom panel of figure 4.4. We use a lagged credit score to avoid joint endogeneity of credit score and investment activity or default behavior. Following industry practices, we consider the following categories: Deep Subprime (300–499 VantageScore), Subprime (500–600 VantageScore), Near Prime (601–660 VantageScore), Prime (661–780 VantageScore) and Super Prime (781–850 VantageScore).[7] Prime and Near Prime borrowers exhibit the strongest investor activity during the boom as well as the most sizable rise in the fraction of investors during that period. At the beginning of the sample, Prime and Near Prime borrowers have a fraction of investors equal to 11% and 10%, respectively. This fraction rises to 14% in 2009Q2 for Prime borrowers, and to 12% for Near Prime borrowers. It then declines, stabilizing at 12% in 2010 for Prime borrowers. The decline for Near Prime borrowers is more substantial and prolonged, leading to a fraction of investors of about 8% in 2011 and 2012. Super Prime borrowers start the sample with their fraction of investors at 8%. This fraction rises to approximately 10% in 2007Q4 and stabilizes at that level for the rest of the sample. Clearly, for these borrowers the recession did not have a negative impact on investor activity, even if this activity intensified during the 2004–2006 boom. The fraction of investors among Subprime borrowers is relatively stable during the entire sample period, averaging about 7% during the boom and falling to 6% in mid-2009 and for the remaining period.[8]

7. The VantageScore is Experian's primary credit scoring model, based on Experian credit report data. It varies from 300 to 850. As with other credit scores, it ranks borrowers based on their probability of incurring a 90+ day delinquency in the subsequent twenty-four quarters. It is very similar to the FICO score and the Equifax Risk Score. Throughout the analysis, we use VantageScore 3.0. For more information see https://www.vantagescore.com/meet-vantagescore.

8. The fraction of investors among Deep Subprime borrowers starts at 5% and rises to approximately 7% between the end of 2009 and early 2011, when it starts declining, reaching

Taken together, these results suggest that investor activity is prevalent among high income, middle age, high credit score borrowers. However, during the 2004–2006 boom, there was a significant intensification of investor activity for relatively young borrowers as well as Near Prime and Prime borrowers. Since there was virtually no rise in investor activity for borrowers in the lowest three quintiles of the income distribution over this period, this suggests that even relatively young and Near Prime borrowers who became investors during the 2004–2006 boom tended to have high income.

Dynamics of Investment Activity

To gain a better understanding of investment activity, we examine the one-quarter-ahead transitions from zero, one, two, three, and four or more first mortgages. We first consider the upward transitions, that is, the ones that correspond to an increase in the number of first mortgages, which are plotted in figure 4.5.

The rate at which borrowers who have one first mortgage increase their number of first mortgages is quite low. Between 2004 and the end of 2006, approximately 3% obtain an additional mortgage, and less than 0.5% obtain two or more additional mortgages. Both these fractions drop by more than half between early 2007 and mid-2009 and stabilize at that level until the end of 2012. The bottom panel considers borrowers who have two or three first mortgages. The fraction of those with two first mortgages who acquire one or more additional mortgages in the subsequent quarter is just under 6% between 2004 and early 2007, while the fraction of those with three first mortgages who acquire more is about 11% over that same period. Both these fractions experience a very large drop between 2007 and early 2009. For borrowers with two first mortgages, the fraction who acquire an additional mortgage in the subsequent quarter stabilizes at around 3% after the crisis. The fraction of borrowers with three first mortgages who acquire additional mortgages also drops to 3% at the beginning of 2009 but recovers to about 6% by late 2011.

Clearly, the rate at which borrowers acquire additional first mortgages is increasing with the number of initial first mortgages. The 2007–2009 crisis is associated with a more than 50% decline of the rate at which borrowers acquire additional first mortgages, with the largest drop for borrowers with three first mortgages. These borrowers are also the only ones for whom the rate of acquisition of additional mortgages rebounds, though not completely, after the crisis.

---

preboom values by the end of 2012. This behavior for Deep Subprime borrowers may be driven by investors with initially higher credit scores who defaulted on their mortgages during the crisis.

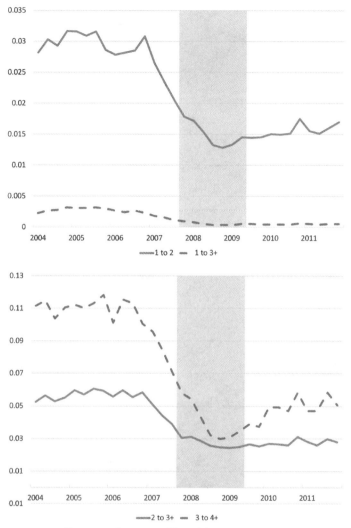

FIGURE 4.5 Fraction of borrowers who acquire additional first mortgages over the next quarter
Source: Author's calculations based on Experian data.

This suggests that there is an investor class of borrowers who are far more likely to acquire or increase their holdings of investment properties.

We now examine transitions to a lower number of first mortgages. Closure of a mortgage may be driven by a sale or foreclosure. The results are shown in figure 4.6. The top panel reports the fraction of borrowers who transition from one to zero, two to one, and two to zero first mortgages in the subsequent quarter. The fraction of borrowers who transition from one to zero first mortgages

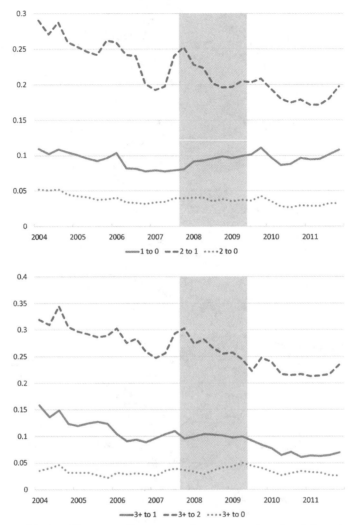

FIGURE 4.6 Fraction of borrowers with one or more first mortgages who reduce their number of first mortgages in the subsequent quarter
Source: Author's calculations based on Experian data.

hovers around 10% between 2004 and mid-2006, before dropping slightly to 8% until early 2008, when it rises to a level just above 10% where it stabilizes. This transition may be driven in part by borrowers paying off their mortgages, but the fact that this increase coincides quite precisely with the rise in the mortgage default rate for borrowers with only one first mortgage suggests that foreclosures do play a role in this transition. Only about 5% of borrowers transition from two to zero first mortgages over the span of one quarter, and this transition rate is quite stable over the sample period. The transition from two to one first mortgages is much higher, averaging around 25% between 2004 and the end of 2006. After dropping by 5% in 2007, this transition rate rises back to 25% between 2007Q2 and 2007Q4. The rate hovers around 20% between mid-2008 and mid-2009 and falls by an additional 2 percentage points in ensuing quarters.

The bottom panel reports transition rates for borrowers with three or more first mortgages. The transition rate from more than three to two is close to 30% between 2004 and early 2006, and the rate from more than three to one averages 13% over the same period. Both rates exhibit a decline in the subsequent year and then experience a sharp increase. This brings the more-than-three to two transition rate to a peak of 30% at the start of the Great Recession, and the more-than-three to one rate to 11% in the same period. Subsequently, both rates decline gradually, stabilizing at 21% and at 6%, respectively, in mid-2010. As for the two to zero rate, the more-than-three to zero rate is below 5% and stable throughout the sample period.

These transition rates suggest that there is a significant amount of churn in investor activity, with investors acquiring additional first mortgages at a rate that is approximately half the rate at which they reduce them both during the housing boom and after the crisis. This pattern may be consistent with investors "flipping" properties to take advantage of rising housing prices during the boom. At the start of the housing crisis, there is a sizable but temporary rise in the rate at which investors reduce their number of first mortgages.

Leverage and Maturity

One factor behind the greater delinquency and foreclosure rate for investors is the fact that they may have higher leverage than noninvestors. This is reflected in figure 4.7, which plots the fraction with a second mortgage and with a home equity line of credit by investor status. The fraction of investors and noninvestors with a second mortgage is about 6% in 2004Q1, and it rises for both groups until 2007Q4. The rise is more pronounced for investors, with a peak of 16%, whereas the fraction with a second mortgage peaks at 13% for noninvestors. During and after the 2007–2009 recession, the fraction with a second mortgage declines for both investors and noninvestors, though the magnitude of the decline is larger for investors. By the end of 2012, approximately 7% of noninvestors and 8.5% of investors have a second mortgage. This pattern is similar but amplified for home equity lines of credit (HELOCs). Approximately 16% of noninvestors hold HELOCs in 2004Q1, and this fraction rises to 24% in 2005Q2, where it stabilizes until mid-2008. It declines thereafter and goes back to 16% by the end of 2012. In 2004Q1, 25% of investors hold HELOCs, and this

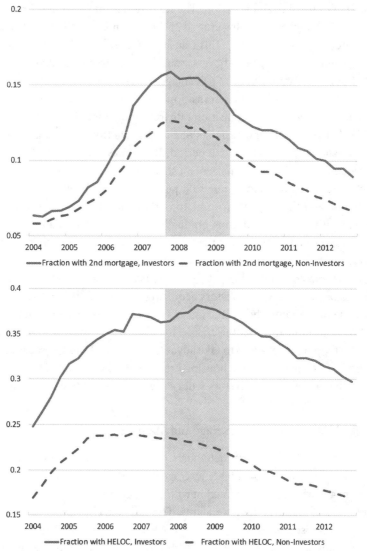

FIGURE 4.7 Fraction with a second mortgage (*top panel*) and with a home equity line of credit (*bottom panel*), by investor status
Source: Author's calculations based on Experian data.

fraction rises rapidly thereafter, reaching a peak of 38% in 2008Q2. This fraction declines during and after the crisis, reaching 30% in 2012Q4.

The fact that investors are more likely to have second mortgages and HELOCs in part reflects their higher income, credit score, and age compared to noninvestors, as shown earlier. However, their additional indebtedness implies that mortgage payments absorb a greater fraction of their income relative to noninvestors. This can be seen in figure 4.8, which plots the monthly mortgage payment to household income ratio for first and second mortgages by investor status. The first mortgage payment to household income ratio is about 17% for noninvestors between 2004 and 2009 and declines by approximately

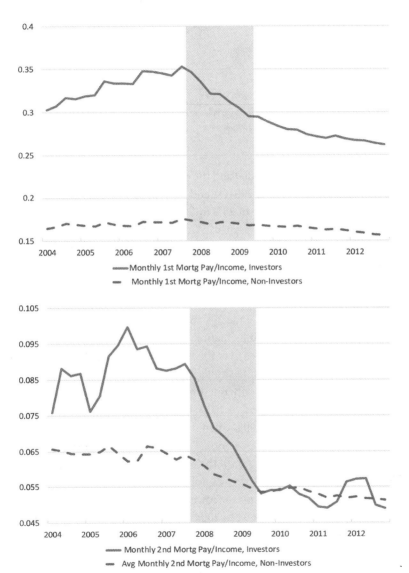

FIGURE 4.8 Ratio of monthly first mortgage (*top panel*) and second mortgage (*bottom panel*) payments to income, by investor status
Source: Author's calculations based on Experian data.

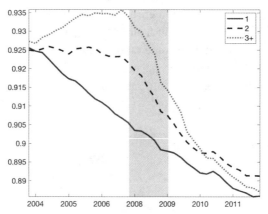

FIGURE 4.9 Residual over initial first mortgage balance by number of first mortgages
Source: Author's calculations based on Experian data.

2 percentage points between 2009 and the end of the sample period. For investors, this ratio starts at 30% in 2004Q1 and rises to a peak of 35% in 2007Q4. It then declines, reaching a value of 26% by 2012Q4. This sizable decline is likely associated with the loss of properties in foreclosure experienced by investors. For second mortgages, the ratio of monthly payments to income is about 8% in 2004–2005 for investors and rises to a peak of 10% in 2006Q1. After the 2006 peak, it declines very sharply, reaching a value of close to 5% between mid-2009 and the end of the sample. For noninvestors, this ratio is stable at 6.5% in 2004–2007 and then declines to just under 5% toward the end of the sample.

Figure 4.9 provides some information on leverage, specifically the ratio of current first mortgage balances over the initial credit at the start of the loan. In 2004Q1, this measure is quite similar by number of first mortgages, close to 93%. For borrowers with only one first mortgage, it declines steadily in value, reaching 88% by the end of 2012. For borrowers with two first mortgages, it is stable until early 2008, when it begins to gradually decline, reaching 89% at the end of 2012. By contrast, for borrowers with three or more first mortgages, this ratio rises until the end of 2007, when it reaches a peak of 94%. After that, it declines very rapidly, so that by the end of the sample it is very similar to the value for borrowers with one or two first mortgages. This difference in behavior between 2004 and 2007 may reflect that investors, and especially borrowers with three or more first mortgages, do not reduce or even increase the principal on their first mortgages. This may be a result of higher incidence of no amortization mortgages or balloon mortgages among this class of borrowers.

Default Behavior

The fact that the difference between investors and noninvestors in foreclosure rates is greater than for delinquency rates suggests that investors are less likely to cure a delinquency, compared to noninvestors. This can be seen in figure 4.10, which displays the transition from a new 90+ day mortgage delinquency to foreclosure. Until 2006Q2, the rate is quite similar for borrowers with one and two first mortgages, around 20%, though it averages 35% for borrowers with three or more first mortgages over the same period. However, starting in 2006Q3 there is a strong divergence. For borrowers with only one first mortgage, the rate rises to a peak of 32% in 2008Q1 and declines to precrisis values by the end of 2009. For borrowers with two first mortgages, the rise is much steeper, to a peak of 48% by 2007Q4, with a much slower decline, so that the rate stabilizes at around 30% only in 2011. For borrowers with three or more first mortgages, the peak of the transition from a mortgage delinquency to foreclosure is 62% in mid-2008. The transition declines very slowly, reaching precrisis values only in mid-2011.

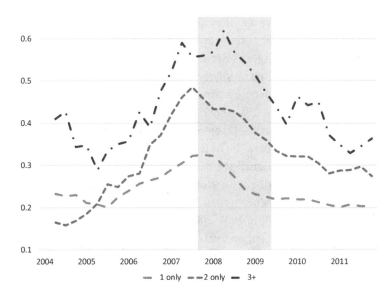

FIGURE 4.10 Fraction of borrowers with a new 90+ day mortgage delinquency who experience a new foreclosure in the subsequent four quarters, three-quarter moving averages by number of first mortgages
Source: Author's calculations based on Experian data.

TABLE 4.1 Partial default by investors

Number of mortgages	Foreclosures fewer than mortgages		Foreclosures on smallest mortgage	
	2	3+	2	3+
2004Q1–2006Q4	0.87	0.78	0.63	0.46
2007Q1–2010Q4	0.75	0.84	0.47	0.51
2011Q1–2012Q4	0.75	0.84	0.63	0.66

Source: Author's calculations based on Experian data.
Note: Fraction with foreclosed first mortgage trades smaller than number of first mortgages and fraction with foreclosure on smallest first mortgage trade; period averages by number of first mortgages.

Multiple Defaults

We now examine whether borrowers with multiple first mortgages default on all the first mortgages and, if not, on which ones. Table 4.1 reports the fraction of borrowers who do not foreclose on all their first mortgage trades and the fraction among those who foreclose on the smallest mortgage trade by number of first mortgages. The fact that borrowers do not show a foreclosure on all first mortgage trades may reflect that the cost of defaulting on different mortgages vary, and that they can continue to make payments on at least one mortgage. The fact that borrowers foreclose on first mortgages with small balances may reflect that they are more likely to default on a vacation or investment property, since those are typically lower in value for borrowers with multiple first mortgages. A decline in the fraction of borrowers who do not foreclose on all their first mortgages and the fraction who default on their smallest mortgages may denote a rise in the intensity of financial distress.

The table shows that in 2004–2006, the fraction of borrowers with two first mortgages who do not foreclose on both is at its highest at 87%, whereas it drops to 75% in the subsequent period. The fraction of these borrowers who foreclose on the mortgage with the smallest balances is 63% in 2004–2006, dropping to 47% in 2007–2010, and rising again to precrisis levels subsequently. For borrowers with three or more first mortgages, the fraction who do not foreclose on all their first mortgages is 78% in 2004–2006, and it rises to 84% in the remaining period. The fraction of these borrowers who default on the smallest mortgages is 46% in 2004–2006, rising to 51% in 2007–2010 and to 66% in 2011–2012.

Strategic Default

The greater transition rates from mortgage delinquency to foreclosure for investors relative to noninvestors and investors' tendency to not default on all their first mortgages may be consistent with a pattern of strategic default by investors, that is, a mortgage default that occurs with a straight roll from current to severe mortgage delinquency, without delinquencies on other non–real estate trades.[9] Identifying the incidence of strategic default is important from a practical and policy prospective, as borrowers who default strategically may be able to repay their debt. To prevent moral hazard, loan modification programs and other government-led interventions to alleviate the cost of mortgage default should arguably not be available to these borrowers. On the other hand, for borrowers who experience a distressed default, such forms of relief may be optimal.

We now provide a formal definition of strategic and distressed default, as well as two other categories of default used in the industry, cash-flow management and pay-down. The definition of strategic default is based on the concept of a straight roll, which occurs when a borrower who is current on mortgage trades in some quarter $t - 1$ becomes 180+ days past due or derogatory either at $t + 1$ or $t + 2$. A borrower then experiences strategic default if they straight-roll and display no other delinquency at quarters $t + 1$ and $t + 2$. A borrower experiences distressed default if they display a 60–180 days past due on mortgage at t and are at most 30 days past due at $t - 1$, including a straight roll, and at least one delinquency on non–real estate trades at $t + 1$ and $t + 2$. A cash-flow manager is a borrower who is 60–180 days past due on mortgage trades at t and at most 30 days past due at $t - 1$ without a straight roll and shows no other type of delinquency at $t + 1$ and $t + 2$. Finally, a pay-down occurs if a borrower is 60–180 days past due on mortgage trades at t and at most 30 days past due at $t - 1$, including a straight roll, and displays no mortgage delinquency in $t + 1$ and $t + 2$.

A cash-flow manager is a borrower who temporarily misses payments, perhaps due to a liquidity shortfall, but is able to cure this delinquency. This pattern of behavior may be recurrent, as no straight roll is allowed for this category of default. This pattern may be considered strategic since the borrower misses payments on the mortgage but is able eventually to resume making payments. A pay-down experiences a more protracted period of missed payments but eventually cures the delinquency. Table 4.2 presents the average share of defaults by type over the entire sample period. Whereas the share of strategic defaults is only 8% for borrowers with one first mortgage, this share rises to 17% and 23% for borrowers with two and three or more first

---

9. For example, Wyman (2010), following industry practices, identifies strategic defaulters as borrowers who "continued to pay their other credit obligations for 6 months after going 60 days past due on their mortgage and who go straight from current to default on their mortgage."

TABLE 4.2 Defaults by type

# of mortgages	Strategic	Cash-flow managers	Distressed	Pay-downs	No non-real estate trades
1	0.074	0.146	0.555	0.116	0.108
2	0.165	0.195	0.470	0.115	0.055
3+	0.232	0.212	0.143	0.101	0.042

Source: Author's calculations based on Experian data.
Note: Share of defaults by type, by number of first mortgages, 2004Q2–2015Q2 averages.

mortgages, respectively. The share of distressed defaults is 56% for borrowers with only one first mortgage and drops to 47% and 41% for borrowers with two and two or more first mortgages. The share of cash-flow managers also rises with the number for first mortgages, whereas the share of pay-downs is quite similar by number of first mortgages. Finally, just over 4%–11% of borrowers who default on their mortgage in a given quarter t do not display any non–real estate trades in quarters $t-1$, t, $t+1$, $t+2$, and therefore cannot be classified.

Figure 4.11 displays the evolution over time of the share of default types by number of first mortgages. Until 2006Q1, the share of strategic defaults for borrowers with one first mortgage is close to 4%, while it already starts climbing for investors for whom it reaches a peak of 24% and of 33% for borrowers with two and with three or more first mortgages, respectively. For borrowers with one first mortgage, the maximal share of strategic defaults is only 10% in 2007Q3. The share of strategic defaults declines slowly for all borrowers after the crisis. It reaches precrisis levels by mid-2013 for borrowers with only one first mortgage, while it drops only to 15%–20% for borrowers with two or more in 2013–2015.

Cash-flow managers are also disproportionately present among investors, though the share of this class of defaults converges across types of borrowers at the height of the crisis. For borrowers with only one first mortgage, cash-flow managers comprise about 5% of all defaults until 2007Q2, when they start rising, reaching a peak of 18% of all defaults in 2008Q4, when they stabilize. The pattern is similar for borrowers with two first mortgages until 2008Q3, when for these borrowers the share of these defaults continues to rise, reaching 25% in 2009Q1–2012Q1 and rising further to 28%–30% in 2014. For borrowers with three or more first mortgages, the share of cash-flow managers declines from 23% to approximately 5% between 2004 and mid-2007, and then starts rising, reaching approximately 30% by 2010, after which it fluctuates at this high level.

Turning to distressed default, the share is quite similar by number of first mortgages before 2007Q2, ranging between 60% and 70% for borrowers with

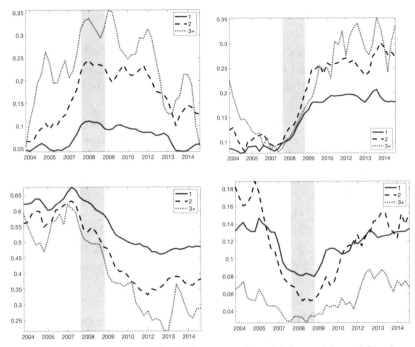

FIGURE 4.11 Share of strategic (*top left*), cash-flow manager (*top right*), distressed (*bottom left*), and pay-down (*bottom right*) defaults by number of first mortgages
Source: Author's calculations based on Experian data.

only one first mortgage, and between 50% and 62% for investors. The share of these defaults declines for all borrowers during the crisis, dropping to 50% in early 2012 from a high of 67% for borrowers with only one first mortgage, to 35% from a high of 62% for those with two first mortgages over the same period. For borrowers with three or more first mortgages, the share of distressed defaults drops to 23% by 2013Q3 after which it rises by 10 percentage points by the end of the sample. The share of pay-downs is substantially lower for borrowers with three or more mortgages relative to those with one and two throughout the sample period. It drops from 7% to 2% before the crisis for those borrowers and only starts rising substantially in early 2012, peaking at around 8% at the end of 2013. For borrowers with one and two first mortgages, the share of pay-downs is 15% or higher before the crisis and in 2012 and later years. During the crisis, the share drops to a low of 8% for borrowers with only one first mortgage and to 5% for borrowers with two.

The higher incidence of strategic and cash-flow management default among investors, especially those with three or more first mortgages, suggests that these borrowers were likely able to continue making payments on their mortgages but decided not to as part of an optimizing financial strategy. The lower incidence of distressed default for all borrowers during the crisis may reflect a higher sensitivity to fluctuations in housing values over this period, consistent with evidence discussed above that mortgage delinquency was higher in areas with large fluctuations in housing values. Finally, the lower incidence of pay-down defaults for investors is consistent with their higher likelihood to transition from mortgage delinquency to foreclosure, as discussed above. We are limited to measuring financial distress based on information on credit reports. Using Panel Study of Income Dynamics (PSID) data, Gerardi et al. (2013) find that job loss, low levels of liquid assets, and severe negative equity were primarily responsible for mortgage defaults during the housing crisis, and, conditional on negative equity, unemployment increases the probability of default by a factor of three. On this basis, they argue that strategic default is not an important factor in the foreclosure crisis. However, they do not examine investors, which, given the size of their sample, are likely to be underrepresented.

In summary, the evidence on default behavior by number of first mortgages suggests that investors are more likely to experience mortgage delinquency, more likely to experience foreclosure in conjunction with mortgage delinquencies and less likely to cure such delinquencies, with the gap relative to noninvestors increasing substantially during the crisis. Investors are also more likely to exhibit strategic default. Borrowers with two first mortgages display default behavior that is intermediate between borrowers with only one and those with three or more first mortgages, consistent with the notion that, for some of these borrowers, their second first mortgage may correspond to a vacation home, for which the incentives to default are more similar to those of a primary residence.

The Geography of Investor Activity

Investor activity exhibits substantial geographical variation. As an illustration, figure 4.12 plots the fraction of borrowers with one or more first mortgages (left panel), and the fraction with two or more first mortgages (right panel) among borrowers with at least one for the ten largest metropolitan statistical areas (MSAs) in 2010. New York–Newark–Jersey City (NY) is the largest MSA and it displays the lowest fraction of borrowers with a first mortgage for most of the sample period, with a peak of 31% in 2007. The Washington–Arlington–Alexandria (DC) is the area with the highest fraction of borrowers with a first mortgage throughout the sample period, with a peak of 47% in 2007. All MSAs display a modest increase in the fraction of borrowers with a

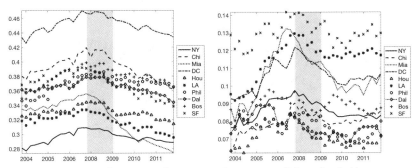

FIGURE 4.12 Fraction of borrowers with one or more first mortgages (*left panel*) and with two or more first mortgages (*right panel*) among those with at least one, in the top ten metropolitan statistical areas by 2010 population

Source: Author's calculations based on Experian data.

Note: In order of population size, the MSAs include NY = New York–Newark–Jersey City, LA = Los Angeles–Long Beach–Anaheim, Chi = Chicago–Naperville–Elgin, Phil = Philadelphia–Camden–Wilmington, Mia = Miami–Fort Lauderdale–West Palm Beach, Dal = Dallas–Fort Worth–Arlington, DC = Washington–Arlington–Alexandria, Bos = Boston–Cambridge–Newton, Hou = Houston–The Woodlands–Sugar Land, SF = San Francisco–Oakland–Hayward.

first mortgage between 2004 and 2007; the largest such rise occurs in the NY area, where it increases by approximately 10%. During and after the 2007–2009 crisis, the fraction with first mortgages declines, returning to preboom values by the end of the sample, except for the Miami area where it drops to 5 percentage points below the 2004 value in 2012.

The increase in the fraction of investors in 2004–2007 displays even more geographical variation and is everywhere much larger than the rise in the fraction with a first mortgage. San Francisco (SF), Los Angeles–Long Beach–Anaheim (LA), DC, and Miami start with the highest fraction of investors and also experience the largest increases in investor activity between 2004 and 2007. Miami experiences the largest rise from 11% in 2004 to 18% by early 2008. The other MSAs start with a fraction of investors just below 10% in 2004 and experience a rise of 2–3 percentage points. The four metropolitan areas with the largest rise also experience the largest decline in the fraction of investors after the 2007–2009 crisis, with Miami and DC returning to preboom levels by 2010. For San Francisco and LA, the fraction of investors declines by about half of the rise during the boom by mid-2009. In the other metropolitan areas, investor activity returns to preboom levels more gradually.

Figure 4.13 distinguishes between borrowers with only two and with three or more first mortgages. Among the MSAs with the largest increase in investor activity, San Francisco experiences only a modest rise in the fraction with two first mortgages but a very dramatic rise in the fraction with three or more. LA

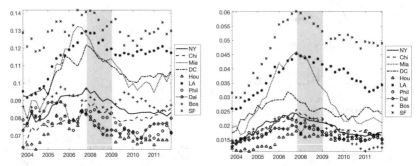

FIGURE 4.13 Fraction of borrowers with two (*left panel*) and three or more (*right panel*) first mortgages among borrowers with one or more first mortgages in the top ten metropolitan statistical areas by 2010 population
Source: Author's calculations based on Experian data.
Note: See figure 4.12 for MSA abbreviations.

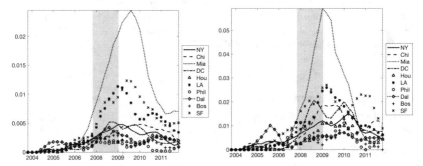

FIGURE 4.14 Fraction of borrowers with a new foreclosure in the last four quarters by one (*left panel*) and two or more (*right panel*) first mortgages in the top ten metropolitan statistical areas by 2010 population
Source: Author's calculations based on Experian data.
Note: See figure 4.12 for MSA abbreviations.

and Miami instead experience a similar percentage point rise in the fraction with only two and with three or more first mortgages, whereas DC experiences a rise in the fraction with two first mortgages which is about twice as large as the rise of those with three or more. The other major metropolitan areas display a common pattern during the boom, with the rise in the fraction with two first mortgages about twice as large as the rise of those with three or more.

Figure 4.14 displays the foreclosure rates for investors and noninvestors in the same metropolitan areas. In all metropolitan areas considered, the foreclosure rate is substantially higher for investors, though the difference displays some geographical variation. Miami displays the highest foreclosure rate for both investors and noninvestors, with a peak of 6.5% and 3.8%, respectively. In all metropolitan areas, the foreclosure rate for investors seems to peak earlier than for noninvestors.

To better understand the spatial variation in investor activity and default behavior, I examine the relation between investor activity and a number of important economic and demographic controls at the MSA and zip code level.

Factors in Geographical Dispersion

The analysis begins from the MSA level, restricting attention to the three hundred largest MSAs by 2010 population. Figure 4.15 presents a scatter plot of the 2000–2010 change in population and the population density in 2010 based on census data. Clearly, population grew more in MSAs with higher population density, reflecting the growing concentration of the population in urban areas. The figure also plots the change in the Corelogic house price index between 2001Q4 and 2006Q4 and between 2006Q4 and 2009Q4 against the change in population. The 2004–2006 change in house prices is positively related to the change in population, while the 2007–2009 change is negatively related. This suggests that high population density areas with increasing populations experienced a more pronounced boom-bust in housing values over the sample period.

Figure 4.16 plots the fraction with first mortgages and the fraction of investors in 2004Q1 against the population density. There is a positive relation between population density and these two variables, which is consistent with the concentration of high-income households in urban areas (see Couture and Handbury 2017 and Gyourko, Mayer, and Sinai 2013), with the slope of this relation steeper for the fraction with two or more first mortgages. The figure also presents the relation between the fraction with first mortgage in 2004Q1 and the fraction of investors in the same period, reflecting a positive correlation, consistent with the notion that factors leading particular metropolitan areas to be attractive to households also render them attractive to investors.

Figure 4.17 illustrates the relation between population density and the 2000–2010 change in population and investor activity during the boom. The top panel is a scatter plot of the 2004–2007 change in the fraction with two and three or more first mortgages against population density. There is a positive relation, stronger in magnitude for three or more first mortgages. The bottom panel suggests a similar pattern for the 2000–2010 population change. Both figures also display the 2004–2007 change in the fraction with a first mortgage. There is no relation between this variable and population density or the population change, which is consistent with the notion that there was little variation in the fraction of borrowers with a first mortgage during the boom.

We now turn to the relation with house price fluctuations. Figure 4.18 shows scatter plots of the log change in house prices in 2001Q4–2006Q4 and in 2006Q4–2009Q4 and the 2004Q1–2007Q4 log change in the fraction of borrowers with one or more first mortgages, two first mortgages, and three or more first mortgages. The figure clearly shows a negative relation between the change in house prices during the bust and the change in investor activity

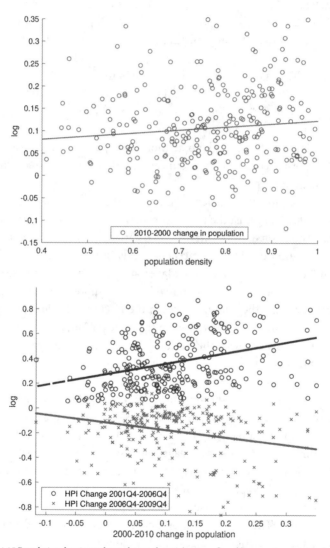

FIGURE 4.15 Population density and population change (*top panel*) and house price variation by population change (*bottom panel*) for the top three hundred MSAs by population

Source: Author's calculations based on Experian, census, and Corelogic data.

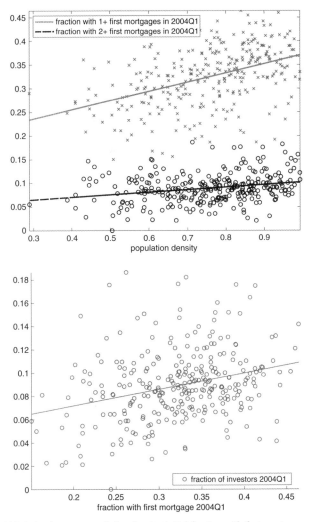

FIGURE 4.16 Relation between population density, initial fraction with first mortgages, and investor activity for the top three hundred MSAs by population
Source: Author's calculations based on Experian and census data.

between 2004 and 2007. There is also a positive relation between the change in house prices during the boom and the change in the fraction of borrowers with three or more first mortgages. This suggests that the surge in investor activity was positively related to the amplitude of house price fluctuations, especially for borrowers with three or more first mortgages.[10] The positive

10. Since the fraction of investor activity is positively related to the initial fraction of investors, these results are consistent with Garcia (2018) who, using Home Mortgage Disclosure Act

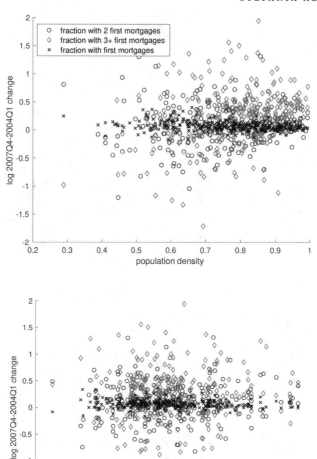

FIGURE 4.17 Relation between population density, population change, and change in fraction with one, two, and three or more first mortgages for the top three hundred MSAs by population
Source: Author's calculations based on Experian and census data.

relation between the magnitude of house price fluctuations and the incidence of investor activity is consistent with Chinco and Mayer (2015), who find that demand from out-of-town second-house buyers during the mid-2000s predicted house price appreciation rates.

data, finds that preboom intensity of investor activity is positively related to the occurrence and size of a boom in house prices.

Figure 4.19 plots the relation between the 2007–2009 and the 2001–2006 changes in housing values and the 2007–2009 log change in foreclosure rates by number of first mortgages. The graph suggests that the metropolitan areas that experienced the biggest house price fluctuations also experienced the biggest rise in foreclosure rates during the 2007–2009 crisis, and that this relation holds for both investors and noninvestors.

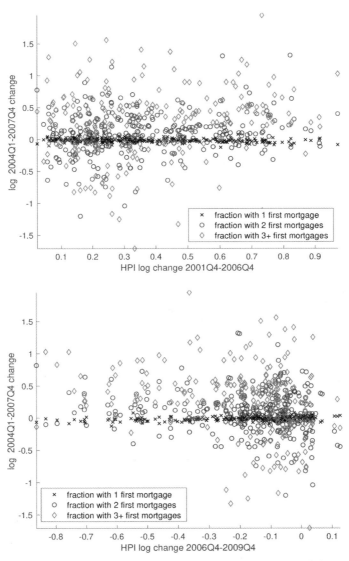

FIGURE 4.18 Relation between fluctuations in housing values and the 2004Q1–2007Q4 change in the fraction with at least 1, 2, and 3 or more first mortgages for the top three hundred MSAs by population
Source: Author's calculations based on Experian data.

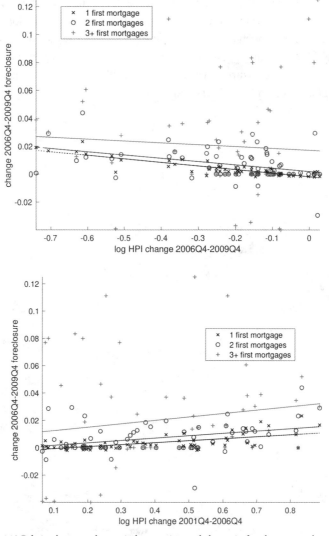

FIGURE 4.19 Relation between changes in house prices and change in foreclosure rates by number of first mortgages for the top three hundred MSAs by population
Source: Author's calculations based on Experian, census, and Corelogic data.

Conclusion

This chapter provides varied sets of evidence on the role of real estate investors in the 2007–2009 housing crisis. We show that investors, especially those with three or more first mortgages, are primarily responsible for the mortgage crisis. Despite the fact that they have higher income and higher credit scores than noninvestors, they display much higher default rates than noninvestors, and this gap grows dramatically in 2007–2009. Investors are more highly leveraged than noninvestors, and they are substantially more likely to default strategically rather than due to financial distress. There is substantial geographical dispersion in investor activity, which is higher in metropolitan areas with high population density in 2000 and strong 2000–2010 population growth. Areas with high homeownership rates also display high investor activity and a stronger rise during the 2004–2006 boom. We find that the magnitude of the rise in default rates is positively correlated with the magnitude of the rise in house prices during the boom and the magnitude of their decline during the crisis.

The evidence raises important questions on the mechanisms driving some of the most important and surprising patterns. For example, was the surge in investor activity by relatively young borrowers, which was the only notable change in the characteristics of investors during the housing boom, driven by an increase in supply of credit to these borrowers, loosening of credit standards, or a rise in income of young professional college graduates? Was the strong positive relation between population density, 2000–2010 population growth, house price fluctuations and investor activity at the MSA level driven by investor activity, or was investor activity a consequence of the dynamics in housing values? What role did exogenous changes in local economic structure, such as concentration of employment in top occupations and growing industries, play? (On this last, see Rossi-Hansberg et al. 2009; Ferreira and Gyourko 2011; Liebersohn 2017.) Finally, are lower investor activity and default rates in judicial nonrecourse states, where arguably borrowers benefit most from foreclosure, due to equilibrium lending conditions response? The higher incentive to default would lead to higher mortgage rates, tighter lending standards in equilibrium, which would induce lower leverage and lower default rates, as observed in the data. Albanesi (2018) develops a quantitative equilibrium model of housing and mortgage markets with investors that can be used to explore these questions.

REFERENCES

Acemoglu, Daron, and David Autor. 2011. Skills, Tasks and Technologies: Implications for Employment and Earnings. Handbook of Labor Economics 4: 1043–1171.

Albanesi, Stefania. 2018. Real Estate Investors: A Quantitative Analysis. In progress, University of Pittsburgh.

Albanesi, Stefania, Giacomo DeGiorgi, and Jaromir Nosal. 2017. Credit Growth and the Financial Crisis: A New Narrative. NBER Working Paper 23740.

Chinco, Alex, and Christopher Mayer. 2015. Misinformed Speculators and Mispricing in the Housing Market. Review of Financial Studies 29 (2): 486–522.

Couture, Victor, and Jessie Handbury. 2017. Urban Revival in America, 2000 to 2010. NBER Working Paper 24084.

Eeckhout, Jan, Christoph Hedtrich, and Roberto Pinheiro. 2019. Automation, Spatial Sorting, and Job Polarization. In IZA 2019 Meeting Papers. Society for Economic Dynamics.

Elul, Ronel, Sebastian G. Tilson, and Aaron Payne. 2019. Owner-Occupancy Fraud and Mortgage Performance. Federal Reserve Bank of Philadelphia Working Paper No. 19-53.

Ferreira, Fernando, and Joseph Gyourko. 2011. Anatomy of the Beginning of the Housing Boom: U.S. Neighborhoods and Metropolitan Areas, 1993–2009. NBER Working Paper 17374.

Foote, Christopher L., and Paul S. Willen. 2016. The Subprime Mortgage Crisis. In Garet Jones, ed., Banking Crises, 324–36. London: Palgrave Macmillan.

Garcia, Daniel. 2018. Property Investors and the Housing Boom and Bust. Manuscript, Federal Reserve Board.

Gerardi, Kristopher, Kyle Herkenhoff, Lee E. Ohanian, and Paul Willen. 2013. Unemployment, Negative Equity, and Strategic Default. Federal Reserve Bank of Atlanta Working Paper 2013-04.

Ghent, Andra C., and Marianna Kudlyak. 2011. Recourse and Residential Mortgage Default: Evidence from US States. Review of Financial Studies 24 (9): 3139–86.

Guerrieri, Veronica, Daniel Hartley, and Erik Hurst. 2013. Endogenous Gentrification and Housing Price Dynamics. Journal of Public Economics 100: 45–60.

Gyourko, Joseph, Christopher Mayer, and Todd Sinai. 2013. Superstar Cities. American Economic Journal: Economic Policy 5 (4): 167–99.

Haughwout, Andrew, Donghoon Lee, Joseph S. Tracy, and Wilbert Van der Klaauw. 2011. Real Estate Investors, the Leverage Cycle, and the Housing Market Crisis. Federal Reserve Bank of New York Staff Reports, no. 514.

Keys, Benjamin J., Tomasz Piskorski, Amit Seru, and Vikrant Vig. 2012. Mortgage Financing in the Housing Boom and Bust. In Edward L. Glaeser and Todd Sinai, eds., Housing and the Financial Crisis, 143–204. Chicago: University of Chicago Press.

Kindermann, Fabian, and Sebastian Kohls. 2016. Rental Markets and Wealth Inequality in the Euro-Area. Technical report, University of Bonn.

Liebersohn, Jack. 2017. Housing Demand, Regional House Prices and Consumption. Manuscript, MIT.

Rossi-Hansberg, Esteban, Pierre-Daniel Sarte, et al. 2009. Firm Fragmentation and Urban Patterns. International Economic Review 50 (1): 143–86.

Wyman, Oliver. 2010. Understanding Strategic Default in Mortgages. Experian report.

Comment by Fernando Ferreira

There is an old and ugly narrative about poor and minority subprime borrowers causing the housing crisis and subsequent Great Recession. The narrative mostly arose from talking-head media rants that mistakenly put blame for the housing problems on the shoulders of the people who actually suffered

Fernando Ferreira is the C. F. Koo Professor, professor of real estate, and professor of business economics and public policy at the Wharton School, University of Pennsylvania.

the most dire consequences of the economic crisis. A somewhat similar theory developed on the academic side: The very early work of Mian and Sufi (2009) claimed that neighborhoods with a large share of subprime families took too much credit in the 2000s and that led to the foreclosure crisis.

These stories have been thoroughly debunked by many researchers. Adelino, Schoar, and Severino (2016) showed that the 2000s mortgage expansion happened across the entire income distribution. Then Foote, Loewenstein, and Willen (2016) actually showed that more debt was issued to wealthy households, and Albanesi, De Giorgi, and Nosal (2017) revealed that credit growth was concentrated in the prime segment. Ferreira and Gyourko (2015) concluded that subprime mortgages mostly displaced government-sponsored mortgages, and that prime foreclosures represented more than two-thirds of the overall distress after the Great Recession. Finally, minorities bought housing properties very late in the cycle, at the worst possible time (Bayer, Ferreira, and Ross 2016), and were the first to suffer the negative consequences of the Great Recession unemployment shock.

This new and exciting work by Stefania Albanesi drives yet another stake through the heart of the old narrative. First, Albanesi describes that investors, who correspond to approximately 14% of all borrowers, had a much larger share of foreclosures than previously known—almost 50% of foreclosures during crisis peak! This little-known fact further minimizes the role of households, subprime or otherwise, in the housing crisis. Moreover, she shows that investors are more likely to default strategically, which exacerbated the housing crisis and ensuing negative equity problems for standard homeowners.

There are a couple of avenues to improve the credibility of these results, and Albanesi is perfectly equipped to accomplish the task. Her definition of investors is based on homeowners with at least two mortgage transactions for different properties. But it would be interesting to compare that with other definitions used in the literature, such as flippers who quickly resell investment homes. Also, it is likely that more professional investors, organized as LLPs for example, are not part of her sample. Such comparisons will not only strengthen the work but also help guide future research using different data.

Similarly, it would be important to compare the advantages and costs of her definition of strategic default, and how strategic default fits in a model where investors care about portfolio decisions, not just the units occupied by their families. Those estimates are critical input for policy makers, as the desirability of bailout policies are highly dependent on the potential redistribution and moral hazard.

Revisiting the housing boom and bust also highlights that it takes a village to fully understand certain economic phenomena. Many other stylized facts about the housing boom and bust have emerged from a diverse set of research: (A) Housing booms started at local levels in the mid- to late 1990s and spread out over a decade (Ferreira and Gyourko 2011); (B) Booms were a middle-class event with a mix of fundamental (Glaeser and Gyourko 2018) and behavior factors (Shiller 2005; Soo 2018); (C) The financial sector contributed to the boom with a lag (Favara and Imbs 2015; Keys et al. 2010); (D) Investors and speculators added to existing demand (DeFusco, Nathanson, and Zwick 2017); and (E) The foreclosure crisis first impacted poor/minorities because of real job losses and because of investors that defaulted strategically.

Given that we are still learning about many aspects of the crisis, and the inherent difficulties of accounting for the vast set of causes and consequences, researchers can certainly benefit from an extra dose of humility when presenting early results about any economic event. This is even more important in the age of Facebook/Twitter, where it may be quite difficult to explain all nuances of empirical research in economics.

Overall, this chapter is a great step in the direction of understanding what has been the most important economic event of this century to date. I look forward to reading more from Albanesi, as there are still many challenges related to uncovering all the interconnected mechanisms that fueled the boom and bust.

REFERENCES

Adelino, Manuel, Antoinette Schoar, and Felipe Severino. 2016. Loan Originations and Defaults in the Mortgage Crisis: The Role of the Middle Class. Review of Financial Studies 29 (7): 1635–70.
Albanesi, Stefania, Giacomo De Giorgi, and Jaromir Nosal. 2017. Credit Growth and the Financial Crisis: A New Narrative. NBER Working Paper 23740.
Bayer, Patrick, Fernando Ferreira, and Stephen L. Ross. 2016. The Vulnerability of Minority Homeowners in the Housing Boom and Bust. American Economic Journal: Economic Policy 8 (1): 1–27.
DeFusco, Anthony A., Charles G. Nathanson, and Eric Zwick. 2017. Speculative Dynamics of Prices and Volume. NBER Working Paper 23449.
Favara, Giovanni, and Jean Imbs. 2015. Credit Supply and the Price of Housing. American Economic Review 105 (3): 958–92.
Ferreira, Fernando, and Joseph Gyourko. 2011. Anatomy of the Beginning of the Housing Boom: U.S. Neighborhoods and Metropolitan Areas, 1993–2009. NBER Working Paper 17374.
———. 2015. A New Look at the U.S. Foreclosure Crisis: Panel Data Evidence of Prime and Subprime Borrowers from 1997 to 2012. NBER Working Paper 21261.
Foote, Cristopher L., Lara Loewenstein, and Paul S. Willen. 2016. Cross-Sectional Patterns of Mortgage Debt during the Housing Boom: Evidence and Implications. NBER Working Paper 22985.
Glaeser, Edward, and Joseph Gyourko. 2018. The Economic Implications of Housing Supply. Journal of Economic Perspectives 32 (1): 3–30.

Keys, Benjamin J., Tanmoy Mukherjee, Amit Seru, and Vikrant Vig. 2010. Did Securitization Lead to Lax Screening? Evidence from Subprime Loans. Quarterly Journal of Economics 125 (1): 307–62.

Mian, Atif, and Amir Sufi. 2009. The Consequences of Mortgage Credit Expansion: Evidence from the U.S. Mortgage Default Crisis. Quarterly Journal of Economics 124 (4): 1449–96.

Shiller, Robert J. 2005. Irrational Exuberance. 2nd ed. Princeton, NJ: Princeton University.

Soo, Cindy K. 2018. Quantifying Sentiment with News Media across Local Housing Markets. Review of Financial Studies 31 (10): 3689–3719.

5

Bank Capital before and after Financial Crises

ÒSCAR JORDÀ, BJÖRN RICHTER,
MORITZ SCHULARICK, AND ALAN M. TAYLOR

> A well-run bank needs no capital. No amount of capital will rescue a badly run bank.
> WALTER BAGEHOT, *Lombard Street* (1873)

The regulatory response to the global financial crisis followed a well-known playbook. New policies include managing statutory loan-to-value and debt-to-income ratios; extending financial regulation beyond banks to other financial institutions; stress-testing the balance sheets of the largest lenders; closely monitoring systemically important intermediaries; and setting up countercyclical capital buffers together with a macroprudential authority to administer them.[1] These are some of the most common changes implemented internationally to limit leverage in the financial system.

Underlying this wide-ranging regulatory response lies one core belief: raise bank capital because the more equity at stake, the more carefully its owners will monitor whom and how much the bank lends to—shareholders have more "skin in the game." In addition, a bigger capital buffer should provide banks with greater capacity to absorb loan losses and continue in the business of lending. The key question is whether higher levels of bank capital will prevent the next crisis as a result. And if they do not, the follow-up

Òscar Jordà is professor of economics at the University of California, Davis, and a senior policy advisor at the Federal Reserve Bank of San Francisco. Björn Richter is assistant professor of finance at Universitat Pompeu Fabra. Moritz Schularick is professor of economics at Sciences Po and the University of Bonn, and a fellow at the Institute for New Economic Thinking. Alan M. Taylor is distinguished professor of economics and finance at the University of California, Davis.

1. A countercyclical capital buffer consists of raising/lowering capital requirements for the banking system as a whole depending on economic conditions. The macroprudential authority is tasked with making that determination. This differs from microprudential policy, where the determination is made for individual institutions.

question is whether the additional loss-absorbing capacity will facilitate recovery from the inevitable crisis.

Our overarching goal is to investigate how the banking system's capital structure affects its ability to take on and manage risk. Because financial crises are rare events, we turn to 150 years of modern financial history across seventeen advanced economies. In particular, we construct a new aggregate data set that covers three main categories of the funding mix of financial intermediaries: capital, deposits, and other (no-deposit) debt instruments. The new data directly complement our previous work (Jordà, Schularick, and Taylor 2017b) on the asset side of the banking system.

In thinking about bank capital and financial crises, Bagehot's quip is a reminder that trouble starts when a bank decides what to lend for and to whom—no amount of capital can make up for poor business decisions. But the liability side of banks, and the composition of their funding in particular, are also important determinants of their solvency and liquidity with important ramifications for financial stability. Higher capital ratios should serve as a buffer against loan defaults just as higher levees protect against major floods.

There is an alternative view to the skin-in-the-game role of bank capital, however. In a credit boom, banks may not fully appreciate the buildup of risk in their balance sheets. Recent research documents overoptimism by insiders and market-wide neglect of crash risk during credit booms.[2] These findings are consistent with an older literature[3] and with recent theoretical work.[4] In this view, capital ratios can do little to stem systemic waves of overoptimism. Banks are not behaving carelessly because they do not have skin in the game. Like everyone else, they underestimate the risk they are undertaking.

In fact, the evidence so far seems to suggest that more capital does not mean fewer crises. Haldane (2010) shows that regulatory capital ratios before the crisis do not explain which banks suffered the most thereafter. Barth, Caprio, and Levine (2006) arrived at the same conclusion based on a large cross section of countries. Rajan (2018) reminds us that while equity holders are the first to bear losses, in a crisis it is the public that ends up footing most of the bill. Historically Anderson, Barth, and Choi (2018) find little evidence that double-liability banks took fewer risks before the Great Depression.[5]

2. Baron and Xiong 2017; Fahlenbrach, Prilmeier, and Stulz 2016; as well as Cheng, Raina, and Xiong 2014.

3. Kindleberger 1978; Minsky 1977, 1986; Shiller 2000.

4. Bordalo, Gennaioli, and Shleifer 2018; Simsek 2013; Greenwood, Hanson, and Jin 2016.

5. Jaremski and Wheelock (2017) also present mixed evidence about the disciplining force of double liability in the World War I agricultural commodity price boom.

The long sweep of history provides perspective on the ever-changing business of banking. Capital ratios declined rapidly from about 30% at the start of our sample until World War II. From then onward they have remained eerily stable over time and across countries in a tight range of about 5% to 10%. If anything, capital ratios rose slightly during the lead-up to the recent crisis, dispelling a widely held belief to the contrary.

Perhaps the most striking development of the twentieth century happened in regard to the funding structure of banks. In 1950, bank debt funding consisted almost entirely of deposits. But starting sometime in the 1970s, the share of outside funding began to increase so that on the eve of the financial crisis in 2007, the deposit share of funding had shrunk to 50% of total debt liabilities. All of a sudden, large chunks of a bank's balance sheet were exposed to abrupt liquidation. Nondeposit financing is highly "runnable" and shows up in our analysis as one of the nascent indicators of financial risk.

In contrast, there is no evidence that more capital prevents systemic banking crises. The literature identifies systemic banking crises narratively as periods when significant parts of the banking system fail or have to be rescued by government intervention.[6] More capital, whether measured at market or book values, does not affect the chances of a crisis in either the pre– or the post–World War II eras.

Yet there may be a different rationale for boosting capital. Even if a crisis cannot be prevented with more capital, is the recovery facilitated by it? Existing evidence indicates this to be the case. Evidence from the Great Depression is provided by Bernanke (1983) and for Japan in the mid-1990s and the Great Recession (Peek and Rosengren 2000; Khwaja and Mian 2008; Jordà, Schularick, and Taylor 2013). This is precisely what the historical record shows.

A more weakly capitalized financial sector is associated with a deeper recession and a slower recovery. The differences in social costs are economically sizable, showing as much as 4 percentage points higher real GDP five years after the start of the crisis. Historical evidence across countries lines up well with evidence for the United States.[7]

The mechanism is easy to grasp. Higher loss absorption capacity places banks in a better position to issue credit again once the worst of the crisis passes. In poorly capitalized systems, demand for credit is stunted by the inability of banks to issue new loans.

6. See Schularick and Taylor 2012; Laeven and Valencia 2012; Jordà, Schularick, and Taylor 2017b.

7. See Cecchetti, King, and Yetman 2011 and Berkmen, Gelos, Rennhack, and Walsh 2012 for the 2007 crisis and its aftermath.

The takeaway can be simply stated. Boost capital to restart credit following the crisis and facilitate the recovery. But don't rely on higher capital as protection against financial crises. Vigilance needs to rest on a variety of other indicators, two of the most important being the growth of credit relative to the economy, and the funding mix of the banking system—in particular, reliance on outside short-term wholesale funding.

Understanding a Bank's Balance Sheet

The balance sheets of U.S. banks in 1929 and in 2007 provide some perspective on the evolution of this business. On the asset side, banks primarily hold cash and securities, and issue loans. On the liability side, banks fund themselves largely through customer deposits, outside short-term wholesale borrowing, and equity issued (or capital). The categories are somewhat imprecisely defined, but they paint the big picture accurately enough. Core liabilities are deposits and capital; the rest is lumped into the noncore category.

On the asset side, not a great deal has changed since 1929. Banks manage with lower levels of cash in hand today than in the past, but that is to be expected given developments in payment technology. The share of loans is virtually unchanged.

Changes on the liability side are more interesting. Although capital levels are similar (11% in 1929 vs. 8% in 2007), the share of noncore liabilities has risen considerably, from just under 10% to nearly one-third. It turns out that many banking systems have experienced a similar shift in the composition of liabilities, with consequences that we will explore in more detail below.

Several key balance-sheet ratios of financial intermediaries are central in any analysis of financial stability. The most well-known is the capital ratio, defined like today's Basel III "leverage ratio," that is, the ratio of capital over total assets. Next the ratio of loans to deposits is often considered a measure of banking sector illiquidity or vulnerability.[8] Finally, the share of other liabilities (excluding capital) is a measure of the stability of the bank's funding. In order to avoid confusion, we will refer to this measure as the noncore ratio, that is, the ratio of other liabilities over the sum of deposits and other liabilities.

Perspective on how capital and the composition of liabilities affect the stability of the banking system requires data, lots of it in fact, because financial crises do not happen very often. To this end, we collected nearly 150 years of data (from 1870 to 2015) for seventeen advanced economies on the main

8. See Cecchetti, King, and Yetman 2011.

components of the liability side of the balance sheet. Details on how the data were collected and the formal definitions of all the variables are available in Jordà, Richter, Schularick, and Taylor (2017a).

The Long View on Bank Liabilities

Nearly 150 years of data provide a sharper focus on the main trends in the business of banking. Start with the capital ratio discussed earlier. Figure 5.1 shows that the cross-country average aggregate capital ratio decreased steadily from around 30% to less than 10% right after World War II, before fluctuating in the range of 5% to 10% over subsequent decades and up to the present. In other words, bank leverage rose dramatically from 1870 until the mid-twentieth century.

This decline in capital ratios likely reflects the evolution of commercial banking—a fairly new business model in the nineteenth century. Bank creditors back then required large amounts of equity funding as a buffer against the risk they attached to this new business. Over time, financial innovation led to higher liquidity in markets. And increasing sophistication of financial instruments allowed banks to better hedge against uncertain events. As a result, banks became safer investments overall, thus reducing the need for large capital buffers.[9]

In addition, central banks progressively took on the role of lender of last resort, allowing banks to manage short-term liquidity disruptions by borrowing directly from the central bank.[10] The second main innovation in the twentieth century was the introduction of deposit insurance. Deposit insurance mitigates the risks of self-fulfilling panic-based bank runs[11] and today is the norm in almost all countries around the world.[12] Of course, one could also argue that too-big-to-fail banks enjoy an additional implicit guarantee since authorities are loath to let these institutions fail for fear of contagion.[13]

Figure 5.2 turns to the composition of the balance sheet by plotting the share of capital, deposits, and noncore liabilities over time. While deposits make up the largest share of funding at all times, the patterns have changed substantially since World War II. Until about 1950, the share of deposits in

9. See Kroszner 1999; Merton 1995.
10. See Calomiris, Flandreau, and Laeven 2016.
11. As explained in Diamond and Dybvig 1983.
12. See Demirgüç-Kunt, Kane, and Laeven 2014.
13. Haldane (2010) puts the annual implicit subsidy at several hundred billion dollars for global systemically important banks.

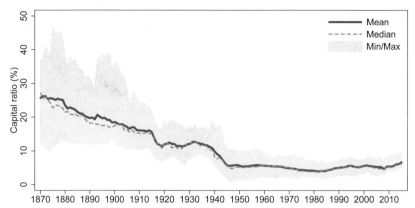

FIGURE 5.1 Capital ratio, averages by year for seventeen countries, full sample
Note: The solid line plots the mean of capital ratios in the sample countries between 1870 and 2015. The dashed line refers to the median of the sample countries. The gray area is the min-max range for the seventeen countries in the sample.

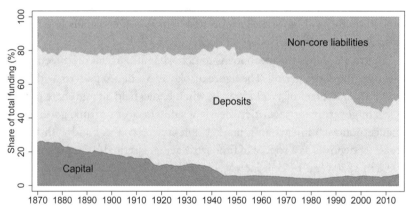

FIGURE 5.2 Composition of liabilities, averages by year for seventeen countries, full sample
Note: This figure plots the shares of capital, deposits, and noncore liabilities in total funding. Categories add up to 100%.

total funding increased as the capital ratio decreased. There was little change in the share of noncore liabilities. Deposits made up 80% of all liabilities. But by the early 2000s, the share of deposits had fallen to little more than 50%.[14]

In banking textbooks, banks intermediate funds between borrowers and savers. This intermediation entails a maturity transformation—banks borrow

14. The increasing importance of noncore (e.g., wholesale) funding sources is central to the growing separation of money and credit in the post–World War II period discussed by Schularick and Taylor (2012) as well as Jordà, Schularick, and Taylor (2013).

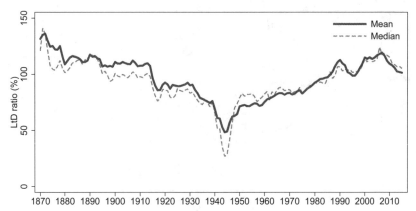

FIGURE 5.3 Loans to deposits ratio, averages by year for seventeen countries, full sample
Note: This figure plots the average of the aggregate loan-to-deposit ratio over all sample countries from 1870 to 2015.

short and lend long. Thus, the loans to deposit ratio is a common metric of bank illiquidity. A higher level means that banks would typically find it more difficult to withstand large deposit outflows.

Figure 5.3 shows the mean loans to deposits ratio for all seventeen countries over the entire period. The figure displays a V-shaped pattern, with a low near 50% at the end of World War II, when banks held a large share of their assets in government securities, clearly a side-effect of wartime government finance policies rather than a market outcome. Hand in hand with the increase of deposits as a source of funds, the average ratio declined from above 100% in 1870 until 1945. It increased afterward, from 75% in the early 1950s to more than 100% before the global financial crisis. After the crisis, the ratio has decreased as banks have deleveraged and reduced noncore funding.

Bank Capital Structure before and after the Crisis

How does capital structure affect bank risk-taking and the likelihood of financial crises? If bankers have an incentive to take excessive risks,[15] then more skin in the game should lead to more prudent behavior, improve screening and monitoring incentives, and thereby reduce the probability that financial institutions face large and life-threatening losses.[16] Empirically, some studies report evidence consistent with this hypothesis[17] while others have found

---

15. See Merton 1977; Jensen and Meckling 1976.
16. Holmstrom and Tirole 1997; Mehran and Thakor 2011.
17. Esty 1997; Gan 2004; Landier, Sraer, and Thesmar 2011.

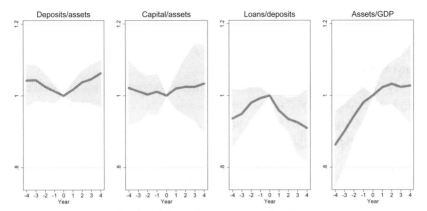

FIGURE 5.4 Event study of key bank balance-sheet ratios centered on the crisis year
Note: This figure presents the path of balance-sheet ratios around financial crises. Year 0 corresponds to a systemic financial crisis. The values of the respective variable are scaled to equal 1 in year 0. The solid line corresponds to the mean and the gray bands to the interquartile range.

little empirical support.[18] Yet others argue that leverage can be beneficial because uninsured short-term creditors monitor and discipline bankers more effectively.[19] Market discipline imposed through risk-adjusted funding costs will ensure that the capital structure of a bank reflects the riskiness of its assets. In fact, some studies argue that imposing higher capital requirements can perversely increase bank risk.[20]

One way to gauge these competing views is to consider the dynamics of banking sector balance sheets in the run-up to and in the aftermath of systemic financial crises. Systemic banking crises are periods when significant parts of the banking system fail or have to be rescued by government intervention.[21] Importantly, financial crises relate to systemic distress rather than to a single institution only.

Figure 5.4 presents the paths of the three average balance-sheet ratios defined earlier and the size of the banking sector relative to GDP around crises. All ratios are shown here relative to their value in the year of the systemic financial crisis, where the value in the crisis year 0 is normalized to 1.

18. See, e.g., Gropp, Hakenes, and Schnabel 2011 for banks and Gilje 2016 for nonfinancial firms.

19. See, e.g., Calomiris and Kahn 1991; Diamond and Rajan 2001.

20. Hellmann, Murdock, and Stiglitz 2000; Blum 1999; Besanko and Kanatas 1996; Gale 2010. Adrian, Friedman, and Muir (2015) show that return-on-equity targeting is indeed a widespread industry practice.

21. Laeven and Valencia 2012; Jordà, Schularick, and Taylor 2017b; Schularick and Taylor 2012.

The first two panels show the behavior of deposits and capital. Before a financial crisis, banks turn to nontraditional funding sources to finance credit expansion. These funds dry up in the wake of the crisis, after which banks turn again to deposits as a source of funds.

For equity capital, the patterns are much less clear. Before a financial crisis, book capital ratios are more or less stable. After a financial crisis, banks rebuild their capital base relative to precrisis levels. This reaction seems plausible since after a financial crisis, creditors may penalize low levels of capitalization. Equally, a financial crisis may lead to changes in the regulatory environment. However, as a first pass, it is hard to identify large ex ante downward shifts in capital ratios in the years just prior to financial crises.

On the asset side, the third panel of figure 5.4 shows that the loan-to-deposit ratio increases before a financial crisis and falls afterward. This behavior partly mirrors the path of deposits presented above, but it also mirrors the growing share of loans in total assets. The fourth panel shows that the size of aggregate banking assets (or liabilities) relative to GDP grows markedly before a financial crisis. The typical credit boom pattern before a crisis is clearly visible in the event windows.

Bank Capital and the Odds of Crisis

It is time to explore the bank capital structure of the banking system and its effect on the odds of a financial crisis, using a battery of experiments that we now describe.

A first pass We calculate the odds of a financial crisis using the three balance-sheet ratios introduced earlier individually—the capital ratio, loans to deposits, and the noncore ratio—with respect to the average annual change over the previous five-year window of the ratio of credit to GDP. Schularick and Taylor (2012) found this to be the most useful predictor of a financial crisis.

Beyond the first pass Next, we also consider market rather than book values of capital. We include variables that control for asset prices (such as housing prices), macroeconomic risks (such as the volatility of output, inflation, or mortgage rates), and the riskiness of balance sheets.

Voluntary capital expansions The predictive ability of bank capital could be masked by the fact that regulators can force banks to raise more capital if they perceive that the bank's loans are getting riskier. Thus capital might increase in anticipation of a crisis.

In order to address this masking effect, one can turn to variation in capital due to retained earnings only. Retained earnings are one of the major sources of bank equity financing.[22] As of 2018Q3, undivided profits account for 37.8% of total bank equity capital of commercial and savings banks in the United States, which is slightly below the average share for the post-1984 period.[23]

Well-capitalized credit booms   Rapid balance-sheet expansions—credit booms—lie at the heart of financial crisis risk. If more skin in the game induces prudent behavior by banks, we should expect to find that credit booms occurring at high levels of bank equity are considerably less likely to end in a crisis than credit booms financed with less equity. That is, interacting credit growth with bank capital should reveal if this is the case.

Deposit insurance   Deposit insurance affects the bank's incentives to take on risk, and therefore how much capital creditors will require. One way to assess the impact of the introduction of deposit insurance and its effect on bank capital and the likelihood of financial crisis is to split the sample into two groups depending on whether in a given country-year pair there is deposit insurance. Deposit insurance schemes were introduced at different times in different countries.

Concentration of risk   Aggregate capital ratios could mask substantial heterogeneity within banking systems and risks could be highly concentrated in a few, systemically important institutions or in a subset of banks with very low capital ratios. Here we rely on evidence from Italy, where the Historical Archive of Credit (Natoli, Piselli, Triglia, and Vercelli 2016) contains micro-level balance-sheet data for the near-universe of banks over more than eighty years, between 1890 and 1973.

Capitalization of the largest and systemically important banks matters for financial crisis risks. As a matter of fact, current regulations contain capital surcharges for large and interconnected institutions. To examine this proposition, we examined whether low or falling capital ratios of the largest banks signal growing financial fragility using microdata[24] for a subset of the largest

22. Cohen and Scatigna (2016) show that retained earnings have been the most important source of bank capital increases in advanced economies after the financial crisis and that banks also retained a significant fraction of earnings pre-2007.

23. Numbers are based on data from "FDIC—Quarterly Banking Profile Time Series Spreadsheets."

24. Collected and kindly shared by Mazbouri, Guex, and Lopez (2017).

banks in Belgium, France, Germany, Italy, Switzerland, and the United Kingdom for the period 1890 to 1970 and extended with data for France, Germany, Switzerland, and the United Kingdom. We also added recent data from statistics for large commercial banks in the Organisation for Economic Co-operation and Development Banking Statistics, plus hand-collected additional data for Denmark, Sweden, Norway, and the Netherlands.

The takeaway   Evidence that equity capital has a disciplining effect on bank risk-taking is thin. Credit booms are equally dangerous whether levels of bank capital are high or low. The disciplining and monitoring effects are absent when they presumably matter most. This finding fits well with work that points to overoptimism of insiders and market-wide neglect of crash risk during credit booms,[25] rather than supporting the skin-in-the-game hypothesis.

A potential explanation for the missing link between capital and crises in recent data is that banks simply increase the riskiness of their assets once capital ratios are regulated. However, capital and crises are unrelated across a wide range of regulatory and economic environments. There is neither a link in a pre-1914 sample, when regulation was at its infancy, nor in a sample of countries that had already introduced deposit insurance. This core result is also robust to a whole battery of controls for asset and macroeconomic risk factors, and it does not change when we account for the possibility that banks finance themselves with more equity capital when crisis risks are elevated.

Market-based capital ratios do not perform much better than book measures in this regard. From a historical perspective, this carries a lot of plausibility. Just as in 2006–2007, bank equity prices in general tend to be boosted by the increased profitability during the boom. Equity investors typically fail to spot the risks that are built up during credit booms.[26] This result in particular raises further doubts about the efficacy of market discipline. Credit booms are often triggered by increasing bank profitability[27] and hence retained earnings allow banks to hold capital ratios stable during the boom, even when assets are growing fast.[28]

Liquidity matters, however. Rising loan-to-deposit ratios and nondeposit funding often presage banking crises. Growing maturity mismatch and expo-

---

25. See, e.g., Kindleberger 1978; Minsky 1986; Shiller 2000; Bordalo, Gennaioli, and Shleifer 2018; Cihak and Schaeck 2010; Barth, Caprio, and Levine 2006.

26. As Baron and Xiong (2017) have shown.

27. See Richter and Zimmermann 2018.

28. He and Krishnamurthy (2013) argue in a similar way that intermediary leverage is countercyclical.

sure to uninsured short-term debt pose a measurable threat to financial stability.[29] Liquidity regulation did not feature prominently in the original Basel
process that started in the 1970s. Our findings suggest that this was a consequential and potentially costly omission.[30]

Bank Capital and the Recovery from the Crisis

When significant parts of the banking sector are in trouble, does it matter
whether banks are better capitalized? Is the severity of the crisis diminished,
and the recovery sped up? Our new data provide a unique laboratory answer
to these questions. The long historical sample provides much greater heterogeneity in capital ratios than would otherwise be available. The natural
measure of economic performance is real GDP per capita so as to adjust for
inflation and varying demographic trends.

Specifically, consider recession episodes. We split these episodes into normal and financial recessions (that is, recessions associated with a financial
crisis in a ±2-year window). Finally, we split financial recessions into two bins
based on the level of the bank capital ratio before the recession, high or low,
as measured with respect to a country-specific average.

The left panel of figure 5.5 shows the average economic performance over
subsequent years following recessions under different scenarios. The right
panel shows the same results but adjusted for a variety of variables that could
explain the patterns displayed in the left panel. These variables include the
values of the growth rates of real GDP per capita, real investment per capita,
Consumer Price Index inflation, short- and long-term interest rates, and the
current account to GDP ratio leading up to the recession.

It is clear that financial recessions tend to be worse than normal recessions in terms of the depth of output loss and the speed of economic recovery, regardless of the bank capital ratio. However, while an economy with an
above-average capitalized banking sector (dashed line) recovers after year 2
(and thereafter grows at a speed similar to that of a normal recession), an
economy with a below-average capitalized banking sector (dotted line) sees a
more protracted slump and recovers more slowly: output per capita is more
than 4 percentage points lower relative to a normal recession after five years.

In sum, over the five-year period after the peak of economic activity, the
cumulative GDP costs of a financial crisis hitting a below-average capitalized banking sector amount, on average, to a loss of more than 12 percentage

---

29. In line with the seminal insights by Diamond and Dybvig (1983).

30. For a history of the early years of the Basel committee see Goodhart 2011.

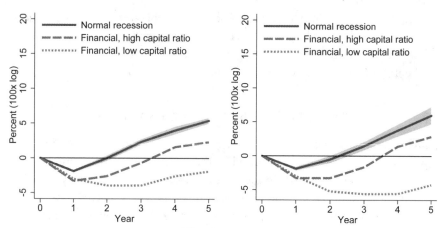

FIGURE 5.5 Normal versus financial recessions, real GDP per capita by capital ratio
Note: The average effect after a financial recession with an above- (or below-) average capitalized banking sector. These outcomes are shown by the dashed and dotted lines, respectively; the solid line shows
normal recession. The gray area is the 90% confidence region for the normal recession path. Full sample
results: 1870–2013, excluding world wars and five-year windows around them.

points of cumulative GDP per capita compared to a financial crisis hitting an
above-average capitalized banking sector: compare −25.23% with −12.49%.

Inspecting the Mechanism: The Credit Channel

The previous section showed that there is robust evidence of an economically
and statistically significant relationship between prerecession capital ratios
and economic recovery following the crisis. An explanation could come from
the inability of highly levered intermediaries to extend credit after an initial
shock to their balance sheets in line with the literature on real effects of bank
distress.[31] We examine this proposition by estimating what happens to real
private credit per capita following a downturn depending on whether capital
ratios beforehand are high or low.

Turning to figure 5.6, we see first that, after a business cycle peak, credit
growth in a typical financial crisis recession is on average lower than during a normal recession. Furthermore, capital matters. Similar to the dynamics of aggregate output, below-average capitalized banking systems extend
much less credit for several years during a financial crisis recession. These
results therefore complement recent microevidence on the role of capital for

31. See Peek and Rosengren 2000; Khwaja and Mian 2008; Chodorow-Reich 2014.

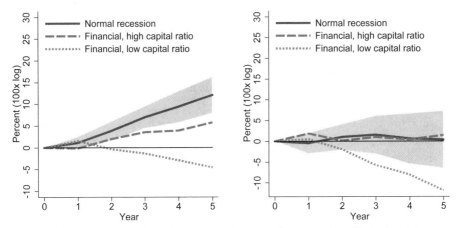

FIGURE 5.6 Normal versus financial recessions, real private credit per capita binned by bank capital, no controls included

Note: The solid line reports the average path after normal recessions. The gray area corresponds to the 90% confidence region around the recession path. The dashed line corresponds to the sum of the average recession coefficient and the financial recession coefficient when the precrisis capital ratio was high. The dotted line corresponds to the sum of the average recession coefficient and the financial recession coefficient when the precrisis capital ratio was low.

lending[32] and provide evidence that impairments to credit creation appear to be an important vector from low bank capital ratios to the slow pace of postcrisis economic recovery.

Conclusions

In the era of modern finance, systemic banking crises continue to strike unannounced. A growing macrofinance literature emphasizes that banking crises tend to follow periods of easy credit. Not surprisingly, research has mostly focused on the asset side of banks' balance sheets. We redress this neglect in this chapter.

Higher capital reduces risk-taking behavior at the level of the individual bank. With more skin in the game, shareholders have an incentive to monitor who the bank lends to or risk losing their investment. Not surprisingly, the regulatory response to the global financial crisis has, by and large, embraced higher capital buffers and regulation of bank leverage. But the question of whether more capital protects the system as a whole against systemic events

32. See Peek and Rosengren 2000; Carlson, Shan, and Warusawitharana 2013; Gambacorta and Marques-Ibanez 2011.

remained largely unanswered. This has not been the first time capital ratios have been raised in response to a systemic banking crisis.[33] Despite higher capital, crises have not gone away.

One hundred fifty years of data across seventeen advanced economies provide a clearer picture of the main trends in modern central banking that help us understand this disconnect. In most countries, banking sector capital ratios declined rapidly before World War II but have remained low and stable since. However, perhaps counterintuitively, there does not seem to be an obvious association between capital ratios and the likelihood of a systemic financial crisis.

Over the past few decades, loan-to-deposit ratios have become a stronger predictor of vulnerability, as some theories predict. Importantly, the role of noncore liabilities has also emerged as a risk factor that departs markedly from the preceding century of modern finance.

However, even if ineffective in preventing a financial crisis, well capitalized systems allow the economy to recover faster following a financial crisis and thus result in significantly shallower recessions. One reason appears to be that the recovery of credit is greatly facilitated by boosting the loss absorption capacity of lenders as a whole rather than individually—higher capital ratios in banking systems can bring about more resilience. History lends support for a precautionary approach to capital regulation. Its main role appears to lie not so much in eliminating the chances of systemic financial crises but rather in mitigating their social and economic costs—a distinct but arguably more important benefit.

REFERENCES

Adrian, Tobias, Evan Friedman, and Tyler Muir. 2015. The Cost of Capital of the Financial Sector. FRBNY Staff Report 755.

Anderson, Haelim, Daniel Barth, and Dong Beom Choi. 2018. Reducing Moral Hazard at the Expense of Market Discipline: The Effectiveness of Double Liability before and during the Great Depression. Unpublished.

Baron, Matthew, and Wei Xiong. 2017. Credit Expansion and Neglected Crash Risk. Quarterly Journal of Economics 132 (2): 713–64.

Barth, James, Gerard Caprio, and Ross Levine. 2006. Rethinking Bank Regulation: Till Angels Govern. Cambridge: Cambridge University Press.

Berkmen, Pelin S., Gaston Gelos, Robert Rennhack, and James P. Walsh. 2012. The Global Financial Crisis: Explaining Cross-Country Differences in the Output Impact. Journal of International Money and Finance 31 (1): 42–59.

Bernanke, Ben S. 1983. Nonmonetary Effects of the Financial Crisis in the Propagation of the Great Depression. American Economic Review 73 (3): 257–76.

33. As Grossman (2010) reports.

Besanko, David, and George Kanatas. 1996. The Regulation of Bank Capital: Do Capital Standards Promote Bank Safety? Journal of Financial Intermediation 5 (2): 160–83.

Blum, Jürg. 1999. Do Capital Adequacy Requirements Reduce Risks in Banking? Journal of Banking and Finance 23 (5): 755–71.

Bordalo, Pedro, Nicola Gennaioli, and Andrei Shleifer. 2018. Diagnostic Expectations and Credit Cycles. Journal of Finance 73 (1): 199–227.

Calomiris, Charles, Marc Flandreau, and Luc Laeven. 2016. Political Foundations of the Lender of Last Resort: A Global Historical Narrative. CEPR Discussion Paper 11448.

Calomiris, Charles W., and Charles M. Kahn. 1991. The Role of Demandable Debt in Structuring Optimal Banking Arrangements. American Economic Review 81 (3): 497–513.

Carlson, Mark, Hui Shan, and Missaka Warusawitharana. 2013. Capital Ratios and Bank Lending: A Matched Bank Approach. Journal of Financial Intermediation 22 (4): 663–87.

Cecchetti, Stephen G., Michael R. King, and James Yetman. 2011. Weathering the Financial Crisis: Good Policy or Good Luck? BIS Working Paper 351.

Cheng, Ing-Haw, Sahil Raina, and Wei Xiong. 2014. Wall Street and the Housing Bubble. American Economic Review 104 (9): 2797–2829.

Chodorow-Reich, Gabriel. 2014. The Employment Effects of Credit Market Disruptions: Firm-Level Evidence from the 2008–09 Financial Crisis. Quarterly Journal of Economics 129 (1): 1–59.

Cihak, Martin, and Klaus Schaeck. 2010. How Well do Aggregate Prudential Ratios Identify Banking System Problems? Journal of Financial Stability 6 (3): 130–44.

Cohen, Benjamin, and Michela Scatigna. 2016. Banks and Capital Requirements: Channels of Adjustment. Journal of Banking and Finance 69 (S1): S56–S69.

Demirgüç-Kunt, Asli, Edward Kane, and Luc Laeven. 2014. Deposit Insurance Database. World Bank Policy Research Working Paper 6934.

Diamond, Douglas W., and Philip H. Dybvig. 1983. Bank Runs, Deposit Insurance, and Liquidity. Journal of Political Economy 91 (3): 401–19.

Diamond, Douglas W., and Raghuram G. Rajan. 2001. Liquidity Risk, Liquidity Creation, and Financial Fragility: A Theory of Banking. Journal of Political Economy 109 (2): 287–327.

Esty, Benjamin C. 1997. Organizational Form and Risk Taking in the Savings and Loan Industry. Journal of Financial Economics 44 (1): 25–55.

Fahlenbrach, Rüdiger, Robert Prilmeier, and René M. Stulz. 2016. Why Does Fast Loan Growth Predict Poor Performance for Banks? NBER Working Paper 22089.

Gale, Douglas. 2010. Capital Regulation and Risk Sharing. International Journal of Central Banking 23: 187–204.

Gambacorta, Leonardo, and David Marques-Ibanez. 2011. The Bank Lending Channel: Lessons from the Crisis. Economic Policy 26 (66): 135–82.

Gan, Jie. 2004. Banking Market Structure and Financial Stability: Evidence from the Texas Real Estate Crisis in the 1980s. Journal of Financial Economics 73 (3): 567–601.

Gilje, Erik P. 2016. Do Firms Engage in Risk-Shifting? Empirical Evidence. Review of Financial Studies 29 (11): 2925–54.

Goodhart, Charles. 2011. The Basel Committee on Banking Supervision: A History of the Early Years 1974–1997. Cambridge: Cambridge University Press.

Greenwood, Robin, Samuel G. Hanson, and Lawrence J. Jin. 2016. A Model of Credit Market Sentiment. Harvard Business School Project on Behavioral Finance and Financial Stability Working Paper, no. 2016-02.

Gropp, Reint, Hendrik Hakenes, and Isabel Schnabel. 2011. Competition, Risk-Shifting, and Public Bail-out Policies. Review of Financial Studies 24 (6): 2084–2120.

Grossman, Richard S. 2010. Unsettled Account: The Evolution of Banking in the Industrialized World since 1800. Princeton, NJ: Princeton University Press.

Haldane, Andrew G. 2010. The $100 Billion Question. BIS Review 40.

He, Zhiguo, and Arvind Krishnamurthy. 2013. Intermediary Asset Pricing. American Economic Review 103 (2): 732–70.

Hellmann, Thomas F., Kevin C. Murdock, and Joseph E. Stiglitz. 2000. Liberalization, Moral Hazard in Banking, and Prudential Regulation: Are Capital Requirements Enough? American Economic Review 90 (1): 147–65.

Holmstrom, Bengt, and Jean Tirole. 1997. Financing as a Supply Chain: The Capital Structure of Banks and Borrowers. Quarterly Journal of Economics 112 (3): 663–91.

Jaremski, Matthew, and David C. Wheelock. 2017. Banking on the Boom, Tripped by the Bust: Banks and the World War I Agricultural Price Shock. Working Papers 2017-36, Federal Reserve Bank of St. Louis.

Jensen, Michael C., and William H. Meckling. 1976. Theory of the Firm: Managerial Behavior, Agency Costs and Ownership Structure. Journal of Financial Economics 3 (4): 305–60.

Jordà, Òscar, Björn Richter, Moritz Schularick, and Alan M. Taylor. 2017a. Bank Capital Redux: Solvency, Liquidity, and Crisis. NBER Working Paper 23287.

Jordà, Òscar, Moritz Schularick, and Alan M. Taylor. 2013. When Credit Bites Back. Journal of Money, Credit and Banking 45 (2): 3–28.

———. 2017b. Macrofinancial History and the New Business Cycle Facts. NBER Macroeconomics Annual 2016, 31: 213–63.

Khwaja, Asim Ijaz, and Atif Mian. 2008. Tracing the Impact of Bank Liquidity Shocks: Evidence from an Emerging Market. American Economic Review 98 (4): 1413–42.

Kindleberger, Charles P. 1978. Manias, Panics, and Crashes: A History of Financial Crises. New York: Basic Books.

Kroszner, Randall. 1999. The Impact of Consolidation and Safety-Net Support on Canadian, US and UK Banks: 1893–1992: Comment. Journal of Banking and Finance 23 (2): 572–77.

Laeven, Luc, and Fabian Valencia. 2012. Systemic Banking Crises Database; An Update. IMF Working Papers 12/163.

Landier, Augustin, David Sraer, and David Thesmar. 2011. The Risk-Shifting Hypothesis: Evidence from Subprime Originations. Unpublished.

Mazbouri, Malik, Sebastian Guex, and Rodrigo Lopez. 2017. University of Lausanne. Project— Swiss Data Bank of International Bank Data (1890–1970). Available at http://www.unil.ch /hist/placefinanciere.

Mehran, Hamid, and Anjan Thakor. 2011. Bank Capital and Value in the Cross-Section. Review of Financial Studies 24 (4): 1019–67.

Merton, Robert C. 1977. An Analytic Derivation of the Cost of Deposit Insurance and Loan Guarantees: An Application of Modern Option Pricing Theory. Journal of Banking and Finance 1: 3–11.

———. 1995. Financial Innovation and the Management and Regulation of Financial Institutions. Journal of Banking and Finance 19 (3): 461–81.

Minsky, Hyman P. 1977. The Financial Instability Hypothesis: An Interpretation of Keynes and an Alternative to "Standard" Theory. Challenge 20 (1): 20–27.

———. 1986. Stabilizing an Unstable Economy. New Haven, CT: Yale University Press.

Natoli, Sandra, Paolo Piselli, Ivan Triglia, and Francesco Vercelli. 2016. Historical Archive of Credit in Italy. Bank of Italy Economic History Working Papers 36.

Peek, Joe, and Eric S. Rosengren. 2000. Collateral Damage: Effects of the Japanese Bank Crisis on Real Activity in the United States. American Economic Review 90 (1): 30–45.

Rajan, Raghuram G. 2018. Liquidity and Leverage. Speech at the AEA/AFA Joint Luncheon, January 5. Unpublished.

Richter, Björn, and Kaspar Zimmermann. 2018. The Profit-Credit Cycle. Unpublished.

Schularick, Moritz, and Alan M. Taylor. 2012. Credit Booms Gone Bust: Monetary Policy, Leverage Cycles, and Financial Crises, 1870–2008. American Economic Review 102 (2): 1029–61.

Shiller, Robert J. 2000. Irrational Exuberance. Princeton, NJ: Princeton University Press.

Simsek, Alp. 2013. Belief Disagreements and Collateral Constraints. Econometrica 81 (1): 1–53.

Comment by Anna Kovner

In their work, "Bank Capital before and after Financial Crises," Òscar Jordà, Björn Richter, Moritz Schularick, and Alan Taylor analyze the relationship between bank capital ratios, recessions, and financial crises using a long, hand-collected, cross-country time series data set. The authors establish two stylized facts: First, that bank capital ratios are not associated with financial crises (or more precisely that bank capital ratios do not add predictive power over and above the predictive power of changes in debt). Second, conditional on entering a financial crisis, economies with higher bank capital are likely to experience faster recoveries. By carefully putting together this long cross-country time series of bank balance sheets and financial crises, as well as making that data available to other researchers, the authors deepen our understanding of how varying amounts of bank capital have coincided with financial recessions and how vulnerabilities in the banking sector can amplify macroeconomic outcomes. In this piece, I offer observations on how to interpret this evidence. These cautions are meant to inform how policy should be promulgated in response to these facts. However, this should not be interpreted as challenges to the stylized facts presented in the work.

The advantage of the long time period and cross-country approach is the increase in statistical power to forecast rare events. However, without a structural model or exogenous change to capital, it's important to note that a number of critical factors changed over time and across countries. The relationships documented between capital and financial recessions may reflect omitted variables that could bias the results (or simply make them less generalizable). Possibilities include differences in the nonbank provision of credit, the amount of bank supervision, as well as the underlying amount

Anna Kovner is policy leader of financial stability at the Federal Reserve Bank of New York.

of bank competition. Other possible omitted variables include changes in the separation of ownership and control (Jensen and Meckling 1976), bank competition and franchise value (Keeley 1996), as well as perhaps changing economies of scale (Hughes and Mester 2013). Further, bank business models have changed dramatically over the last century. Analyzing a long time series of data, it is natural to assert that a capital ratio of 15% in 1920 is higher than a capital ratio of 8% today. But if banks are more diversified, then current capital ratios of 8% could effectively be higher than a ratio of 15% on a risk-adjusted basis.[1] Alternatively, if banks increasingly engage in riskier noninterest income-generating activities such as trading, perhaps current capital ratios are even lower than the numbers show.

Thinking about differences in risk naturally leads to questions about measuring bank capital. Unfortunately, there are practical trade-offs between having a long time series of data and having the right data to understand whether current capital standards will prevent financial crises. The main measure of bank capital looked at in this analysis is the ratio of book equity to book assets. However, the binding capital ratio for most banks today is common equity tier 1 (CET1) / risk-weighted assets. This matters because it is unclear if the value of bank capital is as an absolute benefit (to equity investors) or because of regulation (having more capital than required means a greater ability to lend). The difference between book assets and risk-weighted assets is particularly meaningful in considering the appropriate measure for bank capital, as would be the difference between book equity and a market-based leverage measure (see, e.g., Baron and Xiong 2017).

The United States regulatory data illustrate the trade-offs between the longer time series and the binding capital requirements. Figure 5C.1 presents the time series of equity capital and risk-weighted assets based on data presented in the Federal Reserve Bank of New York's Quarterly Trends for Consolidated Banking Organizations.[2] As shown in figure 5C.1, the past decades' pattern is different depending on the definition of leverage. A second concern about the leverage metric is in capturing the role of nonbank financial intermediation in financial crises. Countries that have a significant amount of intermediation by nonbanks such as the United States and the United Kingdom need analysis that includes the capital of nonbank financial intermediaries. For example,

1. This is true even if capital is calculated relative to risk-weighted assets, because risk-weighted assets do not necessarily capture risk factors such as geographic diversification. It would be more closely captured in a measure such as Z-score or distance to default.

2. Available at https://www.newyorkfed.org/research/banking_research/quarterly_trends .html.

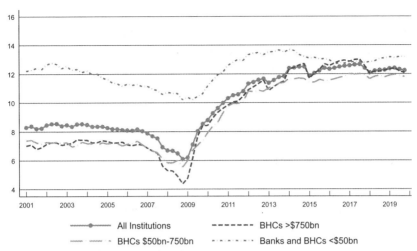

FIGURE 5c.1 CET1 and Tier 1 common equity ratio as percentage of risk-weighted assets
Source: FFIEC031/041; FY Y-9C; Federal Reserve Bank of New York.

most of the business debt in the United States is not held by banks, and a significant amount of risky business debt issuance after the financial crisis has come from high-yield bonds and leveraged loans sold to nonbanks.

The authors interpret their results as evidence that more skin in the game (by having more capital) will not result in more prudent bank behavior. I am reluctant to draw conclusions on microeconomic theories from macroeconomic time series evidence. Even if aggregate skin in the game does not curtail tail risk in aggregate, bank capital may induce lower risk at individual banks. For example, Jimenez et al. (2017) examine a dynamic provisioning capital experiment in Spain, documenting that banks that are required to increase capital reduce the supply of credit. However, they also find that borrowers substitute to less capital constrained banks and, in aggregate, credit may even flow to riskier firms. Similarly, Acharya et al. (2018) examine the impact of stress testing in the United States and find that while stress-tested banks reduce the supply of credit, non-stress-tested banks more than make up for the change. It is notable that a focus in these microstudies is on the impact of bank capital on loan growth, the key variable that does appear to predict financial crises. Even if aggregate capital is not associated with financial crises, I would be cautious in extrapolating this finding to draw conclusions about the role of bank capital and risk-taking at a bank level.

Perhaps the most important contribution of this work is to allow us to rule out some commonly held views. For example, is it likely that increasing bank capital requirements will lean against the wind and perhaps reduce the probability of a financial crisis? That does not appear to have been the case in the historical data. On the other hand, higher amounts of bank capital may serve to mitigate financial recessions, contingent on entering one.

REFERENCES

Acharya, Viral V., Allen N. Berger, and Raluca A. Roman. 2018. Lending Implications of U.S. Bank Stress Tests: Costs or Benefits? Journal of Financial Intermediation 34: 58–90.

Bagehot, Walter. 1873. Lombard Street: A Description of the Money Market. London: H. S. King.

Baron, Matthew, and Wei Xiong. 2017. Credit Expansion and Neglected Crash Risk. Quarterly Journal of Economics 132 (3): 713–64.

Hughes, Joseph P., and Loretta J. Mester. 2013. Who Said Large Banks Don't Experience Scale Economies? Evidence from a Risk-Return-Driven Cost Function. Journal of Financial Intermediation 22: 559–85.

Jensen, Michael C., and William H. Meckling. 1976. Theory of the Firm: Managerial Behavior, Agency Costs and Ownership Structure. Journal of Financial Economics 3 (4): 305–60.

Jimenez, Gabriel, Jose-Luis Peydro, Steven Ongena, and Jesus Saurina. 2017. Macroprudential Policy, Countercyclical Bank Capital Buffers, and Credit Supply: Evidence from the Spanish Dynamic Provisioning Experiments. Journal of Political Economy 125 (6): 2126–77.

Keeley, Michael C. 1990. Deposit Insurance, Risk, and Market Power in Banking. American Economic Review 80 (5): 1183–1200.

PART THREE

Mispricing Risks:
Credit Booms and Risk Premia

6

Beliefs and Risk-Taking

ALESSIA DE STEFANI AND KASPAR ZIMMERMANN

The global financial crisis and its fallout have shaped macrofinancial research over the last ten years. Driven by newly available data and methods, a consensus is emerging that marks fluctuations in private credit as a key driver of financial and economic instability. High credit growth predicts a heightened risk of financial turmoil (Schularick and Taylor 2012) and low growth (Mian et al. 2017), and it amplifies the effects of financial shocks on the real economy (Jordà, Schularick, and Taylor 2013, 2016; Mian and Sufi 2009). In the aftermath of the crisis, macroprudential regulation has aimed at curbing the credit cycle. The design and effectiveness of policy is, however, constrained by an incomplete understanding of the underlying drivers of cyclical variation in credit.

One popular interpretation of the recent boom-bust episode in the U.S. housing market maintains that its roots lay in excessive risk-taking on the side of lenders. According to this view, bankers were aware of the likelihood of a market downturn but did not fully internalize the risks associated with a widespread wave of mortgage defaults. As a consequence, their incentives leaned toward excessive lending to risky borrowers, even if this was clearly suboptimal from a systemic perspective. This narrative certainly carries some weight in explaining the events occurring in the run-up to 2007. However, recent empirical evidence suggests that this account of the U.S. boom-bust cycle is incomplete, for two reasons.

Alessia De Stefani is an economist at the International Monetary Fund. Kaspar Zimmermann is a postdoctoral researcher at the Leibniz Institute for Financial Research SAFE.

First, most financial intermediaries simply did not see the crisis coming. Bank CEOs levered up on risk independent of their incentive structures during the boom and then also incurred large personal losses once the crisis hit (Fahlenbrach and Stulz 2011). Similarly, mid-level managers involved in the mortgage securitization business made no attempt to time the housing market and were personally invested in real estate ahead of the downturn (Cheng, Raina, and Xiong 2014). Evidence that lenders and bank equity investors fail to anticipate looming crises is not confined to the U.S. experience, or to the housing market in particular, but spans across countries and time (Baron and Xiong 2017).

Second, the buildup of household debt ahead of 2007 was not limited to poor, financially constrained, or subprime borrowers. Rather, it occurred across the entire span of the income distribution. Relatively wealthy housing investors, with good credit ratings, made up the bulk of defaults after 2007 (Adelino, Schoar, and Severino 2016; Albanesi, De Giorgi, and Nosal 2017). This evidence is difficult to explain exclusively through the lens of excessive risk-taking of banks, lending to subprime borrowers who were living beyond their means (Adelino, Schoar, and Severino 2018b). A recent body of work has therefore turned to an alternative narrative: that before 2007 both borrowers and lenders had overoptimistic expectations about the future prospects for the housing market (Case, Shiller, and Thompson 2012; Foote, Gerardi, and Willen 2012; Kaplan, Mitman, and Violante 2020; Mian and Sufi 2021; Piazzesi and Schneider 2009).

In this chapter, we discuss the role of expectations in driving credit booms and busts, drawing from recent research. We derive three main takeaways. First, expectations of agents can at times deviate substantially from rational predictions based on economic fundamentals. This bias in beliefs is not the product of random shocks. Rather, it is systematic and often closely linked to past observed fundamentals. Second, expectations matter for credit originations and drive both borrowing and lending activity. Third, market sentiment has macroeconomic implications: elevated sentiment tends to be followed by reversals in asset prices and output. Finally, we argue that in order to properly understand the role that expectations play in credit and asset price cycles, it is necessary to study the effects and interactions of both borrowers' and lenders' beliefs.

Expectation Formation

Asset prices move more than their underlying fundamentals. Boom-bust cycles in asset valuations are a recurring feature across all major asset classes, countries, and time (Shiller 1981; Jordà et al. 2015b; Kuvshinov 2018). So far, no single explanation for these fluctuations is universally accepted. Rational models vary risk or its price by introducing habit (Campbell and Cochrane 1999), rare disasters (Barro 2009), or long-run risk (Bansal and Yaron 2004). Behavioral models attribute the observed excess volatility to time-varying expectations of economic agents (Barberis et al. 2015, 2018). These theories of irrational exuberance largely build on a simple intuition: people look at their recent experiences to form their expectations about the future.

Expectations are inherently difficult to observe. Researchers are therefore increasingly turning to survey data to study how agents form their beliefs about future states of the economy. Due to issues with measurement error and reporting incentives, part of the profession remains critical of the use of survey data for testing economic theories in general and models of belief formation in particular. For example, Cochrane (2011, 2017) challenges the notion that survey data on expectations are inconsistent with observed asset prices and suggests that people report risk-neutral return expectations rather than their true measure mean. This critique was recently countered by Adam et al. (2018), who showed that expected excess returns from surveys are predictable—a pattern that should not hold if these were true measures of risk neutral probabilities. While this debate is still ongoing, there is a growing body of evidence suggesting that survey data on expectations are more than just noise: overall, beliefs are highly correlated across surveys and are predictive of agents' behavior (Greenwood and Shleifer 2014; Giglio et al. 2019).

A large empirical literature focuses on the formation of house price expectations. Overoptimistic beliefs about this particular asset class may have played a pivotal role during the house price boom of the 2000s. Even though consumers were fairly well informed about their local housing market, they exhibited unrealistic long-run beliefs. In some cities, the average expected annual house price growth over a five-year horizon exceeded 10 percentage points per year at the peak of the boom (Case et al. 2012). This evidence can be explained by extrapolation from recently experienced house price growth, which affects not only point estimates but also belief dispersion (Kuchler and Zafar 2019). Consumers appear to overreact to news about the housing market over the medium run and neglect mean reversion (Armona et al. 2019). As a result, forecast errors in house price expectations are systematically predictable by recently experienced house price trends (De Stefani 2021). Figure 6.1 shows the time trend in house price forecast errors of respondents to the Michigan Survey of Consumers (De Stefani 2021). Expectations are overoptimistic at the onset of the crisis and reverse afterward. Interestingly, errors are persistently negative up to very recent quarters. Households appear to

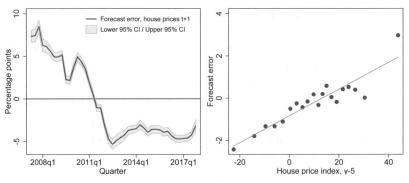

FIGURE 6.1 Average forecast error in house price expectations: U.S. households
Source: De Stefani (2021).
Note: This figure displays, in the left panel, the evolution over time of average forecast errors in house price expectations among U.S. consumers; in the right panel, individual forecast errors are regressed on an index of average housing appreciation over the prior five years in the MSA of residence of the respondent. Expectations are measured by the Michigan Survey of Consumers as the percentage expected house price change at the one-year horizon; house price growth for Metropolitan Statistical Areas is measured by the Federal Housing Finance Association quarterly index. Forecast errors are constructed as the difference between individual expectations and ex post house price growth in the city of residence of individual respondents.

systematically underestimate the recovery of the U.S. housing market in the aftermath of the Great Recession.

Since housing transactions are relatively infrequent from the point of view of individual investors, this evidence may be explained either by a sluggish updating of information or by low incentives for survey respondents to provide a precise forecast. However, extrapolation from recent experience is also widely documented for more sophisticated agents, including professionals and other asset classes. Forecast errors in CFOs' earnings expectations are predictable from past earnings (Gennaioli et al. 2016). Along similar lines, sophisticated investors' expectations about stock market returns are correlated with past returns; even professional analysts fail to predict mean reversion in the stock market (Bordalo et al. 2019; Greenwood and Shleifer 2014). Richter and Zimmermann (2019) use aggregate survey data to link past credit market outcomes to the expectations of financial intermediaries and show that forecast errors in bank CFOs' profit expectations are predictable with past fundamentals. Managers become overoptimistic about their companies' financial prospects after periods of either good fundamentals or low loan losses.

These departures from a rational benchmark require a theoretical framework that can account for the systematic predictability of forecast errors from publicly available data. One recent approach builds on the representativeness heuristic, originally proposed by Kahneman and Tversky (1972). In this framework, agents overweight the probability of outcomes similar to those they have recently witnessed: this leads them to become overoptimistic following a string of good news and vice versa. Barberis et al. (1998) show that, under representativeness, both overreaction to news in the long run and underreaction in the short run can arise in equilibrium. Furthermore, people may consistently underestimate the probability of a market downturn following good times (Bordalo et al. 2019).[1]

In this world, a belief reversal can occur even in the absence of a clear downward revision in economic fundamentals: A slowdown in growth rates may be sufficient. To the extent that expectations are positively correlated with leverage and investment, the systematic component of overoptimism and overpessimism based on diagnostic expectations has the power to endogenously generate asset price and credit bubbles (Barberis et al. 2015; Bordalo et al. 2018).

Expectations and the Credit Cycle

The hypothesis of an expectation-led credit cycle goes back to the work of Minsky (1977). According to Minsky (1977), the credit cycle starts with an initial improvement in fundamentals. This displacement generates a boom in asset prices, credit, and output. As investors observe initial price increases, they revise their beliefs and become excessively optimistic. Once the boom runs out of steam and optimistic expectations are not realized, investors reverse their beliefs and start leaving the market. Prices decline and, eventually, a panic breaks out. We review new empirical evidence that has revived and substantiated these early ideas of sentiment-driven credit cycles.

As a first step we document that expectations of borrowers and lenders are indeed closely aligned with the credit cycle. The top panel of figure 6.2 displays bank CFOs' optimism about their company's financial prospects vis-à-vis subsequent one-year-ahead credit growth in the United States. The bottom panel plots households' one-year-ahead house price expectations and credit growth in the next year. Both expectation measures are highly correlated with subsequent credit developments both before and during the crisis (Richter and Zimmermann 2019).

1. New work reconciles this evidence with underreaction in consensus forecasts of macroeconomic indicators (Coibion and Gorodnichenko 2012, 2015). Bordalo et al. (2018a) show that if all actors overreact to private news, and all signals are on average informative, on average the economy will appear as if it were underreacting to news shocks. This is because actors do not react enough to the average information or the signals of other agents.

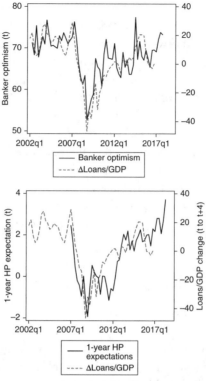

FIGURE 6.2 Credit growth and the expectations of borrowers and lenders
Source: *Top panel*: Richter and Zimmermann (2019).
Note: The top panel shows the evolution of financial CFOs' optimism about their firm's financial prospects and subsequent four-quarter loans / GDP changes. The Duke CFO Global Business Outlook (2018) asks bank CEOs to rate their optimism about the financial prospects of their own company on a scale from 0 to 100, with 0 being the least optimistic and 100 being the most optimistic. The bottom panel shows households' one-year-ahead house price expectations from the Michigan Survey and subsequent credit market developments.

What is the systematic evidence on a link between credit growth and investors' expectations beyond this stylized fact? Following Baker and Wurgler (2007), we differentiate between two approaches to understand and quantify the effects of expectations or sentiment. The "bottom-up" approach relies on the actual expectations reported by individual agents and links these to their economic decisions. The "top-down" approach is in its nature macroeconomic. It builds on reduced-form aggregate measures of sentiment and studies the effects on the economy as a whole.

The top-down approach has proven to be highly influential in shaping the academic debate (see, e.g., Gennaioli and Shleifer 2018 or Mian and Sufi 2018). Yet it suffers from two shortcomings. First, it "backward engineers" market participants' expectations from macroeconomic data instead of measuring actual expectations. This makes it difficult to pin down the precise expectation formation process and to achieve a clear identification of the channels through which sentiment affects behavior. Second, it implicitly assumes an alignment of expectations throughout the economy. A proper understanding of the aggregate consequences of sentiment and its transmission mechanism will therefore require both bottom-up and top-down evidence. We start with a discussion of top-down evidence in the next section and move on to bottom-up research in the following sections.

Credit Market Sentiment and the Credit Cycle

We identify two main results in the top-down literature linking the credit cycle to aggregate measures of sentiment. First, credit market sentiment predicts reversals in asset prices and output. Aggregate sentiment proxies are typically constructed from asset price and quantity data and ex post rationalized with their predictive power for future asset returns. Greenwood and Hanson (2013) show that a high share of risky corporate debt issuance in total debt issuance forecasts low excess returns for corporate bondholders. Similarly, low bond spreads, or a small difference in expected default probabilities of high- and low-quality bonds, are followed by rising spreads and low returns in the future. López-Salido et al. (2017) show that these bond market sentiment proxies not only predict bond returns but also future economic activity. Elevated bond market sentiment is followed by lower GDP growth over the next three years. Baron and Xiong (2017) study bank equity returns in credit booms and busts. High credit growth predicts low bank equity returns over the next years. Even though bank stock prices rally leading up to the peak of a credit boom, investors seem to neglect the crash risks of credit expansions. Sentiment-driven cycles can also be observed at the industry level: high profits in shipping are associated with high prices for existing ships and increased investment in new ships but also with low future returns (Greenwood and Hanson 2015).

Second, financial conditions are "calm before the storm." Danielsson et al. (2018) show that financial crises tend to follow periods of low volatility in the stock market, and Krishnamurthy and Muir (2017) document exceptionally low corporate bond market spreads before financial crises. Along similar lines, Richter and Zimmermann (2019) find that the run-up to a financial crisis is characterized by low loan losses and high profits for banks. Focusing on fundamentals alone does not seem to paint an accurate picture of systemic financial risks in the economy. Financial risks build up when risks appear low—the boom sows the seeds of the bust.

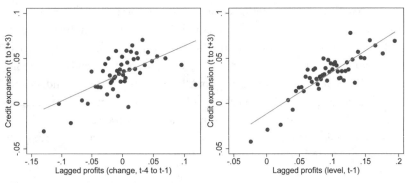

FIGURE 6.3 The profit-credit cycle

Source: Richter and Zimmermann (2019).

Note: This figure relates bank profitability and subsequent three-year changes in credit to GDP for a sample spanning seventeen countries and 145 years. Observations are collapsed into fifty equal-sized bins according to their profitability. Each point represents the group-specific means of profitability and credit expansion after controlling for a vector of net worth and macroeconomic variables. Fitted regression lines illustrate the correlation between bank profitability and subsequent credit expansion. For graphical purposes the variables have been winsorized at the 2.5% level.

Encouraged by the emerging evidence on expectation formation and credit market sentiment, a new theoretical literature is emerging that explains the credit cycle by incorporating nonrational expectation formation in macro and finance models (Bordalo et al. 2018, 2021; Greenwood et al. 2019; Kaplan et al. 2020). In Bordalo et al. (2018), agents form their expectations about future fundamentals in a diagnostic fashion. They overweight future outcomes that become more likely in light of incoming data. Incorporating these diagnostic expectations into a credit cycle model allows them to match some of the most important empirical features: as in Greenwood and Hanson (2013), credit spreads become excessively volatile and are subject to predictable reversals. Greenwood et al. (2019) go one step further and assume that lenders extrapolate default rates of their borrowers instead of aggregate fundamentals. This assumption generates a lead-lag relationship between credit markets and the real economy in their model. When default rates are low, lenders will demand lower credit spreads. These lower credit spreads will temporarily lower default probabilities and bolster the credit market when fundamentals are already deteriorating.

This mechanism can actually be observed in the data. Low corporate bond defaults today are positively correlated with elevated bond market sentiment going forward (Greenwood et al. 2019). Richter and Zimmermann (2019) find a similar pattern for bank credit: rising bank profits are followed by an expansion in credit over the next three years (see fig. 6.3). This profit-credit cycle is not driven by bank revenue or administrative expenses but rather by the loan loss component of the income statement. The predictive power of profits, or loan losses, for credit growth over the next year connects nicely with the models of Greenwood et al. (2019) and Bordalo et al. (2018). Decreasing loan losses inflate the perceived probability of states with low defaults. These low expected losses then enter into the credit assessments of banks and create an incentive to extend lending. Richter and Zimmermann (2019) also show that the profit-credit cycle cannot be fully explained by a relaxation of net worth constraints or rational expectations of good future fundamentals: the relationship remains strong when looking at paid out profits (dividends), and high profitability predicts low equity returns and elevated crisis probabilities going forward.

Lenders' Expectations and Credit Growth

Studying lenders' expectations explicitly is complicated by two challenges. First, it is inherently difficult to measure "institutional expectations." Existing studies rely on the expectations of the management (CEOs or CFOs) or employees in charge of borrowing decisions (loan officers). Second, micro data on the expectations of bankers are difficult to come by. As a consequence, researchers turn to revealed measures of investors' optimism, such as option holdings of managers after vesting period, or study how institutional and personal experience shapes the business strategy of a financial intermediary.

Past institutional experience matters for lending practices, possibly through a belief channel: Bouwman and Malmendier (2015) find that a significant loss event shapes a bank's risk-taking in the lending business for years to come, and Berger and Udell (2004) show that banks ease their lending standards as the memory of past loan defaults fades. Similarly, Koudijs and Voth (2016) use a case study from eighteenth-century Amsterdam to show that even a past threat of major loss can shape financial intermediary leverage and willingness to take risks. Central banks are also not immune to the bias derived from personal experience: the relative hawkishness of monetary policy decisions is shaped by the macroeconomic circumstances experienced by governors during their youth (Malmendier et al. 2017).

Fahlenbrach et al. (2017) combine equity price data and bank accounting information to study the expectations of investors and bankers. They show that high loan growth is on average followed by low equity returns, low profitability, and high loan losses going forward. High credit growth does not only predict poor equity performance across countries and time but also across banks (Baron and Xiong 2017; Fahlenbrach et al. 2017). This evidence suggests that bank managers and investors do not recognize that fast loan growth results from riskier loans and do not charge high enough compensations for these loans.

Furthermore, there are a number of papers that use the options-based CEO overconfidence measure developed by Malmendier and Tate (2005, 2008) to study lending behavior of overoptimistic bank CEOs during the housing bubble. Managers that are overoptimistic about their firm's financial prospects are more likely to keep deep-in-the-money stock options of their firm after the vesting period. Ho et al. (2016) and Ma (2015) find that banks with optimistic CEOs increased their mortgage debt exposure by more during the run-up to the crisis and subsequently suffered more during the downturn.

Taken together, the above evidence shows that actions of financial intermediaries are strongly influenced by past credit market outcomes. Biased expectations are gaining prominence as a potential explanation for these patterns.

House Price Beliefs, Housing Investment, and Mortgage Credit

As mortgages constitute a large and growing fraction of household debt in developed economies (Jordà et al. 2016), financial stability is becoming increasingly dependent on the state and health of the real estate market (Jordà et al. 2015a, 2015b). This has sparked a wide interest in the role of sentiment in driving house prices and mortgage leverage.

Aggregate measures of housing sentiment have predictive power for house price developments (Piazzesi and Schneider 2009; Soo 2018). Soo (2018) constructs a sentiment index from the qualitative tone of local news reports about the housing market. This sentiment measure leads house price developments across major U.S. cities. Optimism explains subsequent growth in house prices above and beyond market fundamentals. Microlevel evidence confirms that a more optimistic outlook on the housing market makes people more likely to invest in real estate (Adelino et al. 2018a; Armona et al. 2019; Bailey et al. 2018). Bailey et al. (2018) combine housing transaction data, local house prices, and social network information from Facebook. Positive house price shocks within an individual's social network increase house price expectations and, through beliefs, affect the likelihood to transition into homeownership, buy larger houses, and pay higher prices for a given home.

Based on this evidence, it would seem natural to expect that mortgage leverage will also comove with house price beliefs (Geanakoplos 2010; Simsek 2013). Bailey et al. (2019) show that this is not always the case. Using the same social network data as in Bailey et al. (2018), they show that a pessimistic outlook on the housing market leads U.S. home buyers to leverage more on the houses they purchase. This result can be rationalized through a model

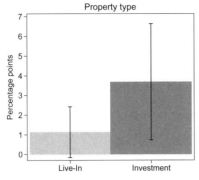 

FIGURE 6.4 Effect of house price expectations on mortgage loan-to-value ratios

Source: Adapted from De Stefani (2021).

Note: This figure shows the causal effect of a percentage point increase in house price expectations on mortgage leverage ratios, estimated through a 2SLS regression. House price expectations are measured as the city-quarter averages of the responses recorded in the Michigan Survey of Consumers between 2007 and 2017, for expected percentage price growth over a five-year horizon. Loan-level data on new mortgage originations stems from Freddie Mac's Single-Family Loan-Level data set, over the same time frame. Estimations include a set of covariates for borrowers' demographics and partial out time-varying shocks to lenders.

in which housing is not only an asset class but also a consumption good. If people see housing as a consumption good, or a necessity, they will require a certain home size. These consumers will not necessarily buy less housing when their expectations deteriorate. But they will decrease down payments, leading to an increase in mortgage leverage. The opposite holds when housing is primarily perceived as an investment. In this scenario, leverage will comove with beliefs, as optimism leads people to leverage up and buy more, in the expectation of a positive return on investment.

De Stefani (2021) confirms this theoretical distinction by linking regional measures of house price expectations to loan-level data on new mortgage originations. Housing sentiment increases leverage on investment properties but not on live-in homes, where the consumption aspect of housing is likely to dominate (see left panel of fig. 6.4). Also, a shift in optimism does not change leverage on home purchases but significantly increases the size of refinancing mortgages, which are commonly used to finance nonhousing consumption (right panel of fig. 6.4).

The evidence suggests that optimistic house price expectations drive the buildup of leverage if the share of consumers with an investment motive is large enough in the aggregate. Of course, this share is endogenous to macroeconomic circumstances: the fraction of investors is likely to be much larger in a boom than in a bust. This is particularly true if the boom is triggered by a shift in credit supply, which may encourage housing speculation and detach the expectations of housing investors from those of other agents in the economy (Mian and Sufi 2021).

Firms' Expectations and Investment

Making informed choices on the basis of an unknown future is a core aspect of firm management and entrepreneurship. Managers' expectations and experience can therefore shape the financial prospects of their firms. Optimistic CEOs overpay for firm acquisitions (Malmendier and Tate 2008), overinvest in internal funds (Malmendier and Tate 2005), and choose to finance their firms excessively through short-term debt (Landier and Thesmar 2008).

Managers' expectations also fluctuate over the business cycle and overreact to recent experiences. Gennaioli et al. (2016) show that CFOs who recently experienced a more rapid growth in profits not only become systematically overoptimistic about future firm performance but also invest more aggressively. Gulen et al. (2019) study the firm-level effects of heightened aggregate credit market sentiment using credit market sentiment proxies from Greenwood and Hanson (2013) and firm-level data from Compustat. Periods of elevated credit market sentiment are associated with high investment and debt issuance in the short run but also with a reversal of both over the medium run.

Inexperienced managers may be more susceptible to these miscalculations. For example, less-experienced mutual fund managers were more heavily invested in equity at the peak of the technology bubble (Greenwood and Nagel 2009) and had a stronger exposure to the housing market at the peak of the housing bubble (Chernenko et al. 2016). The psychology of belief formation provides a lens to understand this evidence: recent experience is more important when data points are scarce (Malmendier and Nagel 2011). However, even experienced CFOs are not immune to overconfidence and miscalibration of potential future outcomes: their overconfidence drives them to invest and leverage more (Ben-David et al. 2013). Despite strong incentives for managers to provide accurate estimates of future fundamentals, biased beliefs appear to have an important role in firms' investment and financing decisions.

Borrowers' or Lenders' Expectations?

The evidence presented so far suggests that both borrowers' and lenders' expectations matter for aggregate credit dynamics. Even if overoptimistic households or firms want to overborrow, they are constrained by rising spreads, if lenders are rational. Similarly, overoptimistic banks are constrained in their

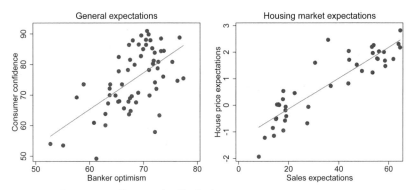

FIGURE 6.5 Comovement of borrowers' and lenders' expectations
Note: The left panel depicts the correlation between the average consumer sentiment index recorded by the Michigan Survey of Consumers and a measure of lenders' optimism from the Duke CFO survey; quarterly frequency 2002–2017. The right panel depicts the correlation between average expected house price growth (percentage points, one-year horizon) recorded by the Michigan Survey and a measure of home builders' optimism about sales growth looking ahead, recorded by NAHB / Wells Fargo Housing Market Index. The frequency is quarterly, 2007–2017.

funding if households remain rational. As a consequence, most of the theoretical and empirical literature implicitly assumes that the expectations of borrowers and lenders align.

Indeed, beliefs of consumers and lenders are positively correlated. The left panel of figure 6.5 plots the consumer confidence index from the Michigan Survey of Consumers and an optimism measure of bank CFOs about the financial prospects of their institutions. The right panel focuses on house price expectations. We plot average one-year-ahead house price expectations from the Michigan Survey against the one-year ahead sales expectations of real estate professionals, recorded by the National Association of Home Builders (NAHB) and Wells Fargo Survey. Both the general and the domain-specific measures of sentiment are highly correlated. This descriptive evidence corroborates earlier work documenting a strong correlation of equity return expectations across various surveys (Greenwood and Shleifer 2014).

A more systematic study of the joint dynamics of borrower and lender expectations over the credit cycle is complicated by a lack of comparable data. While household surveys have become widely established and available, firms' expectation surveys remain scarce (Coibion et al. 2018). Similarly, data on financial intermediaries' expectations are restricted to senior loan officer surveys, the Duke CFO survey and, requiring a number of assumptions, surveys of professional forecasters.

And yet, evidence from economic theory suggests that the degree of comovement and relative effects of lender and borrower sentiment might be important. Kaplan et al. (2020) show that a joint shift in sentiment of both borrowers and lenders is a necessary condition for a housing boom-bust cycle to arise. Using a structural macroeconomic model, they show that shifts in credit conditions alone cannot account for the joint dynamics of debt and house prices in the U.S. economy. While optimistic beliefs play a key role for aggregate buildup of private debt, house price dynamics cannot be explained without elevated consumer sentiment (Kaplan et al. 2020). Similarly, Bordalo et al. (2021) build a real business cycle model with diagnostic expectations of borrowers and lenders and show that having diagnostic borrowers but rational lenders does not generate sharp reversals in credit spreads around financial crises as observed in the data.

Moving forward, we hope to witness further implementation of systematic surveys that pose comparable questions to different economic agents (consumers, firms, and lenders) about different macroeconomic outcomes and asset classes.[2] Ideally, these surveys will contain a panel component at the individual level in order to ascertain how different agents approach the same type of information, along the lines of Coibion and Gorodnichenko (2015). These data will enable future researchers to study the effects and joint dynamics of both borrower and lender beliefs.

Conclusions

There is growing evidence that expectations matter for the credit cycle: they drive investment, lending, and borrowing activity. Nevertheless, many open questions remain regarding the role of biased beliefs in shaping financial booms and busts.

We identify four main areas for future research. The first relates to potential asymmetries at different stages of the credit cycle. Existing contributions tend to focus on the credit boom phase, but it is not clear ex ante that the primary role of biased expectations lies in shaping upswings. There are good reasons to think that excessively pessimistic expectations during the downturn might be at least as important. Credit market expectations are focused on negative tail risks due to the asymmetric payoff structure of debt contracts. While neglect of tail risk can be important during credit booms, attaching a too high weight to the tail of the distribution could have even larger effects during the bust. Overpessimism might also be important in shaping asset price developments. For example, households' house price expectations

---

2. In a way similar to the equity return forecasts used in Greenwood and Shleifer (2014).

and forecast errors remained overly pessimistic for years after the burst of the housing bubble (see fig. 6.1).

Second, existing top-down studies of sentiment largely assume that there is one economy-wide sentiment factor. However, Kuvshinov (2018) shows that market sentiment of different assets does not necessarily comove. While asset returns are highly predictable with their own valuation ratios, there is no predictability of returns across asset classes. This challenges the notion that there is an economy-wide exuberance driving valuations across assets and credit markets. Going forward, we will need to understand in more detail what this domain-specificity implies for our understanding of the joint dynamics of fundamentals, credit, and asset prices.

Third, we have not yet gained a good understanding of the quantitative importance of behavioral factors for the credit cycle. Do behavioral biases create first-order macroeconomic effects? New work is already proceeding in this direction with Ma et al. (2019) and Barrero (2021) quantifying the effects of biased managerial expectations on economy-wide resource allocation and Bordalo et al. (2021) incorporating diagnostic expectations into a real business cycle model with heterogeneous firms and default.

Fourth, as briefly discussed above, we identify a lack of empirical evidence that explicitly studies the relative role of borrowers' and lenders' expectations within a unified framework. Are expectations of borrowers and lenders aligned during credit booms and busts? What happens when expectations of borrowers and lenders diverge from each other? Does a common shift in domain-specific expectations suffice to create a credit boom (e.g., a common increase in house price growth expectations)? We advocate for the collection of surveys with questions that are consistent across consumers, firms, and lenders, to answer these questions in the future.

REFERENCES

Adam, Klaus, Dmitry Matveev, and Stefan Nagel. 2021. Do Survey Expectations of Stock Returns Reflect Risk-Adjustments? Journal of Monetary Economics 117: 723–40.
Adelino, Manuel, Antoinette Schoar, and Felipe Severino. 2016. Loan Originations and Defaults in the Mortgage Crisis: The Role of the Middle Class. Review of Financial Studies 29 (7): 1635–70.
———. 2018a. Perception of House Price Risk and Homeownership. NBER Working Paper 25090.
———. 2018b. The Role of Housing and Mortgage Markets in the Financial Crisis. Annual Review of Financial Economics 10: 25–41.
Albanesi, Stefania, Giacomo De Giorgi, and Jaromir Nosal. 2017. Credit Growth and the Financial Crisis: A New Narrative. NBER Working Paper 23740.
Armona, Luis, Andreas Fuster, and Basit Zafar. 2019. Home Price Expectations and Behavior: Evidence from a Randomized Information Experiment. Review of Economic Studies 86 (4): 1371–1410.

Bailey, Michael, Ruiqing Cao, Theresa Kuchler, and Johannes Stroebel. 2018. The Economic Effects of Social Networks: Evidence from the Housing Market. Journal of Political Economy 126 (6): 2224–76.

Bailey, Michael, Eduardo Dávila, Theresa Kuchler, and Johannes Stroebel. 2019. House Price Beliefs and Mortgage Leverage Choice. Review of Economic Studies 86 (6): 2403–52.

Baker, Malcolm, and Jeffrey Wurgler. 2007. Investor Sentiment in the Stock Market. Journal of Economic Perspectives 21 (2): 129–52.

Bansal, Ravi, and Amir Yaron. 2004. Risks for the Long Run: A Potential Resolution of Asset Pricing Puzzles. Journal of Finance 59 (4): 1481–1509.

Barberis, Nicholas, Robin Greenwood, Lawrence Jin, and Andrei Shleifer. 2015. X-CAPM: An Extrapolative Capital Asset Pricing Model. Journal of Financial Economics 115 (1): 1–24.

———. 2018. Extrapolation and Bubbles. Journal of Financial Economics 129 (2): 203–27.

Barberis, Nicholas, Andrei Shleifer, and Robert Vishny. 1998. A Model of Investor Sentiment. Journal of Financial Economics 49 (3): 307–43.

Baron, Matthew, and Wei Xiong. 2017. Credit Expansion and Neglected Crash Risk. Quarterly Journal of Economics 132 (2): 713–64.

Barrero, José Maria. 2021. The Micro and Macro of Managerial Beliefs. Journal of Financial Economics, forthcoming.

Barro, Robert J. 2009. Rare Disasters, Asset Prices, and Welfare Costs. American Economic Review 99 (1): 243–64.

Ben-David, Itzhak, John R. Graham, and Campbell R. Harvey. 2013. Managerial Miscalibration. Quarterly Journal of Economics 128 (4): 1547–84.

Berger, Allen N., and Gregory F. Udell. 2004. The Institutional Memory Hypothesis and the Procyclicality of Bank Lending Behavior. Journal of Financial Intermediation 13 (4): 458–95.

Bordalo, Pedro, Nicola Gennaioli, Rafael La Porta, and Andrei Shleifer. 2019. Diagnostic Expectations and Stock Returns of Finance 74 (6): 2839–74.

Bordalo, Pedro, Nicola Gennaioli, Yueran Ma, and Andrei Shleifer. 2020. Over-reaction in Macroeconomic Expectations. American Economic Review 110: 2748–82.

Bordalo, Pedro, Nicola Gennaioli, and Andrei Shleifer. 2018. Diagnostic Expectations and Credit Cycles. Journal of Finance 73 (1): 199–227.

Bordalo, Pedro, Nicola Gennaioli, Andrei Shleifer, and Stephen J. Terry. 2021. Real Credit Cycles. NBER Working Paper 28416.

Bouwman, Christa H. S., and Ulrike Malmendier. 2015. Does a Bank's History Affect Its Risk-Taking? American Economic Review 105 (5): 321–25.

Campbell, John Y., and John H. Cochrane. 1999. By Force of Habit: A Consumption-based Explanation of Aggregate Stock Market Behavior. Journal of Political Economy 107 (2): 205–51.

Case, Karl E., Robert J. Shiller, and Anne K. Thompson. 2012. What Have They Been Thinking? Homebuyer Behavior in Hot and Cold Markets. Brookings Papers on Economic Activity 265–315.

Cheng, Ing-Haw, Sahil Raina, and Wei Xiong. 2014. Wall Street and the Housing Bubble. American Economic Review 104 (9): 2797–2829.

Chernenko, Sergey, Samuel G. Hanson, and Adi Sunderam. 2016. Who Neglects Risk? Investor Experience and the Credit Boom. Journal of Financial Economics 122 (2): 248–69.

Cochrane, John H. 2011. Presidential Address: Discount Rates. Journal of Finance 66 (4): 1047–1108.

———. 2017. Macro-finance. Review of Finance 21 (3): 945–85.

Coibion, Olivier, and Yuriy Gorodnichenko. 2012. What Can Survey Forecasts Tell Us about Information Rigidities? Journal of Political Economy 120 (1): 116–59.

———. 2015. Information Rigidity and the Expectations Formation Process: A Simple Framework and New Facts. American Economic Review 105 (8): 2644–78.

Coibion, Olivier, Yuriy Gorodnichenko, and Saten Kumar. 2018. How Do Firms Form Their Expectations? New Survey Evidence. American Economic Review 108 (9): 2671–2713.

Danielsson, Jón, Marcela Valenzuela, and Ilknur Zer. 2018. Learning from History: Volatility and Financial Crises. Review of Financial Studies 31: 2774–2805.

De Stefani, Alessia. 2021. House Price History, Biased Expectations and Credit Cycles: The Role of Housing Investors. Real Estate Economics 49: 1238–66.

Duke CFO Global Business Outlook. 2018. Accessed May 25, 2018.

Fahlenbrach, Rüdiger, Robert Prilmeier, and René M. Stulz. 2017. Why Does Fast Loan Growth Predict Poor Performance for Banks? Review of Financial Studies 31 (3): 1014–63.

Fahlenbrach, Rüdiger, and René M. Stulz. 2011. Bank CEO Incentives and the Credit Crisis. Journal of Financial Economics 99 (1): 11–26.

Foote, Christopher L., Kristopher S. Gerardi, and Paul S. Willen. 2012. Why Did So Many People Make So Many Ex Post Bad Decisions? The Causes of the Foreclosure Crisis. NBER Working Paper 18082.

Geanakoplos, John. 2010. The Leverage Cycle. NBER Macroeconomics Annual 24 (1): 1–66.

Gennaioli, Nicola, Yueran Ma, and Andrei Shleifer. 2016. Expectations and Investment. NBER Macroeconomics Annual 30 (1): 379–431.

Gennaioli, Nicola, and Andrei Shleifer. 2018. A Crisis of Beliefs: Investor Psychology and Financial Fragility. Princeton, NJ: Princeton University Press.

Giglio, Stefano, Matteo Maggiori, Johannes Stroebel, and Stephen P. Utkus. 2021. Five Facts about Beliefs and Portfolios. American Economic Review 111 (5): 1481–1522.

Greenwood, Robin, and Samuel G. Hanson. 2013. Issuer Quality and Corporate Bond Returns. Review of Financial Studies 26 (6): 1483–1525.

———. 2015. Waves in Ship Prices and Investment. Quarterly Journal of Economics 130 (1): 55–109.

Greenwood, Robin, Samuel G. Hanson, and Lawrence J. Jin. 2019. Reflexivity in Credit Markets. NBER Working Paper 25747.

Greenwood, Robin, and Stefan Nagel. 2009. Inexperienced Investors and Bubbles. Journal of Financial Economics 93 (2): 239–58.

Greenwood, Robin, and Andrei Shleifer. 2014. Expectations of Returns and Expected Returns. Review of Financial Studies 27 (3): 714–46.

Gulen, Huseyin, Mihai Ion, and Stefano Rossi. 2019. Credit Cycles, Expectations, and Corporate Investment. CEPR Discussion Paper 13679.

Ho, Po-Hsin, Chia-Wei Huang, Chih-Yung Lin, and Ju-Fang Yen. 2016. CEO Overconfidence and Financial Crisis: Evidence from Bank Lending and Leverage. Journal of Financial Economics 120 (1): 194–209.

Jordà, Òscar, Moritz Schularick, and Alan M. Taylor. 2013. When Credit Bites Back. Journal of Money, Credit and Banking 45 (S2): 3–28.

———. 2015a. Betting the House. Journal of International Economics 96: S2–S18.

———. 2015b. Leveraged Bubbles. Journal of Monetary Economics 76: S1–S20.

———. 2016. The Great Mortgaging: Housing Finance, Crises and Business Cycles. Economic Policy 31 (85): 107–52.

Kahneman, Daniel, and Amos Tversky. 1972. Subjective Probability: A Judgment of Representativeness. Cognitive Psychology 3 (3): 430–54.

Kaplan, Greg, Kurt Mitman, and Giovanni L. Violante. 2020. The Housing Boom and Bust: Model Meets Evidence. Journal of Political Economy 128 (9): 3285–3345.

Koudijs, Peter, and Hans-Joachim Voth. 2016. Leverage and Beliefs: Personal Experience and Risk-Taking in Margin Lending. American Economic Review 106 (11): 3367–3400.

Krishnamurthy, Arvind, and Tyler Muir. 2017. How Credit Cycles across a Financial Crisis. NBER Working Paper 23850.

Kuchler, Theresa, and Basit Zafar. 2019. Personal Experiences and Expectations about Aggregate Outcomes. Journal of Finance 74 (5): 2491–2542.

Kuvshinov, Dmitry. 2018. The Time Varying Risk Puzzle. Working paper.

Landier, Augustin, and David Thesmar. 2008. Financial Contracting with Optimistic Entrepreneurs. Review of Financial Studies 22 (1): 117–50.

López-Salido, David, Jeremy C. Stein, and Egon Zakrajšek. 2017. Credit-Market Sentiment and the Business Cycle. Quarterly Journal of Economics 132 (3): 1373–1426.

Ma, Yueran. 2015. Bank CEO Optimism and the Financial Crisis. Working paper.

Ma, Yueran, Tiziano Ropele, David Sraer, and David Thesmar. 2020. A Quantitative Analysis of Distortions in Managerial Forecasts. NBER Working Paper 26830.

Malmendier, Ulrike, and Stefan Nagel. 2011. Depression Babies: Do Macroeconomic Experiences Affect Risk Taking? Quarterly Journal of Economics 126 (1): 373–416.

Malmendier, Ulrike, Stefan Nagel, and Zhen Yan. 2021. The Making of Hawks and Doves: Inflation Experiences on the FOMC. Journal of Monetary Economics 117: 19–42.

Malmendier, Ulrike, and Geoffrey Tate. 2005. CEO Overconfidence and Corporate Investment. Journal of Finance 60 (6): 2661–2700.

———. 2008. Who Makes Acquisitions? CEO Overconfidence and the Market's Reaction. Journal of Financial Economics 89 (1): 20–43.

Mian, Atif R., and Amir Sufi. 2009. The Consequences of Mortgage Credit Expansion: Evidence from the US Mortgage Default Crisis. Quarterly Journal of Economics 124 (4): 1449–96.

———. 2018. Finance and Business Cycles: The Credit-driven Household Demand Channel. Journal of Economic Perspectives 32 (3): 31–58.

———. 2021. Credit Supply and Housing Speculation. Review of Financial Studies, forthcoming.

Mian, Atif R., Amir Sufi, and Emil Verner. 2017. Household Debt and Business Cycles Worldwide. Quarterly Journal of Economics 132 (4): 1755–1817.

Minsky, Hyman P. 1977. The Financial Instability Hypothesis: An Interpretation of Keynes and an Alternative to "Standard" Theory. Challenge 20 (1): 20–27.

Piazzesi, Monika, and Martin Schneider. 2009. Momentum Traders in the Housing Market: Survey Evidence and a Search Model. American Economic Review 99 (2): 406–11.

Richter, Björn, and Kaspar Zimmermann. 2019. The Profit-Credit Cycle. Working paper.

Schularick, Moritz, and Alan M. Taylor. 2012. Credit Booms Gone Bust: Monetary Policy, Leverage Cycles, and Financial Crises, 1870–2008. American Economic Review 102 (2): 1029–61.

Shiller, Robert J. 1981. The Use of Volatility Measures in Assessing Market Efficiency. Journal of Finance 36 (2): 291–304.

Simsek, Alp. 2013. Belief Disagreements and Collateral Constraints. Econometrica 81 (1): 1–53.

Soo, Cindy K. 2018. Quantifying Sentiment with News Media across Local Housing Markets. Review of Financial Studies 31 (10): 3689–3719.

Comment by Yueran Ma

In the decade after the Great Recession, research on credit cycles and research on expectations are among the most vibrant areas of study in economics. De Stefani and Zimmermann (2021) summarize research progress at the intersection of these two important literatures, where the central question is to understand the role of expectations in credit cycles. My discussion amplifies the theme in their review: recent work offers accumulating evidence that imperfectly rational expectations are frequently a key component of credit cycles, and there are many interesting open questions for future investigation.

Since the global financial crisis, there is increasing—and by now perhaps unanimous—recognition that credit cycles are central to economic fluctuations (Schularick and Taylor 2012; Jordà, Schularick, and Taylor 2013; Mian and Sufi 2009, 2014; López-Salido, Stein, and Zakrajšek 2017). But why do boom-and-bust cycles in credit arise?

As De Stefani and Zimmermann (2021) point out, expectations have emerged as a promising candidate. Several other contributions in this volume also point to this direction. I think there are several important dots that connect together.

First, evidence shows that distorted incentives do not seem to explain everything, as highlighted by Fahlenbrach and Stulz (2011) and Cheng, Raina, and Xiong (2014), among others.

Second, a set of influential work, following Schularick and Taylor (2012), looks to history and finds that credit cycles happen repeatedly and are not confined to a particular institutional setting (such as originate-to-distribute). Previous scholars who looked to history such as Minsky and Kindleberger (though in a more episodic and less quantitative way) also postulated that credit cycles seem to originate from overoptimism leading to credit and investment booms.

Third, a long literature in behavioral finance considers biased expectations to be central to asset price fluctuations, which traditionally focused on the stock market instead of credit markets. Since Shiller (1981) and De Bondt and Thaler (1985) in the 1980s, one way to understand fluctuations in the

Yueran Ma is assistant professor of finance at the Booth School of Business, University of Chicago.

158   YUERAN MA

stock market is that investors have biased beliefs that lead them to overreact to news. More recently, there is more direct evidence using expectations data from surveys of investors (Greenwood and Shleifer 2014; Amromin and Sharpe 2014; Bordalo, Gennaioli, La Porta, and Shleifer 2019).

Against this backdrop, over the past few years, several papers have provided important empirical evidence on the role of biased expectations in credit cycles. First, Greenwood and Hanson (2013) show that low issuer quality predicts low or negative excess corporate bond returns, and issuer quality tends to decline after periods of low default. The result suggests that credit market investors may extrapolate default rates, which is further explored in Greenwood, Hanson, and Jin (2019). Second, Baron and Xiong (2017) demonstrate that credit expansions increase bank equity crash risk, but bank stockholders do not appear to foresee the crash risk. Third, Fahlenbrach, Prilmeier, and Stulz (2018) find that fast loan growth predicts poor bank performance, but banks and analysts do not seem to anticipate the poor performance. Finally, Richter and Zimmermann (2019) show that high past profits of banks lead to credit expansions and overoptimism of bank CFOs. Overall, the first two papers provide evidence based on dynamics in market prices, while the last two papers use direct data on expectations. The overarching finding is that expectations in credit markets appear imperfectly rational, which can drive boom/bust cycles. In addition to the empirical papers, new models of expectations are also developed and applied to credit cycles (Bordalo, Gennaioli, and Shleifer 2018).

In the following, I first briefly summarize the general lessons from research on expectations: What are the consistent features of expectations we observe in the data across different domains? I then transition to applications of expectations in the research on credit cycles and discuss some special elements in analyzing credit cycles. I will also outline some open questions in understanding expectations and credit cycles.

EXPECTATIONS AND ECONOMIC ACTIVITIES: AN OVERVIEW

For decades, the benchmark framework of expectations in economics research has been rational expectations (RE). While RE is an important theoretical construct, it is not necessarily an empirical description of economic decision makers. In recent years, interest has grown in understanding the empirical features of expectations formation, using data on expectations from surveys of decision makers. These studies find accumulating evidence that (1) expectations can be meaningfully elicited and measured in the data,

(2) expectations in the data have significant explanatory power for economic decisions, and (3) expectations in many domains appear imperfectly rational, but deviations from RE have some consistent patterns.[1]

What is the structure of deviations from perfectly rational forecasts in the data? One common theme in the data, across different domains, is that people tend to overextrapolate recent shocks or trends (Greenwood and Shleifer 2014; Piazzesi, Salomao, and Schneider 2015; Bordalo, Gennaioli, and Shleifer 2018; Bordalo, Gennaioli, Ma, and Shleifer 2020; Gennaioli, Ma, and Shleifer 2016; Richter and Zimmermann 2019; De Stefani 2021; Afrouzi et al. 2019). Correspondingly, forecast errors are predictable: forecasts tend to be overoptimistic when current conditions are good, and vice versa. Figure 6C.1 shows a few examples. Panel A shows predictable forecast errors in credit spread forecasts by analysts in financial institutions (using data from the Blue Chip Financial Forecasts data set) from Bordalo, Gennaioli, and Shleifer (2018): when current credit spreads are low, financial analysts tend to underestimate future credit spreads, and vice versa. Panel B shows predictable forecast errors in earnings growth forecasts by CFOs from major nonfinancial firms (using data from the Duke CFO survey): when current earnings are high, CFOs tend to overestimate future earnings growth. The predictability in forecast errors indicates deviations from rational expectations, in the direction of overextrapolation. The extrapolative tendencies in expectations can be important for understanding credit cycles and help explain why credit booms and excess lending may arise in good times, sowing the seeds for subsequent crises.

To further flesh out the impact of expectations on economic decisions, recent research also provides ample evidence on the link between expectations measured in the data and economic activities. For instance, investors with more optimistic expectations of stock returns hold more stocks in their

1. This body of work by now covers several domains, including the following:

Financial markets: expectations of stock returns (Greenwood and Shleifer 2014; Amromin and Sharpe 2014; Andonov and Rauh 2021; Giglio, Maggiori, Stroebel, and Utkus 2021; Nagel and Xu 2021), bond yields (Piazzesi, Salomao, and Schneider 2015; Cieslak 2018), and credit spreads (Bordalo, Gennaioli, and Shleifer 2018)

Macroeconomic outcomes: expectations of inflation and GDP (Malmendier and Nagel 2016; Coibion and Gorodnichenko 2012, 2015; Bordalo, Gennaioli, Ma, and Shleifer 2020; Broer and Kohlhas 2019; Fuhrer 2018)

Firms: expectations of earnings and sales (Gennaioli, Ma, and Shleifer 2016; Bordalo, Gennaioli, La Porta, and Shleifer 2019; Bouchaud, Krueger, Landier, and Thesmar 2019; Richter and Zimmermann 2019; Rossi, Gulen, and Ion 2021; Ma, Ropele, Sraer, and Thesmar 2019)

Households: expectations of income and house prices (Rozsypal and Schlafmann 2019; De Stefani 2021)

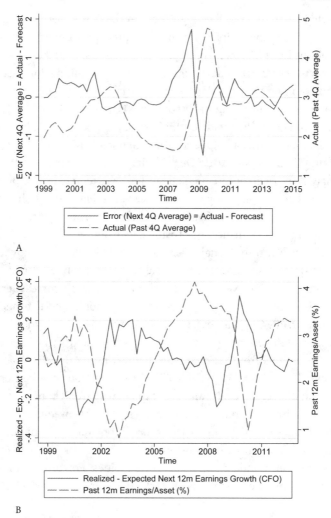

FIGURE 6C.1 Predictability in forecast errors. (A) Financial analyst forecast errors of credit spreads. (B) CFO forecast errors of future earnings growth.
Note: In panel A, the dashed line is the average credit spreads in the past four quarters; the solid line is mean forecast errors (realized minus forecast) of average credit spreads in the next four quarters. In panel B, the dashed line is corporate earnings (normalized by book assets) in the past twelve months; the solid line is mean forecast errors (realized minus forecast) of earnings growth in the next twelve months.

portfolios (Andonov and Rauh 2021; Giglio, Maggiori, Stroebel, and Utkus 2021). Firms with more optimistic expectations of future earnings make more investments (Gennaioli, Ma, and Shleifer 2016; Ma, Ropele, Sraer, and Thesmar 2019; Richter and Zimmermann 2019). Accordingly, biases in expectations transmit into decisions and shape real outcomes.

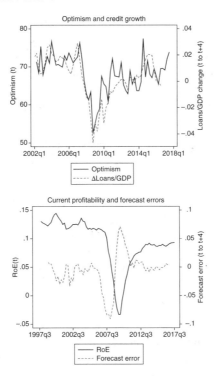

FIGURE 6C.2 Evidence on expectations and credit cycles. Bank CFO expectations and lending growth (*top panel*). Overextrapolation in bank CFO expectations (*bottom panel*).
Source: Richter and Zimmermann (2019).

EXPECTATIONS AND CREDIT CYCLES

Putting everything together, there is an emerging narrative of biased beliefs and credit cycles supported by empirical evidence. The narrative generally goes as follows. First, some good fundamental shocks arise. Then, the good shocks feed into overextrapolation and overoptimism and lead to (excessive) credit expansions. Next, credit booms and excessive lending eventually turn into losses. Finally, the moment of recognition comes, and credit crises take place.

One paper that has traced out these steps most fully is the recent work by Richter and Zimmermann (2019). Using historical data across seventeen countries as well as recent data on expectations of bank executives, they show the following important links. First, high past profits tend to lead to overoptimism in bank CFOs' expectations about future profitability. As shown in the bottom panel of figure 6C.2, when current return on equity (ROE) is high, bank CFOs tend to overestimate future ROE. Second, optimistic expectations of bank CFOs are accompanied by high credit growth, as shown by the top panel of figure 6C.2. Finally, high credit growth predicts a higher probability of credit crisis.

While the recent advancement in research offers many new insights, there are a number of open questions for future work. I summarize some of them below.

First, what triggers reversals in optimistic beliefs and turns the tide to panics? Do beliefs revert because overoptimism gradually fades on its own, or because losses from excessive lending eventually become overwhelming?

Second, while empirical analyses show that expectations overall play an important role in driving economic decisions, further work is needed to assess the impact of the biased component of expectations.

Third, the narrative of boom-and-bust cycles in investment driven by biased expectations can in principle apply to any type of firm (not just banks). What are the special features of credit cycles and debt contracts?

As De Stefani and Zimmermann (2021) highlight, in the context of lending, both beliefs of borrowers and beliefs of lenders can play a role. Lessons from theoretical analyses (Simsek 2013) suggest that borrowers' optimism about the upside (of an asset or a project they try to finance), or lenders' optimism about the downside, tends to be most powerful. When borrowers are optimistic about the upside, they have high willingness to buy the asset and are happy to accept the terms lenders offer. When lenders are optimistic about the downside, they think default is unlikely and are willing to expand the quantity of credit or offer attractive terms. Most of the data on expectations so far measure beliefs about conditional means or central tendencies, not beliefs about the tails. Future work may advance our understanding of beliefs about the tails. Future work may also advance our understanding of whether credit cycles generally involve biased beliefs among all parties or primarily biased beliefs among lenders (who drive credit supply).

In the context of credit markets, one can also ask whether there are potentially interesting interactions between biased expectations and financial frictions. Do financial frictions dampen the impact of biased expectations (e.g., by making it harder for people to act on their beliefs) or amplify them (e.g., through financial acceleration)?

CONCLUSIONS

Research on credit cycles and on expectations has made substantial progress since the global financial crisis. Evidence is accumulating that expectations in practice tend to be imperfectly rational, often in the direction of overextrapolation. And from the work on credit cycles, we are learning that extrapolative expectations appear to be an important driver of lending booms and eventual crises. A number of interesting open questions remain for the years ahead. With advancement in both modeling and data collection, the interaction between work on credit cycles and on expectations is an exciting enterprise. There are high expectations for this investment, and one can be hopeful that it will yield high returns.

REFERENCES

Afrouzi, Hassan, Spencer Y. Kwon, Augustin Landier, Yueran Ma, and David Thesmar. 2021. Overreaction in Expectations: Evidence and Theory. Columbia University working paper.

Amromin, Gene, and Steven A. Sharpe. 2014. From the Horse's Mouth: Economic Conditions and Investor Expectations of Risk and Return. Management Science 60: 845–66.

Andonov, Aleksandar, and Joshua D. Rauh. 2021. The Return Expectations of Institutional Investors. Stanford University Graduate School of Business Research Paper No. 18-5.

Baron, Matthew, and Wei Xiong. 2017. Credit Expansion and Neglected Crash Risk. Quarterly Journal of Economics 132: 713–64.

Bordalo, Pedro, Nicola Gennaioli, Rafael La Porta, and Andrei Shleifer. 2019. Diagnostic Expectations and Stock Returns. Journal of Finance 74: 2839–74.

Bordalo, Pedro, Nicola Gennaioli, Yueran Ma, and Andrei Shleifer. 2020. Overreaction in Macroeconomic Expectations. American Economic Review 110: 2748–82.

Bordalo, Pedro, Nicola Gennaioli, and Andrei Shleifer. 2018. Diagnostic Expectations and Credit Cycles. Journal of Finance 73: 199–227.

Bouchaud, Jean-Philippe, Philipp Krueger, Augustin Landier, and David Thesmar. 2019. Sticky Expectations and the Profitability Anomaly. Journal of Finance 74: 639–74.

Broer, Tobias, and Alexandre Kohlhas. 2019. Forecaster (Mis-)behavior. 2019 Meeting Papers 1171, Society for Economic Dynamics.

Cheng, Ing-Haw, Sahil Raina, and Wei Xiong. 2014. Wall Street and the Housing Bubble. American Economic Review 104: 2797–2829.

Cieslak, Anna. 2018. Short-Rate Expectations and Unexpected Returns in Treasury Bonds. Review of Financial Studies 31: 3265–3306.

Coibion, Olivier, and Yuriy Gorodnichenko. 2012. What Can Survey Forecasts Tell Us about Information Rigidities? Journal of Political Economy 120: 116–59.

———. 2015. Information Rigidity and the Expectations Formation Process: A Simple Framework and New Facts. American Economic Review 105: 2644–78.

De Bondt, Werner F. M., and Richard Thaler. 1985. Does the Stock Market Overreact? Journal of Finance 40: 793–805.

De Stefani, Alessia. 2021. House Price History, Biased Expectations and Credit Cycles. Real Estate Economics 49: 1238–66.

De Stefani, Alessia, and Kaspar Zimmermann. 2021. Expectations and Credit Cycles: What Role for Overoptimism of Borrowers and Lenders? Paper 10 at Institute for New Economic Thinking NextGen.

Fahlenbrach, Rüdiger, Robert Prilmeier, and René M. Stulz. 2018. Why Does Fast Loan Growth Predict Poor Performance for Banks? Review of Financial Studies 31: 1014–63.

Fahlenbrach, Rüdiger, and René M. Stulz. 2011. Bank CEO Incentives and the Credit Crisis. Journal of Financial Economics 99: 11–26.

Fuhrer, Jeffrey C. 2018. Intrinsic Expectations Persistence: Evidence from Professional and Household Survey Expectations. Federal Reserve Bank of Boston working paper, 18–19.

Gennaioli, Nicola, Yueran Ma, and Andrei Shleifer. 2016. Expectations and Investment. NBER Macroeconomics Annual 30: 379–431.

Giglio, Stefano, Matteo Maggiori, Johannes Stroebel, and Stephen Utkus. 2021. Five Facts about Beliefs and Portfolios. American Economic Review 111: 1481–1522.

Greenwood, Robin, and Samuel G. Hanson. 2013. Issuer Quality and Corporate Bond Returns. Review of Financial Studies 26: 1483–1525.

Greenwood, Robin, Samuel G. Hanson, and Lawrence J. Jin. 2019. Reflexivity in Credit Markets. NBER Working Paper 25747.

Greenwood, Robin, and Andrei Shleifer. 2014. Expectations of Returns and Expected Returns. Review of Financial Studies 27: 714–46.

Jordà, Òscar, Moritz Schularick, and Alan M. Taylor. 2013. When Credit Bites Back. Journal of Money, Credit and Banking 45: 3–28.

López-Salido, David, Jeremy C. Stein, and Egon Zakrajšek. 2017. Credit-Market Sentiment and the Business Cycle. Quarterly Journal of Economics 132: 1373–1426.

Ma, Yueran, Tiziano Ropele, David Sraer, and David Thesmar. 2019. Do Managerial Forecasting Biases Matter? University of Chicago working paper.

Malmendier, Ulrike, and Stefan Nagel. 2016. Learning from Inflation Experiences. Quarterly Journal of Economics 131: 53–87.

Mian, Atif, and Amir Sufi. 2009. The Consequences of Mortgage Credit Expansion: Evidence from the U.S. Mortgage Default Crisis. Quarterly Journal of Economics 124: 1449–96.

———. 2014. What Explains the 2007–2009 Drop in Employment? Econometrica 82: 2197–2223.

Nagel, Stefan, and Zhengyang Xu. 2021. Asset Pricing with Fading Memory. Review of Financial Studies, forthcoming.

Piazzesi, Monika, Juliana Salomao, and Martin Schneider. 2015. Trend and Cycle in Bond Premia. Stanford University working paper.

Richter, Björn, and Kaspar Zimmermann. 2019. The Profit-Credit Cycle. Universitat Pompeu Fabra working paper.

Rossi, Stefano, Huseyin Gulen, and Mihai Ion. 2021. Credit Cycles, Expectations, and Corporate Investment. Purdue University working paper.

Rozsypal, Filip, and Kathrin Schlafmann. 2019. Overpersistence Bias in Individual Income Expectations and Its Aggregate Implications. Danmarks Nationalbank working paper.

Schularick, Moritz, and Alan M. Taylor. 2012. Credit Booms Gone Bust: Monetary Policy, Leverage Cycles, and Financial Crises, 1870–2008. American Economic Review 102: 1029–61.

Shiller, Robert J. 1981. Do Stock Prices Move Too Much to Be Justified by Subsequent Changes in Dividends? American Economic Review 71: 421–36.

Simsek, Alp. 2013. Belief Disagreements and Collateral Constraints. Econometrica 81: 1–53.

7

A New Approach to Measuring Banks' Risk Exposure

JULIANE BEGENAU

The financial crisis of 2008/2009 sent shock waves through the banking industry, regulators, and academia. Why did nobody see it coming? Where did all the risk suddenly emerge from? This event forcefully highlighted how important measuring banks' risk exposure is, but measuring that exposure is not an easy undertaking. Banks' balance sheets are large and complicated. Publicly available data offer a rather coarse and typically backward-looking view on banks' risk exposure. Forward-looking stock return data have the problem that it is often difficult to differentiate between investors' beliefs/expectations and banks' fundamental risks. This piece shows that the replicating portfolio methodology used to value securities and firms offers a simple yet powerful way of measuring the risk exposures of banks.

At its core, the replicating portfolio method is just an application of the law of one price. Similar things should demand a similar price, that is, have a similar value. Random fluctuations in value are due to realized risks. If two things are alike, their values move alike. In other words, they have similar risk exposures. Take, for example, a U.S. Treasury (UST) bond portfolio and assume that bonds with maturities of ten and twelve years are traded while eleven-year-term bonds are not. Even though, in this hypothetical example, an eleven-year UST bond is not traded, we can figure out its value and risk exposure as a linear combination of the traded ten- and twelve-year UST bonds.

Juliane Begenau is associate professor of finance at the Graduate School of Business, Stanford University, a faculty research fellow at the National Bureau of Economic Research, and a research affiliate at the Centre for Economic Policy Research.

Going a step further, many financial securities, including bonds, share a common factor structure.[1] This just means that their values are driven by the same sources of risk, say, for example, shocks to the level of interest rates or shocks to the business cycle. The securities' sensitivity to the factors may differ across securities, but they all answer to the same factor realizations. Financial valuation methods use this fact to describe the value and risk of securities as a linear combination of these factors. For example, one can show that the universe of UST bonds can be described very precisely with a single bond. What does "very precisely" mean? It means that over 95% of the variation in UST bond returns can be described (i.e., replicated) by a single UST bond, say the five-year UST bond. Bonds with a different maturity may have different "loadings" (i.e., sensitivities) from the five-year UST bond factor.

Why is this relevant for measuring the risk exposure of banks? The balance sheet of banks resembles a levered bond portfolio. Cash and securities make up roughly 30%, loans 53%, and trading assets 10% of bank holding companies' assets. Less than 60% of bank holding companies' funding stems from deposits and 26% from capital market debt. This means that we can compare banks to a highly levered bond portfolio in order to figure out their risk exposure.[2] Since bonds follow a factor structure, we can then summarize the risk exposure of banks' complex portfolios as the risk exposure of the portfolio that replicates banks' portfolios with a small number of factors.

In Begenau, Piazzesi, and Schneider (2015), we apply the portfolio mimicking logic to banks in order to study their risk exposure. The key steps are as follows. First, we exploit the factor structure of the fixed-income securities banks hold (e.g., mortgages, treasuries, corporate bonds, interest rate derivatives) to express their return as a linear combination of the returns to the factors. Second, we use the information from the FR-Y-9C filings to express each balance-sheet position as a bond portfolio. The idea is that a shock to the underlying factors will change the value of the balance-sheet item in the same way as it will change the value of the bond portfolio.

The replicating portfolio approach to measure bank risk differs in three important ways from existing methods. First, it does not rely on bank accounting returns. Bank accounting returns are much smoother than market value

---

1. The bond pricing literature (e.g., Litterman and Scheinkman 1991; Duffie and Kan 1996; Cochrane and Piazzesi 2005; Piazzesi 2010) has shown that treasuries follow an affine linear factor structure.

2. Banks' cash and securities holdings are literally a bond portfolio. Loans are very similar to bonds: they promise an income stream over a contractually agreed upon period. The income stream reflects the interest rate exposure and credit risk.

returns would be, because banks do not need to report valuation changes for their assets.[3] Moreover, accounting rules tend to be backward looking (see Begenau, Bigio, Majerovitz, and Vieyra 2019). Table 7.1 below demonstrates how difficult it is to measure risk from accounting returns. The intuition is easiest explained with an analogous example. The stock return is driven by dividends and capital gains (i.e., the change in the stock's value). Suppose we wanted to measure the riskiness of a stock with its equity return volatility. This includes variation in capital gains (valuations) and dividends. If we were to apply accounting rules, those value fluctuations would be ignored. Thus, we would measure the riskiness of a stock by the riskiness of its dividends. Those tend to be very stable and predictable, thus not very risky. In other words, measuring banks' risk exposure using accounting variables alone can lead to grossly underestimating it.

The second difference from existing methods is that it does not rely on bank stock returns data. Though bank stock returns are forward looking and therefore overcome one of the key concerns with using accounting data, they also mix investors' expectations and beliefs with bank fundamental risk exposures. In Begenau and Stafford (2019), we show that in the aggregate, banks' credit risk and interest rate exposure appear not to be priced, even though banks clearly bear both. Instead, bank stocks often trade similar to nonfinancial stocks, indicating that common investor beliefs (which are not bank specific) perhaps matter more for movements in aggregate bank stock returns.

Finally, the approach here is also different from value-at-risk (VaR) measures that banks usually report for their trading books. VaR measures focus on a narrow (albeit important) part of the bank balance sheet and do not aggregate across positions within a bank or across banks as factor exposures do. This can make it difficult to get a sense for the total risk exposure of an institution or the banking sector as a whole. A great advantage of the replicating portfolio method is that it easily aggregates positions within a bank as well as positions across banks, thereby creating a transparent and flexible measure of banks' risk exposures.

Related Literature

A traditionally popular way of measuring banks' risk exposure has been to regress bank stock returns on a risk factor. The risk factor typically measured

---

3. Bank securities are reported at fair value. Although this concept is closer to a market value, banks still do not have to report valuation changes on securities unless they are realized. Unrealized gains and losses are instead reported in equity.

interest rate risk (see, e.g., Flannery and James 1984). A more recent example is English, Van den Heuvel, and Zakrajšek (2018). This approach is similar to the mimicking portfolio approach and can in principle accommodate additional factors such as credit risk. The key difference is that, instead of using bank stock returns directly, the mimicking portfolio constructs each bank position from the bottom up. Thus, one does not need to rely on the assumption that the stock market has priced banks accurately. This appears to be relevant for both the aggregate (see Begenau and Stafford 2019) and the cross section (see Gandhi and Lustig 2015); bank equity does not load much on either credit or interest rate factors.

Another more recently popular approach to studying bank risk is by looking at banks' accounting returns. Meiselman, Nagel, and Purnanandam (2020) study net-income measures directly, while Gomez, Landier, Sraer, and Thesmar (2021) and Drechsler, Savov, and Schnabl (2018) consider the changes in interest income or earnings as a fraction of assets.

Risk exposures of a mimicking portfolio (see Begenau, Piazzesi, and Schneider 2015 and Begenau and Stafford 2019) are additive risk measures that are comparable across positions and banks. This is an advantage over nonadditive measures of risk such as value-at-risk constraints (VaR) that are often used by banks to measure their trading book risk exposures (see, e.g., Acharya, Pedersen, Philippon, and Richardson 2017 for discussions of tail risk measures and Adrian and Boyarchenko 2012 for the macroeconomic effects of VaR constraints).

The replicating portfolio approach is similar in spirit to the stress tests conducted by bank regulators (see Brunnermeier, Gorton, and Krishnamurthy 2012). Similar to a stress test, a replicating portfolio can be stressed with various factor shocks that represent different adverse scenarios.

This document is organized as follows. I first describe the data. Then I discuss the methodology and its advantage over using bank equity or bank accounting returns alone. Before concluding, I discuss a few limitations.

Data

For this research, I use detailed data from the quarterly regulatory filings (FR-Y-9C) of U.S. bank holding companies (BHCs). To obtain additional information on the maturity composition of bank balance sheets I link each BHC to its commercial banks that file forms FFIEC 031 and FFIEC 041 each quarter. I focus on the BHCs because they represent the entire financial institution, which is also the entity that is publicly traded.

For a longer time horizon, I also use aggregate data on FDIC-insured commercial and savings banks in the United States from the FDIC Historical Statistics on Banking (HSOB). These data are reported at an annual frequency from 1934 through 2018 and include information on the number of institutions and some detail on their structure, as well as financial data from income statements and balance sheets.

I also use the returns and market capitalization of publicly traded BHCs, from the Center for Research in Security Prices (CRSP). The Federal Reserve provides a table for linking the bank regulatory data with CRSP. In addition, I use a variety of additional capital market data on UST bonds, U.S. corporate bond indexes, and bond index portfolios available to retail investors through Vanguard and accessed through CRSP.

Methodology: Bank Mimicking Portfolio

As described in detail in Begenau, Piazzesi, and Schneider (2015), bank regulatory reports provide fairly detailed information about banks' balance-sheet positions. Begenau, Piazzesi, and Schneider (2015) and Begenau and Stafford (2019) use this information to construct a bank mimicking portfolio. Then, for each balance-sheet position, the combination of bond factors is chosen such that the replicating portfolio has approximately the same cash flow process as the bank position that it replicates.

The key steps are as follows. First, one has to decide which factors to include. One can use the information from the FR-Y-9C filings to classify assets according to which factors they likely are exposed to. For example, banks' U.S. Treasury holdings are exposed to interest rate risk and therefore an interest rate factor is well suited to replicate their cash flows. Loans are likely exposed to interest rate risk and credit risk. In Begenau, Piazzesi, and Schneider (2015), we consider an interest rate factor and in Begenau and Stafford (2019) we add to it a market factor. Then for various fixed-income securities, we find the factor loadings by regressing market returns for a particular fixed-income security R_t^i with term m and credit rating k on the chosen interest rate risk R_t^{IRR} and credit factor R_t^{CR}:

$$R_t^i = \alpha^i + \beta^{i,IRR} R_t^{IRR} + \beta^{i,CR} R_t^{CR} + \varepsilon_t^i.$$

This regression tells us how many units of the interest rate factor and credit risk factor are necessary to replicate the factor exposure of one dollar of security i, which says how much the return of i changes with changes in the underlying factors.

The second step is then to calculate the dollar amount of the replicating portfolio positions. In most cases, one cannot simply use the dollar amount of the balance-sheet position since banks report most of their positions in terms of amortized costs (hold-to-maturity accounting) that do not quite capture the actual dollar amount at risk. For securities, the data provide both amortized cost as well as fair value measures. For loans, Begenau, Piazzesi, and Schneider (2015) propose an algorithm that is more easily explained with the following example.

A typical loan involves regular payments following an amortization schedule that depends on the interest rate of the loan, its term, and payment frequency. Consider a one-year $5,000 loan issued at the end of May in 2019 with quarterly payments and an annual interest rate of 4%. Based on the annuity formula, this loan involves four regular payments in the amount of $1,281.41. The first payment is due at the end of August 2019, the following is due at the end of November 2019, then another payment is due at the end of February 2020, and the final payment is due at the end of May in 2020. Each payment can be thought of as the face value of a zero-coupon bond with a three-month, six-month, nine-month, or twelve-month term. Thus, each loan can be represented as a portfolio of zero-coupon bonds with the same face value but different maturities. This is useful, because it is straightforward to replicate a portfolio of zero-coupon bonds as long as one knows the underlying risk structure. The idea is that a shock to the underlying factors will change the value of the balance-sheet item in the same way as it will change the value of the zero-coupon bond portfolio.

How can one gauge the underlying risk structure of specific balance-sheet items? Bank loans entail credit risk and interest rate risk exposure. While imperfect, banks' regulatory filings provide a range of useful information that we use as an input to calculate how much interest rate risk and credit risk each balance-sheet position contains.

For credit risk, one can use the information about risk-weighted assets from the FR-Y-9C filings. For each balance-sheet category (say loans), banks report how many dollars of the balance-sheet item in question (e.g., loans) have a risk weight of 0%, 20%, 40%, . . . 100%, and more than 100%.[4] The instructions to the FR-Y-9C provide a mapping from risk weights into credit ratings. Begenau, Piazzesi, and Schneider (2015) use this information to map bank loans to the appropriate credit market risk as captured by corporate bond spreads.

---

4. The exact risk weight categories changed over the sample period.

To calculate how much interest rate risk exposure a loan has, one needs to know its term. The bank holding company filings (FR-Y-9C) do not provide that information. This information is provided through the call reports (FFIEC 031 and FFIEC 041 filings) that commercial banks have to file quarterly. Therein, banks report the term distribution of loans and securities according to different buckets: less than three-month, three-month up to one year, one year to three years, three years to five years, five years through fifteen years, and more than fifteen years. The term distribution here denotes over what time period the interest rate is contractually fixed. That is, a fifteen-year floating-rate mortgage would be reported in the less than three-month bucket. It is fairly straightforward to aggregate the commercial bank information to the bank holding company level. Since almost all loans and securities that are not held for trading are held by the subsidiary commercial banks, the commercial bank's loans and securities maturity distribution reflects the maturity distribution of loans and securities at the bank holding company level.

The credit rating and term of each fixed-income balance-sheet position allows us to ascertain which factor loadings from the first step to use. In the final step, one just needs to multiply the factor loadings with the respective dollar amounts of the replicating position. This number then represents the dollar exposure to a specific factor. We can also calculate gains and losses that result from various factor shocks. In fact, we can trace out the entire distribution of banks' portfolio changes to changes in factor realizations.

Advantage Over Using Bank Accounting Returns

A recent literature (e.g., Meiselman, Nagel, and Purnanandam 2020; Gomez, Landier, Sraer, and Thesmar 2021; and Drechsler, Savov, and Schnabl 2021) uses bank accounting returns to make statements about banks' risk-taking and risk exposure. There are two potential drawbacks of using banks' accounting returns alone to measure banks' risk exposure.

First, banks do not have to report unrealized valuation changes of their balance-sheet positions on the income statement, with the partial exception of trading assets. This excludes any capital gains or losses from the return calculation. The following example illustrates why this is an issue for risk-exposure measures. Suppose we were to calculate the risk exposure of the U.S. value-weighted stock market. It is well documented that once firms pay dividends, they tend to smooth dividends over time. That is, the dividends time series of the S&P 500 is much smoother than the time series of its price index. If prices were ignored in the risk-exposure measurement of the S&P 500, we would estimate a market beta of less than 1 in a capital-asset-pricing

TABLE 7.1 How accounting changes interest rate sensitivity

	Accounting	Market value
12 months		
FFR loading	0.0006	0.0271
t-stat.	3.52	9.85
R^2	0.29	0.31
18 months		
FFR loading	0.0002	0.0333
t-stat.	1.31	8.59
R^2	0.07	0.25
24 months		
FFR loading	0.0001	0.0385
t-stat.	0.98	7.89
R^2	0.03	0.22
30 months		
FFR loading	0.002	0.0431
t-stat.	1.24	7.34
R^2	0.03	0.2
N	238	238

Note: This table presents results from monthly regressions of
market value and accounting value U.S. Treasury portfolio
returns on changes of the Federal Funds rate. The data
ranges from 1997/01 until 2018/09.

model (CAPM) regression even though economically the coefficient should
be 1. The CAPM just regresses any security (here the S&P 500 return) on the
market return, that is, the S&P 500 return. Obviously, capital gains (i.e., the
valuation changes) also need to be taken into account to fully gauge the risk
exposure of stocks. The same also holds for assets banks hold. I provide a
concrete example in table 7.1.

Table 7.1 presents ordinary least square regression results that show how
the inference about the interest rate risk exposure of treasury portfolios to
changes in the Federal Funds rate (FFR) varies depending on measuring the
treasury portfolio returns in terms of market value returns or accounting
value returns. The column headed "Market value" represents the standard
market value return, while the column headed "Accounting" represents the
accounting return. I calculate an accounting value (or book value [BV]) of the
bond portfolio using the standard capital accumulation rule:

$$BV_{t+1} = BV_t + \text{interest income}_{t+1} - \text{purchases}_{t+1} + \text{proceeds}_{t+1},$$

where purchases and proceeds are measured at market transaction value and
interest income is earned periodically according to the bond coupon terms.
This results in the portfolio book value ignoring the effects of fluctuating

interest rates on the market values of the bonds in the portfolio, implicitly assuming that their values equal par. This is equivalent to the hold-to-maturity accounting rules that most banks' balance sheets follow.

I construct various treasury bond portfolios that differ according to their average term. Take, for example, the first rows of table 7.1. This treasury portfolio has an average maturity of twelve months. That means that this portfolio buys each month two-year treasuries and holds them until maturity. The average term is therefore one year.

Economically, treasuries are clearly exposed to changes in market rates (as measured by the FFR). This is also shown by the last column of table 7.1. The FFR coefficient (change in the Federal Funds rate) of the treasury portfolio's market value is always larger than its book value. The longer the term of the portfolio, the smaller the accounting coefficient and the smaller its statistical significance. In other words, if we were to use the accounting returns of the treasury portfolio and regress these on changes in the FFR, we would find that the treasury portfolio is not exposed to interest rate risks. Of course, if we use the proper market value returns of the treasury portfolio, we find economically large and statistically significant interest rate exposures. This shows how accounting rules and therefore accounting returns can mask the underlying risk exposure.

The second (related) issue is that the income statement is highly managed.[5] The discrepancy between book and market equity reflects bank accounting practices that give banks discretion on when to acknowledge losses. Banks can delay acknowledging losses on their books (e.g., Laux and Leuz 2010), because banks are not required to mark-to-market the majority of their assets. There are many incentives to delay book losses. In practice, a key metric for measuring success of a bank is the book return on equity (ROE). For example, J. P. Morgan's 2016 annual report states "the Firm will continue to establish internal ROE targets for its business segments, against which they will be measured" (p. 83 of the report). Given that ROE is a measure of success, manager compensation is linked to book value performance. Moreover, shareholders and other stakeholders may base their valuations on information from book data. Finally, banks are required to meet capital standards based on book values.

---

5. Banks' annual reports include an entire section about how they manage various risks, including market risk, credit risk, and interest rate risk. So clearly, it is important to them to convey that banks are exposed to little risk. Interestingly, they discuss interest rate risk exposure in terms of earnings rather than value.

Banks' ability to "massage" their accounts is studied extensively in the accounting literature (Bushman 2016 and Acharya and Ryan 2016 review the literature on this issue). In practice, banks can record securities on the books using two methodologies: either amortized historical cost (the security is worth what it cost the bank to buy it with appropriate amortization) or fair value accounting. Fair value accounting can be done at three levels: Level 1 accounting uses quoted prices in active markets. Level 2 uses prices of similar assets as a benchmark to value assets that trade infrequently. Level 3 is based on models that do not involve market prices (e.g., a discounted cash-flow model). Banks are required to use the lowest level possible for each asset. In practice, most assets are recorded at historical cost. The majority of fair value measurements are Level 2 (Laux and Leuz 2010). Recent work has shown that the stock market values fair value assets less if they are measured using a higher level of fair value accounting. This leaves room to misprice assets on books. Particularly during 2008, Level 2 and Level 3 measures of assets were valued substantially below 1 (Goh et al. 2015; Kolev 2009; Song et al. 2010). Laux and Leuz (2010) document sizable reclassifications from Levels 1 and 2 to Level 3 during this period. They highlight the case of Citigroup, which moved $53 billion into Level 3 between the fourth quarter of 2007 and the first quarter of 2008 and reclassified $60 billion in securities as held-to-maturity which enabled Citi to use historical costs. In addition to mispricing securities, another degree of freedom is the extent to which banks can acknowledge impairments: banks have the right to delay acknowledging impairments on assets held at historical cost, if they deem those impairments as temporary (i.e., they believe the asset will return to its previous price). This gives banks substantial leeway and led banks to overvalue assets on the books during the crisis.

Huizinga and Laeven (2012) find that banks used discretion to hold real estate–related assets at values higher than their market value. Laux and Leuz (2010) note some notable cases of inflated books during the crisis: Merrill Lynch sold $30.6 billion of collateralized debt obligations for 22 cents on the dollar while the book value was 65% higher than its sale price. Similarly, Lehman Brothers wrote down its portfolio of commercial mortgage-backed securities by only 3%, even when an index of commercial MBS was falling by 10% in the first quarter of 2008. Laux and Leuz (2010) also document substantial underestimation of loan losses in comparison to external estimates.

Harris, Khan, and Nissim (2013) construct an index, based on information available in the given time period, that predicts future losses substantially better than the allowance for loan losses. The allowance for loan losses is the stock variable corresponding to the flow variable provision for loan

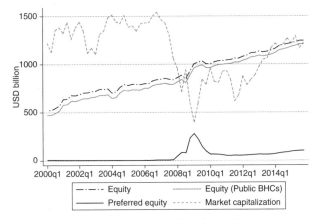

FIGURE 7.1 Aggregate book equity versus aggregate bank market equity
Source: Begenau, Bigio, Majerovitz, and Vieyra (2019).

losses. This implies that the allowance for loan losses is not capturing all of the information available to estimate losses. This may in part be strategic manipulation, but there may also be a required delay in acknowledging loan losses. Under the "incurred loss model" that was the regulatory standard during the crisis, banks are only allowed to provision for loan losses when a loss is "estimable and probable" (Harris, Khan, and Nissim 2013). Thus, even if banks know that many of their loans will eventually suffer losses, they were not supposed to update their books until the loss was imminent.

Figure 7.1 presents another important piece of evidence for banks' ability to smooth income and therefore bank equity. This figure plots market equity (market capitalization), book equity, and preferred equity for the aggregate banking sector. The banking sector is very concentrated. This implies that book equity for public BHCs (typically the largest banks) is nearly identical to the book equity for all BHCs. The figure shows that there is a large discrepancy between market and book equity. By just focusing on book equity, one would have missed that the 2008–2009 event was one of the worst financial crises of the century. The discrepancy between book and market equity cannot be explained by preferred equity, which is included in book equity but not in market capitalization. Preferred equity rose temporarily during the crisis due to the Troubled Asset Relief Program. The aggregate pattern is mainly influenced by the four largest banks (Bank of America, J. P. Morgan, Citigroup, and Wells Fargo). Citigroup (not shown here) is an extreme example of the discrepancy between book and market values. The bank lost 90% in terms of its market capitalization. But according to its book equity measure, Citigroup did just fine. Its book equity continued to grow as it had before the crisis.

Advantage Over Using Bank Stock Returns

The previous section has made the case that risk-exposure measures based on accounting returns and accounting (book) equity may not in fact capture banks' risk exposures. Figure 7.1 suggests that market equity and therefore bank stock return regressions could be used to reveal banks' true risk exposures. This has in fact been a long-standing approach to studying banks' risk exposure (e.g., Flannery and James 1984; English, Van den Heuvel, and Zakrajšek 2018). While these regressions are very useful and complementary to a replicating banks' balance-sheet approach, they rely on the assumption that the market prices banks correctly.

A piece of evidence that the market may not fully recognize banks' risk exposures is provided by table 7.2. This table presents monthly value-weighted bank stock return regressions on different factors. The market factor is the value-weighted return on the S&P 500. The term factor is the term spread between a five-year U.S. Treasury bond and the three-month U.S. Treasury bill. The investment grade credit factor (IG) is the spread between the return on an investment-grade corporate bond index and the return on a portfolio of short-term U.S. treasuries. The speculative credit factor (HY) is the spread between the return on a speculative / high yield corporate bond index and the return on a portfolio of medium-term U.S. treasuries. It shows that the largest explanatory power comes from the market factor and not from interest rate or credit-risk factors. In a longer time series, for example, going back to the early 1990s, both the credit and the interest rate slope factor come out as significant, but they do not increase the explanatory power by much. In other words, bank stocks in the aggregate trade closely to nonfinancial stocks.[6]

This could mean two things. One possibility is that banks hedged out all interest rate or credit risk exposure. This seems inconsistent with the events of the financial crisis and banks' own accounts of what and how they hedge. In particular for interest rate risk, banks state explicitly in their annual reports that they hedge earnings and not value. But movements in interest rates have the opposite implication for earnings than they have for value. When interest rates go up, banks' net-interest margins improve but the value of their portfolios declines. By stating that they hedge earnings (i.e., net-interest margins), banks' hedging activity goes in the other direction of what would be required to hedge their portfolios against interest rate movements. In the following

---

6. Table 1 in Gandhi and Lustig (2015) makes a similar point. For most banks, neither the credit factor nor the interest rate factor come out significant. If they do, the coefficient is economically small and statistically marginally significant.

TABLE 7.2 Factor exposures of aggregate value-weighted bank stock returns

Intercept	Market	Term	IG	HY	R^2/N
0.00	1.10				0.62
(−0.40)	(20.94)				264
0.00	1.1	−0.18	−0.87	0.09	0.63
(−0.09)	(15.35)	(−0.68)	(−1.38)	(0.43)	264.00

Data source: Center for Research in Security Prices. Period: 1997/01 to 2018/12.
Note: This table presents the results from regressing monthly value-weighted
bank stock returns on different factors. The market factor is the value-
weighted return on the S&P 500. The term factor is the term spread between
a five-year U.S. Treasury bond and the three-month U.S. Treasury bill. The
investment grade credit factor (IG) is the spread between the return on an
investment-grade corporate bond index and the return on a portfolio of short-
term U.S. Treasuries. The speculative credit factor (HY) is the spread between
the return on a speculative/high yield corporate bond index and the return on
a portfolio of medium-term U.S. Treasuries.

section, I provide more evidence that is inconsistent with this interpretation.
A second possibility seems to be that bank stocks are priced similarly to non-
financials stocks. That is, the bulk of the common variation is due to common
stock market movements.

Robustness of the Mimicking Portfolio Approach to Measuring Bank Risk

A key challenge of the mimicking portfolio approach to measuring the risk
of banks is that risk exposures are read off capital market objects. The entire
strength of the method relies on how closely bank positions mirror traded
capital market objects.

Begenau and Stafford (2019) show that a large share of banks' balance-sheet
items are closely mapped by maturity-matched U.S. Treasury portfolios. In
fact, only a small fraction of banks' assets (19%), trading assets, and bank services, and 40% of bank funding (i.e., transaction deposits) cannot be matched
with a U.S. Treasury portfolio or combinations of traded credit portfolios.

The fact that bank loans are well matched by a maturity and credit-risk–
matched traded capital market portfolio is especially surprising. Bank loans,
as they are typically thought of, go to borrowers that have few alternatives.
Take, for example, a business loan. Businesses borrowing from banks tend to
be smaller and unrated. For this reason, it has often been assumed that their
loan risk profile differs drastically from the risk profile of larger corporate
borrowers that can issue corporate bonds on the capital market. Figure 7.2
calls this assumption into question.

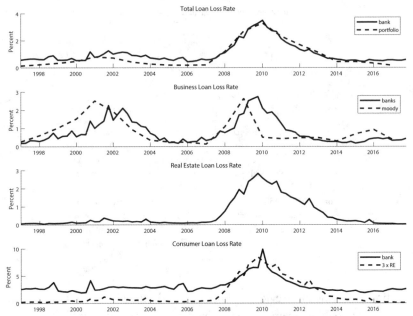

FIGURE 7.2 Comparing aggregate BHC loan losses with corporate bond loan losses

Note: This figure presents loan loss rates. The solid line represents net charge-offs (charge-offs minus recoveries) on all commercial and industrial loans of the aggregate bank holding company sector as an annualized percentage of commercial and industrial loans. The data source is FR-Y-9C. The dashed line represents the net-loss rates on a corporate bond portfolio that consists of 70% investment-grade corporate bonds and 30% speculative-grade corporate bonds.

Figure 7.2 represents aggregate loan loss rates of commercial and industrial loans made and held by banks (solid line) and corporate bonds traded in the capital market (dashed line). The solid line represents net-charge-offs (charge-offs minus recoveries) on all commercial and industrial loans of the aggregate bank holding company sector as an annualized percentage of commercial and industrial loans. The data source is FR-Y-9C. The dashed line represents the net-loss rates on a corporate bond portfolio that consists of 70% investment-grade corporate bonds and 30% speculative-grade corporate bonds. This proportion implies that the investment-grade and speculative-grade corporate bond portfolio mix has the same average loss rate as the business loans portfolio of banks.

The figure shows that the size of losses and the time series shape of both series are remarkably similar even though bank losses lag the capital market-based series. This is because banks only charge off losses once they are fully realized. But, in general, the time series pattern and size of losses are almost identical, implying that the credit risk in banks' business loans is not that different from the credit risk of a corporate bond portfolio once the average loss rate is matched.

Conclusion

How can we measure the risk of banks? This is a challenging and exciting area to work in. The literature has approached this question from different angles, from bank equity return regressions through VaR analyses, stress tests, and studying banks' accounting returns. I argue that the portfolio mimicking approach combines both market data and bank accounting data in a useful way to make progress on this question. The resulting risk measures are transparent, additive, and can be used to subject banks, their positions, or the entire system to various adverse scenarios.

REFERENCES

Acharya, Viral V., Lasse H. Pedersen, Thomas Philippon, and Matthew Richardson. 2017. Measuring Systemic Risk. Review of Financial Studies 30: 2–47.

Acharya, Viral V., and Stephen G. Ryan. 2016. Banks' Financial Reporting and Financial System Stability. Journal of Accounting Research 54: 277–340.

Adrian, Tobias, and Nina Boyarchenko. 2012. Intermediary Leverage Cycles and Financial Stability. Becker Friedman Institute for Research in Economics Working Paper 2021-010.

Ang, Andrew, and Monika Piazzesi. 2003. A No-Arbitrage Vector Autoregression of Term Structure Dynamics with Macroeconomic and Latent Variables. Journal of Monetary Economics 50: 745–87.

Begenau, Juliane, Saki Bigio, Jeremy Majerovitz, and Matias Vieyra. 2020. A Q-theory of Banks. NBER Working Paper 27935.

Begenau, Juliane, Monika Piazzesi, and Martin Schneider. 2015. Banks' Risk Exposures. NBER Working Paper 21334.

Begenau, Juliane, and Erik Stafford. 2019. Do Banks Have an Edge? Available at https://ssrn.com /abstract=3095550.

Brunnermeier, Markus K., Gary Gorton, and Arvind Krishnamurthy. 2012. Risk Topography. NBER Macroeconomics Annual 26: 149–76.

Bushman, Robert M. 2016. Transparency, Accounting Discretion, and Bank Stability. Economic Policy Review (August): 129–49.

Cochrane, John H., and Monika Piazzesi. 2005. Bond Risk Premia. American Economic Review 95: 138–60.

Drechsler, Itamar, Alexi Savov, and Philipp Schnabl. 2021. Banking on Deposits: Maturity Transformation without Interest Rate Risk. Journal of Finance 76 (3): 1091–1143.

Duffie, Darrell, and Rui Kan. 1996. A Yield-Factor Model of Interest Rates. Mathematical Finance 6: 379–406.

English, William B., Skander J. Van den Heuvel, and Egon Zakrajšek. 2018. Interest Rate Risk and Bank Equity Valuations. Journal of Monetary Economics 98: 80–97.

Flannery, Mark J., and Christopher M. James. 1984. The Effect of Interest Rate Changes on the Common Stock Returns of Financial Institutions. Journal of Finance 39: 1141–53.

Gandhi, Priyank, and Hanno Lustig. 2015. Size Anomalies in US Bank Stock Returns. Journal of Finance 70: 733–68.

Goh, Beng Wee, Dan Li, Jeffrey Ng, and Kevin O. Yong. 2015. Market Pricing of Banks' Fair Value Assets Reported under SFAS 157 since the 2008 Financial Crisis. Journal of Accounting and Public Policy 34 (2): 129–45.

Gomez, Matthieu, Augustin Landier, David Sraer, and David Thesmar. 2021. Banks' Exposure to Interest Rate Risk and the Transmission of Monetary Policy. Journal of Monetary Economics 117: 543–70.

Harris, Trevor S., Urooj Khan, and Doron Nissim. 2018. The Expected Rate of Credit Losses on Banks' Loan Portfolios. Accounting Review 93 (5): 245–71.

Hirtle, Beverly J. 1997. Derivatives, Portfolio Composition, and Bank Holding Company Interest Rate Risk Exposure. Journal of Financial Services Research 12: 243–66.

Huizinga, Harry, and Luc Laeven. 2012. Bank Valuation and Accounting Discretion during a Financial Crisis. Journal of Financial Economics 106: 614–34.

Keim, Donald B., and Robert F. Stambaugh. 1986. Predicting Returns in the Stock and Bond Markets. Journal of Financial Economics 17: 357–90.

Kolev, Kalin S., 2019. Do Investors Perceive Marking-to-Model as Marking-to-Myth? Early Evidence from FAS 157 Disclosure. Quarterly Journal of Finance 9 (2): 1950005.

Laux, Christian, and Christian Leuz. 2010. Did Fair-Value Accounting Contribute to the Financial Crisis? Journal of Economic Perspectives 24: 93–118.

Litterman, Robert, and Jose Scheinkman. 1991. Common Factors Affecting Bond Returns. Journal of Fixed Income 1: 54–61.

Meiselman, Ben S., Stefan Nagel, and Amiyatosh K. Purnanandam. 2020. Judging Banks' Risk by the Profits They Report. Available at https://ssrn.com/abstract=3169730.

Piazzesi, Monika, 2010. Affine Term Structure Models. In Handbook of Financial Econometrics: Tools and Techniques, 691–766. Amsterdam: North Holland.

Saunders, Anthony, and Pierre Yourougou. 1990. Are Banks Special? The Separation of Banking from Commerce and Interest Rate Risk. Journal of Economics and Business 42: 171–82.

Song, Chang Joon, Wayne B. Thomas, and Han Yi. 2010. Value Relevance of FAS No. 157 Fair Value Hierarchy Information and the Impact of Corporate Governance Mechanisms. Accounting Review 85 (4): 1375–1410.

Comment by Nina Boyarchenko

"A New Approach to Measuring Banks' Risk Exposure" argues that the correct way to measure the economic risk exposure of banks is to map balance-sheet components to risk-factor-mimicking portfolios. In this comment, I discuss some of the caveats to this approach, focusing on the complications created by the limited nettability between the asset and liabilities side of the bank balance sheet as well as limits-to-arbitrage more generally. Furthermore, in

Nina Boyarchenko is research officer at the Federal Reserve Bank of New York and a fellow at the Centre for Economic Policy Research.

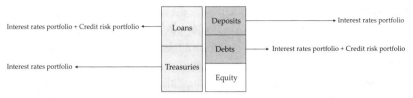

FIGURE 7C.1 Stylized representation of a bank balance sheet and mapping to risk exposures

an economy where banks are the marginal intermediary, the market prices of the risk-factor-mimicking portfolios are affected by the banks' constraints.

RISK EXPOSURE OF BANKS

What is the right way to measure the risk exposures of banks? Through accounting values, market value of bank equity, market value of bank debt? The chapter argues that the right way is to think of banks (or financial institutions more generally) as portfolios of exposures to particular sources of risk, as illustrated in figure 7C.1. That is, suppose we are interested in understanding how banks are exposed to interest rate and credit risk. Then we can think of the treasuries held on the asset side of the bank balance sheet as loading on interest rates of different maturities, loans held as loading on interest rates at different maturities and credit risk at different maturities and different ratings, deposits issued as loading on interest rates of different maturities, debt issued as loading on interest rates at different maturities and credit risk at different maturities and different ratings. The chapter shows that, for example, this approach generates a realistic time series pattern of bank loan loss rates, suggesting that this portfolio representation of bank balance sheets may be a promising approach to understanding how bank riskiness varies over time.

In my comments, I first highlight the fundamental assumptions underlying the portfolio representation approach to measuring bank risk exposures. Second, I argue that the appropriate measure of bank risk exposures is stakeholder-specific. That is, for example, bank equity holders may be interested in measuring different types of risk exposures than depositors. Finally, I discuss the connections to the intermediary asset pricing literature.

LIMITS TO ARBITRAGE

The portfolio approach to measuring bank risk exposures relies on two fundamental assumptions. The first is that there are no violations of arbitrage: two securities that provide the same risk exposure are priced the same way. This is the assumption that allows us to represent the asset side and the liabilities side of the bank balance sheet as portfolios of interest rate and credit risk exposures. The second is that the asset side and the liabilities side of the bank balance sheet are nettable: once we represent each as a portfolio of exposures, the exposure of the bank as a whole is just the difference between the asset exposures and the liabilities exposures. The second assumption will be violated if, for example, there are synergies between different banking activities, such as complementarity between deposit-taking and loan-issuing functions of a traditional commercial bank. In this comment, I would like to put aside the other potential frictions, such as active internal capital markets and differences in liquidity between asset-side and liabilities-side exposures, that would violate the nettability assumption and focus instead on the no-arbitrage assumption.

Under the classical no-arbitrage assumptions (see, e.g., Sharpe and Alexander, 1990), opportunities to simultaneously purchase and sell the same, or essentially the same, security in two different markets for advantageously different prices should not exist. Thus, an exposure to interest rate risk taken through, for example, treasury securities and the same exposure to interest rate risk taken through interest rate swaps should be priced the same. However, as noted in, for example, Shleifer and Vishny (1997), Gromb and Vayanos (2002), Liu and Longstaff (2004), and Gromb and Vayanos (2010), arbitrage trades are rarely risk-free, with institutions participating in such trades exposed to convergence risk, position financing costs, basis risk, and other sources of "limits to arbitrage." A large and growing empirical literature documents that limits to arbitrage do in fact prevent basis spread convergence.

On the equity side, Mitchell and Pulvino (2001) examine the systematic risk priced in merger arbitrage strategies while Mitchell et al. (2002) study arbitrage in situations where both the parent company and a subsidiary are publicly traded. In both of these types of equity arbitrage strategies, the papers find evidence of limits-to-arbitrage. Duarte et al. (2007) consider the alphas generated by five types of fixed-income arbitrage trades that were prevalent prior to the financial crisis and find that arbitrage trades that require the most leverage generate the highest alpha, consistent with arbitrageurs being compensated for using their limited capital.

A number of recent studies have demonstrated that regulatory constraints create limits to arbitrage for banks, perpetuating deviations from arbitrage in particular in markets in which banks are important intermediaries. Avdjiev et al. (2016) show that deviations from covered interest rate parity (CIP) are strongly correlated to the dollar financing costs of global banks. In a related paper, Du et al. (2018) argue that the expected profitability of CIP trades is much lower after proxying for banks' balance-sheet costs.

Similarly, Boyarchenko et al. (2018c) and Boyarchenko et al. (2018d) show that, after the introduction of Supplementary Leverage Ratio in the United States, the break-even levels of treasury-swaps spreads and credit bases are much lower (more negative) than prior to the crisis. Extending this intuition, Boyarchenko et al. (2018b) document that the increase in the absolute value of the basis and the decrease in the implied return-on-equity is biggest for trades that experienced the largest increases in capital requirements postcrisis. In the equity market, Jylhä (2018) shows that tighter leverage constraints—induced by changing initial margin requirements—correspond to a flatter relationship between market betas and expected returns.

In the sovereign fixed-income market, Fleckenstein and Longstaff (2018) argue that the difference between the market repo rate on U.S. treasuries and the implied repo rate from U.S. Treasury futures proxies for the balance-sheet costs of regulated institutions in the United States and shows that that spread is related to other fixed-income bases, such as the treasury-swap spread. Similarly, Pelizzon et al. (2018) study the sovereign bond futures basis for European sovereigns and argue that regulatory constraints on the banking sector prevent a market-neutral implementation of large-scale asset purchase programs.

To summarize, the recent literature on the relationship between bank regulatory constraints and deviations from no arbitrage casts doubt on the applicability of the no-arbitrage assumption in valuing elements of bank balance sheets. If banks are too constrained to narrow the equilibrium basis between treasuries and interest rate swaps, why should we expect to be able to value a bank's interest rate portfolio under the assumption that the basis is zero? Indeed, Boyarchenko et al. (2018a) document that, at least for corporate credit risk exposures, banks earn differential trading income when trading only in corporate bonds, through a combination of corporate bonds and credit default swaps (CDS), or through only CDS.

WHOSE EXPOSURES ARE WE MEASURING?

Let's take a step back from the specifics of how the portfolio approach to measuring bank risk exposures operates and consider instead whose risk exposures it measures. A bank potentially has many different types of stakeholders that care about different types of risks. For example, retail depositors, who are FDIC-insured up to the national deposit guarantee limits, may perceive any bank as being risk-free for their purposes. Wholesale depositors and other debt holders more generally are primarily concerned with bank insolvency and illiquidity risks, potentially making bank CDS spreads the appropriate measure of bank riskiness for them. Holders of publicly traded bank equity would consider measures such as the Sharpe ratio of the return on traded equity; management and other inside equity holders are concerned with return-on-equity, as well as the risk that the institution would violate a regulatory constraint. By measuring bank risk as a portfolio of exposures to interest rate and credit risk, the chapter is implicitly measuring the risk exposure of a hypothetical investor that holds the entire capital structure of the bank. That is, the portfolio approach to measuring risk exposure of banks measures the exposure of a social planner that may be required to fully replicate the bank, not of any individual stakeholder in the bank.

INTERMEDIARY ASSET PRICING

Finally, the portfolio approach to bank risk exposures has interesting and potentially complicated intersections with the intermediary asset pricing literature. In the intermediary asset pricing view (see, e.g., Fostel and Geanakoplos 2008; Brunnermeier and Pedersen 2009; Gertler and Kiyotaki 2012; He and Krishnamurthy 2012; Adrian and Boyarchenko 2012; He and Krishnamurthy 2013; Brunnermeier and Sannikov 2014, and others), financial intermediaries are marginal investors in all risky assets in the economy. Thus, risk premia and asset expected returns are determined by the relative health of the marginal financial intermediary. If we combine this with the portfolio approach to bank risk exposures, this implies that we are pricing the risk exposures using Lagrange multipliers of the same risk exposures.

From a theoretical perspective, this problem may not always have a fixed-point equilibrium. From a practical perspective, if there are only a few institutions that matter for setting asset prices—for example, the "G14" derivatives dealers for derivatives exposures—bank risk exposures measured using the portfolio approach may be just as manipulatable as accounting-based measures of exposure.

CONCLUSION

The portfolio approach to measuring bank risk exposures provides an important alternative to accounting- and market-securities-based approaches. As with the latter two approaches, however, the portfolio approach is not completely assumption-free, with violations of the no-arbitrage assumption posing one of the biggest challenges. Thus, the approach to measuring bank risk exposures proposed in the chapter is likely to be a complement, not a substitute, to previously proposed approaches in creating a holistic view of financial institution health.

REFERENCES

Adrian, Tobias, and Nina Boyarchenko. 2012. Intermediary Leverage Cycles and Financial Stability. Staff Report no. 567, Federal Reserve Bank of New York.

Avdjiev, Stefan, Wenxin Du, Catherine Koch, and Hyun S. Shin. 2016. The Dollar, Bank Leverage and the Deviation from Covered Interest Parity. Working paper, Bank for International Settlements.

Boyarchenko, Nina, Anna M. Costello, and Or Shachar. 2018a. Credit Market Choice. Staff Report no. 863, Federal Reserve Bank of New York.

Boyarchenko, Nina, Thomas M. Eisenbach, Pooja Gupta, Or Shachar, and Peter Van Tassel. 2018b. Bank-Intermediated Arbitrage. Staff Report no. 858, Federal Reserve Bank of New York.

Boyarchenko, Nina, Pooja Gupta, Nick Steele, and Jacqueline Yen. 2018c. Negative Swap Spreads. Economic Policy Review of the Federal Reserve Bank of New York 24: 1–14.

———. 2018d. Trends in Credit Market Arbitrage. Economic Policy Review of the Federal Reserve Bank of New York 24: 15–37.

Brunnermeier, Markus K., and Lasse H. Pedersen. 2009. Market Liquidity and Funding Liquidity. Review of Financial Studies 22: 2201–38.

Brunnermeier, Markus K., and Yuliy Sannikov. 2014. A Macroeconomic Model with a Financial Sector. American Economic Review 104: 379–421.

Du, Wenxin, Alexander Tepper, and Adrien Verdelhan. 2018. Deviations from Covered Interest Rate Parity. Review of Financial Studies 73: 915–57.

Duarte, Jefferson, Francis A. Longstaff, and Fan Yu. 2007. Risk and Return in Fixed-Income Arbitrage: Nickels in Front of a Steamroller? Review of Financial Studies 20: 769–811.

Fleckenstein, Matthias, and Francis A. Longstaff. 2018. Shadow Funding Costs: Measuring the Cost of Balance Sheet Constraints. NBER Working Paper 24224.

Fostel, Ana, and John Geanakoplos. 2008. Leverage Cycles and the Anxious Economy. American Economic Review 98: 1211–44.

Gertler, Mark, and Nobuhiro Kiyotaki. 2012. Banking, Liquidity, and Bank Runs in an Infinite Horizon Economy. Working paper, Princeton University and New York University.

Gromb, Denis, and Dimitri Vayanos. 2002. Equilibrium and Welfare in Markets with Financially Constrained Arbitrageurs. Journal of Financial Economics 66: 361–407.

———. 2010. A Model of Financial Market Liquidity Based on Intermediary Capital. Journal of the European Economic Association 8: 456–66.

He, Zhiguo, and Arvind Krishnamurthy. 2012. A Model of Capital and Crises. Review of Economic Studies 79: 735–77.

———. 2013. Intermediary Asset Pricing. American Economic Review 103: 732–70.

Jylhä, Petri. 2018. Margin Requirements and the Security Market Line. Journal of Finance 73: 1281–1321.

Liu, Jun, and Francis A. Longstaff. 2004. Losing Money on Arbitrage: Optimal Dynamic Portfolio Choice in Markets with Arbitrage Opportunities. Review of Financial Studies 17: 611–41.

Mitchell, Mark, and Todd Pulvino. 2001. Characteristics of Risk and Return in Risk Arbitrage. Journal of Finance 56: 2135–75.

Mitchell, Mark, Todd Pulvino, and Erik Stafford. 2002. Limited Arbitrage in Equity Markets. Journal of Finance 57: 551–84.

Pelizzon, Loriana, Marti G. Subrahmanyam, Davide Tomio, and Jun Uno. 2018. Central Bank-Driven Mispricing. Working Paper no. 226, Sustainable Architecture for Finance in Europe.

Sharpe, William E., and Gordon J. Alexander. 1990. Investments. Englewood Cliffs, NJ: Prentice Hall International.

Shleifer, Andrei, and Robert W. Vishny. 1997. The Limits of Arbitrage. Journal of Finance 52: 35–55.

8

Is Risk Mispriced in Credit Booms?

TYLER MUIR

Credit booms tend to precede financial crises (Jordà et al. 2011; Schularick and Taylor 2012). A key question is how expectations of agents and their attitudes toward risk may drive credit booms. This chapter studies how those expectations and attitudes toward risk may manifest themselves in asset prices. I take the asset pricing framework that expected risk premiums should equal quantity of risk times price of risk (e.g., "effective risk aversion") and then study how each of these channels moves in a credit boom. The main conclusion, echoing and summarizing a broader literature, is that risk premiums fall in credit booms while quantity of risk appears to rise, suggesting a very low price of risk.

I begin by summarizing, and then extending, the existing literature on credit booms, asset prices, and financial crises. In an international panel spanning seventeen countries over 140 years, credit growth negatively forecasts excess returns on housing and equity returns, meaning risk premiums are low in credit booms. The relationship is economically large: a 1 standard deviation increase in credit growth is associated with about a 2% lower expected excess return for equities and 1%–1.5% lower return for housing. Thus, as a broader literature has found, asset prices appear to be significantly elevated in credit booms and in the run-up to financial crises so that expected returns going forward are low. Krishnamurthy and Muir (2018) document low credit spreads in the years preceding a financial crisis (about 25% lower than average levels) and show that low spreads actually positively forecast crises. Baron and Xiong (2017) find that credit growth significantly negatively forecasts bank equity

Tyler Muir is associate professor of finance at the Anderson School of Management, University of California, Los Angeles.

returns, suggesting mispricing of bank equity in the lead-up to crises. Brunnermeier et al. (2019) find that high equity and real estate price rises appear
to contribute to increased systemic risk. López-Salido et al. (2017) find high
credit growth negatively predicts returns on corporate bonds.

Next, I analyze the quantity of risk channel during credit booms. High
credit growth predicts financial crises (Jordà et al. 2011; Schularick and Taylor 2012) as well as drops in economic activity (e.g., GDP) and it also predicts
heightened probability of a significant decline in asset values for multiple
broad asset classes, consistent with the work of Baron and Xiong (2017), who
focus on bank stocks. This is important because it signifies that the low-risk
premiums are not easily explained by low future risk in asset returns, that
is, by the quantity of risk channel. Taken together, low-risk premiums and
higher risk suggest that the pricing of risk (effective risk aversion in the economy) appears very low in credit booms. This is an important feature that
equilibrium asset pricing models should aim to match.

Mispricing is always difficult to cleanly document, as one needs a model
of "correct" prices (Fama 1970).[1] This chapter takes several views to think
about the possibility that risk is mispriced—and in particular underpriced
during credit booms. However, there is no definitive evidence of mispricing
without taking a stronger view on agents' effective risk aversion, which may
vary through time (e.g., low enough risk aversion from agents can rationalize
a higher quantity of risk and lower risk premium). Thus, a main open question is whether this lower effective risk aversion is due to belief distortions (so
that it reflects mispricing), or whether it is consistent with rational models of
risk pricing with time-varying risk aversion.

In my analysis, there is no "smoking gun" to rule out stories of time-
varying risk aversion without more structure: while average returns are quite
low when credit growth is high, they do not appear robustly negative. Hence,
there is still some positive price of risk that can rationalize these episodes,
so it is difficult to say definitively that there is a clear underpricing of risk.
Note that this conclusion differs from Baron and Xiong (2017), who reliably
forecast negative returns for bank stocks when credit growth is above a speci-
fied threshold (which appears inconsistent with any positive price of risk,
and hence clearly indicates mispricing), but this is because I consider equity
returns and housing returns broadly rather than just bank stocks. However,
the low-risk premiums do not seem to be driven by standard models with
time-varying risk aversion (e.g., Campbell and Cochrane 1999). This leads

---

1. See Santos and Veronesi (2018) for an example where many results can obtain in a fric-
tionless setting with time-varying risk aversion.

me to explore what factors drive credit booms and if they are instead consistent with more behavioral views of mispricing.

A main result is that low past risk in asset returns is positively associated with credit booms despite the fact that booms predict increased future risk. Putting these facts together paints a potential story for the financial crisis episode and boom-bust cycle in credit, though I don't argue it is the only potential story.

Low measures of risk in the past (e.g., low volatility of asset returns) may lead agents to view the world as safe and to be overoptimistic about risk going forward, resulting in low premiums. In doing so they may take excessive leverage, resulting in a credit boom and high asset prices. The result of this collective action is increased fragility through increased leverage and can result in higher risk ex post. This would explain why low past risk predicts credit booms, which are associated with low-risk premiums, but predict increased quantity of risk going forward (see Gennaioli et al. 2012; Greenwood et al. 2019; and Moreira and Savov 2014 for models along these lines, and similar arguments in Minsky 1977; Kindleberger and Aliber 2011; and Reinhart and Rogoff 2009). However, as with the rest of the results in this chapter, the results are meant to be suggestive, and I do not claim the regressions show that low volatility causes credit growth (see Gomes et al. 2018b or Santos and Veronesi 2018).

These results relate to the work on credit growth and crises more broadly.[2] However, the focus here is specifically on asset price movements associated with credit growth, most closely in the vein of Baron and Xiong (2017), Brunnermeier et al. (2019), López-Salido et al. (2017), and Krishnamurthy and Muir (2018). The closest paper is Baron and Xiong (2017), who focus mostly on pricing of bank stocks, though I extend much of their analysis to the broader equity market, real estate returns, and credit markets. Because this is a short chapter and this literature is large, many more relevant references are omitted to save space.

The chapter proceeds as follows. First, I outline a general framework for thinking about asset prices as linking risk premiums, quantity of risk, and price of risk. The next section describes the data, followed by documentation showing empirically that credit growth is associated with low-risk premiums

2. A nonexhaustive list includes Bordo et al. 2001; Cerra and Saxena 2008; Reinhart and Rogoff 2009; Claessens et al. 2010; Bordo and Haubrich 2012; Jordà et al. 2011; Schularick and Taylor 2012; Romer and Romer 2015 studying the aftermath of financial crises, and Schularick and Taylor 2012; Jordà et al. 2011; Baron and Xiong 2017; López-Salido et al. 2017; Mian et al. 2017 studying credit growth.

and higher future risk. I then revisit the price of risk from the perspective of standard models and consider which models best match the facts.

Framework

To better consider mispricing of risk, we need to start with a benchmark model of how agents should price risk. For simplicity, the analysis can't consider all possible models of risk pricing, though still my goal is for a simple benchmark framework that captures the main features of such models. I begin with a broad framework where risk premiums are determined by quantity and price of risk. That is,

$$(\text{Risk Premium})_t = (\text{Quantity of Risk})_t \times (\text{Price of Risk})_t$$

For example, in a classic mean-variance representative agent equilibrium, this equation would be $(\text{Risk Premium})_t = \sigma^2 \times \gamma$ where γ is the agent's risk aversion and σ_t^2 is the conditional variance of returns and measures the quantity of risk (see Merton 1980). The prediction is that, all else being equal, higher quantity of risk or higher risk aversion should lead to higher risk premiums.

For $(\text{Quantity of Risk})_t$ I consider downside risk, or risk of a crash, as the main object of interest, that is, the chance of significant drops in asset returns going forward. The crash probability captures "left tail" events and is the object of interest in models with rare disasters (Barro 2006; Wachter 2013), though it is also related to volatility or variance. I focus on real economic activity (e.g., GDP) and asset returns being below roughly the 10th percentile for each asset class as an indicator of quantity of risk. One can look at lower percentiles as well, though this gives me substantially more power in my tests. This is also strongly related to volatility of asset returns as well, so I choose to focus mainly on this indicator for the analysis.

Admittedly, the object $(\text{Price of Risk})_t$ is even harder to assess without significantly more structure due to the joint hypothesis problem (Fama 1970). That is, we need a null hypothesis on the pricing of risk to make progress. In the most basic economic models (e.g., representative agent models with CRRA preferences), the object $(\text{Price of Risk})_t$ is equal to a fixed constant γ and does not vary through time. I argue that this can't be consistent with the credit boom facts because it appears both that risk premiums fall and quantity of risk, if anything, rises. However, many models feature time-varying risk aversion. I characterize the pricing of risk behavior consistent with the data and then see how much progress can be made by comparing this to predictions of such models. Many rational models predict a positive association between the quantity of risk and risk aversion which is inconsistent with the evidence in credit booms.

Data Description

Data are from Jordà et al. (2017) who construct a database on macro quantities, including credit and GDP, together with returns for housing and equities as well as dividend yields (dividend to price) and rental yields (rent to price). The database covers seventeen advanced economies since 1870 on an annual basis (see http://www.macrohistory.net/data/). I omit summary statistics or other descriptive statistics to save space. The data set also includes dates for financial crises—periods where the banking system suffered large losses, bank runs, and bank failures. Return data are winsorized at the 0.1% level. This has implications only for equity returns where the nonwinsorized data show one or two major outliers (in particular, Germany in the early 1920s shows equity returns of several thousand percent, which I remove).

I study excess returns as the (log) returns minus the (log) risk-free rate taken as the short-term interest rate in each country. Excess log returns are of interest because this measures the risk premium, but practically this also deals with the fact that returns are given in nominal units and are in different currencies and the log excess returns net these effects out. I also construct real per capita GDP growth and define credit to GDP as the log of total loans divided by GDP (both nominal). I consider three- and five-year changes in credit to GDP as measures of credit growth, that is, of indicators that credit in the economy is growing.

I supplement these data with data on credit spreads from Krishnamurthy and Muir (2018), though these data do not allow me to construct credit returns. The main reason is that I don't have data on observed defaults so we can't assess the actual returns from spreads alone. Still, I will use the spread as a proxy for expected returns in keeping with a longer literature that finds variation in credit spreads is driven more by risk premiums rather than by default (see Giesecke et al. 2012). Another limitation of the credit spread (and quantity data) is that at the aggregate level it doesn't allow me to study cross-sectional dispersion in credit quality per Gomes et al. (2018a).

In all regressions below I include a dummy for pre- and postwar data, that is, I include a dummy that takes the value of 1 after 1945. This is important in capturing different means of returns and differences in economic growth rates before and after this period. Further, I include country-fixed effects to account for cross-country differences in means. Finally, I drop the major world wars (1914–1918 and 1939–1945) from the analysis.

Empirical Analysis

PREDICTING RISK AND RETURNS IN CREDIT BOOMS

Table 8.1 regresses future excess returns for housing and equities on lags of credit growth. I use cumulative returns over three years for both housing and equities, though one-year returns give qualitatively similar results. I construct credit to GDP following Schularick and Taylor (2012) and consider the level of credit to GDP, as well as the three- and five-year changes in this variable. In addition, I consider controls for the predictive regressions which include the equity dividend yield and housing rental yield (rent to price) as both are known forecasters of returns, as well as country-fixed effects and a dummy for the postwar period (post 1945). The point here is not to say that credit growth drives out these predictors but to assess if it has some additional forecasting power beyond these variables.

In both cases, credit growth strongly negatively forecasts returns. That is, credit booms are followed by lower than average stock and housing returns. This result is robust to including the asset class predictors (equity dividend yield and housing rental yield). Returns are in percent and credit growth is standardized in all cases, so the coefficients represent the drop in risk premiums from a 1 standard deviation change in credit growth. The results are economically large: for equity returns, a 1 standard deviation change in credit growth implies about 2% lower excess returns, while for housing the coefficient implies about a 1% drop (unconditional excess equity and housing returns are both around 5%, so this is high relative to the mean).

While intriguing, nothing in these regressions rules out, or even addresses, a basic risk-based story. Perhaps credit booms predict low returns because they also predict low risk. That is, if periods of high credit growth are associated with safer future returns, then it makes sense that investors would require low premiums for holding these assets. In the language of the framework earlier, perhaps the quantity of risk drops to explain the fall in risk premiums, leaving the pricing of risk unchanged.

Table 8.2 indicates that this is not the case. Panel A runs regressions of financial crisis indicators on credit growth, confirming the findings of Jordà et al. (2011) who find high credit growth predicts financial crises (similar results are found using probit or logit specifications, though I stick to ordinary least squares [OLS] for this analysis). Thus credit growth is associated with high future macroeconomic risk, possibly due to fragility created by leverage in the credit growth episode. Panels B and C run regressions of future crashes

TABLE 8.1 Forecasting excess returns with credit growth

	(1)	(2)	(3)	(4)	(5)	(6)
A. Predicting equity excess returns						
credit/gdp	−2.01			−1.40		
	(0.98)			(0.91)		
Δ_3(credit/gdp)		−2.26			−2.47	
		(0.71)			(0.80)	
Δ_5(credit/gdp)			−1.99			−2.41
			(0.68)			(0.77)
dividend yield				1.93	2.07	2.13
				(0.37)	(0.41)	(0.40)
N	1,614	1,588	1,561	1,546	1,521	1,496
R^2	0.05	0.07	0.07	0.10	0.13	0.13
B. Predicting housing excess returns						
credit/gdp	−1.60			−0.45		
	(0.38)			(0.30)		
Δ_3(credit/gdp)		−0.98			−0.49	
		(0.29)			(0.27)	
Δ_5(credit/gdp)			−1.26			−0.66
			(0.34)			(0.31)
rental yield				1.54	1.54	1.53
				(0.19)	(0.19)	(0.19)
N	1,401	1,384	1,367	1,394	1,377	1,361
R^2	0.17	0.16	0.17	0.31	0.31	0.31

Note: I run predictive regressions of returns on lagged credit to GDP across countries. I consider the level of credit to GDP as well as three- and five-year changes. As dependent variables I use the equity risk premium and housing risk premium over a three-year period (each computed as log total return over short-term interest rates). Standard errors in parentheses are double clustered by country and time.

(a crash in any of the next three years) in equity and housing returns over the following three years (again, using one-year results produces qualitatively similar results). I define "crashes" for equities as a dummy indicator of returns being below −20% in a given year. This occurs in about 10% of the years in my sample, so should not be viewed as an abnormally large crash. Similarly, a housing crash is defined as housing returns being below −5%—the lower threshold is due to the lower standard deviation of housing returns, though this definition also means a housing crash occurs in about 10% of the years in the sample. More severe crashes give fairly similar results though the trade-off is that there are then fewer observations.

A 1 standard deviation increase in credit growth suggests a crash over the next three years is about 10% more likely (slightly smaller for equities and slightly larger for housing, depending on controls). These results echo

TABLE 8.2 Forecasting crises and crashes with credit growth

	(1)	(2)	(3)	(4)	(5)	(6)
A. Predicting financial crises						
credit/gdp	4.94			4.32		
	(1.95)			(2.28)		
Δ_3(credit/gdp)		5.58			6.45	
		(1.26)			(1.24)	
Δ_5(credit/gdp)			4.58			5.51
			(1.16)			(1.22)
dividend yield				0.10	−0.31	−0.25
				(1.05)	(1.04)	(1.07)
rental yield				−1.55	−1.96	−1.94
				(0.82)	(0.83)	(0.82)
N	2,114	2,030	1,978	1,531	1,499	1,481
R^2	0.06	0.08	0.07	0.07	0.10	0.09
B. Predicting equity crashes						
credit/gdp	10.00			7.11		
	(4.87)			(4.78)		
Δ_3(credit/gdp)		7.23			8.41	
		(2.68)			(2.87)	
Δ_5(credit/gdp)			4.65			5.84
			(2.03)			(2.39)
dividend yield				−7.56	−8.14	−8.35
				(1.63)	(1.81)	(1.80)
N	1,671	1,645	1,618	1,598	1,573	1,548
R^2	0.08	0.08	0.08	0.12	0.12	0.12
C. Predicting housing crashes						
credit/gdp	9.16			0.85		
	(4.51)			(4.75)		
Δ_3(credit/gdp)		12.11			8.71	
		(3.37)			(3.63)	
Δ_5(credit/gdp)			13.77			9.63
			(3.75)			(4.06)
rental yield				−11.37	−10.72	−10.89
				(3.27)	(3.29)	(3.33)
N	1,445	1,428	1,411	1,438	1,421	1,405
R^2	0.09	0.11	0.12	0.16	0.18	0.18

Note: I run predictive regressions of crash and crisis indicators (defined as a financial crisis in the next three years or a crash in returns in the next three years) on lagged credit to GDP across countries. I consider the level of credit to GDP as well as three- and five-year changes. Standard errors in parentheses are double clustered by country and time.

the findings in Baron and Xiong (2017), who use similar dummies to assess credit growth on crash risk and find elevated probability of a crash following high credit growth. We thus see for both housing and equity returns that credit growth has information for the left tail of the return distribution: a crash is more likely if credit growth is high. This gets directly at the rare disaster-type story and suggests that low-risk premiums during credit booms are not only reflecting the likelihood of a crash. Of course, it does not say that time-varying risk premiums more generally (e.g., outside credit booms) don't relate to agents' view of disaster probabilities.

Table 8.3 repeats this analysis using declines in consumption and GDP over the next three years where a significant drop is defined as consumption

TABLE 8.3 Forecasting consumption and GDP drops with credit growth

	(1)	(2)	(3)	(4)	(5)	(6)
A. Predicting GDP declines						
credit/gdp	3.50			1.28		
	(3.73)			(4.04)		
Δ_3(credit/gdp)		5.41			4.51	
		(2.54)			(2.73)	
Δ_5(credit/gdp)			5.02			3.97
			(2.35)			(2.72)
dividend yield				0.47	0.27	0.20
				(1.74)	(1.71)	(1.86)
rental yield				−2.94	−2.75	−3.09
				(1.75)	(1.82)	(1.82)
N	1,882	1,853	1,824	1,412	1,396	1,382
R^2	0.16	0.17	0.18	0.14	0.15	0.16
B. Predicting consumption declines						
credit/gdp	4.67			0.90		
	(3.86)			(4.50)		
Δ_3(credit/gdp)		6.70			6.09	
		(3.09)			(3.46)	
Δ_5(credit/gdp)			6.32			4.77
			(3.97)			(4.77)
dividend yield				3.27	3.35	3.12
				(1.51)	(1.41)	(1.48)
rental yield				−5.41	−4.94	−5.22
				(2.51)	(2.31)	(2.33)
N	1,825	1,799	1,772	1,389	1,373	1,359
R^2	0.23	0.23	0.23	0.23	0.24	0.24

Note: I run predictive regressions of an indicator for a substantial decline in consumption and GDP (defined as a significant drop in each series in the next three years) on lagged credit to GDP across countries. I consider the level of credit to GDP as well as three- and five-year changes and include controls for dividend yields and rental yields. Standard errors in parentheses are double clustered by country and time.

or GDP growth being below 2.5% (again this threshold is chosen to represent about the 10th percentile for both series). For GDP, higher credit growth signifies an elevated chance of a decline. For consumption, the results also go in the same direction, though they are notably noisier.

Taken together, both results indicate credit booms are associated with lower average returns but effectively more risk in terms of a more spread-out distribution of returns with increased probability of a downside event in terms of returns, a financial crisis, or a decline in consumption or GDP. These results suggest a standard risk story alone is unlikely in driving the predictability results; one needs variation in the pricing of risk or risk aversion to account for these facts.

I next summarize the behavior of credit spreads during credit expansions and preceding crises. I then turn to risk premium stories where the pricing of risk, rather than its quantity, varies over time due to changes in effective risk aversion of agents.

CREDIT SPREAD DATA

I use data from Krishnamurthy and Muir (2018) on credit spreads for the same set of countries, though the data set is much more limited than what is presented here. The data constructs the equivalent of riskier (higher yield) bonds over government bonds for the same set of countries, thus giving a sense of the pricing of credit risk.

I provide evidence straight from the tables in Krishnamurthy and Muir (2018) which in many ways echoes the above findings and is presented in table 8.4. First, credit spreads before a financial crisis are low, around 23% lower than their average as shown in the table. Importantly, we control for a postcrisis dummy as well, which is equal to 1 in the five years after a crisis. This means the precrisis dummy should be judged relative to other "normal times" and is not mechanically low because spreads during crises are high.

Second, the flip side of this result is that low spreads (in conjunction with high credit growth) are a significant predictor of financial crises. That is, periods where credit grows strongly and risk premiums in credit markets are low suggest a significantly higher chance of a crisis going forward.

This is notable for a few reasons. First, though we don't observe data on realized defaults, it is reasonable to assume that, if anything, they increase during financial crises. That implies that the low spreads before a crisis are not easily reconciled by the expected default channel. This implies—just as in the other asset price data seen so far—that the credit risk premium is low and

TABLE 8.4 Spreads before a crisis

	(1)	(2)	(3)
$1_{t-5,t-1}$	−0.23		
	(0.11)		
$1_{t-5,t-1} \times$ Severe		−0.43	
		(0.20)	
$1_{t-5,t-1} \times$ Mild		−0.18	
		(0.11)	
$1_{t-5,t-1} \times \Delta Credit_{t-1}$			−1.58
			(0.72)
$\Delta Credit_{t-1}$	0.98	0.92	1.18
	(0.58)	(0.52)	(0.70)
ΔGDP_{t-1}	−0.16	−0.18	−0.22
	(1.68)	(1.68)	(1.54)
Observations	621	621	621
R^2	0.40	0.40	0.40
Country FE	Y	Y	Y
Year FE	Y	Y	Y

Note: This table is reproduced from Krishnamurthy and Muir (2018).
Are spreads before a crisis too low? We run regressions of our normalized spreads on a dummy which takes the value 1 in the five years before
a financial crisis (labeled $1_{t-5,t-1}$) in order to assess whether spreads going
into a crisis are low. Importantly, we control for a postcrisis dummy as
well, which is equal to 1 in the five years after a crisis. For the interpretation, this means the precrisis dummy should be judged relative to other
"normal times" and is not mechanically low because spreads during crises
are high. We show the univariate results, as well as the results controlling
for time-fixed effects. We then add changes in credit growth and GDP to
control for fundamentals that could drive spreads. We then split this result
by severe versus mild crises based on the median drop in GDP in a crisis.
It thus asks whether spreads are especially low before crises which are
particularly severe. Standard errors clustered by country in parentheses.

the quantity of risk is high in the lead-up to a crisis. This would imply that the
pricing of risk is especially low.

Second, credit spreads appear to decouple from fundamentals in these
periods. More specifically, in our paper we regress credit spreads regressed on
GDP growth and other variables that track the macroeconomy and correlate
with spreads. We take the residual from this regression as the "abnormal"
spread. The information in predicting crises seems to come from the abnormal spread piece—that is, crises are especially likely when abnormal spreads
appear low. Again, this suggests a pricing of risk channel that is distinct from
the usual channels we consider to be driving macroeconomic measures of
risk pricing.

PRICING OF RISK IN CREDIT BOOMS

Taken together, these results suggest that the object (Risk Premium)$_t$ is lower during credit booms. Further, the evidence is that the object (Quantity of Risk)$_t$ does not appear to be lower during credit booms, and in most of the specifications appears to be higher if anything. Thus, from the framework (Risk Premium)$_t$ = (Quantity of Risk)$_t$ × (Price of Risk)$_t$, it appears that the price of risk must be substantially lower in credit booms. This is important because it indicates that one cannot easily view asset price behavior in these episodes from the view of a constant risk aversion type of model.

Is this low pricing of risk rational or does it reflect "mispricing" in the sense that risk is underpriced during these episodes? This is hard to fully gauge as one needs a model for what the price of risk should be (the "Joint Hypothesis Problem"; Fama 1970). A leading theory is the habits model (Campbell and Cochrane 1999) where risk premiums are low when the economy is booming and specifically when consumption growth in the past has been high. If credit booms are associated with economic booms in general, it is therefore natural that risk premiums could be low in such episodes.

To assess this issue, I next see whether the results change if I include past GDP growth or consumption growth in the regressions as a proxy for the time-varying risk aversion coming from a Campbell and Cochrane (1999) model. In that model, surplus consumption (defined as cumulative consumption relative to a habit level) drives risk premiums where high surplus consumption implies low effective risk aversion (though it is worth noting in the main calibration of their model this also implies low asset volatility going forward, which we don't appear to see in credit booms). I consider cumulative GDP growth over the past five years as a control in the predictive regressions (past lags beyond this don't appear to change the results, nor does including lags of GDP growth individually by year). This is imperfect, though the results indicate that credit growth continues to provide about the same forecasting power as before (results are omitted to save space, though see Muir 2017 for a more in-depth treatment using consumption data rather than GDP and considering other models with time-varying risk aversion). Hence, there is no indication that the price of risk is low in credit booms simply because the economy has been strong in the credit boom episodes. It is also worth noting that these predictions are at odds with models of intermediation and financial frictions driving risk premiums (He and Krishnamurthy 2013) because those models generally predict higher risk premiums when the likelihood of a crisis is high. Those models do, however, well describe the behavior of risk premiums during a financial crisis episode (see Muir 2017).

A full answer to the mispricing story would make even weaker assumptions on the rational pricing of risk. In particular, Baron and Xiong (2017) use the weak restriction that in standard asset pricing models (Price of Risk)$_t \geq 0$. That is, risky assets always deserve a weakly positive premium. They then show that high thresholds of credit growth (e.g., above the 95th percentile) actually forecast negative returns, violating the above inequality. However, they show this primarily for bank stock returns. In the housing and equity return data that I have available, this prediction doesn't appear to be true. If I condition on credit growth being above 1.5 standard deviations above its mean (but condition on no other factors), I find mean returns for stocks to be about −1% (not statistically significant) and for housing to be about 2%, where both have unconditional average returns near 5%. Thus, there is evidence that mean returns are quite low following a credit boom and even negative for equities. Further, given the increased risk associated with these episodes, this would imply a much lower price of risk than average. However, it does not provide any "smoking gun" evidence for mispricing since the average returns are not reliably negative in a statistical sense.

In summary, I don't find direct evidence for the idea that the price of risk inferred from models of time-varying risk aversion explains why credit growth predicts returns with a negative coefficient. However, using weak restrictions on prices of risk does not lead me to the conclusion that risk is clearly underpriced either.

To make more progress on this issue, I turn to explicit models of mispricing to assess whether they are able to account for these facts, and specifically I analyze behavioral stories where agents extrapolate from past returns.

BEHAVIORAL STORIES WITH RETURN EXTRAPOLATION

I explore whether extrapolation from past returns can help us understand credit booms (Barberis et al. 2015; Malmendier and Nagel 2011). That is, perhaps agents see high past returns and then view future returns as being high. This may lead them to push up prices even further and possibly to take on more risk. Are credit booms associated with high past returns in the data? I find mixed results. Regressions of credit growth on cumulative asset returns over the past five years don't provide strong evidence for this channel.

Column (1) of table 8.5 presents these results where I regress future credit growth over the coming five years on lags of GDP growth and returns over the previous five years. There is not much evidence that high returns are associated with high future credit growth. This cuts against the extrapolation

TABLE 8.5 What drives credit growth?

	(1)	(2)	(3)	(4)
Past GDP growth	0.58		0.73	0.49
	(0.46)		(0.48)	(0.46)
Past equity returns	0.10		0.08	0.11
	(0.07)		(0.08)	(0.07)
Past housing returns	−0.14		−0.11	−0.10
	(0.19)		(0.18)	(0.18)
Past GDP volatility		0.08	−0.39	
		(0.39)	(0.41)	
Past equity volatility		−1.91	−1.63	
		(0.79)	(0.75)	
Past housing volatility		−13.52	−3.75	
		(20.11)	(21.34)	
Past equity crash				−0.03
				(0.02)
Past housing crash				−0.06
				(0.02)
Past financial crisis				−0.09
				(0.02)
Observations	1,275	1,275	1,275	1,275
R^2	0.09	0.09	0.10	0.13

Note: This table runs regressions of credit growth over five years on lags of GDP growth
and returns over the trailing five years to see if credit growth is high following a period of
high economic growth or high returns in asset markets (column 1). Columns 2 and 3 repeat
this exercise but instead use trailing volatility of each of these series to see if low volatility is
associated with high future credit growth. Column 4 uses dummies for whether there has
been a crash in equity markets or housing markets or a financial crisis over the past five
years. The result is that periods of low risk are associated with higher credit growth whereas
high past growth or high returns themselves do not appear to be. Standard errors in parentheses are double clustered by country and time.

story based on past experience of good times as being associated with low
pricing of risk, high credit growth, and lower future risk premiums.

DRIVERS OF CREDIT GROWTH AND LOW VOLATILITY

I now explore the idea that low volatility is a key driver of credit booms. The
idea is that if the economy looks relatively safe, then agents may view the
quantity of risk to be low (overoptimism), leading them to take excess risk
in the form of leverage and also driving risk premiums down. This increased
borrowing can generate a credit boom. What I have in mind, however, is that
the act of taking leverage generates endogenous risk which is not properly

accounted for since high leverage can lead to more fragility in the system (see Gennaioli et al. 2012). Thus, even though things look fairly safe, they may actually be fairly risky through the fragility created by leverage.

To assess this story, I run regressions of future credit growth on lags of volatility in GDP growth, stock returns, and housing returns over the trailing five years. The main prediction is that low volatility positively predicts credit growth. Table 8.5 columns (2) and (3) present these results, which are mixed to some extent. Equity market volatility is associated with future credit growth, meaning low equity volatility is associated with a credit boom. Similarly, past crashes in asset markets for both equity and housing are negatively associated with credit growth, as is past incidence of a crisis.

These regressions support the idea that perhaps agents extrapolate the quantity of risk dimension. That is, suppose agents base their expectations on the quantity of risk based on past experience. Then it seems natural they will take more leverage and borrow and lend more aggressively, possibly resulting in a credit boom. However, this could lead to more fragility from the resulting higher leverage and actually generate more risk in the future. Thus, the objective quantity of risk going forward could be high even though things have looked safe in the past. This would mean the agents' subjective view of the quantity of risk is below the true objective quantity of risk going forward through the channel of endogenous actions. This would then show up empirically as an abnormally low price of risk in credit booms. While more work would be needed to fully flesh out this channel, the results here indicate this may be a promising avenue. Models consistent with this view include Gennaioli et al. (2012), who study neglected risk, Moreira and Savov (2014), who study an agent who learns about disaster probabilities over time, and Greenwood et al. (2019).

RISK PREMIUMS AFTER A CRISIS

So far, the analysis documents low-risk premiums during high credit growth periods and in the run-up to financial crises. I now study the behavior of risk premiums after a financial crisis. The results presented here mirror those in Muir (2017), though using slightly different data on dividend yields and rental yields over somewhat different countries to be consistent with the analysis presented in the rest of this chapter. However, the conclusions are the same. Specifically, I run regressions of the dividend yield, rental yield, and credit spreads on an indicator for whether there was a financial crisis in the last five years. I control for five lags of GDP growth in the regressions as well. This is very important because it helps differentiate whether financial crises are "special" for risk premiums or not. That is, if risk premiums just go

TABLE 8.6 Risk premiums after a financial crisis

	(1) Dividend yield	(2) Rental yield	(3) Credit spread
Crisis past five years	0.28	0.15	0.31
	(0.10)	(0.13)	(0.13)
Observations	1,628	1,437	682
R^2	0.31	0.57	0.14

Note: I run regressions of measures of risk premiums for stocks, housing, and credit, on a dummy equal to 1 if a financial crisis has occurred in the last five years. Included are lags of each variable before the crisis began (e.g., five-year lags), as well as GDP growth for each of the last five years. The latter is important in distinguishing financial crises from other bad times like recessions. In particular, the coefficient below indicates how high-risk premiums are even controlling for the fact that GDP growth is low through a financial crisis. Standard errors in parentheses are double clustered by country and time.

up when the economy is doing poorly, and financial crises are just instances where the macroeconomy declines, then the rise in premiums may have little to do with the crisis. Other analysis pursued in Muir (2017) includes recession dummies to compare the financial crises, whereas here I just include GDP declines directly in the analysis though this produces similar results. Thus, one can't explain the increase in risk premiums during financial crises just through the lens of the economy doing poorly. This result supports models of risk premiums in crisis episodes such as He and Krishnamurthy (2013).

Table 8.6 gives the results. We see significant increases in the dividend yield and credit spreads after a crisis of close to 30%. The point estimate for rental yields suggests an increase though this is not statistically significant.

These results paint a clearer picture of the earlier observations: financial crises are preceded by credit growth which is associated with low-risk premiums. Hence, asset prices are high leading into a crisis and credit spreads are low. However, these effects on risk premiums dramatically shift after the crisis begins, and spreads and risk premiums appear to rise substantially (which also means prices and realized returns will fall dramatically). This would not speak to pricing of risk stories if crises themselves were not predictable, though the evidence indicates that they are. This is also in keeping with the quantity of risk facts that high credit growth appears to predict both low mean returns as well as heightened chances of a significant decline in asset values. Further, it suggests that agents update their view on risk following crisis episodes. These results put more structure on the time-varying risk aversion stories, as risk aversion needs to fluctuate substantially to be very low in the lead-up to a crisis and then spike to high levels following a crisis. The dramatic shift in risk premiums is also consistent with agents significantly updating beliefs in a crisis as in the behavioral models mentioned earlier.

Conclusion

This chapter studies the pricing of risk during credit booms by studying the behavior of equities, housing, and credit spreads in these episodes. It summarizes and echoes much of the empirical work on asset prices in credit market booms. First, credit growth negatively predicts asset market returns for stocks and housing and is associated with low credit spreads before a financial crisis. These results all indicate low-risk premiums in a credit boom. However, at the same time, the quantity of risk, defined by considering left tail events in returns, appears to rise during credit booms.

The way to square these facts is with the pricing of risk by agents in the economy: that is, by effective risk aversion in the economy being abnormally low in credit booms. Because the risk premium falls and risk itself rises, effective risk aversion needs to fall substantially to reconcile the evidence. This provides an important piece of evidence for asset pricing models aimed at explaining these episodes. Using only the restriction that effective risk aversion must be positive, I cannot definitively rule out a risk pricing story because the evidence doesn't support reliable forecasts of negative returns, only that returns are well below average in credit expansions. At the same time, there is not strong evidence of time-varying risk aversion from typical structural asset pricing models that match the data. Thus, whether the evidence points to behavioral biases or low rational effective risk aversion remains open. The results do support the idea of neglected risk (Gennaioli et al. 2012, among others) and suggests neglected risk may come from low past risk (rather than, say, high past returns). In particular, because low asset volatility in part predicts credit growth, a potential explanation is that agents update their views on risk based on the past and are overoptimistic about risk going forward. This could lead them to take excessive risk, resulting in fragility and raising the future likelihood of a bad event. At the same time, it could explain why risk premiums appear low in credit booms. While more work would be needed to fully flesh out this channel, the results here indicate this may be a promising avenue for future work.

REFERENCES

Barberis, Nicholas, Robin Greenwood, Lawrence Jin, and Andrei Shleifer. 2015. X-CAPM: An Extrapolative Capital Asset Pricing Model. Journal of Financial Economics 115 (1): 1–24.

Baron, Matthew, and Wei Xiong. 2017. Credit Expansion and Neglected Crash Risk. Quarterly Journal of Economics 132 (2): 713–64.

Barro, Robert J. 2006. Rare Disasters and Asset Markets in the Twentieth Century. Quarterly Journal of Economics 121 (3): 823–66.

Bordo, Michael, Barry Eichengreen, Daniela Klingebiel, and Maria Soledad Martinez-Peria. 2001. Is the Crisis Problem Growing More Severe? Economic Policy 16 (32): 51–82.

Bordo, Michael D., and Joseph G. Haubrich. 2012. Deep Recessions, Fast Recoveries, and Financial Crises: Evidence from the American Record. NBER Working Paper 18194.

Brunnermeier, Markus K., Simon C Rother, and Isabel Schnabel. 2019. Asset Price Bubbles and Systemic Risk. NBER Working Paper 25775.

Campbell, John Y., and John Cochrane. 1999. By Force of Habit: A Consumption-Based Explanation of Aggregate Stock Market Behavior. Journal of Political Economy 107 (2): 205–51.

Cerra, Valerie, and Sweta Chaman Saxena. 2008. Growth Dynamics: The Myth of Economic Recovery. American Economic Review 98 (1): 439–57.

Claessens, Stijn, M. Ayhan Kose, and Marco E. Terrones. 2010. The Global Financial Crisis: How Similar? How Different? How Costly? Journal of Asian Economics 21 (3): 247–64.

Fama, Eugene F. 1970. Efficient Capital Markets: A Review of Theory and Empirical Work. Journal of Finance 25 (2): 383–417.

Gennaioli, Nicola, Andrei Shleifer, and Robert Vishny. 2012. Neglected Risks, Financial Innovation, and Financial Fragility. Journal of Financial Economics 104 (3): 452–68. Market Institutions, Financial Market Risks and Financial Crisis.

Giesecke, Kay, Francis A. Longstaff, Stephen Schaefer, and Ilya Strebulaev. 2012. Macroeconomic Effects of Corporate Bond Default Crises: A Long-Term Perspective. NBER Working Paper 17854.

Gomes, Joaõ F., Marco Grotteria, and Jessica Wachter. 2018a. Cyclical Dispersion in Expected Defaults. Review of Financial Studies 32 (4): 1275–1308.

———. 2018b. Foreseen Risks. NBER Working Paper 25277.

Greenwood, Robin, Samuel G. Hanson, and Lawrence J. Jin. 2019. Reflexivity in Credit Markets. NBER Working Paper 25747.

He, Zhiguo, and Arvind Krishnamurthy. 2013. Intermediary Asset Pricing. American Economic Review 103 (2): 732–70.

Jordà, Òscar, Moritz Schularick, and Alan M. Taylor. 2011. Financial Crises, Credit Booms, and External Imbalances: 140 Years of Lessons. IMF Economic Review 59 (2): 340–78.

———. 2017. Macrofinancial History and the New Business Cycle Facts. NBER Macroeconomics Annual 31 (1): 213–63.

Kindleberger, Charles P., and Robert Z. Aliber. 2011. Manias, Panics and Crashes: A History of Financial Crises. London: Palgrave Macmillan.

Krishnamurthy, Arvind, and Tyler Muir. 2017. How Credit Cycles across a Financial Crisis. NBER Working Paper 23850.

López-Salido, David, Jeremy C. Stein, and Egon Zakrajšek. 2017. Credit-Market Sentiment and the Business Cycle. Quarterly Journal of Economics 132 (3): 1373–1426.

Malmendier, Ulrike, and Stefan Nagel. 2011. Depression Babies: Do Macroeconomic Experiences Affect Risk Taking? Quarterly Journal of Economics 126 (1): 373–416.

Merton, Robert C., 1980. On Estimating the Expected Return on the Market: An Exploratory Investigation. Journal of Financial Economics 8 (4): 323–61.

Mian, Atif, Amir Sufi, and Emil Verner. 2017. Household Debt and Business Cycles Worldwide. Quarterly Journal of Economics 132 (4): 1755–1817.

Minsky, Hyman P. 1977. The Financial Instability Hypothesis: An Interpretation of Keynes and an Alternative to "Standard" Theory. Challenge 20 (1): 20–27.

Moreira, Alan, and Alexi Savov. 2014. The Macroeconomics of Shadow Banking. NBER Working Paper 20335.

Muir, Tyler. 2017. Financial Crises and Risk Premia. Quarterly Journal of Economics 132 (2): 765–809.

Reinhart, Carmen M., and Kenneth S. Rogoff. 2009. This Time Is Different: Eight Centuries of Financial Folly. Princeton, NJ: Princeton University Press.

Romer, Christina D., and David H. Romer. 2015. New Evidence on the Impact of Financial Crises in Advanced Countries. NBER Working Paper 21021.

Santos, Tano, and Pietro Veronesi. 2018. Leverage. Columbia Business School Research Paper No. 17–1.

Schularick, Moritz, and Alan M. Taylor. 2012. Credit Booms Gone Bust: Monetary Policy, Leverage Cycles, and Financial Crises, 1870–2008. American Economic Review 102 (2): 1029–61.

Wachter, Jessica A. 2013. Can Time-Varying Risk of Rare Disasters Explain Aggregate Stock Market Volatility? Journal of Finance 68 (3): 987–1035.

PART FOUR

Financial Crises:
Reconsidering the Origins and Consequences

9

Historical Banking Crises:
A New Database and a Reassessment of
Their Incidence and Severity

MATTHEW BARON AND DANIEL DIECKELMANN

What Do We *Not* Know about Historical Banking Crises?

A large and well-known body of research (e.g., Reinhart and Rogoff 2009; Schularick and Taylor 2012; Laeven and Valencia 2013, 2020) studies banking crises of the past to better understand why they occur and how to prevent them in the future. Given this extensive literature, it may be tempting to think that the study of historical banking crises is on relatively solid foundations.

Readers outside this field will therefore likely be surprised that there is considerable disagreement over basic questions, even such as when historical banking crises happened. In a recent paper, Baron, Verner, and Xiong (2021)—hereafter abbreviated BVX—show that the existing classifications often disagree, sometimes drastically, on which episodes are banking crises. Table 9.1, reproduced from BVX, shows that, in Germany, for example, there is striking disagreement when one lines up six prominent banking crisis chronologies. BVX show that this disagreement also arises for many other countries in their sample. These six prominent narrative-based approaches, which BVX collectively refer to as the set of "narrative crises," are Bordo et al. (2001), Caprio and Klingebiel (2003), Demirgüç-Kunt and Detragiache (2005), Reinhart and Rogoff (2009), Schularick and Taylor (2012), and Laeven and Valencia (2013, 2020). Their inability to agree on the incidence of banking crises calls into question whether many of the episodes from these chronologies are indeed banking crises. As banking crises may be quite heterogeneous in

---

Matthew Baron is assistant professor of finance at the Johnson Graduate School of Management, Cornell University. Daniel Dieckelmann is a financial stability expert at the European Central Bank. The views expressed in this chapter are those of the authors alone and do not necessarily represent the views of the European Central Bank.

TABLE 9.1 Narrative-based banking crises in Germany

Reinhart Rogoff	Schularick Taylor	Laeven Valencia	Bordo et al.	Caprio Klingebiel	Demirgüç-Kunt Detragiache
0	1873				
1880	0				
1891	1891		0		
1901	1901		1901		
0	1907		0		
1925	0		0		
1929	1931		1931		
1977	0	0	0	late 1970s	
2008	2008	2008		0	

Note: This table, reproduced from Baron, Verner, and Xiong (2021), illustrates disagreement among narrative-based chronologies regarding the occurrence of historical banking crises, focusing on the case of Germany (similar results hold for other countries; see appendix table 1 in Baron, Verner, and Xiong 2021). It lists the occurrence of banking crises according to six prominent papers. Years listed correspond to the starting year of the banking crisis, according to each paper. A zero means that the source reports no banking crisis in a given year, while a blank cell means that the crisis is not covered in the sample period. Note that Demirgüç-Kunt and Detragiache (2005) focus on the period 1980–2002 and do not report any crises for Germany during this period.

their characteristics (featuring a mix or absence of bank runs, bank failures, nonperforming loans, credit contractions, government policy interventions, etc.), how do we best define a banking crisis? And with different severities of these characteristics, what threshold should we use to distinguish between major crises, minor crises, and no crises? These issues are difficult to solve because many of these prior narrative approaches, with the notable exception of Laeven and Valencia (2013, 2020), have minimal documentation to back up their classifications of banking crises, making it difficult for other researchers to reconcile differences between crisis chronologies or even to assess the basic facts of what happened during each crisis.[1]

This chapter starts by describing some of the reasons for this disagreement on banking crisis incidence and severity. We then survey recent contributions that use quantitative and systematic methods to better catalog historical crises

1. Reinhart and Rogoff (2009) and Caprio and Klingebiel (2003) write only a few sentences about each crisis, while the database of Bordo et al. (2001) contains some macroeconomic variables but no historical documentation for their coding of episodes. Schularick and Taylor (2012) did not originally provide historical documentation but now do so in a recent online appendix (2021). Laeven and Valencia (2013, 2020) do provide extensive narrative documentation and systematically quantify various aspects of banking crises, but their database only starts in 1970.

and quantify their macroeconomic consequences. We highlight the approach of BVX, in addition to those of Jalil (2015), Romer and Romer (2017), and Krishnamurthy and Muir (2020), which together address many of the biases and limitations of the prior literature in identifying and studying historical banking crises.

At the same time, the advantages of quantitative approaches in identifying banking crises should in no way minimize the use of historical narratives to better understand these episodes, as narrative historical approaches offer insights that can complement quantitative approaches. Therefore, we also present a new historical database of the causes, bank failures, creditor panics, policy responses, and consequences of banking crises in forty-seven countries since 1870. Consistent with our belief that the optimal approach combines the best of systematic quantitative analyses with insights from economic historians, this database is built on the list of banking crises put forth by BVX, which are identified systematically by historical bank equity returns, bank failures, and creditor panics.

Our database has two components: (1) narrative historical documentation and summaries for each crisis episode in each country, and (2) a quantitative component of the causes, crisis characteristics, and policy responses. In the first component, we provide curated narrative summaries for every recorded bank distress event for each country based on the chronology of BVX, with subsections on each of the following aspects: the macroeconomic and political background at the time, the main causes of the crisis, the description of the crisis's main events, a summary of the recorded bank failures, the responses and countermeasures taken by the banking system and by policy makers, and the economic and regulatory consequences. For many episodes in our database, especially those outside the United States, the United Kingdom, and other well-studied developed economies, the history of these episodes has often been forgotten or simplified in the modern English-language economics literature. We thus bring together for the first time a variety of key sources, including both primary sources (such as newspaper articles, research reports, and government documents written around the time of each crisis or shortly thereafter) and secondary sources. These secondary sources are usually authored by country-specific historians, are sometimes not in English, and are often older publications potentially forgotten by modern economists. In the second component, we build a coded quantitative database—similar to Laeven and Valencia's (2013, 2020) but extended back from 1970 to 1870—of crisis causes, characteristics, and policy interventions.

Our goal is to make the episodes obscured by the past vibrant and accessible in one place. Previously, for many episodes—such as in nineteenth-century

Australia, early twentieth-century Spain, or 1990s Thailand—it has been difficult to find basic institutional details, even such as which specific banks failed and why. Beyond that, we want to know: What were the likely causes of the crisis? Who were the key bankers and government officials? At what point was the system threatened (if at all) by widespread creditor panics? The goal of this research is to zoom in to *all* the banking crises of the past century and a half—not just the well-studied ones in the United States, United Kingdom, and other developed countries—to fully understand the unfolding drama and institutional backdrop with as much clarity as when we study the 2008 global financial crisis.

Our banking crises database can be found at the following link: https://www.quantfinhistory.org.

Limitations of Existing Banking Crisis Chronologies

We first highlight in more detail some of the limitations of existing chronologies of banking crises, as argued in recent papers by Romer and Romer (2017), Krishnamurthy and Muir (2020), and BVX. We also describe how these papers have overcome some of the limitations they identify in the prior literature. Then, in the next section, we dive deeper into the approach of BVX.

Recall the six prominent previous chronologies of banking crises are Bordo et al. (2001), Caprio and Klingebiel (2003), Demirgüç-Kunt and Detragiache (2005), Reinhart and Rogoff (2009), Schularick and Taylor (2012), and Laeven and Valencia (2013, 2020). Their first limitation, as pointed out by Romer and Romer (2017), is that many of the prior approaches are subjective, qualitative, and retrospective in how they identify historical crises. As a result, Romer and Romer (2017) suggest these approaches may lead to a "look-back bias," meaning they may be more likely to select crises that were ex post more macroeconomically severe, leading the literature to overstate the average severity of banking crises and to forgo periods of bank distress that had little to no macroeconomic ramifications in hindsight. Thus, economic historians may unintentionally minimize episodes of bank distress that are not followed by severe output losses.[2] Romer and Romer (2017) attempt to overcome potential

2. Additionally, BVX point out that, because narrative-based approaches tend to focus on salient crisis symptoms and are retrospectively identified, narrative approaches might neglect some banking crisis episodes that may have initially appeared bad but quickly recovered, perhaps due to aggressive policy interventions, and are thus forgotten by narrative approaches because they "went away." Historians may be more likely to focus on crises that led ex post to bad macroeconomic outcomes, like the U.S. Great Depression—and be less likely to study crises that were quickly averted, because in some sense these crises never happened. Such episodes are

biases from these backward-looking accounts by constructing a real-time measure of financial distress from contemporaneous economic reports from the Organisation for Economic Co-operation and Development (OECD) for twenty-four advanced economies starting in 1967. However, the approach of Romer and Romer (2017) is limited by the fact that OECD narrative accounts, written by outside observers, may still be subjective and do not cover historical banking crises before 1967 or outside OECD economies.

BVX point out another related problem. Because existing accounts tend to focus on salient crisis symptoms such as panics, bank failures, and government interventions, these approaches may not capture episodes without these salient features.[3] As BVX point out, historically there have been many "quiet crises"—episodes in which no overt creditor panics or bank failures occurred, usually due to a forceful government liquidity backstop or interventions in banks about to fail, but in which the banking sector nevertheless suffers large losses. Because there are no salient features like depositor runs, these episodes again might be understated or even missed by historians, even though they may be followed by large credit contractions and severe recessions.

A third and perhaps even more basic problem is that in many of the previous narrative-based approaches, there is no precise definition of what a banking crisis is; instead, scholars often adopt a "know it when you see it" approach, which allows for excessive discretion in identifying banking crises. As banking crises might be heterogeneous in their characteristics, the exact criteria used to label each episode a banking crisis remain unclear. In addition, narrative accounts also view crises as discrete, binary events, when instead one might want a continuous quantitative measure (as suggested by Romer and Romer 2017) to know which crises are more severe than others and along which dimensions.

Fourth, BVX point out that the existing narrative crisis chronologies tend to include a surprising number of clear-cut historical errors, due to what they call a "hearsay bias." That is, many crisis chronologies call an episode a banking crisis because previous chronologies do, without actually looking at primary sources or quantitative data. This leads to the perpetuation of historical errors or the overemphasis on minor panics. For example, BVX point out that

---

important to study precisely because they were successfully averted. Bank equity returns, as used by BVX, can help identify such episodes for more systematic study.

3. For example, Bordo et al. (2001), Reinhart and Rogoff (2009), and Schularick and Taylor (2012) identify banking crises based on narrative accounts, looking for events such as bank runs and bank failures. Laeven and Valencia (2013, 2020) have a more precise definition of a banking crisis, focusing specifically on government interventions in various forms.

Reinhart and Rogoff (2009) call Italy in 1935 a banking crisis, because Bordo et al. (2001) consider it a crisis, because, in turn, Bernanke and James (1991) consider it a crisis, though it is unlikely that any banking crisis, however defined, started in 1935.[4] A related issue is that many currency, monetary, or sovereign debt crises are commonly—but sometimes spuriously—labeled as banking crises as well, even if there is little evidence of a large negative impact on the banking sector.[5] This bias can lead the literature to overstate the incidence of so-called twin or triple crises described by Kaminsky and Reinhart (1999). These clear-cut historical errors in part explain the large disagreement between the various narrative chronologies.

As a result of these limitations, Romer and Romer (2017), BVX, and others (including Laeven and Valencia 2013, 2020 before them) promote the use of systematic and quantitative definitions of banking distress and banking crises. BVX, in particular, emphasize that no single correct definition of a banking crisis exists: banking crises are multidimensional, and a banking crisis chronology should report quantitative measures along multiple dimensions, to provide data for each episode on observed characteristics and their severity. BVX thus classify various types of banking crises according to whether there are creditor panics, widespread bank failures, large bank equity declines (which they view as proxying for large aggregate bank losses), and other characteristics.

Readers should not, however, take away the conclusion that only quantitative information, like bank equity returns, is useful for studying historical banking crises. The limitations described above are mostly directed at *particular* narrative approaches, not narrative information in general. Information from narrative historical accounts can be useful, as long as it is systematically collected and extensively documented. Laeven and Valencia (2013, 2020), Jalil (2015), and Romer and Romer (2017) are excellent examples of the uses of systematically collected and extensively documented narrative information.

4. As BVX write, Bernanke and James (1991) consider this a crisis mainly due to a sharp drop in bank credit in the League of Nations banking statistics, though the drop is likely a data artifact. In fact, the main banking crisis in Italy erupted in 1930 and by 1935 was principally resolved (the entire banking sector had largely been nationalized). The only bank to fail in 1935 was Credito Marittimo, which had been nationalized years earlier and was only finally liquidated by the government in 1935.

5. One problem inherent in many older accounts of crises, as BVX describe, is that the terms "financial crisis" and "panic" are used to describe interchangeably monetary crises, currency crises, sovereign debt crises, or often even just stock market crashes, without being clear about what they are describing. These other types of nonbanking crises often get conflated with banking crises in secondary sources that cite these original historical accounts.

Jalil (2015) arguably presents the best systematic approach for the United States, although his study only covers pre-1929 panics due to data limitations. Jalil (2015) systematically counts reports of banking panics using articles in the *Niles Weekly Register,* the *Merchants' Magazine and Commercial Review,* and the *Commercial and Financial Chronicle.* From these data, Jalil (2015) reports both major and minor banking panics, classified by cities and regions in the United States. Jalil's (2015) series is, at times, different from other U.S.-based series, although, like BVX, he points out there is also a lot of disagreement across these earlier series. Jalil (2015) points out various clear-cut historical errors in earlier accounts (e.g., the United States in 1825). Likewise, Jalil (2015) shows that his measure of a banking crisis forecasts persistent output gaps measured in terms of industrial production.

Before turning in depth to the approach of BVX, it is important to note a related approach from Krishnamurthy and Muir (2020), who use credit spread data to study banking crises and forecast their consequences. Like bank equity data used by BVX, credit spread data are objective, quantitative, and real-time. Thus, Krishnamurthy and Muir (2020) argue that their approach overcomes the problem of binary classification of crises, along with potential look-back biases in narrative accounts. Krishnamurthy and Muir (2020) show that the macroeconomic severity of a crisis can be predicted by the size of credit losses (as measured by the change in spreads) interacted with the fragility of the financial sector (as measured by precrisis credit growth). They also find that spreads decline in advance of crises and appear too low, suggesting that (1) credit booms preceding crises tend to be driven by increased credit supply, and (2) bond market investors tend to systematically underestimate the inherent risk of credit booms and that crises come as surprises to bond markets.[6]

---

6. At the same time, one potential downside of the analysis in Krishnamurthy and Muir (2020) is that it is mostly a *conditional* analysis, meaning the forecasting is conditional on the set of Schularick and Taylor (2012) crises. Thus, unlike in BVX, their analysis does not identify banking crises de novo. Another potential downside of their approach is that credit spread data are historically limited. As described in BVX, bond markets in many countries have only developed in recent decades. In most of the postwar period, corporate bond markets mainly existed only in the United States and the United Kingdom, while in most other non-Anglophone advanced economies, corporate bond markets were very limited or nonexistent until deregulation in the 1980s. As a result, Krishnamurthy and Muir (2020) analyze a more limited sample, since they do not have corporate credit spreads for emerging market countries or even for many advanced economies in the modern period.

New Data and New Approaches from BVX

In response to potential biases in narrative chronologies of banking crises, BVX take a different approach to studying banking crises and use bank equity returns. In this section, we summarize their findings related to crisis frequency and severity. Their approach is based on gathering bank equity returns data covering forty-six countries from 1870 to 2016 to study the relationship between the banking sector and the broader economy.[7] Using bank equity returns combined with other structurally gathered information (widespread bank failures and creditor panics), BVX—like Jalil (2015), Romer and Romer (2017), and Krishnamurthy and Muir (2020) before them—help provide systematic answers to the questions: When did crises happen and how severe were they?

BVX argue that bank equity returns as a measure of banking losses and banking distress offer several advantages in the study of historical crises. First, bank equity returns provide an objective, quantitative, and real-time measure, overcoming the aforementioned look-back biases of the narrative-based approaches. Second, bank equity returns are theoretically motivated: In a broad class of theoretical models of constrained financial intermediaries, banking sector equity is a key state variable that determines banks' capacity to intermediate funds from savers to firms and households, as large declines in banking sector net worth constrain banks' ability to lend (e.g., Gertler and Kiyotaki 2010; Brunnermeier and Sannikov 2014; Rampini and Viswanathan 2019). Consistent with theory, BVX find empirically, across a wide historical sample of over forty-six countries, that large declines in bank equity, even controlling for nonfinancial equity, predict large persistent credit contractions and output gaps. Third, historical bank equity price and dividend data are readily available from historical financial newspapers in many countries going back to 1870, which BVX use to build country-level bank equity index returns. Fourth, bank equity returns have high temporal resolution and allow for a precise analysis of the turning points of historical crises and the dynamics of how crises evolve, as understood in real-time by equity investors. Fifth, bank equity returns allow one to uncover the full spectrum of banking crises,

---

7. Reinhart and Rogoff (2009) suggest taking such an approach, writing that "the relative price of bank stocks (or financial institutions relative to the market) would be a logical indicator to examine." However, they do not take this approach due to the "lack of long-range time series data that would allow us to date banking or financial crises quantitatively."

including "quiet crises" (i.e., episodes of large banking sector losses without creditor panics or bank failures). A bank equity–based approach can thus obtain a more complete sample of crises for analyzing many important issues, such as whether panics are necessary for severe crises and whether early aggressive policy interventions can successfully avert crises.

With this approach, BVX put forward several key findings regarding the severity of historical banking crises, which we discuss below in detail. Then, they discuss the incidence of banking crises throughout history.

BANK EQUITY DECLINES PREDICT LARGE OUTPUT GAPS AND CREDIT CONTRACTIONS

BVX construct a new historical data set of country-level bank equity index real total returns at the annual level for forty-six advanced and emerging economies going back to 1870, building off earlier bank equity index returns from Baron and Xiong (2017). To control for broader stock market conditions, they also construct a new country-level index of nonfinancial stocks over the same sample.

BVX's analysis first shows, using their full sample, that large declines in bank equity, while controlling for nonfinancial equity, forecast negative macroeconomic outcomes. BVX write that, by testing whether bank equity returns have predictive content for future macroeconomic dynamics beyond the information contained in nonfinancial equities, their result confirms that bank equity declines contain useful information about banking sector distress and the future macroeconomy. Specifically, they find that bank equity declines predict persistently lower output. For example, as BVX explain, a decline in bank equity of at least 30% predicts 3.4% lower real output after three years. At the same time, bank equity declines predict sharp and persistent contractions in bank credit to the private sector. Three years after a bank equity decline of at least 30%, bank credit-to-GDP declines by 5.7 percentage points, relative to periods without a decline. BVX show that the relation between bank equity returns and future output and credit growth is nonlinear: declines in bank equity predict future output and credit contractions, whereas increases in bank equity do not predict stronger economic performance. These estimates control for nonfinancial equity returns which capture investor expectations about broader macroeconomic conditions.

A nonlinearity in crisis severity can be observed by looking at figure 9.1, which is reproduced from BVX and examines the predictability of large bank equity declines for subsequent GDP growth and bank credit-to-GDP growth.

To generate figure 9.1, BVX estimate the following Jordà (2005) local projection specification for horizons $h = 1, \ldots, 6$:

$$(1) \ \Delta_h y_{i,t+h} = \alpha_i^h + \gamma_t^h + \sum_j \beta_j^h \, 1[r_{i,t}^B \in B_j] + \sum_j \delta_j^h \, 1[r_{i,t}^N \in B_j] + \Gamma^h X_{i,t} + \varepsilon_{i,t}^h,$$

where $\Delta_h y_{i,t+h}$ is real GDP growth from year t to $t + h$, α_i^h is a country-fixed effect, γ_t^h is a year-fixed effect, and $1[r_{i,t}^B \in B_j]$ and $1[r_{i,t}^N \in B_j]$ are indicator variables for whether the bank equity return and nonfinancial equity return, respectively, in year t are within a range defined by bin B_j. To examine the predictability across the full distribution of returns, they include eight evenly spaced bins, B_j, for both bank and nonfinancial returns: less than −45%, −45% to −30%, −30% to −15%, −15% to 0%, 0% to 15%, 15% to 30%, 30% to 45%, and greater than 45%.

As described in BVX, the top left plot in figure 9.1 depicts the cumulative response of real GDP to bank equity return innovations (controlling for nonfinancial equity returns, which are plotted in the top right panel). The bottom two panels of figure 9.1 present estimates with the change in bank credit-to-GDP as the dependent variable, demonstrating that the response of credit-to-GDP to bank equity return shocks is highly nonlinear. As BVX explain, this nonlinearity in credit growth is consistent with models in which banks are financially constrained. Larger shocks to bank net wealth are more likely to force banks against their capital constraint and therefore to contract the asset side of their balance sheets (as in He and Krishnamurthy 2013; Brunnermeier and Sannikov 2014; Rampini and Viswanathan 2019).

ANALYSIS CONDITIONAL ON BANKING CRISES DEFINED BY NARRATIVE APPROACHES

BVX also show that, *conditional* on "narrative crisis" episodes (defined as the combination of all banking crisis episodes from the six prominent prior chronologies), the magnitude of the peak-to-trough bank equity decline of each episode is associated with increased severity both in terms of crisis characteristics and macroeconomic outcomes. Specifically, BVX show that, conditional on a narrative crisis, a (hypothetical) 100% peak-to-trough decline in bank equity returns is associated with a 13.9% decline in real GDP. Banking crises with larger bank equity declines are associated with significantly larger declines in bank deposits, an increased incidence of failure of the largest banks, and higher nonperforming loans. Moreover, bank equity declines predict an increased probability of various forms of government intervention including significant liability guarantees, liquidity support, bank nationalizations, and government equity injections.

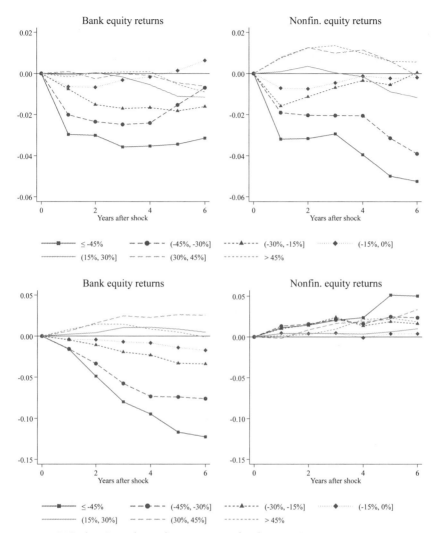

FIGURE 9.1 Bank equity crashes predict output gaps and credit contraction

Note: This figure, reproduced from BVX, plots the predictive content of bank equity and nonfinancial equity returns for real GDP (*top*) and bank credit-to-GDP (*bottom*). The responses are estimated using equation (1) and omitting the 0% to 15% indicator variables, which are thought of as returns during "normal times" and serve as baselines. The responses to bank equity and nonfinancial equity returns are estimated jointly, and the specification controls for contemporaneous and lagged real GDP growth and change in credit-to-GDP and country-fixed effects.

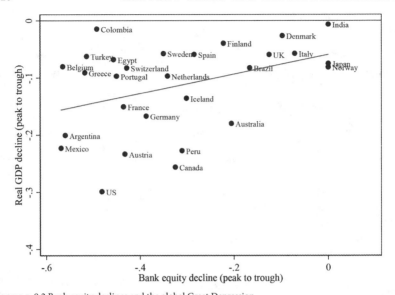

FIGURE 9.2 Bank equity declines and the global Great Depression
Note: This figure, reproduced from BVX, plots the peak-to-trough decline in real GDP against the peak-to-trough bank equity decline over the period 1929–1933. Note that this figure plots all countries in the sample for which data is available, not just those that experienced banking crises. BVX omit from the plot one outlier observation, Chile, which reported a real GDP decline of 48% and a bank equity decline of 30%.

In an extension, BVX showcase the usefulness of their banking crisis intensity measures constructed from bank equity prices by revisiting the banking crises of the Great Depression. While there is no doubt of the presence of severe banking crises in some countries (e.g., Austria and the United States) and their absence in other countries (e.g., Japan and the United Kingdom), there is considerable debate about the presence and severity of banking crises in other countries, as BVX write. For example, in their cross-country study, Bernanke and James (1991) write about their study on the international Great Depression, "a weakness of our approach is that, lacking objective indicators of the seriousness of financial problems, we are forced to rely on dummy variables to indicate periods of crisis" (34).

Figure 9.2, reproduced from BVX, plots the peak-to-trough decline in real GDP against the peak-to-trough bank equity decline over the period 1929–1933. Note that this figure plots all countries in the sample for which data are available, not just those that may have experienced banking crises. As BVX write, figure 9.2 shows large declines in bank equity for well-known examples of severe banking crises: Austria, Belgium, France, Germany, Switzerland, and the United States. In contrast, Japan and the United Kingdom are considered not to have had banking crises during this period and have minimal bank equity declines. BVX are the first to identify banking crises (these do not appear in any of the previous narrative chronologies) in Chile, Colombia, Iceland, and Peru; all these countries experienced large bank stock declines, and the narrative evidence strongly supports widespread and serious bank losses or failures in these countries. BVX also use new evidence from bank equity returns to discuss some other interesting cases (Brazil, Canada, Finland, and the Netherlands) where substantial disagreement exists in the historical literature over the extent of banking distress in these countries.

BVX'S CHRONOLOGY OF BANKING CRISES DEFINED BY LARGE AGGREGATE BANK LOSSES AND BANK FAILURES

BVX provide a new chronology of banking crises. As they argue, there is obviously no single correct definition of a banking crisis, but their goal is to provide one possible construction of clear-cut crisis episodes based on systematic criteria emphasizing three dimensions: bank equity losses, bank failures, and creditor panics. With a database of other banking crisis characteristics, such as the one we present below, one can likewise systematically construct alternative lists of crises based on other dimensions.

To construct their banking crisis chronology, BVX initially construct two nonmutually exclusive chronologies. The first is a chronology of "bank equity crises." As they write, they build this list by first selecting instances of cumulative 30% declines in bank equity, which indicate potential banking crises. To avoid including episodes of bank equity declines purely due to equity market noise, they then only select the subset of these with narrative evidence of widespread bank failures, which they define as the failure of a top-five (by assets) bank or more than five total bank failures above the normal rate of bank failures. The second is a chronology of "panic banking crises."[8] The union of these two overlapping sets is their BVX Crisis List. The BVX Crisis List distinguishes between crises involving bank equity losses and those involving panics (or both), emphasizing that banking crises take various forms.

---

8. BVX define a "panic banking crisis" as "an episode containing any of the following criteria appearing in narrative accounts: (1) severe and sudden depositor or creditor withdrawals at more than one of a country's largest banks or a number of smaller banks that lead these banks to be on the verge of collapse; (2) severe and sudden strains in interbank lending markets; or (3) severe and sudden foreign-currency capital outflows from the banking sector. In short, they define panic episodes as any episode when a significant part of the banking system experienced sudden salient funding pressures" (75–76).

As BVX write, one of the other advantages of such a list is that it helps to identify the surprising number of clear-cut historical errors, potentially due to a hearsay bias. As mentioned earlier, the hearsay bias is the fact that many crisis chronologies call an episode a crisis because previous chronologies do, without looking at primary sources or quantitative data. This leads to the perpetuation of historical errors or the overemphasis on minor panics.[9] After removing these clear-cut historical errors, BVX find that previous narrative-based approaches actually slightly *understate* the average crisis severity, contrary to the conclusion of Romer and Romer (2017), due to the inclusion of many spurious or minor events.

The approach in BVX helps to resolve the large disagreement between the various narrative chronologies. As they write, with the help of large bank equity declines as a screening tool, BVX are able to uncover a number of "forgotten" banking crises that are strongly backed by the historical narrative. It is quite remarkable that this approach rediscovers banking crises unknown to some of the great modern historians of banking crises. The authors document in their paper several interesting newly rediscovered crises, including Belgium in 1876, Japan in 1922, and Portugal in 1876.

A New Database of Historical Banking Crises

Building on the list of banking crises put forth by BVX, we present a new database of the causes, bank failures, creditor panics, policy responses, and consequences of banking crises in forty-seven countries since 1870.[10] We comprehensively revisit the economic history literature—and unearth hundreds of new sources—for the forty-seven countries. In the process, we discover new periods of bank distress, uncover artifacts in the existing historiography, and present sometimes divergent views from different scholars on the causes and consequences of specific banking crises.

The database has two components: (1) narrative historical documentation and summaries for each crisis episode in each country and (2) a quantitative component that codes the causes, crisis characteristics, policy responses, and macroeconomic consequences. We describe its two components in turn.

---

9. Some examples of likely historical errors from prior crisis chronologies in which no banking crisis seems to have occurred are the Netherlands in 1897, France in 1907, and Germany in 1977.

10. We add an additional country, China, to BVX's forty-six countries to yield forty-seven countries. BVX do not include China due to lack of bank equity data before the mid-1990s.

NARRATIVE SUMMARIES
AND DETAILED DOCUMENTATIONS

In the first component, we provide curated narrative summaries for every recorded bank distress event for each country. The country summaries represent the full set of information we gathered on each bank distress event curated in a condensed form.[11] For each episode, we provide information on the macroeconomic and political background at the time, the main causes of the crisis, a description of the crisis's main events, a summary of the recorded bank failures, the responses and countermeasures taken by the banking system and policy makers, and the economic and regulatory consequences. We list all our main sources, as well, in a curated bibliography.

Alongside the curated summaries, we provide detailed documentation which contains all narrative information we were able to gather on bank distress periods within each country. This detailed documentation contains direct quotes, tables, and book excerpts with information beyond what we can fit into the summaries. Together, the narrative summaries and the detailed documentations provide future scholars with a guide to the historical literature on each of these banking crises.

QUANTITATIVE DATABASE OF THE CAUSES AND
CHARACTERISTICS OF BANKING CRISES

In the second component, we extend the quantitative information from BVX. While BVX provide information on *whether* there were widespread bank failures or banking panics in the aggregate, we provide more detailed variables on the likely causes of the banking distress, the extent of bank losses and failures, which policy measures were taken, and the macroeconomic consequences. In particular, we code the following variables.

First, we code the likely causes of banking distress as indicated by the economic history literature. We identify major categories of causes, some of which have associated subcategories, and we highlight some of the indicator

---

11. In addition to the set of episodes that BVX call banking crises, the database also includes historical information on a wider set of episodes, including (1) nonbanking crises (episodes perhaps erroneously called banking crises by other chronologies, in order to better understand the evidence of why such an episode may likely not be a banking crisis), (2) minor episodes of bank distress (events that do not meet the crisis thresholds set out by BVX but are still economically important), and (3) averted crises (episodes that may have developed into a banking crisis but were prevented by forceful policy interventions).

variables we create, as follows. *Credit booms* are banking crises that are preceded by a period of sustained above-average growth in private credit—particularly bank credit—and a subsequent collapse of the boom. We have a similar variable for *real estate booms. Commodity shocks* are sudden and drastic changes in international commodity prices with particular relevance to a country's economy. We also count bad harvests as commodity shocks. Shocks to international trade that hit a particular country hard, either related to global recessions or tariffs and embargoes, we categorize as *trade shocks.* Prior to the abandonment of the gold standard, *monetary gold shocks* are defined as events of large in- or outflows of monetary gold or silver with relevance for banking stability. *Financial flow shocks* are defined as a range of destabilizing events that are related to the in- and outflow of financial capital of both public and private nature, which we further distinguish into several subcategories. *Natural disasters*—such as earthquakes, extreme weather events, and epidemics—as key triggering events of banking crises are classified in their own separate category. Another is the start of *wars*—either at home or abroad and including civil wars. All other types of drastic political changes of both sudden and structural nature that trigger banking crises are categorized as *political shocks* and include unexpected disruptions like revolutions or military coups.

Second, we document which banks failed and when. We use this information to present data on the extent of losses in the banking system such as the percentage of failed banks in relation to the banking system's total assets or deposits, whether any of the country's largest banks failed, the decline in the banking system's total deposits, depositor losses in relation to the size of the banking system, and the banking system's nonperforming loans ratio at its peak. Naturally, not all of these data series are available for each bank distress event, but we put substantial effort into locating or estimating them to the extent possible.

Third, we code policy measures in response to banking distress along six categories as binary variables: significant liability guarantees, significant liquidity guarantees, banks nationalized, government equity injections, deposit freezes, and bank holidays. In this way, we adopt an approach close to Laeven and Valencia's (2013, 2020) who define a very similar set of categories of policy measures. We draw heavily from their database as a key source that covers the period from 1970 to 2017.

Fourth and last, we collect data on the macroeconomic consequences of bank distress events. Building on the BVX data, we compute quantities such as the peak-to-trough changes in the credit-to-GDP ratio and in real GDP.

Conclusion

This chapter discusses limitations and potential biases of existing narrative approaches to identifying banking crises and showcases the potential of new quantitative methods. At this point, researchers may ask which chronologies of banking crises and types of approaches one should use going forward. We would suggest the following guidelines, noting that these are simply rules of thumb from the authors' experiences.

If one is performing in-sample analysis of banking crises and needs a set of clear-cut episodes to examine the dynamics *within*, we would suggest using Laeven and Valencia's (2013, 2020) database for the 1970–2017 period because it identifies crises based on systematic criteria, is extremely well documented, and covers more than 160 countries. For pre-1929 panics in the United States, we would recommend Jalil (2015) for being the most systematic and carefully documented. For historical crises in other countries going back to 1870, we would recommend BVX as a refinement of the six other prominent narrative chronologies, as BVX is based on systematic criteria and carefully documented. BVX also contains quantitative measures of crisis intensities, which the other narrative approaches do not. Schularick and Taylor (2012) is an alternative refinement of existing approaches that one can use: it contains a more limited set of (what the authors subjectively assess as) systemic crises in seventeen advanced economies and may thus be of interest to researchers who want to focus on systemic events. Importantly, it should be noted that Laeven and Valencia's (2013, 2020) and Schularick and Taylor's (2012) lists are similar to BVX's list for the subsamples over which they overlap. Thus, for certain types of in-sample studies, it may not even matter much which of these three lists one chooses.

However, if one is looking instead to estimate quantities on the entire universe of crises (e.g., to investigate the average severity of banking crises), then one should be very concerned about potential biases, as argued by Romer and Romer (2017). In this case, we would recommend researchers to use objective, continuous, and real-time measures, such as bank equity returns (as in BVX), credit spread measures (as in Krishnamurthy and Muir 2017), or credit distress measures (as in Romer and Romer 2017), rather than relying on discrete historical episodes drawn from narrative approaches.

Beyond the question of crisis incidence, the new database we present in this chapter is the first to reconcile the various existing chronologies by asking *what exactly happened* during bank distress events of the past 150 years around the globe. While our new database builds upon the crisis dating methodology of BVX, it does not specifically take a stand on which events qualify as banking crises but instead enables future researchers themselves to take a stand by providing them with the most comprehensive collection of economic knowledge on historical banking crises to date.

REFERENCES

Baron, Matthew, Emil Verner, and Wei Xiong. 2021. Banking Crises without Panics. Quarterly Journal of Economics 136 (1): 51–113.

Baron, Matthew, and Wei Xiong. 2017. Credit Expansion and Neglected Crash Risk. Quarterly Journal of Economics 132 (2): 713–64.

Bernanke, Ben, and Harold James. 1991. The Gold Standard, Deflation, and Financial Crisis in the Great Depression: An International Comparison. In R. Glenn Hubbard, ed., Financial Markets and Financial Crises, 33–68. Chicago: University of Chicago Press.

Bordo, Michael, Barry Eichengreen, Daniela Klingebiel, and Maria Soledad Martinez-Peria. 2001. Is the Crisis Problem Growing More Severe? Economic Policy 16 (32): 52–82.

Brunnermeier, Markus, and Yuliy Sannikov. 2014. A Macroeconomic Model with a Financial Sector. American Economic Review 104 (2): 379–421.

Caprio, Gerard, and Daniela Klingebiel. 2003. Episodes of Systemic and Borderline Banking Crises. In Daniela Klingebiel, and Luc Laeven, eds., Managing the Real and Fiscal Effects of Banking Crises, 31–49. Washington, DC: World Bank.

Demirgüç-Kunt, Asli, and Enrica Detragiache. 2005. Cross-Country Empirical Studies of Systemic Bank Distress: A Survey. National Institute Economic Review 192 (1): 68–83.

Gertler, Mark, and Nobuhiro Kiyotaki. 2010. Financial Intermediation and Credit Policy in Business Cycle Analysis. In B. M. Friedman and F. H. Hahn, eds., Handbook of Monetary Economics 3: 547–99. Oxford: Elsevier.

Jalil, Andrew. 2015. A New History of Banking Panics in the United States, 1825–1929: Construction and Implications. American Economic Journal: Macroeconomics 7 (3): 295–330.

Jordà, Òscar. 2005. Estimation and Inference of Impulse Responses by Local Projections. American Economic Review 95 (1): 161–82.

Kaminsky, Graciela, and Carmen Reinhart. 1999. The Twin Crises: The Causes of Banking and Balance-of-Payments Problems. American Economic Review 89 (3): 473–500.

Krishnamurthy, Arvind, and Tyler Muir. 2020. How Credit Cycles across a Financial Crisis. NBER Working Paper 23850.

Laeven, Luc, and Fabian Valencia. 2013. Systemic Banking Crises Database. IMF Economic Review 61 (2): 225–70.

———. 2020. Systemic Banking Crises Database II. IMF Economic Review 68 (2): 307–61.

Rampini, Adriano, and S. Viswanathan. 2019. Financial Intermediary Capital. Review of Economic Studies 86 (1): 413–55.

Reinhart, Carmen, and Kenneth Rogoff. 2009. This Time Is Different: Eight Centuries of Financial Folly. Princeton, NJ: Princeton University Press.

Romer, Christina, and David Romer. 2017. New Evidence on the Impact of Financial Crises in Advanced Countries. American Economic Review 107 (10): 3072–3118.

Schularick, Moritz, and Alan Taylor. 2012. Credit Booms Gone Bust: Monetary Policy, Leverage Cycles and Financial Crises, 1870–2008. American Economic Review, 102 (2): 1029–61.

Comment by Mark Carlson

The chapter "Historical Banking Crises: A New Database and a Reassessment of Their Incidence and Severity" by Matthew Baron and Daniel Dieckelmann provides an overview of research by Baron, Verner, and Xiong (2021, hereafter BVX) that uses newly created indexes of bank stock prices to study the timing of banking crises and the impact of deteriorations in bank condition on the macroeconomy. The data panel from BVX that has been assembled is notable for both its length and breadth. The stock price indexes are based on prices of publicly traded stocks of banks located in financial centers of forty-six countries over the period from 1870 to 2016. Annual data is available for all countries and monthly data is available for some periods. Similar indexes are constructed for nonfinancial firms. As described in the chapter, BVX use this index to develop a new chronology for banking crises by first selecting episodes in which the equity price indexes decline by at least 30% and then by reviewing historical narratives of these periods to better understand the event and determine whether it was indeed a crisis. Based on this approach, BVX present a revised crisis chronology and identify some "quiet crises" in which there are declines in bank equities but no reaction by depositors.

The authors of the chapter also describe how BVX use the index to investigate the impact of deteriorations in the condition of banks on the macroeconomy by estimating how changes in both bank and nonfinancial equity price indexes are related to changes in GDP and bank credit. The results of the investigations in BVX indicate that, even after controlling for changes in nonfinancial equity prices, large declines in bank equity prices are associated with significant declines in economic activity, especially when those declines are associated with banking panics. Increases in bank equity are not found to have similar predictive power.

Overall, the overview provided in the chapter describes a variety of interesting and thought-provoking results. To more fully understand the value of the analysis, how it relates to other literature on financial crises, and how the reader should think about how changes over time in the banking sector impact the analysis, it is useful to consider the analysis in the context of a simple model of the banking sector. Such a simple model is illustrated in figure 9C.1. Here, banks issue equity and raise uninsured deposits to fund their operations. Banks' assets consist of loans to businesses as well as cash and liquid assets. Nonfinancial businesses issue equity and borrow from banks (or from

Mark Carlson is adviser, Board of Governors of the Federal Reserve System.

Non-financial firms   Commercial Banks

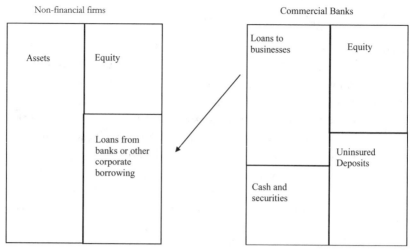

FIGURE 9c.1 Stylized model of the banking sector

securities markets) to fund their operations, which may be producing, distributing, or retailing goods.

In this simple framework, economic deteriorations of different magnitudes (or an economic decline that slowly becomes more severe) should produce a predictable ordering of responses in the prices of financial securities associated with different parts of the capital structure of the nonfinancial and financial institutions. The securities that should be affected by mild economic deteriorations that reduce the assets of nonfinancial businesses are the equities of those firms. Next, if the economic deterioration is such that losses in the nonfinancial sector become severe enough, there could be losses to the liability holders of these firms—either corporate bond holders or bank lenders—depending on who had been providing funds to the nonfinancial firms. If there were losses on bank loans, then that should result in declines in the equity prices of banks. Finally, in the most severe economic declines, when problems in the nonfinancial sector are severe enough to cause significant losses to their lenders such that bank equity has been notably depleted, then bank depositors might become concerned about the value of their claims and withdraw their funds from the banks and possibly cause bank runs. Depending on the distribution of claims and concentration of losses, the responses in asset prices may only be apparent for particular subsets of entities. This might be the case if the losses in the nonfinancial sector were concentrated in a particular industry, such as the mining or land development industry.

This model helps provide context for several results reported in the chapter. In this model, if real economic declines cause crises, the expected order in which securities prices would respond should be (1) nonfinancial equities, (2) bank equities, (3) deposits. BVX report observing this pattern in the nineteenth century, the time period when this simple model is most likely to accurately describe the banking sector. However, BVX note that they do not observe this pattern later in the sample, a point to which I return below. This model also suggests that it is amid the most severe economic declines that depositor outflows should be observed; again, this is consistent with the reported results. Finally, in this model, since bank equity holders essentially hold a debt claim on the nonfinancial sector, declines in bank equity should be more informative about the condition of the economy than increases (consistent with the structure of payoffs of a debt contract). This prediction is again consistent with the reported findings.

This chapter compares the BVX crisis chronology to other chronologies, especially those based on narrative evidence, and identifies differences. The model described above suggests that one potential source of differences might be differences in the security prices that are being considered. To that extent, it might also be worthwhile to compare the crises identified by BVX to those identified using alternative quantitative metrics such as corporate bond spreads (Mishkin 1991; Krishnamurthy and Muir 2017) or sudden and widespread deposit outflows (Calomiris and Gorton 1991; Mitchener and Richardson 2019). Looking at bank equity declines is an important complement to this previous research. One would expect differences in the list of identified events based on these alternative securities considered, but those differences themselves might be informative.

The model described above also provides a way of thinking about how some of the developments in the banking sector in the past 150 years might be particularly relevant for the analysis.[1] The first development that may be relevant is the spread of deposit insurance, which would reduce the responsiveness of depositors to concerns about the extent to which bank assets were impaired by any decline in economic activity. Calomiris and Chen (2018) discuss the spread of insurance over the past ninety years. BVX note this development but could say more. In particular, it points to the value of looking at bank distress through the lens of bank equity since the responsiveness of equity holders, who are typically not protected by the safety net, to troubles in the banking sector is more likely to be consistent over time. Moreover, the

---

1. There are of course other developments that may also be important. For instance, some countries had some form of extended liability for bank equity holders around the time of the beginning of the sample but that ended at some point. That change could have implications for the responsiveness of bank equity.

authors should indicate whether the spread of deposit insurance has resulted in "quiet crises" becoming more common.

A second development that might cause the pattern of responses across assets to differ from the one predicted in the model discussed above is a change in banks' role in financial intermediation. One aspect of that change is that, as has been noted by a variety of authors and is apparent in figure 9C.2, bank lending has shifted away from loans to businesses and toward real estate–related loans (see, e.g., Hancock and Wilcox 1997; Jordà, Taylor, and Schularick 2016). Another aspect is that bank lending has gradually declined

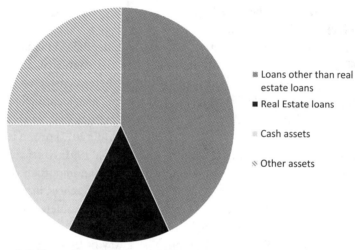

FIGURE 9C.2A Composition of bank assets in 1896

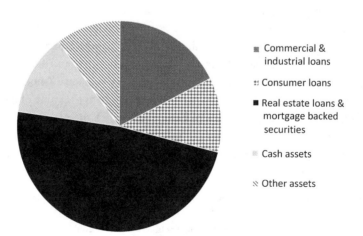

FIGURE 9C.2B Composition of bank assets in 2019

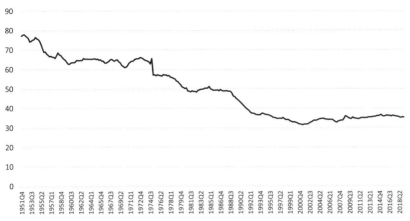

FIGURE 9C.3 Ratio of bank assets to total household and nonfinancial business liabilities

as a share of total financial intermediation (a trend suggested in figure 9C.3), partly as other financial intermediaries have increased in importance and partly as banks have conducted more of their business off balance sheet.

These developments give rise to several questions that the authors might want to consider. First, has the timing of declines in bank equity shifted relative to declines in nonfinancial business equity? When the timing of declines in these indexes differs notably, does that signal that the source of the stress is outside the private nonfinancial sector (such as a real estate–related crisis, a currency crisis, or a natural resource–related crisis)? Second, is the bank index more meaningful in countries or periods in which banks represent a larger share of financial intermediation? It is not obvious that it should be. Even if banks are a smaller share of total financial intermediation, they may remain at the heart of the financial sector and changes in their condition may still have just as much impact on the economy. The data that the authors have assembled should be able to shed some light on these questions; any insights the authors are able to provide would be extremely valuable.

REFERENCES

Baron, Matthew, Emil Verner, and Wei Xiong. 2021. Banking Crises without Panics. Quarterly Journal of Economics 136 (1): 51–113.
Calomiris, Charles W., and Sophia Chen. 2018. The Spread of Deposit Insurance and the Global Rise in Bank Asset Risk since the 1970s. NBER Working Paper 24936.
Calomiris, Charles W., and Gary Gorton. 1991. The Origins of Banking Panics: Models, Facts, and Bank Regulation. In R. Glenn Hubbard, ed., Financial Markets and Financial Crises. Chicago: University of Chicago Press.

Hancock, Diana, and James Wilcox. 1997. Bank Capital, Nonbank Finance, and Real Estate Activity. Journal of Housing Research 8 (1): 75–105.

Jordà, Òscar, Moritz Schularick, and Alan Taylor. 2016. The Great Mortgaging: Housing Finance, Crises and Business Cycles. Economic Policy 85: 107–40.

Krishnamurthy, Arvind, and Tyler Muir. 2017. How Credit Cycles across a Financial Crisis. NBER Working Paper 23850.

Mishkin, Frederic. 1991. Asymmetric Information and Financial Crises: A Historical Perspective. In R. Glenn Hubbard, ed., Financial Markets and Financial Crises. Chicago: University of Chicago Press.

Mitchener, Kris, and Gary Richardson. 2019. Network Contagion and Interbank Amplification during the Great Depression. Journal of Political Economy 127 (2): 465–507.

10

Was the U.S. Great Depression a Credit Boom Gone Wrong?

NATACHA POSTEL-VINAY

> Men of business in England do not . . . like the currency question. They are perplexed
> to define accurately what money is: how to count they know, but what to count they do
> not know.
>
> WALTER BAGEHOT (1857)

For a decade now since the financial crisis of 2008–2009, credit has been moving closer to the center of economic debate. At the time the crisis was unfolding, it was already clear that the growth of credit in the 2000s, both in the United States and in Europe, was at the root of many of our economic woes. Perhaps paradoxically, however, until then the idea of credit as a potential source of profound imbalances in the economy had attracted only limited attention (Bernanke 1983; Bernanke and Gertler 1995; Kiyotaki and Moore 1997). This may be because, bar a few exceptions, business cycle downturns in the postwar developed world seemed not to owe much to credit issues. The "money view" strongly implied that the economy was under control as long as the money supply was kept under control (Friedman and Schwartz 1963).

In popular discourse, however, the Great Depression of the 1920s and 1930s had still very much remained an example of a "credit boom gone wrong," a version of history popularized by Galbraith's *The Great Crash, 1929* (1954; see also Eichengreen and Mitchener 2003). When the 2008 crisis hit, many were quick to draw links between the 2000s credit boom and that of the 1920s. While making such parallels is tempting, one must ask the degree to which

Natacha Postel-Vinay is assistant professor of economic history at the London School of Economics.

This chapter was written to be presented at the Institute of New Economic Thinking's "Private Debt Initiative" conference on June 20–21, 2019, in New York. I thank Kris Mitchener and Kilian Rieder for useful conversation on the question, as well as participants at the conference. Oliver Bush, Mark Carlson, Barry Eichengreen, Enrique Jorge-Sotelo, Albrecht Ritschl, Moritz Schularick, Loukis Skaliotis, and Eugene White have provided insightful comments.

this comparison can be made. As a matter of fact, Galbraith's work was mostly based on only one aspect of the economic boom—the 1929 stock market boom and crash—and economic historians since then have insisted that the direct consequences of the crash on the U.S. economy were minor, and that a serious depression started only a year later, in autumn 1930 (Temin 1976).

The main contribution of this review is to document the tremendous credit growth that occurred in the 1920s and suggest that it created significant vulnerabilities in the U.S. economy. The credit boom likely led to asset price inflations, as opposed to general inflation, the extent of which monetary authorities failed to fully grasp. Those inflations were often out of sync with the fundamentals of the economy, and there is some evidence to suggest that they may have impaired household, corporate, and bank balance sheets (Calomiris and Mason 1997, 2003; Mishkin 1978).

Critically, this chapter presents new data showing that credit growth went hand in hand with another form of deterioration of the banking system—a fall in liquidity. Toward the end of the decade, while deposit creation was still full steam ahead, liquid reserves at commercial banks failed to keep up and indeed fell. This can be seen in a slowdown in the pace of broad money growth, normally interpreted as a sign of robust economic growth. Such an interpretation would indeed mask significant shifts in the health of the financial system's balance sheet: in effect loans, and therefore deposits, were growing faster than banks' liquid reserves, and thus faster than broad money as whole. In the wake of the 2008 financial crisis, Schularick and Taylor (2012) suggested that a distinctive feature of post-1945 industrial economies is a decoupling of credit growth from the growth of broad money.[1] While the underlying explanations likely differ, this chapter suggests that a decoupling of credit from money growth had already occurred in the run-up to the U.S. Great Depression.

Broad money did grow fast in the first phase of the credit boom, from the end of the First World War to about 1926. This growth was in great part a consequence of the international economic situation resulting from World War I. After the war, the United States emerged stronger, not weaker, and not as a debtor, as it had been in the past, but as the world's primary creditor. Current account surpluses allowed currency and gold to flow in, enabling the Federal Reserve to keep interest rates relatively low (Eichengreen 1992).

Money growth slowed somewhat afterward. This was noted long ago by Friedman and Schwartz (1963, 298), who conceded that the 1920s were a relatively stationary decade in monetary terms, with a possible link to low

1. That is, M2 or M3.

general inflation. What Friedman and Schwartz failed to emphasize, however, is the extent to which the total amount of credit continued to grow past 1926, up to 1929. In this second phase of the boom, domestic credit expanded independently of gold inflows (Robbins 1934; see also Hayek 1932; Rothbard 1963; and Palyi 1972). And while loans and deposits continued to grow, liquid reserves fell, which compromised banks' preparedness for a liquidity shock. U.S. capital outflows also grew, spurred by high European interest rates and the Dawes Plan, thereby fueling credit booms in already indebted Germany, Austria, and other central European countries (Aldcroft 1977; Ritschl 2002, 2012).

While monetary authorities managed to keep inflation in check, they struggled to control credit and the more localized inflations. In response to speculation in New York, the Federal Reserve tightened rates in 1928. These interest rate hikes failed to quell the speculative boom at home, however, and, in some cases, such as in the brokers' loans market, even encouraged it by attracting funds from abroad.[2] Indeed a combination of high interest rates in New York and recessionary trends in Germany and central Europe caused a great reversal of capital flows back into the United States, adding fuel to an already overheated market (Eichengreen 1992).[3] This in turn only aggravated the German recession.

The consequences of the credit boom were severe (Eichengreen and Mitchener 2003). Geographically heterogeneous asset price inflations occurred in areas such as real estate and the stock market. Once economic actors realized that some assets were overvalued, they started a process of intense deleveraging which spurred deflation (Fisher 1933). Although New York banks were not heavily affected by the brokers' loans market, corporations which had heavily invested in it likely were.[4] Households burdened with first and second mortgages defaulted on their loans (Postel-Vinay 2017).

---

2. The expansion of credit was emphasized early on by Hayek (1932), Robbins (1934), Rothbard (1963), and Palyi (1972). Most of these authors described the Federal Reserve as having maintained artificially low interest rates, making it the primary culprit in the overexpansion of credit. As the rest of this chapter suggests, it seems difficult to lay the blame solely on Federal Reserve policy rates.

3. Ritschl (2002) even argues that U.S. capital outflows to Germany following the Dawes Plan in 1924 led to bad investment decisions there as well as increased uncertainty regarding international payments. This may have caused the German economy to falter even before the U.S. economy, with a stock market boom ending in 1927. This, in turn, may have led investors to redirect funds from Germany to the United States, thereby contributing to speculation in New York. See also Temin (1963).

4. Corporations heavily invested in the brokers' loans market, although the extent to which they were affected by the stock market fall needs further research (see Smiley and Keehn 2008).

Bank and firm insolvency were not the only issue, however, as the sheer size of credit growth in less liquid assets, such as mortgages, left many banks unable to face demands for liquid funds (Postel-Vinay 2016). The Federal Reserve's continued tight monetary policy only made things worse (Richardson and Troost 2009), although dealing with these solvency and deep liquidity issues would have needed particularly extensive intervention, with potential costs to society down the line in the form of moral hazard and fiscal consolidation.

What could the Federal Reserve have done to keep the domestic credit boom under control? While this chapter does not give a definitive answer, some of the nonmonetary aspects of the boom would tend to suggest that unconventional policy tools in the form of micro- and macroprudential measures should have been used in addition to more traditional ones. This is, of course, easier to say in hindsight, although the Federal Reserve was not unacquainted with policies of so-called direct pressure, which it had experimented with in the 1921 crisis and even used in modest form in 1928 (Rieder 2019). Such policy experiments are in line with others seen in postwar France (Monnet 2014), Britain (Aikman, Bush, and Taylor 2016), or even America (Romer and Romer 1993). The idea that such measures may need to become part of the standard policy toolkit was harnessed earlier on by the Bank for International Settlements (Borio and Lowe 2002) and is buttressed by the concomitant credit booms and absence of inflation in the 2000s.

In what follows I first provide an overview of the credit boom, starting with its relationship with money growth. I also describe the evolution of credit by focusing on the different types of lenders, household balance sheets, and corporate debt. The second section draws on less and more recent works in the literature and asks whether this was a "credit boom gone wrong"—an expression borrowed from the seminal paper by Eichengreen and Mitchener (2003). I first ask whether, given the general lack of inflationary trends, specific asset price inflations—for instance in the real estate and stock markets—may not have themselves been spurred by credit. While definitive conclusions are yet to be reached, there is suggestive evidence in both cases that credit supply played a significant role in addition to demand. A discussion then follows, where the Federal Reserve's difficulty in keeping credit under control in 1928–1929 provides some illustration of the potential limits of monetary policy. Alternatives were tried with only limited success, suggesting the absence of one-size-fits-all macroprudential measures. I then suggest that, at the very least, credit booms made households and banks significantly more vulnerable to price and liquidity shocks than they otherwise would have been in 1929.

The 1920s Credit Boom

THE MACROECONOMY

In their seminal work, Friedman and Schwartz (1963) argued that the Great Depression was primarily a monetary phenomenon. Their argument focused on the years of the depression itself, rather than on the preceding years. They found that a significant contraction in the money supply, whose proximate cause was deposit withdrawals and bank failures between 1930 and 1933, was most likely to explain the severity of the downturn. They held the Federal Reserve and its adherence to the gold standard responsible for the lack of proactive measures designed to help fight the depression. The 1920s are not subject to much inquiry in their analysis. Nevertheless, suggestion is made that the generally deflationary stance of the Federal Reserve in the late 1920s prepared the ground for a downturn and may have even caused it. Indeed, in 1928, faced with a speculative boom in the stock market, the Federal Reserve increased its discount rate from 3.5% to 5%, which not only failed to prick the bubble but actually initiated a slowdown in economic activity, reflected in the fall of the industrial production index from 299 to 240 from February to June 1929 (Friedman and Schwartz 1963, 296–98; Miron and Romer 1990).[5]

This view of the depression is far from uncontested. Many authors, especially in the wake of Peter Temin's work, have argued that factors from the real economy were at play too. Temin (1976) stressed the importance of an "autonomous" fall in consumption in 1929, which he left by and large unexplained, but unrelated to monetary forces. Others have emphasized the saturation of investment opportunities for firms once most potential buyers had already purchased the main new products of the 1920s, such as a car, a washing machine, a vacuum cleaner, a fridge, a radio, and a telephone (Wilson 1948; Gordon 1951; Hansen 1951; Rostow 1963). Difficulties in the agricultural areas, where the wartime boom had given way to a long drawn-out bust that never really seemed to completely end, are also often pointed out (Kindleberger 1973).

Eichengreen and Mitchener (2003) went further. Focusing on several industrial countries (not just the United States) they placed credit at the center of their analysis of the Great Depression, as had Robbins (1934), Hayek

5. In their analysis of the Great Depression, Friedman and Schwartz thus very much exemplified the "money view," according to which monetary forces drive the economy. This view has been reasserted in the context of the Great Recession. See Congdon (2017).

(1932), Rothbard (1963), and von Mises (1971) before them. Drawing on a number of statistical sources, they argued for a strong positive association between the extent of the credit boom in the 1920s and the severity of the ensuing fall in GDP. They meticulously documented the ways in which consumers, firms, and financial institutions increased their leverage throughout the decade, and the negative consequences of such investment behavior in the downturn. Their work can be related to several analyses showing that banks failed in the Great Depression for reasons that were similar to the reasons they had been failing in the 1920s (Temin 1976; White 1984), and more generally due to falls in asset prices as opposed to simple panic-related issues (Calomiris and Mason 1997; Calomiris and Mason 2003). While not denying the importance of monetary forces in explaining the depth of the depression (Das, Mitchener, and Vossmeyer 2018; Mitchener and Richardson 2013, 2019), these works shed light on problems that arose on the asset side of banks' balance sheets. Works by Bernanke (2003) and others reinforced the "credit view," which stressed the role of credit disintermediation during the crisis as an additional downward force in the contraction.

Looking at the figures, what do the trends in money and credit look like for the 1920s? Ever since 1933 commentators have puzzled at the absence of any strong inflationary trends in the 1920s worldwide. Eichengreen and Mitchener (2003) also noted, not without surprise, that M2 relative to GDP had a tendency to fall over the 1920s, and that deviations from trend were minor.[6] As puzzling as it is, this observation fits neatly with Friedman and Schwartz's concession that the 1920s were, if anything, a deflationary decade.[7] Figure 10.1 shows the trend in prices over the 1920s.

6. They included deviations of the money supply as part of their composite indicator of credit. While warning readers that money would be a highly imperfect measure of credit, they justified its inclusion by the fact that banks were still the primary provider of credit at the time, as opposed to nonbank sources of funds.

7. Friedman and Schwartz saw the concomitant money supply stabilization and continued GDP growth of the late 1920s as an anomaly. While emphasizing the "close synchronism" of movements in economic activity and the money supply in other periods (1963, 296), they conceded that "the cyclical expansion from 1927 to 1929 is one of the very few in our record in which prices were a shade lower at the three months centered on the peak than at the three months centered on the initial trough. The stock of money, too, failed to rise and even fell slightly during most of the expansion—a phenomenon not matched in any prior or subsequent cyclical expansion. Far from being an inflationary decade, the twenties were the reverse" (1963, 298). They explained the stabilization of the money supply through the tightening of Federal Reserve policy (see below). But they failed to explain why this didn't translate into a slowdown in economic activity from 1928.

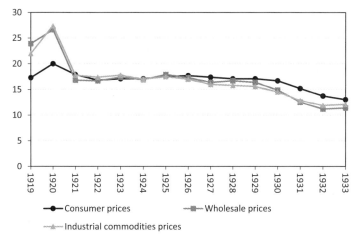

FIGURE 10.1 Consumer, wholesale, and industrial commodities prices
Source: Carter et al. (2006), table Cc1-2: Peter H. Lindert and Richard Sutch, "Consumer Price Indexes, for All Items: 1774–2003"; and table Cc66-83: Christopher Hanes, "Wholesale and Producer Price Indexes, by Commodity Group: 1890–1997 [Bureau of Labor Statistics]."

Looking next at the monetary aggregates, the picture that emerges is one in which broad money rises swiftly up to the middle of the decade, but slows somewhat afterward. Figure 10.2 shows indexes of broad money (M2 and M4) along with loans by commercial banks, mutual savings banks, and building and loan institutions, with 1922 as the base year. From this graph it is clear that the money supply grew very fast until 1926 but slowed afterward, especially in 1928 and 1929. This can be contrasted with the growth of credit, which quickly rose from 1922 to 1927, but continued on its way upward thereafter.

More specifically, two parallel comparisons of money and growth can be made. Just as several measures of broad money coexist (M0, M1, M2, M3, and so on), the same can be said of credit.[8] M2 in Friedman and Schwartz's money stock data only includes deposits at commercial banks, while M4 also includes deposits at savings institutions.[9] Clearly, total bank loans, including

8. One might suggest labeling them C1, C2, C3 and so on; although I refrain from doing so in this chapter.

9. Friedman and Schwartz (1963) see M2 as the most relevant indicator of the money stock at the time; it includes M1 (currency in circulation and demand deposits at commercial banks) and time deposits at commercial banks. M4 includes M1, M2 as well as deposits at mutual savings banks, savings and loan associations, and postal savings banks. Today M1 would also include demand deposits at savings institutions—however at the time savings institutions did not hold demand deposits. M2 would include time deposits only below a certain amount but would include time deposits at savings institutions. The closest version of M2 today would therefore

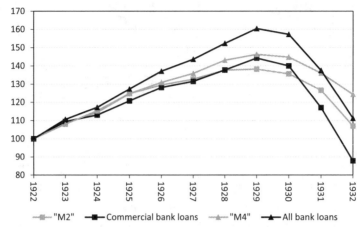

FIGURE 10.2 Estimated money supply (Friedman and Schwartz's M2 and M4), commercial bank loans, and all bank loans (loans of commercial banks, mutual savings banks, and building and loan associations) (1922 = 100)

Sources: Money supply: Friedman and Schwartz (1963), table A1; Carter et al. (2006), table Cj42-48: Richard G. Anderson, "Stock of Money and Its Components: 1867–1947 [Friedman and Schwartz]." Credit: Carter et al. (2006), table Cj251-264: H. Bodenhorn, "Commercial Banks—Number and Assets: 1834–1980"; Carter et al. (2006), table Cj362-374: H. Bodenhorn, "Mutual Savings Banks—Assets and Liabilities: 1896-1977"; Carter et al. (2006), table Cj389-397: H. Bodenhorn, "Savings and Loan Associations—Number, Assets, and Liabilities: 1922–1989 [All Operating Associations]."

Note: M2 includes M1 (currency in circulation and demand deposits at commercial banks) and time deposits at commercial banks. M4 includes M1 and M2, as well as deposits at mutual savings banks, savings and loan associations, and postal savings banks. See text for more information.

loans at savings institutions (what we might call C4), grew substantially faster than M4 as early as 1926, with the difference getting larger from 1927 onward. If we look at commercial bank loans (C2), the difference is smaller but still striking at the peak: in 1929 their pace of growth surpasses that of M2 by a significant amount.

There are therefore really two phases of the boom. In the first phase, the United States benefited from its new postwar international position as the world's creditor. With a current account surplus and gold flowing in continuously at a rapid pace, money was plentiful and could be lent with confidence. In the second phase, gold flows stabilized and even reversed (Robbins

---

be Friedman and Schwartz's M4 which includes deposits at mutual savings banks, savings and loan associations, and postal savings banks (Anderson and Kavajecz 1994). As a comparative benchmark for commercial bank loan growth, M2 seems appropriate. For total bank loans, M4 seems more suitable.

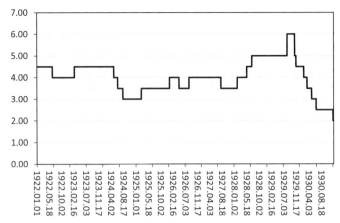

FIGURE 10.3 Federal Reserve discount rate (daily)
Source: Board of Governors of the Federal Reserve System (1922a, 6–7; 1922b–1934); Federal Reserve Bank of St. Louis, DISCOUNT series.

1934, 25). The money supply also slowed,[10] but credit continued on its own course.[11] As a proportion of nominal GDP, total private credit reached 156% in 1929 from 113% in 1912, one of the greatest increases among developed economies at the time (Eichengreen and Mitchener 2003).[12]

This could be partly explained by the Federal Reserve's relaxation of interest rates from 4% to 3% in 1927 following a will to help agricultural areas, and most importantly Britain which was struggling at an overvalued gold standard parity. While the Federal Reserve no doubt holds some responsibility in this, the pace of credit growth was similar before 1927 and afterward, including in 1928 when it tightened its policy in response to the stock market boom. Figure 10.3 shows the Federal Reserve discount rate policy over the course of the 1920s. The pattern of changes would tend to suggest that interest rates may not be the only culprit.

What could explain a noninflationary trend in a booming economy? Kindleberger (1973, 83–107) emphasized world structural deflation as a consequence of overproduction, particularly in primary sectors, itself a result of an underestimation of how fast Europe would recover from the war. While this

10. Friedman and Schwartz (1963) explained the stabilization of the money supply via restrictions in monetary policy, especially in terms of high-powered money (290) and gold sterilization (282–84). But they did not explain why GDP continued to expand over that time.

11. Robbins (1934, 25) already noted that "there was taking place in the United States *an expansion of credit on a declining gold basis*" (emphasis in original).

12. The data on total private credit are from Goldsmith (1958); see the next section. GDP data are from Sutch (2006).

certainly explains deflationary tendencies in South America, Canada, and in the American agricultural sector, it hardly explains the absence of inflation in other commodities and wholesale products in the United States (see fig. 10.1).

An alternative explanation focuses on the distribution of the gains from the upswing. While wages and incomes barely rose throughout the decade, business profits increased tremendously. Between 1925 and 1929 the net profits of 536 firms rose by 42% with wages only increasing by about 5% (Royal Institute of International Affairs 1933, 7). This skewed distribution of profit gains may in turn have subsumed general consumption. An explanation of this kind was put forward by Keynes (see Keynes 1934, 2:190), and is broadly in line with work by Piketty and Saez (2003), who show an increase in U.S. income inequality over the 1920s principally occasioned by a rise in the capital income share. Finally, consumers may have focused their consumption on specific types of assets and goods, leading to more localized bouts of inflation. Further light on this phenomenon will be shed in the following section.

COMMERCIAL BANKS

While explaining the absence of general inflation is not straightforward, finding explanations for the continuance of credit growth is equally treacherous. Let us start with commercial banks. In 1929, commercial bank loans and investments amounted to $49.8 billion. Goldsmith (1958) provided early estimates on commercial and noncommercial bank types of lenders (see table 10.1). It is clear that they all grew very quickly in the 1920s.

Commercial banks saw an unusual increase in assets, peaking in 1928 and 1929. The greatest addition to total intermediary assets from 1923 to 1929, of $20 billion, came from them, although they "only" grew by about half relative to other groups. State-chartered and national banks grew in quite different ways, which partly resulted from different regulations applying to them. For instance, national banks were restricted in the amount of loans they could make on real estate, so they expanded mainly in other stocks and bonds and other loans. State banks, on the other hand, had their greatest increase in mortgage loans as well as other loans (Postel-Vinay 2017).[13] One might speculate that banks expanded their lending in response to competition coming from noncommercial banks.

The increase in commercial banks' assets in 1928–1929 does not seem to have led to an industry-wide increase in leverage in those two years. While the

---

13. Given that state banks had much higher failure rates in the 1930s than national banks, this is worthy of notice (this will be discussed in more detail below).

TABLE 10.1 Estimated total assets at main groups of
intermediaries ($ billions)

	1922	1929
Commercial banks	47.5	66.2
Investment trust companies	18.0	30.0
Insurance companies	11.8	25.0
Mutual savings banks	6.6	9.9
Savings and loan associations	2.8	7.4
Sales finance companies	N/A	2.1

Source: Goldsmith (1958), table 10, pp. 73–74.

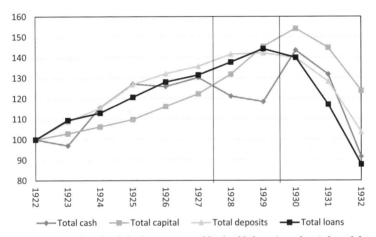

FIGURE 10.4 Estimated total cash (cash, currency, and bankers' balances), total capital, total deposits, and total loans at commercial banks (1922 = 100)
Source: Carter et al. (2006), table Cj251-264: H. Bodenhorn, "Commercial Banks—Number and Assets: 1834–1980."

average equity ratio for all individual banks is unavailable, one can still get a rough idea of the importance of its evolution by looking at indexes of capital and total assets. Figure 10.4 suggests that capital, if anything, rose faster than total loans in 1928–1929; although an increase in leverage may have occurred in preceding years.[14]

Yet commercial bank credit reached a peak in 1929 over and above broad money growth (M2), previously shown in figure 10.2. How could one explain

14. Anecdotal evidence would tend to suggest that some institutions, such as investment trusts, greatly increased their leverage in the last phase of the boom (Galbraith 1954, 82). Interestingly, however, Postel-Vinay (2016) also notes that leverage had a tendency to fall over the 1920s in Chicago.

it? Figure 10.4 may provide a preliminary answer. Loans seem to rise at a similar rate as deposits, which is not unusual. What this chart clearly shows, however, is a *decrease* in liquid reserves among banks in 1928–1929. A large part of the stabilization of broad money (currency + deposits) relative to credit may therefore be explained by a fall in the reserve-deposit ratio and a parallel fall in the currency-deposit ratio,[15] implying a rise in the money multiplier. In other words, deposits, and therefore loans, grew very fast throughout, but cash did not keep up, explaining why the sum of cash and deposits (broad money) did not rise as fast as deposits (and therefore loans) alone.

Friedman and Schwartz (1963, 273–75) already noted a 1920s increase in the money multiplier, which they found difficult to explain in terms of monetary policy. They suggested tentative explanations for the increase in the deposit-reserve ratio, focusing on the decline in actual reserves relative to required reserves, and speculated that this may have been due to the existence of the Federal Reserve as a lender of last resort, "which encouraged banks to trim their reserve balances further than they otherwise would have done" (278). What Friedman and Schwartz did not emphasize is that an increase in the multiplier could mechanically lead to a faster increase of credit than broad money. An emphasis on a multiplier increase leading to greater loan growth combined with loss of liquidity in the 1920s would not have sat easily with their more benign view of bank health in that period.[16]

A closer look at figure 10.4 reveals an additional element to the 1929 peak in credit at commercial banks. Between 1928 and 1929, deposits stopped growing, whereas loans continued to grow fast. Although relatively minor, this increase in credit over and above that in deposits in the last phase of the boom is harder to explain.[17] The increase in capital may have played a role, although several question marks remain.

SAVINGS BANKS

A significant portion of the rise in total credit can also be explained by an increase in credit by mutual savings banks and savings and loans associations

15. The fall in the currency-deposit ratio is not shown on the graph for visibility purposes, but it is substantial.

16. Bernanke (1983) also emphasized the consequences of a change in the currency-deposit ratio from a credit perspective, although he focused on the recession phase. Note that a fall in liquidity occurred before credit and deposits started to grow faster than broad money. This general fall in liquidity and its potentially negative consequences were not emphasized by Friedman and Schwartz despite their remarks on the falling reserve-deposit ratio.

17. It may also be related to the more substantial gap seen at mutual savings banks; see below.

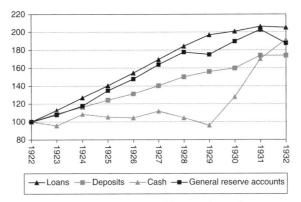

FIGURE 10.5 Estimated total cash, total deposits, total loans, and general reserve accounts at mutual savings banks (1922 = 100)
Source: Carter et al. (2006), table Cj362-374: H. Bodenhorn, "Mutual Savings Banks—Assets and Liabilities: 1896–1977."

(also called building and loans associations or B&Ls). Total private debt, including corporate and individual noncorporate debt, amounted to $161.8 billion, suggesting that about two-thirds of total credit in the economy was coming from noncommercial bank sources (U.S. Bureau of Economic Analysis 1969).

Between 1922 and 1929, mutual savings banks' and B&Ls' assets, which were mostly in the form of mortgages, were respectively multiplied by 0.5 and by 3. In fact, "all bank loans" in figure 10.2 may underestimate the growth of private credit since investment trust and insurance company loans are not shown. Investment trusts resembled today's closed-end mutual funds, and their assets were relatively evenly distributed between debt and equity securities (U.S. Bureau of Economic Analysis 1969, 84).[18] They were the most important other type of intermediary in terms of total assets ($30 billion in 1929), which had almost doubled between 1923 and 1929. Insurance companies held $25 billion in assets in 1929, which had also nearly doubled over that time. There was also a very large share of lending done by individuals (Snowden 2010).

Although evidence on B&Ls is lacking, data on assets and liabilities at mutual savings banks would tend to suggest that the increase in total credit over and above that of M4 broad money is partly a result of a fall in liquidity. Figure 10.5 clearly shows that their deposits grew faster than their total cash. In addition, and more surprisingly, it also evidences a greater growth

18. Their growth has been vividly depicted by Galbraith (1954), who emphasizes their role in stock market speculation due to their capacity to buy stock on margin.

of loans relative to deposits since the beginning of the 1920s, with the gap getting wider over time. Total loans seem to grow in parallel with general reserve funds which form part of mutual savings banks' liabilities. Yet even this item seems to fall in 1929 relative to loans, which keep growing at the same, rapid pace in that year. The source of this widening gap thus remains open to question.

There are several avenues for future research. The aforementioned widening gap at mutual savings banks is one. More generally, potential sources of a liquidity squeeze need to be investigated. An acceleration in the number of panics toward the late 1920s may be one explanation. Others may include a behavioral decline in vigilance among banks in a booming economy.

HOUSEHOLDS

As Mishkin (1978) and Olney (1999) noted some time ago, the increase in lending is reflected partly in the building up of household liabilities in the 1920s. Figure 10.6 shows the rise in nonfarm, noncorporate debt. An increase in consumer debt is noticeable. Individuals would borrow to buy durables such as cars and refrigerators. These could often be bought on an installment basis, and companies themselves would provide these loans. For instance, in 1919 General Motors created its own specialist lending institution, General Motors Acceptance Corporation (GMAC), to allow consumers to buy their cars on credit (Olney 1991). At the peak of the car sales boom about 70% of cars were purchased in this way (Olney 1999).

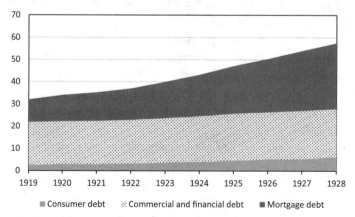

FIGURE 10.6 Estimated private nonfarm, noncorporate debt ($ billions), stacked
Source: Carter et al. (2006), table Cj870-889: John A. James and Richard Sylla, "Net Public and Private Debt, by Major Sector: 1916–1976."

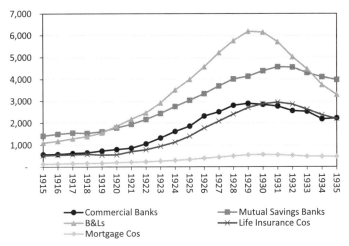

FIGURE 10.7 Estimated residential mortgage debt by type of lender ($ millions)
Source: Grebler, Blank, and Winnick (1956), table N2.

Yet, as can be seen from figure 10.6, consumer debt did not constitute the largest share of household debt at the time, which was in housing. Much of the increase in nonfarm individual debt came in the form of mortgages. Incidentally, the growth in residential mortgage debt illustrates the importance of the growth in noncommercial bank intermediaries. Only a portion of these mortgages came from commercial banks. Figure 10.7 shows the increase in residential mortgage debt by type of lender. Clearly, B&Ls as well as mutual savings banks were the largest creditors in this field. Life insurance companies also played an important role (and so did individual lenders, who are not shown on this graph—see Snowden 2010).

Why did households borrow so much in the 1920s to buy houses? As pointed out previously, nominal wages remained more or less stable throughout the twenties, resulting in only a small improvement in real wages, thanks to the slight deflationary trend. As consumers were already borrowing to buy cars, there is no specific reason to think that they were in a particularly good position to buy houses. Migration to the cities, credit availability, and general optimism must all have figured prominently in individuals' decisions. Many new homeowners had previously migrated from farming areas which were suffering from the postwar boom and bust in agriculture. Migration from the Midwestern plains to Chicago led to a significant property boom there. There were similar booms in Toledo, Cleveland, and Detroit (Allen 1931; Postel-Vinay 2017). State banks would not usually lend more than 50% of the value of the house; however house buyers could easily get a second mortgage from another institution or an individual lender to make up the difference. As a result, consumers could be indebted up to 70% or 80% of the value of the house (Postel-Vinay 2017).

While individual and noncorporate debt increased from $43.9 billion in 1919 to $72.9 billion ten years later, corporate debt rose in a similar way: from $53.3 billion in 1919 to $88.9 billion in 1929. Corporations borrowed from banks and in the bond market to invest in machinery and equipment, which may be partly at the origin of the great productivity increases witnessed in the 1920s (Smiley 2002).

Toward the end of the boom, corporations also became a significant source of funds. Part of their profits were no doubt reinvested in the company, and a portion was directly invested in stocks and bonds. However, over time company profits also became a source of funds for speculation on the stock market (Smiley and Keehn 2008). As we shall see, such unusual sources of funding may have played a significant role in the stock market boom. The general question to which I now turn is the extent to which the rise in credit fueled unsustainable asset price booms and eventually led to their collapse.

A Credit Boom Gone Wrong?

So far, I have shown that the 1920s witnessed a significant credit boom. In this section, I draw on a wide range of studies to suggest three things. First, I provide anecdotal evidence that credit was partly to blame for asset price inflation in certain parts of the economy, notably real estate and the stock market (Keynes 1934; Palyi 1972). While only suggestive, this evidence points to reasons for a disconnect between prices and economic fundamentals, and for the subsequent asset price shocks that occurred in the late 1920s. Second, I suggest that this credit buildup and ensuing inflations made households, banks, and potentially corporations vulnerable to asset price shocks and panics when they started to unfold in 1929.

ASSET PRICE INFLATION: REAL ESTATE
AND THE STOCK MARKET

There was no generalized inflation in the 1920s. Nevertheless, as Keynes (1934) noted, specific areas of the economy were highly inflated. Corporate profits had expanded tremendously. Real estate values had massively increased in certain

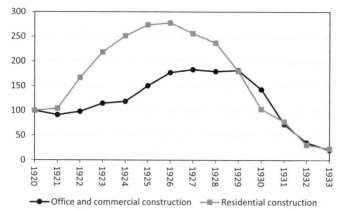

FIGURE 10.8 Value of new office, commercial, and residential construction (1920 = 100)
Source: Grebler, Blank, and Winnick (1956).

parts of the country. And, of course, the stock market witnessed a historic boom. The question I ask in this section is the extent to which the unsustainable real estate and stock market booms were driven by an extraordinary supply of credit.

Real Estate

The 1920s witnessed a significant real estate boom. This was partly helped by migration from the hard-hit agricultural areas and the more widespread use of the automobile. Unfortunately, data on land values is still incomplete (Brocker and Hanes 2014; Fishback and Kollmann 2014). Figure 10.8 gives indexes of traditional estimates of the value of new construction nationwide.[19] New residential construction for the country as a whole likely peaked in 1926 and then receded fairly sharply. At first glance, it would appear that the boom peaked too early to be explained by a surge of credit in the second phase of the credit boom.

Yet figure 10.8 also shows a boom in office and commercial construction, which reached a first peak in 1927 and another one in 1929.[20] This corresponds to the late 1920s growth of skyscrapers described in popular accounts (Allen 1931; Smiley 2002, 9; see also Nicholas and Scherbina 2013). In addition, figure 10.9 shows the rise in housing starts by region. On this graph it appears that

19. Fishback and Kollmann (2014) provide alternative estimates based on this and other series.

20. Brocker and Hanes (2014) also show that the 1925 peak may correspond to single-family houses. The pattern for multifamily units is similar to that of office and commercial construction.

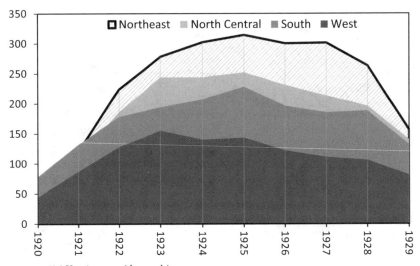

FIGURE 10.9 Housing starts (thousands)
Source: Grebler, Blank, and Winnick (1956).

while most U.S. regions indeed saw a peak in 1925, the suburban areas of
the northeast saw a prolonged boom which lasted until 1927–1928. In terms
of timing, this boom corresponds to the increase in mortgage lending by all
types of lenders already shown in figure 10.7. A cursory look at both graphs
indicates that, at the very least, the construction boom was accompanied by
a large increase in mortgage credit. Data on new mortgages in Cook County,
Illinois, would suggest that the amount of new mortgages made was just as
high in 1928 as in the two preceding years (see fig. 10.10). Finally, the fact that
the housing market started to decline before the start of the Great Depression is in itself an indication that it may be a potent cause of the downturn. A
similar observation has been made regarding the timing of the housing cycle
in the 2000s and the Great Recession (Mian and Sufi 2014).

Several accounts from the contemporary literature also describe housing
supply fast exceeding market demand, implying significant overvaluation of
house prices. In Chicago, immigration predictions had been grossly overesti-
mated: while its population increased by 35% from 1918 to 1926, the number
of lots subdivided rose by over 3,000% (Hoyt 1933, 237). Overbuilding was visible in many suburban areas in a way that was similar to what had happened in
Florida a few years earlier (Vanderblue 1927).[21] Although the evidence is only

21. The Florida boom ended abruptly partly due to a hurricane which caused many casual-
ties. One might speculate that its timing would have followed other regional booms had this
not occurred.

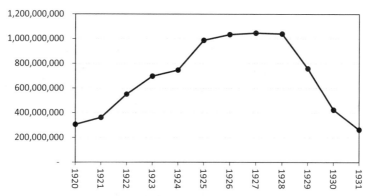

FIGURE 10.10 New mortgages and trust deeds, Cook County, Illinois ($)
Source: Hoyt (1933).

anecdotal, many of those accounts, such as Allen (1931), Simpson (1933), and Sa-kolski (1966), go in the same direction—describing new but empty suburbs (and skyscrapers) in many areas and house values on the way down before 1929 (see also Echols 2017). We also know that some areas saw historic collapses in house prices—Chicago, for example, had witnessed a 50% price decline by 1933 (Hoyt 1933; Postel-Vinay 2016). Brocker and Hanes (2014) find that owner-occupied home values fell by 20% to 48% during 1930–1934, depending on the region.[22]

The fact that housing supply probably exceeded housing demand makes it likely that mortgage supply also exceeded mortgage demand. While some studies have suggested that the contribution of real estate to the national economy was minor (White 2014; Field 2014), it is still possible to ask whether prices and building would have seen such a momentous, unsustainable rise had credit supply not expanded as much as it did. Previous sections of the chapter have shed light on the mortgage credit boom that occurred between 1922 and 1925–1929. Existing evidence would suggest little variation in interest rates (around 6% for first mortgages) over the period, implying a very elastic response of supply to demand (Postel-Vinay 2017). The absence of a rise in interest rates on mortgages questions the idea that demand for loans was the only factor at play. In addition, there is evidence that supply forces played a significant role in the postwar farmland credit boom in agricultural areas (Rajan and Rhamcharan 2015). More suggestive evidence would also tend to point further in this direction (see also Eichengreen and Mitchener 2003), although additional research is arguably needed to settle the issue.

22. A collapse in house prices is not evidence in and of itself of market overvaluation, however.

The Stock Market

The stock market boom and crash has long attracted scholars' attention with regards to several specific questions. Many doubt its importance in terms of causing the subsequent downturn (Friedman and Schwartz 1963; Temin 1976), although Romer (1990) suggested it had a significant impact on uncertainty and consumption. This section of the chapter does not aim to instill doubt about these assertions. Rather, it suggests that the credit boom leading to the stock market bubble may not have been simply demand-led, and it provides a good illustration of the difficulties faced by the Federal Reserve in quelling the credit boom in spite of its monetary policy tightening.

The quality of stock market data—especially relative to real estate data— allows one to say with more certainty that the prices indeed became disconnected from fundamentals. White (1990), for example, shows very clearly that dividends and the Dow Jones index were on the same upward trend from 1922 to 1928 but that they deviated afterward, and quite significantly so. Rappoport and White (1993) confirm this.

Of course, stock prices are always partly based on expected future earnings, which may not be entirely reflected in companies' dividends. And investors had very good reasons to be optimistic about the future. The 1920s had been a decade of outstanding productivity growth, with horsepower per worker increasing by 50% between 1919 and 1929 and manufacturing productivity rising by more than 60% (Aldcroft 1977, 197). Field (2003, 2006) has shown that the 1920s and 1930s were two of the most technologically productive decades in America's history. New technologies such as cars, tractors, radios, refrigerators, and many other appliances were being produced at a rising pace thanks in part to the spread of electricity and the moving assembly line. It was possible to think that companies' prices reflected this and future innovations, relying on the impression that a new era of permanently higher stock prices had come about. However, even if productivity remained high throughout the depression (Nicholas 2008), hindsight would tend to suggest that investors had been overly optimistic. Between 1925 and the peak in 1929 share prices more than doubled while industrial output rose by less than a quarter and profits by less than half (Aldcroft 1977, 196).

Was credit responsible for the bubble? The great proponents of this theory, Galbraith (1954) and Kindleberger (1973), insisted that the rise in brokers' loans, which allowed investors to buy stocks on margin, gave an artificial boost to the boom and led to the overvaluation in prices. Investors interested in buying stocks only had to put down a small amount of cash and borrow the rest, using the stock as collateral for the loan. There was a general assumption that New York banks were especially responsible for this increase in brokers' loans.

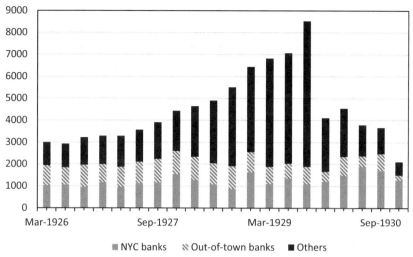

FIGURE 10.11 Estimated sources of brokers' loans ($ thousands) on the New York Stock Exchange
Source: Board of Governors of the Federal Reserve System (1941), table 139.

In a striking graph, White (1990b) showed that the volume of brokers' loans increased at almost exactly the same—extremely fast—pace as stock prices from 1926 up to the peak in 1929. However, he insisted that New York banks could not be held responsible for the greater part of the increase, which occurred in the last months from 1928 to 1929. Brokers' loans at New York banks on their own account actually fell from $1.5 billion in January 1928 to $1.1 billion twelve months later as banks responded to pressure from the Federal Reserve, which increased its discount rate from 3.5% to 5% between January and July.

The increase in the volume of brokers' loans thus came from elsewhere. Figure 10.11 shows that while brokers' loans made by New York banks remained relatively stable, brokers' loans made by "others" increased tremendously between 1928 and 1929. Individual lenders played some role in this. More importantly, in September 1929 14% of brokers' loans came from investment trusts, and an astounding 56% from corporations themselves (Smiley and Keehn 1988). Corporations had experienced a tremendous rise in profits, and in 1928 became attracted to the higher call loan rates, which had gone up 10%–15% in response to demand. They invested heavily in this market, retreating from the market for commercial paper (Smiley and Keehn 1988).[23]

23. See also Wigmore (1985, 94), who points out that "major corporations in the auto, petroleum, and steel industries investment trusts, and utilities built up large portfolios of call loans" while diminishing their time deposits at banks.

There is an extent to which money was tight in the New York market in 1928 (White 1990a, 1990b). Fed discount rates had gone up, and so had open-market sales, which reduced incentives for banks to make brokers' loans.[24] Commercial paper rates had gone up too, and call loan rates as well as margin requirements had increased tremendously partly in response to demand (although not by as much as in the 1907 crisis; see Fohlin 2019). High call loan rates can be seen as resulting from excess demand for brokers' loans.

On the other hand, those high call loan rates in turn attracted lenders into the market. Potential lenders, including some from abroad, were attracted to the higher rates of interest in the call loan market (Smiley and Keehn 1988; Wright 1929; Kindleberger 1973, 112).[25] The attractive power that these high rates exerted on them underscores the extent of the elasticity of supply for loans in this market, which rose very quickly to meet the excess demand. In addition, although corporations lowered their funding supply in the commercial paper market, at the same time banks increased their supply of commercial loans to compensate for this fall (Wright 1929).

Clearly the Federal Reserve had not got complete control over credit markets around that time. There is no doubt that the Federal Reserve was concerned about stock market speculation and wanted to curb it. After all, it was deeply influenced by the "real bills doctrine" which stated that the Federal Reserve should only act to direct credit to productive, as opposed to speculative, purposes. But in 1928 it was caught in a serious dilemma (Kindleberger 1973, 112). On the one hand, increasing the discount rate would make member banks more reluctant to lend—a rather positive outcome at least with regards to the stock market. On the other hand, it might further attract funds to the call market, especially from nonbank sources. In addition, increasing rates would put pressure on European central banks' gold reserves. Aware of these issues, the Federal Reserve still raised the discount rate several times. The effect was, predictably, only felt by the banks, which drastically reduced call loans on their own account. But the brokerage community, which was less constrained by the Federal Reserve's actions, "bid up call loan rates above

24. And although the discount rate was kept constant from mid-1928 to August 1929, the buying rate for bills was raised five times to 5.5% in March 1929, which was 0.5 percentage point above the discount rate (Friedman and Schwartz 1963, 289).

25. Kindleberger noted that interest rates increased "to attract new money" (Aliber and Kindleberger 2015, 94). Galbraith (1954, 49) stated: "In Montreal, London, Shanghai, and Hong Kong there was talk of these rates. Everywhere men of means told themselves that twelve per cent was twelve per cent. [. . .] Corporations also found these rates attractive." A similar increase in call rates occurred in the 1881 stock market boom in France (see Aliber and Kindleberger 2015).

competing rates and [went] beyond the banks to their customers to attract funds the banks would not lend" (Wigmore 1985, 94).

Another solution might have been to apply "direct pressure" to the market.[26] The solution was proposed by Adolph Miller, a prominent member of the Board of Governors of the Federal Reserve System. He suggested that the New York Federal Reserve Bank apply moral suasion and more or less deny access to the discount window member banks who were making brokers' loans for their own accounts.[27] This might also avoid tightening credit to the ordinary businessman.[28] This unconventional type of policy, however, did not deal with the increasing supply of funds coming from other parts of the economy (Kindleberger 1973, 113).[29]

Another form of unconventional policy might have been to increase margin requirements. Margin requirements were not low in 1929: they often reached 40% to 50% (Smiley and Keehn 1988).[30] Nevertheless, they might have been lower in 1928, when most of the increase in brokers' loans took place.[31] Today, even in normal times the *minimum* initial margin requirement is 50%—itself a result of the Securities and Exchange Act of 1934, which gave the Federal Reserve discretion over margin requirement regulation (Regulation T). It is possible that, had it been increased higher and earlier, speculation in the stock market would have been mitigated.[32]

It could be said more generally that traditional tools of monetary policy may have been insufficient to deal with the credit increase in the second half of the 1920s. This occurred independently from the money supply which remained relatively stable, and from inflation which also remained subsumed. Inflation occurred in specific types of assets, and this was not reflected in the general inflation rate. While part of the increase in credit can be explained by

26. See Bernanke's essay in Friedman and Schwartz (2008, 232).

27. At New York banks, only brokers' loans "on their own account" can be considered as loans made by the banks. Brokers' loans made by other financial institutions would appear on their balance sheets, but for these they simply acted as agents between the lender and the borrower—these were called brokers' loans "on account of others." There were also loans on account of out-of-town banks. Friedman and Schwartz (1963, 254–66) described in great detail the disagreements between the New York Federal Reserve and the Board of Governors on this topic.

28. Germany's Reichsbank tried something similar in 1927 (Temin 1963).

29. It is clear from Kindleberger (1973), figure 13, that this policy was successful in terms of curbing New York bank brokers' loans on their own account. The problem was with loans on account of "others."

30. This had in fact already been acknowledged by Galbraith (1954, 58).

31. Smiley and Keehn (1988) do not provide average figures for 1928, and they only note that precautions were taken "some months before the crash."

32. Although note that higher margin requirements might be a form of financial repression.

low interest rates in certain periods, as well as the increase in gold inflows in the early 1920s, the same cannot be said of the later increase. All in all, this would point toward the better use of other policy tools as a potential solution to deal with the problem. Monnet (2014) as well as Aikman, Bush, and Taylor (2018) have shown that central banks in Paris and London made use of such tools post-1945. Rieder (2019) shows that even the Federal Reserve applied "direct pressure" in the 1921 crisis, implying that it may have been more reluctant to do so in 1928 due to the severity of the 1921 crisis, which had often been blamed on its proactivity. Hindsight allows us to say that this reluctance may have been unwarranted.

BANK VULNERABILITY

One of the most striking aspects of the U.S. Great Depression was the bank failure rate. Savings institutions and insurance companies suffered significantly (Courtemanche and Snowden 2011; Fishback, Rose, and Snowden 2013; Rose 2011, 2014, 2016; Echols 2017). Commercial banks failed mostly in four waves, from the first one following the 1930 collapse of Caldwell and Company in Tennessee (McFerrin 1939) to the last one in March 1933, which was nationwide. Overall, more than 9,000 banks failed across the country (Wicker 1996). Almost all authors agree that the inaction of the Federal Reserve Banks aggravated the situation (Richardson and Troost 2009; Carlson, Mitchener, and Richardson 2011; Mitchener and Richardson 2013, 2019). What authors still disagree about is the extent to which individual banks were responsible for their own collapse.

Friedman and Schwartz (1963) saw bank runs as the primary root of the severity of the depression. In their view, banks were not especially vulnerable before those runs occurred. Had the Federal Reserve Bank been more proactive, bank runs could have been avoided. Banks were simply the victims of an exogenous, sudden increase in liquidity risk over which they had no control, and simple Federal Reserve intervention would have done the trick.

Another strand of literature suggests that banks were already vulnerable in 1929, and that such vulnerabilities were not entirely exogenous to the banking system. These authors acknowledge that New York banks were not directly affected by the stock market crash, which, given their controlled involvement in the brokers' loans market discussed above, is unsurprising. Nevertheless, it would be interesting to study the extent to which corporations and other investors were affected by default in this market, since they were so heavily invested in it. At this point the evidence is only suggestive (Galbraith 1956; Smiley and Keehn 2008).

The links to other markets have been more clearly evidenced. While not explicitly drawing a relationship between bank failures and the 1920s credit boom, White (1984) saw parallels between the banks that failed during the first banking crisis (November–December 1930) and those that had failed earlier in the 1920s in agricultural areas. He mentioned "swollen loan portfolios" and their link to the postwar agricultural boom and bust which never seemed to properly end. This is very close to Temin's (1976) interpretation of the crisis.

More recent work by Calomiris and Mason (2003) also showed that banks that failed during panics had ex ante characteristics which differed from those of the banks that survived. Focusing on Chicago, which had the highest urban bank failure rate in the country, Calomiris and Mason (1997) emphasized the similarities between panic failures and nonpanic failures, thereby underlining banks' preexisting weaknesses which made them especially vulnerable to an exogenous liquidity shock.

Often implied in these studies was that ex ante solvency risk was at stake. Some banks had invested in certain assets that had gone bad and were therefore more likely to fail in a liquidity crisis which would exacerbate asset price deflation. Postel-Vinay (2016) went further, asking explicitly which kinds of assets were responsible for leading banks to their failure. In Chicago, these were clearly mortgages. Some banks had invested much more than others in real estate loans throughout the 1920s and were therefore more vulnerable to a liquidity shock when it came (see fig. 10.12).[33] Despite the high foreclosure rate (10%–20% of residential mortgages over the period; see Fishback, Rose, and Snowden 2013), commercial banks likely did not make significant losses on these loans due to their low loan-to-value ratio (50%). However, their illiquid character caused severe problems when banks came to face withdrawals from 1930 onward.[34]

Although central bank action was clearly lacking when the time came for help, Chicago banks' unpreparedness for a liquidity shock suggests that an especially deep form of intervention would have been needed to quell the panic. This might have included, for instance, lending against mortgage collateral or outright purchases of such long-maturity loans. These forms of

33. The liquidity shock was exacerbated by the fact that banks were part of a large and deep network in which they often held liabilities with each other (Mitchener and Richardson 2019).

34. The maturity of first mortgages at commercial banks usually did not exceed five years, but they were frequently rolled over. The negative consequences of such renewal expectations are discussed in Postel-Vinay (2016, 2017).

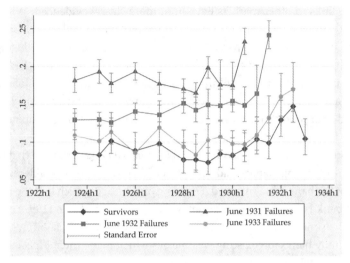

FIGURE 10.12 Real estate loans to total assets at Chicago state banks, by failure window
Source: Postel-Vinay (2016).

intervention would have entailed significant costs to society associated with moral hazard and fiscal consolidation.[35]

What this preliminary evidence suggests is that some banks had made investment decisions in the 1920s that had put them—and society as a whole—in a vulnerable position well before the crisis started. In some cases, it is still unclear whether those investment decisions can themselves be seen as the cause of subsequent declines in certain asset prices. In other cases, it is clear that whatever the subsequent decline in asset prices, banks had originated a credit boom that severely reduced their liquidity and made them vulnerable to any shock. In that sense, the credit boom could be expected to go wrong at any time.

HOUSEHOLD VULNERABILITY

The boom and bust in residential housing left many homeowners in disarray. The contractual form of commercial bank mortgages at the time meant that they were especially likely to default on those. Indeed, the 50% deposit

35. A bank aware of the possibility of such deep intervention would put less care in watching the quality of its long-term loans, making bailouts more likely with, at the very least, significant short- to medium-term fiscal costs to society. Deep liquidity intervention can only come hand in hand with measures mitigating moral hazard, which the developed world is still finding hard to perfectly design.

TABLE 10.2 Real value of household assets and liabilities (in billions of 1958 dollars)

	Household liabilities	Percent change from previous year	Household financial asset holdings	Percent change from previous year
1929	65.3		637.8	
1930	78.1	+20	613.0	−4
1931	79.3	+2	578.6	−6

Source: Mishkin (1978), table 1.

requirement on first mortgages by commercial banks was in most cases very difficult to make, and a large share of house buyers took a second mortgage from another institution or even from an individual to help make the down payment. Those second mortgages, being unregulated, often carried a usurious interest rate and demanded repayment before first mortgages which could in theory be rolled over and only demanded a "balloon" payment at the end. The prevalence of second mortgages increased the probability of foreclosure on first mortgages (Postel-Vinay 2017). With house prices often falling by 30% to 40% in urban areas, foreclosure was not a pleasant experience and significant government help was deployed (Rose 2011).

Irving Fisher's debt-deflation theory states that when price levels fall, the real value of nominal debt increases, which makes it harder to repay. Drawing on data from Goldsmith (1963), Mishkin (1978) provided an overview of the evolution of household balance sheets during the depression and showed that households' real liabilities increased by 12% from 1928 to 1929 and by 20% from 1929 to 1930 (from $65.5 billion to $78.1 billion at 1958 prices). He postulated that most of the increase in real debt during the depression came from the fall in prices (see table 10.2). Since most of the liabilities were in consumer and mortgage debt, as opposed to call loans in the stock market, the increase in real debt must have affected the average consumer at least as much as upper-income groups.

Olney (1999) actually sees consumer debt as exacerbating deflation itself. As consumers focused on paying down their debt, they reduced their consumption of perishable goods, which led to deflation between 1929 and 1930. This may have created a vicious cycle between increases in real debt and deflation.

Conclusion

The U.S. Great Depression was preceded by almost a decade of credit growth. To meet corporate and household demands for loans, credit grew at commercial banks, mutual savings banks, and B&Ls. There were two phases of the boom: the first one, from 1922 to around 1927, when money supply growth matched that of credit; the second one, from 1928 to 1929, when credit growth outpaced money supply growth. Competition from nonbank lenders such as investment trusts and insurance companies may have spurred the second phase. This rise in credit thus occurred in a noninflationary environment.

Still, asset price inflation occurred. Research is still needed to determine the extent to which asset price shocks were endogenous to banks' investment choices. House price data is highly inadequate, although anecdotal evidence would tend to suggest that housing booms were credit fueled and led to over-building. Data quality is better for the stock market. Here it would seem that although the Fed tightened rates in 1928, credit was still relatively easy in certain parts of the economy and aided speculation.

The rise in household debt over the 1920s made households highly vulnerable to deflation when it came about. Due to their investment decisions in the 1920s, some banks were also vulnerable to asset price shocks. Others certainly made themselves particularly vulnerable to liquidity shocks through their expansion of mortgages.

The Federal Reserve was relatively ill-equipped to fight such targeted credit-induced asset price inflations. The inflations occurred when the Federal Reserve both loosened and then tightened its policy. A policy of "direct pressure" was tried but with limited results. Perhaps other kinds of macro- and microprudential tools could have been used.

Many questions remain. The decoupling of credit growth from money growth needs further explanation. The fall in commercial banks' liquidity from 1927 may only be half the picture. Was the 1929 increase in banks' lending linked to the stock market? What happened among savings institutions? Can the commercial bank mortgage boom, which occurred slightly earlier, actually be explained by monetary forces? How should one account for the geographical heterogeneity of the asset price booms? The fact that so many questions can still be raised shows that the debate about the causes of the Great Depression is far from over. To some extent, this chapter raises more questions than it answers.

DATA SOURCES

Board of Governors of the Federal Reserve System. 1922a. Discount Rates of the Federal Reserve Banks, 1914–1921. Washington: Government Printing Office. Digitized and adapted by Kurt Schuler, December 13, 2009.

———. 1922b–1934. Annual Report of the Federal Reserve Board. Washington: Government Printing Office. Digitized and adapted by Kurt Schuler, December 13, 2009.

———. 1941. Banking and Monetary Statistics.

———. 1959. All-Bank Statistics, United States, 1896–1955.

Carter, Susan B., Scott Sigmund Gartner, Michael R. Haines, Alan L. Olmstead, Richard Sutch, and Gavin Wright. 2006. Historical Statistics of the United States, Earliest Times to the Present: Millennial Edition. New York: Cambridge University Press, 2006.

Federal Home Loan Bank Board. 1958. Trends in the Savings and Loan Field.

Federal Reserve Bank of St. Louis. Federal Reserve Economic Data (FRED) database. DISCOUNT series. Downloaded and adapted by Kurt Schuler, December 9, 2009.

Friedman, M., and Anna J. Schwartz. 1963. A Monetary History of the United States, 1867–1960. Princeton, NJ: Princeton University Press.

Grebler, L., D. M. Blank, and L. Winnick. 1956. Capital Formation in Residential Real Estate. Princeton, NJ: University Press.

Sutch, R. 2006. "Gross Domestic Product: 1790–2002 [Continuous Annual Series]." Table Ca9-19, in Susan B. Carter, Scott Sigmund Gartner, Michael R. Haines, Alan L. Olmstead, Richard Sutch, and Gavin Wright, eds., Historical Statistics of the United States, Earliest Times to the Present: Millennial Edition. New York: Cambridge University Press, 2006.

U.S. Bureau of Economic Analysis (formerly Office of Business Economics). 1969. Survey of Current Business (May 1969): 11; (May 1970): 14; (May 1973): 13.

U.S. Bureau of Labor Statistics. Handbook of Labor Statistics, Bulletin number 1,016 (1950). Bulletin number 2,000 (1978).

U.S. Bureau of the Census. 1966. Housing Construction Statistics: 1889 to 1964.

———. 1981. Value of New Construction Put in Place 1964 to 1980, Construction Reports: C30-80S (July 1981).

———. 2000. Current Construction Reports, C30/00-5, Value of Construction Put in Place: May 2000 (issued July 2000).

REFERENCES

Aikman, David, Oliver Bush, and Alan Taylor. 2016. Monetary versus Macroprudential Policies: Causal Impacts of Interest Rates and Credit Controls in the Era of the UK Radcliffe Report. NBER Working Paper 22380.

Aldcroft, Derek. 1977. From Versailles to Wall Street, 1919–1929. Berkeley: University of California Press.

Aliber, Robert, and Charles P. Kindleberger. 2015. Manias, Panics and Crashes: A History of Financial Crises. 7th ed. London: Palgrave.

Allen, Frederick. 1931. Only Yesterday: An Informal History of the Nineteen-Twenties. New York: Harper.

Anderson, Richard G., and Kenneth Kavajecz. 1994. A Historical Perspective on the Federal Reserve's Monetary Aggregates. Federal Reserve Bank of St. Louis Review 76 (March/April 1994).

Bagehot, Walter. 1857. The General Aspect of the Banking Question, no. 1, a letter to the editor of the Economist, February 7, 1857. In N. St. John Stevas, ed., The Collected Works of Walter Bagehot, vol. 9. London: The Economist.

Bernanke, Ben S. 1983. Irreversibility, Uncertainty, and Cyclical Investment. Quarterly Journal of Economics 98 (1): 85–106.

Bernanke, Ben S., and Mark Gertler. 1995. Inside the Black Box: The Credit Channel of Monetary Policy Transmission. Journal of Economic Perspectives 9 (4): 27–48.

Borio, Claudio, and Philip Lowe. 2002. Assessing the Risk of Banking Crises. BIS Quarterly Review 7 (1): 43–54.

Brocker, Michael, and Christopher Hanes. 2014. The 1920s American Real Estate Boom and the Downturn of the Great Depression. In E. N. White, K. Snowden, and P. Fishback, eds., Housing and Mortgage Markets in Historical Perspective, 161–202. Chicago: University of Chicago Press.

Calomiris, Charles W., and Joseph R. Mason. 1997. Contagion and Bank Failures during the Great Depression: The June 1932 Chicago Banking Panic. American Economic Review 87 (5): 863.

———. 2003. Consequences of Bank Distress during the Great Depression. American Economic Review 93 (3): 937–47.

Carlson, Mark, Kris J. Mitchener, and Gary Richardson. 2011. Arresting Banking Panics: Federal Reserve Liquidity Provision and the Forgotten Panic of 1929. Journal of Political Economy 119 (5): 889–924.

Claessens, Stijn, M. Ayhan Kose, and Marco Terrones. 2012. How Do Business and Financial Cycles Interact? Journal of International Economics 87 (1): 178–90.

Congdon, Tim. 2017. Money in the Great Recession: Did a Crash in Money Growth Cause the Global Slump? Buckingham Studies in Money, Banking and Central Banking. Cheltenham: Edward Elgar Publishing.

Courtemanche, Charles, and Kenneth Snowden. 2011. Repairing a Mortgage Crisis: HOLC Lending and Its Impact on Local Housing Markets. Journal of Economic History 71 (2): 307–37.

Das, Sanjiv, Kris Mitchener, and Angela Vossmeyer. 2018. Systemic Risk and the Great Depression. CEPR Discussion Paper 25405.

Echols, Alice. 2017. Shortfall: Family Secrets, Financial Collapse and a Hidden History of American Banking. New York: The New Press.

Eichengreen, Barry. 1992. Golden Fetters: The Gold Standard and the Great Depression, 1919–1939. New York: Oxford University Press.

Eichengreen, Barry, and Kris J. Mitchener. 2004. The Great Depression as a Credit Boom Gone Wrong. Research in Economic History 22: 183–237.

Field, Alexander J. 2003. The Most Technologically Progressive Decade of the Century. American Economic Review 93 (4): 1399–1413.

———. 2006. Technological Change and US Productivity Growth in the Interwar Years. Journal of Economic History 66 (1): 203–36.

———. 2014. The Interwar Housing Cycle in the Light of 2001–2011: A Comparative Historical Approach. In E. N. White, K. Snowden, and P. Fishback, eds., Housing and Mortgage Markets in Historical Perspective, 39–80. Chicago: University of Chicago Press.

Fishback, Price, and Trevor Kollmann. 2014. New Multicity Estimates of the Changes in Home Values, 1920–1940. In E. N. White, K. Snowden, and P. Fishback, eds., Housing and Mortgage Markets in Historical Perspective, 203–44. Chicago: University of Chicago Press.

Fishback, Price, Jonathan Rose, and Kenneth Snowden. 2013. Well Worth Saving: How the New Deal Safeguarded Home Ownership. Chicago: University of Chicago Press.

Fisher, Irving. 1933. The Debt-Deflation Theory of Great Depressions. Econometrica 1: 337.

Fohlin, Caroline. 2019. Monetary Policy Regimes and Money Market Stability: Did the Founding of the Fed Matter? Unpublished paper.

Friedman, Milton, and Anna J. Schwartz. 1963. A Monetary History of the United States, 1867–1960. Princeton, NJ: Princeton University Press.

———. 2008. The Great Contraction, 1929–1933. Princeton, NJ: Princeton University Press.

Galbraith, John Kenneth. [1954] 2009. The Great Crash, 1929. London: Penguin.

Goldsmith, Richard. 1968. Financial Intermediaries in the American Economy since 1900. NBER publications in reprint. New York: Arno Press.

Gordon, Robert A. 1951. Cyclical Experience in the Interwar Period. NBER, Conference on Business Cycles, New York.

Hansen, Bent. 1951. A Study in the Theory of Inflation. London: Allen and Unwin.

Hayek, Friedrich A. 1932. Prices and Production. London: George Routledge and Sons.

Hoyt, Homer. 1933. One Hundred Years of Land Values in Chicago: The Relationship of the Growth of Chicago to the Rise in Its Land Values, 1830–1933. Chicago: University of Chicago Press.

Jordà, Òscar, Moritz Schularick, and Alan M. Taylor. 2013. When Credit Bites Back. Journal of Money, Credit and Banking 45 (s2), 3–28.

Keynes, John M. 1934. A Treatise on Money. London: Macmillan.

Kindleberger, Charles P. 1973. The World in Depression, 1929–1939. London: Allen Lane.

Kiyotaki, Nobuhiro, and John Moore. 1997. Credit Cycles. Journal of Political Economy 105 (2): 211–48.

McFerrin, John B. 1939. Caldwell and Company: A Southern Financial Empire. Chapel Hill: University of North Carolina Press.

Mian, Atif, and Amir Sufi. 2014. House of Debt: How They (and You) Caused the Great Recession, and How We Can Prevent It from Happening Again. Princeton, NJ: Princeton University Press.

Miron, Jeffrey A., and Christina D. Romer. 1990. A New Monthly Index of Industrial Production, 1884–1940. Journal of Economic History 50: 321–35.

Mishkin, Frederic S. 1978. The Household Balance Sheet and the Great Depression. Journal of Economic History 38 (4): 918–37.

Mitchener, Kris J., and Gary Richardson. 2013. Shadowy Banks and Financial Contagion during the Great Depression: A Retrospective on Friedman and Schwartz. American Economic Review 103 (3): 73–78.

———. 2019. Network Contagion and Interbank Amplification during the Great Depression. Journal of Political Economy 127 (2): 465–507.

Monnet, Eric. 2014. Monetary Policy without Interest Rates: Evidence from France's Golden Age (1948 to 1973) Using a Narrative Approach. American Economic Journal: Macroeconomics 6 (4): 137–69.

Nicholas, Tom. 2008. Does Innovation Cause Stock Market Runups? Evidence from the Great Crash. American Economic Review 98 (4): 1370–96.

Nicholas, Tom, and Anna Scherbina. 2013. Real Estate Prices during the Roaring Twenties and the Great Depression. Real Estate Economics 41 (2): 278–309.

Olney, Martha L. 1991. Buy Now, Pay Later: Advertising, Credit, and Consumer Durables in the 1920s. Chapel Hill: University of North Carolina Press.

———. 1999. Avoiding Default: The Role of Credit in the Consumption Collapse of 1930. Quarterly Journal of Economics 114 (1): 319–35.

Palyi, Melchior. 1972. The Twilight of Gold, 1914–1936: Myths and Realities. London: Henry Regnery.

Piketty, Thomas, and Emmanuel Saez. 2003. Income Inequality in the United States, 1913–1998. Quarterly Journal of Economics 118 (1): 1–41.

Postel-Vinay, Natacha. 2016. What Caused Chicago Bank Failures in the Great Depression? A Look at the 1920s. Journal of Economic History 76 (2): 478–519.

———. 2017. Debt Dilution in 1920s America: Lighting the Fuse of a Mortgage Crisis. Economic History Review 70 (2): 559–85.

Rajan, Raghuram, and Rodney Ramcharan. 2015. The Anatomy of a Credit Crisis: The Boom and Bust in Farm Land Prices in the United States in the 1920s. American Economic Review 105 (4): 1439–77.

Rappoport, Peter, and Eugene N. White. 1993. Was There a Bubble in the 1929 Stock Market? Journal of Economic History 53 (3): 549–74.

Reinhart, Carmen, and Kenneth Rogoff. 2009. This Time Is Different: Eight Centuries of Financial Folly. Princeton, NJ: Princeton University Press.

Richardson, Gary, and William Troost. 2009. Monetary Intervention Mitigated Banking Panics during the Great Depression: Quasi-Experimental Evidence from a Federal Reserve District Border, 1929–1933. Journal of Political Economy 117 (6): 1031–73.

Rieder, Kilian. 2019. Should Monetary Policy Lean against the Wind? Quasi-Experimental Evidence from Federal Reserve Policies in 1920–21. Unpublished paper.

Ritschl, Albrecht. 2002. International Capital Movements and the Onset of the Great Depression: Some International Evidence. In H. James, ed., The Interwar Depression in an International Context. Munich: Oldenbourg.

———. 2012. The German Transfer Problem, 1920–33: A Sovereign-Debt Perspective. European Review of History: Revue européenne d'histoire 19 (6): 943–64.

Robbins, Lionel. 1934. The Great Depression. London: Macmillan.

Romer, Christina D. 1990. The Great Crash and the Onset of the Great Depression. Quarterly Journal of Economics 105 (3): 597–624.

Romer, Christina D., and David H. Romer. 1993. Credit Channel or Credit Actions? An Interpretation of the Postwar Transmission Mechanism. NBER Working Paper 4485.

Rose, Jonathan D. 2011. The Incredible HOLC? Mortgage Relief during the Great Depression. Journal of Money, Credit and Banking 43 (6): 1073–1107.

———. 2014. The Prolonged Resolution of Troubled Real Estate Lenders during the 1930s. In E. N. White, K. Snowden, and P. Fishback, eds., Housing and Mortgage Markets in Historical Perspective, 245–84. Chicago: University of Chicago Press.

———. 2016. The Resolution of a Systemically Important Insurance Company during the Great Depression. Finance and Economics Discussion Series 2016-005. Washington: Board of Governors of the Federal Reserve System. http://dx.doi.org/10.17016/FEDS.2016.005.

Rostow, Walt. 1963. Politics and the Stages of Growth. London: Cambridge University Press.

Rothbard, Murray. 1963. America's Great Depression. Princeton, NJ: Van Nostrand.

Royal Institute of International Affairs. 1933. Monetary Policy and the Depression. London: Oxford University Press.

Sakolski, Aaron. 1966. The Great American Land Bubble: The Amazing Story of Land-Grabbing, Speculations, and Booms from Colonial Days to the Present Time. New York: Johnson Reprint.

Schularick, Moritz, and Alan M. Taylor. 2012. Credit Booms Gone Bust: Monetary Policy, Leverage Cycles, and Financial Crises, 1870–2008. American Economic Review 102 (2): 1029–61.

Simpson, Herbert D. 1933. Real Estate Speculation and the Depression. American Economic
    Review 23: 163–71.

Smiley, Gene, and Richard Keehn. 1988. Margin Purchases, Brokers' Loans and the Bull Market
    of the Twenties. Business and Economic History 17: 129–42.

Snowden, Kenneth A. 2010. The Anatomy of a Residential Mortgage Crisis: A Look Back to the
    1930s. NBER Working Paper 16244.

Temin, Peter. 1963. The Beginning of the Depression in Germany. Economic History Review
    24 (2): 240–48.

———. 1976. Did Monetary Forces Cause the Great Depression? 1st ed. New York: Norton.

United Nations. 1955. Foreign Capital in Latin America. New York.

Vanderblue, Homer B. 1927. The Florida Land Boom. Journal of Land and Public Utility Eco-
    nomics 3 (3): 252–69.

White, Eugene N. 1984. A Reinterpretation of the Banking Crisis of 1930. Journal of Economic
    History 44 (1): 119–38.

———. 1990a. When the Ticker Ran Late: The Stock Market Boom and Crash of 1929. In E. N.
    White, ed., Crashes and Panics: The Lessons from History, 143–87. Homewood, IL: Dow
    Jones-Irwin.

———. 1990b. The Stock Market Boom and Crash of 1929 Revisited. Journal of Economic Per-
    spectives 4 (2): 67–83.

———. 2014. Lessons from the Great American Real Estate Boom and Bust of the 1920s. In
    E. N. White, K. Snowden, and P. Fishback, eds., Housing and Mortgage Markets in Histori-
    cal Perspective, 115–61. Chicago: University of Chicago Press.

Wicker, Elmus. 1996. The Banking Panics of the Great Depression. Cambridge: Cambridge Uni-
    versity Press.

Wigmore, Barry. 1985. The Crash and Its Aftermath. Westport, CT: Greenwood Press.

Wilson, Thomas. 1948. Fluctuations in Income and Employment with Special Reference to Re-
    cent American Experience and Post-War Prospects. London: Pitman.

Wright, Ivan. 1929. Loans to Brokers and Dealers for Account of Others. Journal of Business of
    the University of Chicago 2 (2): 117–36.

Comment by Eugene N. White

Since the founding of the Federal Reserve in 1913, the only American economic contraction greater than the Great Recession is, of course, the Great
Depression (1929–1933). While decades of research have answered many
questions about the origins of the depression, the role of the booms and busts
in real estate and the stock market that preceded it deserve more attention.
Natacha Postel-Vinay has offered an important potential explanation for these
events, attributing them to credit booms gone wrong and suggesting that some
macro- and microprudential tools might have kept credit under control. In
this comment, I offer a framework for assessing whether credit caused these
asset booms.

Eugene N. White is professor of economics at Rutgers University.

The stock market boom and bust of 1928–1929 has always played a prominent role as a factor contributing to the beginning of the Great Depression. Galbraith (1956) was one of the first to point to a credit boom as a potential driver for the rapid rise in stock prices, noting the parallel movements in the market for brokers' loans and stock prices (White 1990). The market for brokers' loans was the largest and most liquid of U.S. short-term money markets, with banks and nonbanks supplying funds to stock brokers to hold inventory and provide margin loans to their customers. By doing so, the market tied together the commercial banking system and the securities markets. In this pre-SEC world banks were free to set the interest rate and the margin they required on brokers' loans, measured as the percentage in excess of the value of the loan. Divided into call loans and time loans, they had maturities of one-day (renewable) fixed periods of up to three months.

The plausibility of a credit-supply-driven stock market boom arises from the nearly coincident upward movement of the value of outstanding brokers' loans and the Dow-Jones Industrials and Cowles (a broad index roughly similar to the S&P 500) stock market indexes. However, to properly explain the rise in stocks, the alternative hypothesis of a demand-driven boom needs to be considered. In other words, was the boom propelled by bankers and brokers enticing more people to buy stocks with easier credit and predatory lending practices, inappropriately pricing risk, or by an increasingly and irrationally exuberant public demanding more credit from hesitant lenders?

In several papers (White 1990; Rappaport and White 1993, 1994), I have argued that the stock market boom was demand driven because the lenders in the brokers' loan market grew apprehensive. Prior to the boom, all short-term money market rates were closely aligned, but in 1928 a large premium appeared, rising to average over 6% on call loans and 3% on time loans. Affirming this pricing as an indication of higher risk was the rise in margin rates from approximately 25% to 50%. By doubling the buffer, lenders increased their protection from a drop in the market from a quarter to half of its value. Far from providing easy credit, bank and nonbank lenders made credit more expensive, a fact that favors the demand as the key driver of the boom. While they raised the cost of credit, brokers became more skeptical that the rising market could be sustained; their expectations, reflected in the value of their seats on the New York Stock Exchange, exhibited cumulative abnormal returns of about 20% in the months preceding the crash (White 2009).

While I think that the boom was overwhelmingly driven by a euphoric public rather than by credit, the case can be made for an element of supply factors. Galbraith (1954) and others have offered anecdotal evidence of some shady practices by bankers and brokers that may have enticed some unwary investors. One example of evidence in favor of the supply story is Charles E. Merrill's (Morris 2015) decision to shift his brokers from per sale commissions—common in the boom era, where there was an incentive to increase turnover—to fixed salaries with annual bonuses based on the whole firm's profitability. If brokers' and bankers' efforts to ramp up sales were sufficiently widespread, then a case can be made that a portion of the boom was credit-driven.

Real estate boomed earlier, with housing starts peaking in 1925 then collapsing. However, there is very limited data on housing prices—the Case-Shiller index before 1940 is deeply flawed (White 2014). There is some regional evidence of a boom in housing prices, but it is measured by the rise in the value of new residential construction, peaking in 1925/1926, which, it is argued, was fueled by a rise in mortgage credit. Although of a small magnitude, I argue (White 2014) that the mid-1920s residential housing boom and bust of mid-1920 was similar to the booms and busts in housing of the 1980s and 2000s—with one crucial difference: there was no banking crisis or weakening of other mortgage intermediaries. The case for a credit boom driving the housing boom needs to be considered with other possible factors.

First, one cannot ignore the effects of World War I. Wartime financial repression, redirecting most investment to government bonds, required a recovery of investment in housing. Much of the boom is simply a catch-up. I (White 2014) estimated the value of the wartime deficit in housing to be $4.9 billion. During the postwar recovery, 1921–1925, the surge in construction of $7.3 billion leaves a potential bubble $2.3 billion.

Another possible factor is that the Fed pursued an inappropriately low interest rate policy. Applying a Taylor Rule to short-term rates suggests that in 1925, the discount rate could have been 2% higher, yet the impact on value of construction is negligible. There seems to have been enough market segmentation so that mortgage rates barely moved over a decade. The early Fed may also have created a Greenspan-type put by opening the discount window and enabling banks to take more risk; yet this too was found to have had little effect on construction (White 2014).

Finally, there is the possibility that lending standards fell, encouraging more people to take out mortgages. The existing patchy data show that financial intermediaries maintained high loan-to-value ratios of 40% to 50%, presenting little incentive to borrowers. However, the aggressive building and loans associations (S&L forerunners) offered a second mortgage at 30% loan-to-value ratio after a borrower had an interest-only first mortgage with a 50% loan-to-value ratio, thereby exposing the unwary borrower to greater risk. Even so, defaults did not rise for these loans after the boom ended; only during the Great Depression did borrowers begin to default in large numbers (Fishback, Rose, and Snowden 2013).

To my eye both the real estate and stock market booms were primarily driven by fundamentals—recovery from World War I and a robust economy driven in part by technological innovation. The bubbles on top of the booms were primarily demand-driven by exuberant investors and home buyers. In addition, there may have been some supply-driven increase in demand fueled by opportunistic bankers and brokers. If that is true, what are the appropriate policy remedies? I would argue that macroprudential regulations would not have done the job. During the stock market boom, the New York Fed pressured its member banks to cap brokers' loans. They obeyed, but the interest rates on brokers' loans proved so attractive that nonmember banks, other financial institutions, companies, and individuals filled in the gap almost without a halt. The flexibility of the market thwarted the regulatory effort.

I would argue if a credit boom needs to be restrained, then the most effective reform would be to alter the incentives for financial agents to foster a credit boom (Crockett et al. 2003). Merrill's postcrash reform of broker compensation is a good example. The value of looking at the early twentieth century is that there were no systemic incentives to take risk, no deposit insurance, no Too-Big-to-Fail. Instead there were idiosyncratic incentives—firm level. The mortgage boom was held in check and did not threaten the banking system because directors had significant skin in the game, owning blocks of bank shares with double liability, while meeting once or twice a week to closely monitor lending as well as officers and employees who were often heavily bonded. It has long been claimed that their officers exploited conflicts of interest in 1920s universal banks; while it certainly occurred in some firms, there is no evidence of systematic exploitation (White 1986; Kroszner and Rajan 1994). Capital ratios were high compared to today and bank examiners tested them against probable losses. Even though there were occasional liquidity crises, promoting and monitoring good governance prevented large bank losses in the United States in the late nineteenth and early twentieth century until the Great Depression (White 2013).

REFERENCES

Crockett, Andrew, Trevor Harris, Frederic Mishkin, and Eugene N. White. 2003. Conflicts of Interest in the Financial Services Industry: What Should We Do About Them? London: Centre for Economic Policy Research and the International Center for Monetary and Banking Studies.

Fishback, Price, Jonathan Rose, and Kenneth Snowden. 2013. Well Worth Saving: How the New Deal Safeguarded Homeownership. Chicago: University of Chicago Press.

Galbraith, John Kenneth. 1954. The Great Crash: 1929. Boston: Houghton Mifflin.

Kroszner, Randall, and Ragu G. Rajan. 1994. Is the Glass-Steagall Act Justified? A Study of the US Experience with Universal Banking before 1933. American Economic Review 84 (4): 810–32.

Morris, Edward. 2015. Wall Streeters: The Creators and Corruptors of American Finance. New York: Columbia University Press.

Rappoport, Peter, and Eugene N. White. 1993. Was There a Bubble in the 1929 Stock Market? Journal of Economic History 53 (3): 549–74.

———. 1994. Was the Crash of 1929 Expected? American Economic Review 84 (1): 271–81.

White, Eugene N. 1986. Before the Glass-Steagall Act: An Analysis of the Investment Banking Activities of National Banks. Explorations in Economic History 23 (1): 33–55.

———. 1990. The Stock Market Boom and Crash of 1929 Revisited. Journal of Economic Perspectives 4 (2): 67–83.

———. 2009. Anticipating the Stock Market Crash of 1929: The View from the Floor of the Stock Exchange. In Jeremy Atack, eds., The Development of Financial Institutions and Markets, 294–318. New York: Cambridge University Press.

———. 2013. To Establish a More Effective Supervision of Banking: How the Birth of the Fed Altered Bank Supervision. In Michael D. Bordo and William Robards, eds., A Return to Jekyll Island: The Origins, History and Future of the Federal Reserve, 7–54. New York: Cambridge University Press.

———. 2014. Lessons from the Great American Real Estate Boom and Bust of the 1920s. In Eugene N. White, Kenneth Snowden, and Price Fishback, eds., Housing and Mortgage Markets in Historical Perspective. Chicago: University of Chicago Press.

11

Sectoral Credit Booms and Financial Stability

KARSTEN MÜLLER

At the time of writing, there is an ongoing debate among policy makers in the United States about the potential risks in the leveraged loan market, the market for risky corporate debt. SEC chair Jay Clayton sees "echoes of the 2008 financial crisis" (*Wall Street Journal* 2019), while Federal Reserve chair Jerome Powell stresses that the "financial system appears strong enough to handle potential losses" (Bloomberg 2019).

A natural move is to turn to the historical record and ask: Has rapid growth in corporate debt preceded banking crises? Or more broadly, is a shift in the allocation of credit to particular sectors of the economy a sign of trouble down the line?

Even more than a decade after the onset of the 2008 crisis, I do not think we can answer these questions with certainty. But a growing body of theoretical and empirical work suggests a number of regularities. In this chapter, I discuss what we know and do not know about the anatomy of credit booms and present some new insights based on ongoing work. I argue that changes in the allocation of credit, not just its quantity, are key to understanding the recurring incidence of crises in the financial sector.

I take a data-driven approach to summarize patterns of credit allocation around financial crises, building on ongoing work in Müller and Verner (2019). In particular, I use a large data set on sectoral credit from 1940 to 2014 for 120 countries from Müller and Verner (2020), crossed with data on systemic banking crises from a variety of sources. Based on the existing literature and the results of my empirical tests, I arrive at two major takeaways.

Karsten Müller is assistant professor of finance at the National University of Singapore.

First, credit booms that end in busts are not created equal. Growth in housing-related debt, both on the household and corporate side, seems to be among the more frequent precursors of financial turmoil. A perhaps even clearer result, both on theoretical and empirical grounds, is that expansions of the nontradable service sector often precede crisis episodes. I show that an increase in construction and nontradable sector debt appears to precede crises even after controlling for the growth in lending to other sectors. Although there are other explanations, one reading of this evidence is that pronounced sectoral shifts may coincide with a deterioration of lending standards that ultimately ends badly. Particularly striking is that an allocation toward industrial and infrastructure sectors appears to be associated with a considerably lower crisis probability going forward.

Sectoral credit growth rates also have a somewhat better ability to classify the data into crises and noncrisis episodes than aggregate credit data. I evaluate classification ability using the Area Under the Curve (AUC) statistic, which essentially asks whether a variable is particularly good at identifying true positives compared to false positives.[1] While I interpret these results purely as in-sample correlations, they suggest that studying the link between the distinctive allocative role of credit markets and financial turmoil may be worth further study.

Second, I discuss policy implications. An all too obvious conclusion some may want to draw from these findings is that regulators should use targeted macroprudential tools to rein in the buildup of sectoral risks. I argue that too much confidence in such regulations may be misguided. One obvious reason is that we know very little about why exactly particular types of debt should play a more prominent role in economic fluctuations. The existing empirical evidence is consistent with a number of theories and disentangling these in the data is important for designing policies. We also do not have a good sense about the elasticity of different types of credit to macroprudential tools on a granular level. Credible estimates of these elasticities, however, are key: if macroprudential policy considerably affects the sectors least associated with crises, this might lead to unintended distortions with potential negative welfare consequences. Perhaps even more importantly, time-varying policies are subject to potential political interference. Macroprudential policies targeting

---

1. More precisely, the AUC is an integral over the Receiver Operating Characteristic (ROC) space given by combinations of the true positive rate (true positives divided by true positives and false negatives) and the false positive rate (false positives divided by false positives and true negatives).

specific sectors, for example, are subject to a powerful electoral cycle across countries.

I argue that a better takeaway for policy makers might be to think about transparent time-invariant restrictions on particular types of credit for the largest, systematically important financial institutions. While such approaches may have a myriad of downsides, they are perhaps not as easily reversed as time-varying tools when political pressures arise.

This chapter consists of four parts. In the next section, I discuss existing theory and evidence on the role of credit allocation in periods of financial instability. I also discuss empirical predictions coming out of the existing literature. Following that I present some empirical evidence on patterns of sectoral credit growth around banking crises. Then I discuss these findings in light of policy and further highlight potential challenges to sectoral tools. The final section includes thoughts on future work.

Credit Allocation and Financial Stability: Theory and Evidence

In this section, I discuss theory and evidence which suggest that the *allocation* of credit, not just its quantity or price, might play a role in understanding the deep recessions associated with financial crises. I begin the discussion with two parts: one that focuses on theories that predict a sectoral bias in booms and busts, and one that focuses on empirical evidence. I then derive a synthesis with a number of empirical predictions.

THEORY

At its very core, finance is about the allocation of resources. Thus, the idea that debt booms in some sectors are particularly important for the macroeconomy is as old as the economics discipline itself. However, there is a smaller number of theories with distinct predictions about the allocation of credit.

As a starting point, a sizable literature studies how inefficient private borrowing can generate financial instability (e.g., Lorenzoni 2008; Bianchi 2011; Guerrieri and Lorenzoni 2017; Jeanne and Korinek 2018). Of the many potential sources that may exacerbate deep downturns following crises, downward nominal rigidities (e.g., Farhi and Werning 2016; Schmitt-Grohé and Uribe 2016) and liquidity traps (e.g., Eggertsson and Krugman 2012; Korinek and Simsek 2016) have received special attention. The empirical predictions from these models stand somewhat in contrast to models where the permanent income hypothesis holds. If households smooth permanent income over the cycle, an anticipation of higher income in the future generates a positive link between borrowing today and output tomorrow (e.g., Aguiar and Gopinath 2007).

A first link to sectoral heterogeneity comes from early work on borrowing constraints. In models that follow Kiyotaki and Moore (1997), debt is determined by asset prices and collateral requirements. Changes to collateral requirements, in turn, drive credit cycles (e.g., Eggertsson and Krugman 2012; Guerrieri and Lorenzoni 2017; Jones, Midrigan, and Philippon 2018; also see Bernanke, Gertler, and Gilchrist 1999). This body of work serves as the theoretical backdrop for empirical studies on collateral values, which may differ across sectors (e.g., Chaney, Sraer, and Thesmar 2012). In models with borrowing constraints, higher credit demand puts upward pressure on interest rates. That is, booms coincide with higher borrowing costs, resembling a credit demand shock. Justiniano, Primiceri, and Tambalotti (2019) build a model where a loosening of lending constraints (combined with loosened borrowing constraints) leads to a largely supply-driven boom-bust pattern in credit and house prices.

In models that follow Mendoza (2002), (household) borrowing depends on income from the tradable and nontradable sectors (e.g., Bianchi 2011). This closely ties credit growth to sectoral output and prices. Mian, Sufi, and Verner (2020), for example, use a stylized framework to derive sectoral predictions about credit booms. In their model, shocks to household credit increase nontradable output and prices, while shocks to nontradable (tradable) sector credit decreases (increases) prices. Schneider and Tornell (2004) study a setting with bailout guarantees for lenders and asymmetries between borrowing firms in the tradable and nontradable sectors. In particular, tradable sector firms have access to perfect financial markets while the nontradable sector cannot commit to repay debt. This setup gives rise to endogenous borrowing constraints, a currency mismatch, and a boom-bust cycle. Rognlie, Shleifer, and Simsek (2018) explicitly model how a relaxation of borrowing constraints (due to low interest rates) can lead to a reallocation of resources toward sectors with durable capital, such as housing.

Sectoral booms and busts do not, however, require the existence of collateral constraints. Schmitt-Grohé and Uribe (2016), for example, study an open-economy model where booms drive up the demand for nontradables in a full liability dollarization setup. The key inputs here are downward nominal wage rigidity and currency pegs. These create a negative externality in the bust because real wages cannot adjust downward, which causes unemployment.

A finance-driven key insight comes from recent work by Khorrami (2019). He shows that a shock to the ability of financiers to diversify risks in one sector of the economy can lead to a reallocation of investment toward it.

Because better diversification reduces risk premia (such as during the 2000s U.S. housing boom), financiers borrow more, which leads to an increase in leverage. This ultimately leads to a bust because financiers do not internalize their impact on aggregate risk premia. In Gorton and Ordoñez (2020), boom-bust cycles can arise after positive productivity shocks because lenders do not sufficiently examine the quality of collateral. Because less collateral screening reduces the quality of projects that are financed, an increase in screening can prompt a recession.

EXISTING EMPIRICAL STUDIES

An increasing body of work suggests that debt in some sectors of the economy might be more consequential for macroeconomic downturns than others. Jappelli and Pagano (1994) were perhaps the first to single out a role for household credit. They use an overlapping generations model and cross-country regressions to argue that household debt can decrease aggregate saving rates and economic growth. Radelet et al. (1998) show that, between 1990 and 1996, many countries that were later affected by the East Asian crisis experienced a pronounced shift in lending from agriculture and manufacturing toward household credit and the construction sector. In an early account of the Great Financial Crisis of 2008, Hume and Sentance (2009) argue that the use of credit for the purchase of existing assets was at the heart of the "growth puzzle" of the early 2000s. In what is perhaps the first paper linking sectoral debt to banking crises more systematically, Büyükkarabacak and Valev (2010) study the period 1990 to 2005 in a sample of forty-five mostly developing countries. They find that growth in household debt is associated with the onset of banking crises, and more so than growth in firm debt. Jordà, Schularick, and Taylor (2015a, 2015b) find similar evidence for mortgage vs. total credit for advanced economies. They show that banking crises are more likely and followed by deeper recessions when preceded by a boom in mortgage credit.

Mian, Sufi, and Verner (2017) find that this boom-bust pattern of increases in household debt also holds without conditioning on a banking crisis. Growth in credit to households is accompanied by a predictable short-term boom in consumption, imports, and current account deficits that is followed by a severe bust in output. The same pattern does not hold true for credit expansions to firms. Using state-level banking deregulation in the United States as a quasi-experiment, Mian, Sufi, and Verner (2020) extend these findings. More precisely, deregulation led to a short-term boom in household debt, house prices, and a shift of employment toward the nontradable sector. This boom was followed by a severe bust. Because consumer prices in the nontradable sector increased markedly, they conclude that these patterns are most consistent with credit supply boosting household demand, rather than firm productivity.

Di Maggio and Kermani (2017) exploit the federal exemption from local predatory lending laws as a credit supply shock in the 2000s and find similar evidence along many dimensions. The finding that credit boosts house prices also holds in other settings. Favara and Imbs (2015) use interstate branching deregulation as an exogenous shock and show that it increased mortgage credit and house prices; Adelino, Schoar, and Severino (2012) construct an identification strategy based on nonconforming loan limits. Rajan and Ramcharan (2015) document that credit availability boosted farmland prices during the 1920s boom, that is, an agricultural boom. These studies are important because they suggest that, during booms, credit and real resources are being reallocated toward sectors with a higher dependence on real estate or land. Indeed, there is some direct evidence that rising house prices benefit firms and industries with larger real estate holdings (Chaney, Sraer, and Thesmar 2012; Doerr 2018) and reallocate credit from firms to households (Chakraborty, Goldstein, and MacKinlay 2018).

The pattern that credit booms are accompanied by an expansion of the nontradable sector and real exchange appreciations also create a natural bridge with a large literature on imbalances in international economics (e.g., Calvo, Leiderman, and Reinhart 1996). Bahadir and Gumus (2016) show that, in a sample of emerging markets, household debt is more correlated with macroeconomic variables than firm debt. Household debt booms predict real exchange appreciations and an expansion of the nontradable sector. In an important paper, Gopinath et al. (2017) show that capital inflows into southern Europe since the early 2000s were accompanied by a reallocation toward firms with high net worth but low productivity.

Relatedly, Reis (2013) argues that capital misallocation helps explain the Portuguese crisis experience. More support comes from cross-country panel evidence in Borio et al. (2016), who show that credit booms tend to coincide with a reallocation of employment toward low productivity sectors. Because firms in the nontradable sector are generally less productive, this also meshes well with the cross-country pattern in Kalantzis (2015), who shows that capital inflow episodes are associated with nontradable sector expansions (also see Tornell and Westermann 2005; Giovanni et al. 2017). It is also consistent with the pattern documented in Gorton and Ordoñez (2020) that "bad" credit booms coincide with low productivity growth. Credit allocation during the boom may also have long-term consequences by affecting educational choices across sectors (Charles, Hurst, and Notowidigdo 2018).

Much of the literature on finance and economic growth also makes explicit reference to sectoral heterogeneity. A classic paper by Rajan and Zingales (1998) shows that manufacturing industries with a higher dependence on external financing grow fast in countries with more developed financial sectors. Braun and Larrain (2005) show that these industries are hit harder during recessions; Kroszner, Laeven, and Klingebiel (2007) report that the same holds true for banking crises. Hsu, Tian, and Xu (2014) show that high-tech industries patent more in countries with smaller credit markets (but larger equity markets).

EMPIRICAL PREDICTIONS

Taken together, the existing theoretical and empirical literature is broadly consistent with the following interpretation. Private debt booms ending in crises are often driven by credit supply and can be fueled by capital flows. These booms follow a predictable pattern. As financing conditions loosen, marginal loans are increasingly extended to ex post riskier households and firms with high net worth or particularly collateralizable assets. This is reinforced by debt-fueled household demand for nontradable goods and rising house prices. If a shock brings the boom to a halt, large-scale financial turmoil ensues. But reversing inefficient investments during the boom is costly, particularly in the presence of frictions such as nominal rigidities. This leads to prolonged downturns.

This synthesis has a clear empirical prediction for sectoral credit growth in the run-up to banking crises: lending should expand particularly in nontradable industries and housing-related sectors. It might even be that the *share* of credit to these sectors increases prior to crises, while that of other industries might decline.

There is a clear contrast between this synthesis and the idea that many assets or sectors might be prone to experience "bubbles." Rajan and Ramcharan (2015), for example, write that "[t]he usual difficulty in drawing general lessons from episodes of booms and busts in different countries is that each crisis is sui generis, driven by differences in a broad range of hard-to-control-for factors." Broadly speaking, this view holds that booms are inherently sparked by some novel element that makes their outcomes unpredictable. In the data, Barberis et al. (2018) document a pattern of extrapolation during bubble episodes in different asset classes. In his classic history of financial crises, Kindleberger (1978) revisits episodes resulting from overinvestment in assets as diverse as tulips, railroads, and government bonds. The empirical prediction of the "sui generis" hypothesis is that credit to particular sectors should not be special. Booms and busts could essentially occur in any sector of the economy. In a close to comprehensive sample of banking crises, we should thus not find that lending growth differs systematically across sectors before they hit.

Some Evidence on Sectoral Credit and Crises

DATA

In this section, I discuss some systematic empirical evidence on credit allocation around crises based on work in Müller and Verner (2019). This work extends the previous literature in a few ways. For one, the systematic evidence on banking crises and sectoral debt are based on a limited number of observations. Jordà, Schularick, and Taylor (2015a, 2015b) use a long-run narrow panel of seventeen advanced economies; Büyükkarabacak and Valev (2010) use a broader but short panel of sixteen years. Mian, Sufi, and Verner (2017) use a somewhat larger data set but test for the role of firm vs. household credit in business cycles more broadly, not banking crises (also see Bahadir and Gumus 2016).

A second extension overcomes the limited availability of sectoral data. Existing work has treated corporations as homogeneous. It also does not consistently differentiate between mortgage and household credit. These differences, however, might be important: in related work (Müller 2018), I show that nonmortgage credit is important for understanding the expansion of household debt in emerging economies. Within corporate credit, there has been a secular shift toward real estate and service industries.

Third, the existing network has largely focused on the quantity of credit and not explicitly addressed its allocation. There are, however, good reasons to expect allocation to matter over and above quantities empirically: in an important paper, Greenwood and Hanson (2013) show that the risk of corporate debt issues is higher during credit booms, and this increased risk-taking is not appropriately priced in bond returns. Krishnamurthy and Muir (2017) show that credit spreads are unusually low prior to banking crises.

I extend existing work using the historical sectoral credit data from Müller and Verner (2020). These data cover 120 countries for the period 1940–2014, which notably includes many small open economies that often experience crises (Laeven and Valencia 2018). As a starting point, figure 11.1 plots how corporate and household credit have evolved relative to GDP since 1960 in an unbalanced panel of sixty-six emerging and fifty-four advanced economies (as classified by the World Bank in 2018). Household credit has grown almost uniformly around the world. The ratio of corporate credit to GDP has

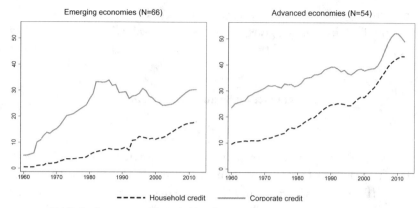

FIGURE 11.1 Ratio of corporate and household credit to GDP, 1960–2014
Data source: Müller and Verner (2020).
Note: This figure plots the average ratio of corporate and household credit to GDP for an unbalanced panel of sixty-six emerging and fifty-four advanced economies, as classified by the World Bank in 2018.

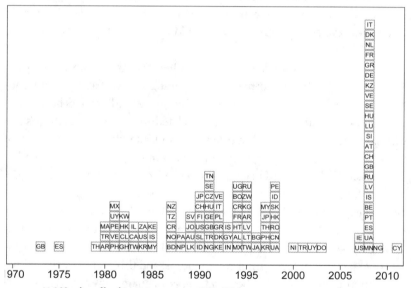

FIGURE 11.2 Number of banking crises per year, 1970–2014
Note: This figure plots the number of systemic banking crises per year used in the sample. I create a "consensus" measure of crises based on the data in Baron, Verner, and Xiong (2021), Laeven and Valencia (2018), Reinhart and Rogoff (2009), and Bordo et al. (2001). See Müller and Verner (2019) for details.

been essentially flat since the mid-1980s but shows a pronounced upward shift during the 2000s, particularly in advanced economies.

For crisis dates, I use multiple sources to maximize data availability. The starting point is the crisis indicator based on bank equity crashes from Baron, Verner, and Xiong (2021). This measure has the advantage that it is motivated by theory and has a consistent definition, in contrast to many existing narrative crisis indicators (Bordo and Meissner 2016). Taken together with the crisis dates in Laeven and Valencia (2018), Reinhart and Rogoff (2009), Bordo et al. (2001), I can construct a panel of credit and systemic banking crises for 108 countries and up to 5,275 country-year observations. There are 107 crises in the sample. Figure 11.2 plots the countries experiencing banking crises in the sample by year; there were no recorded crises between 1940 and 1972.

PATTERNS OF CREDIT GROWTH AROUND CRISES

As a starting point, I plot how different types of credit developed relative to GDP around systemic banking crises (conditional on country-fixed effects). To aid the interpretation, I standardize the change in credit/GDP for each variable to have a mean of 0 and a standard deviation of 1. That means all numbers can be interpreted as changes in standard deviations relative to the country mean.

Figure 11.3 begins by plotting changes in total credit, household credit, and corporate credit. This reveals a distinctive pattern. Relative to the country mean, lending systematically expands in the years prior to banking crises. In the more distant years, household credit expands considerably faster than corporate credit. However, in the immediate run-up to the crisis, corporate credit growth in fact outpaces household lending. This could be read in at least two ways. On one hand, perhaps firms are relatively slower when it comes to "participating" in credit booms. On the other hand, it could be that

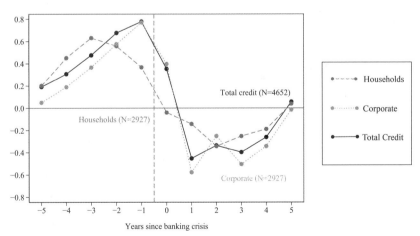

FIGURE 11.3 Changes in credit/GDP around crises, by broad sector
Note: This figure plots changes in credit/GDP relative to the country mean around up to 107 banking crises in 108 countries. Changes are standardized to have a mean of 0 and a standard deviation of 1. See Müller and Verner (2020) for more details.

the spike prior to crises is because firms draw down their credit lines during the early signs of a crisis, which increases total debt. This latter phenomenon was seen, for example, in the most recent crisis episode in the United States.

Figure 11.4 divides household credit into its mortgage and nonmortgage components, where the latter largely reflects consumer lending. Here we can see that, while both mortgages and consumer lending expand prior to crises, increases in household debt mainly reflect mortgage credit.

Figure 11.5 looks at heterogeneity in corporate credit. Based on their patterns around crises, I divide industries into those with a clear "boom-bust" pattern (in panel A) and those without (in panel B). As it turns out, increases in corporate credit prior to crises are mainly driven by construction and real estate, nontradables, and other services. The patterns are considerably more muted for lending to industry (manufacturing and mining), agriculture, and transport and communication.

DOES SECTORAL CREDIT HELP PREDICT CRISES?

To formally investigate which types of credit growth systematically tend to precede crises, I turn to a simple logit prediction framework. These regressions broadly take the following specification:

$$(1)\ P_{it} = \alpha + \beta\Delta_3\text{Credit/GDP}_{it}^{j} + \varepsilon_{it},$$

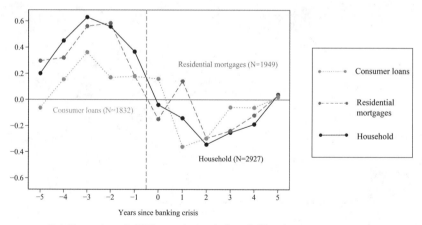

FIGURE 11.4 Changes in credit/GDP around crises, by household credit type
Note: This figure plots changes in credit/GDP relative to the country mean around up to 107 banking crises in 108 countries. Consumer credit refers to household credit other than residential mortgages. Changes are standardized to have a mean of 0 and a standard deviation of 1. See Müller and Verner (2020) for more details.

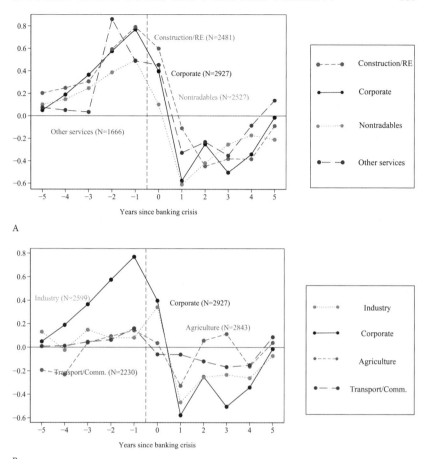

A

B

FIGURE 11.5 Changes in credit/GDP around crises, by industry
Note: This figure plots changes in credit/GDP relative to the country mean around up to 107 banking crises in 108 countries. "Industry" refers to manufacturing and may also include mining. "Nontradables" refers to wholesale and retail trade and restaurants and may include accommodation services. Changes are standardized to have a mean of 0 and a standard deviation of 1. See Müller and Verner (2020) for more details.

where P_{it} is a dummy for the onset of a systemic banking crisis and $\Delta_3 \text{Credit}/\text{GDP}_{it}^j$ is the three-year change in the ratio of credit to GDP for sector j from $t-4$ to $t-1$ (see, e.g., Mian, Sufi, and Verner 2017). I also consider specifications with country-fixed effects, where I run a "horse race" between different types of credit.[2] These fixed effects soak up unobserved heterogeneity across countries; however, they also mean I can only estimate these models

2. Note that, because the subsectors add up to total credit growth, including all credit shares in the same regression is similar to using the *shares* of different credit types.

for countries with at least one crisis. Again, I standardize all credit variables to have a mean of 0 and a standard deviation of 1 in the regression sample; I report marginal effects multiplied by 100 for readability. The error term is assumed to be well-behaved.

Table 11.1 presents the results for a few variants of these logit models. In model 1, I begin with total credit growth. This serves to replicate existing evidence using a larger sample. The results confirm a tight statistical link between credit expansions and future periods of financial turmoil. But how does this relationship vary depending on the type of credit? Models 2 through 4 start by differentiating between corporate, household, and mortgage loans. Note that mortgages here refer to total mortgage credit, as in Jordà, Schularick, and Taylor (2015a, 2015b), not only those for residential purposes.

Interestingly, I find that the estimated marginal effect of lending to corporations is very close to that of household loans. This is also reflected in terms of classification ability (AUC), which are in both cases comparable to that of total credit. This implies that, over the broad sweep of recent banking history around the world, crises have been preceded both by increases in household and corporate debt. The coefficient and AUC for mortgage loans is somewhat smaller.

Models 5 and 6 then differentiate between household loans: residential mortgages and consumer credit. I find that the coefficient for residential mortgages is almost equivalent to that of total household loans in column 3. For consumer loans, the coefficient is somewhat smaller. The AUC of consumer loans is only 0.59 and I cannot reject that it is equal to 0.5, which would mean a coin toss. The AUC for residential mortgages is close to the total household credit estimate in column 3.

Models 7 through 12 in the bottom row investigate heterogeneity in corporate credit. This paints a striking picture. On average, since 1940, lending growth to agriculture and industrial sectors is not a systematic precursor of banking crises. This can be most clearly seen when looking at the AUC, which include a coin toss (0.5) in the 95% confidence interval. Instead, the results for total corporate credit seem to be driven by loans to the construction and services sectors in columns 9, 10, and 12. Importantly, the AUC values for these three sectors—ranging from 0.62 to 0.71—are close to or above those for total credit in the full sample in column 1. Credit to transport and communication is not statistically significant and has an AUC close to a coin toss.

A challenge in interpreting these results is that, during booms, credit growth across different sectors is likely highly correlated. Another issue is that credit growth rates and crisis probabilities may depend on unobserved differences across countries. I thus turn to a "horse race" of different types of credit growth using fixed effects regressions in table 11.2. Here, I focus on

TABLE 11.1 Sectoral credit growth and banking crises

| | Total credit | Corporate credit | Broad sectors | | Household sectors | |
			Household credit	Mortgage credit	Residential mortgages	Consumer credit
	(1)	(2)	(3)	(4)	(5)	(6)
Δ_3 Credit/GDP	0.887***	1.115***	1.115***	0.916***	1.187***	0.757**
	(0.172)	(0.291)	(0.155)	(0.298)	(0.203)	(0.347)
N	5,275	3,279	3,279	1,094	2,182	2,038
Number of countries	108	104	104	36	88	88
Pseudo-R^2	0.04	0.04	0.04	0.03	0.04	0.01
AUC	0.63	0.67	0.65	0.62	0.66	0.59
AUC (95% CI)	[0.57; 0.70]	[0.61; 0.74]	[0.58; .71]	[0.49; .76]	[0.57; 0.74]	[0.49; 0.68]
AUC (Total cr., est. sample)	—	0.67	0.67	0.69	0.73	0.72

| | Agriculture credit | Manufacturing/mining | Corporate sectors | | | |
			Construction loans	Services (nontradable)	Transport/communication	Services (other)
	(7)	(8)	(9)	(10)	(11)	(12)
Δ_3 Credit/GDP	0.412**	0.229	0.820***	1.113***	0.323	0.755**
	(0.184)	(0.333)	(0.174)	(0.289)	(0.320)	(0.213)
N	3,155	2,888	2,779	2,813	2,493	1,852
Number of countries	104	102	101	100	97	86
Pseudo-R^2	0.00	0.00	0.03	0.03	0.00	0.02
AUC	0.56	0.54	0.62	0.71	0.53	0.7
AUC (95% CI)	[0.49; 0.63]	[0.46; 0.62]	[0.55; 0.70]	[0.64; 0.77]	[0.45; 0.61]	[0.62; 0.78]
AUC (Total cr., est. sample)	0.70	0.70	0.70	0.71	0.70	0.73

Note: This table presents the results of logit regressions predicting systemic banking crises. Δ_3 Credit/GDP is the three-year change in the credit-to-GDP ratio from $t - 4$ to $t - 1$ for the sector in the column head. This credit growth measure is standardized to have a mean of 0 and standard deviation of 1 in each regression sample. The reported coefficients are marginal effects multiplied by 100 for readability. "AUC (Total cr., est. sample)" is the AUC statistic for models with the change in total credit to GDP (as in column 1) in the estimation sample. Standard errors in parentheses are clustered by country.

***$p = 0.01$; **$p = 0.05$; *$p = 0.1$.

TABLE 11.2 Fixed effects horse race: credit allocation and banking crises

	(1)	(2)	(3)	(4)	(5)	(6)	(7)	(8)
Δ_3Household credit/GDP	1.115***							9.976***
	(0.155)							(3.536)
Δ_3Agriculture credit/GDP		.0412**						-1.242
		(0.184)						(3.546)
Δ_3Industry credit/GDP			0.229					-11.191**
			(0.333)					(3.799)
Δ_3Construction credit/GDP				0.820***				10.168**
				(0.174)				(4.209)
Δ_3Nontradable services credit/GDP					1.113***			15.514***
					(0.289)			(4.467)
Δ_3Transport and comm. Credit/GDP						0.323		-6.137**
						(0.320)		(2.900)
Δ_3Other services credit/GDP							0.755***	2.890
							(0.213)	(2.542)
N	3,279	3,155	2,888	2,779	2,813	2,493	1,852	1,014
Number of countries	58	51	44	47	49	41	34	34
Pseudo-R^2	0.04	0.00	0.00	0.03	0.03	0.00	0.02	0.16
AUC	0.64	0.56	0.55	0.62	0.071	0.52	0.69	0.76
AUC (95% CI)	[0.57; 0.70]	[0.48; 0.63]	[0.48; 0.63]	[0.54; 0.70]	[0.65; 0.78]	[0.44; 0.59]	[0.60; 0.77]	[0.69; 0.82]
AUC (Total cr., est. sample)	0.66	0.69	0.69	0.70	0.70	0.68	0.71	0.72

Note: This table presents the results of fixed effects logit regressions predicting systemic banking crises. Δ_3Credit/GDP are different sectoral measures of the three-year change in the credit-to-GDP ratio from $t-4$ to $t-1$. These credit growth measures are standardized to have a mean of 0 and a standard deviation of 1 in each regression sample. The reported coefficients are marginal effects multiplied by 100 for readability. "AUC (Total cr., est. sample)" is the AUC statistic for a model that only includes the change in total credit to GDP (as in column 1 of table 11.1) in the estimation sample. Country dummies are not reported. Standard errors are in parentheses.

***$p = 0.01$; **$p = 0.05$; *$p = 0.1$.

a more parsimonious number of sectors to preserve statistical power.[3] The bottom row plots the AUC of a model that only includes the change in total credit/GDP in the estimation sample (as in column 1 of table 11.1).

The results in columns 1 to 7 confirm the main patterns in table 11.1. On average, lending to the agriculture, industry, and transport/communication sectors does not reliably classify periods into crisis and noncrisis episodes, for which the 95% confidence interval for the AUC always includes 0.5. Credit to the nontradable service sector, other services, construction, and households yield the highest AUC. Most importantly, the horse race in column 8 suggests that banking crises are preceded by predictable shifts in the allocation of credit. The coefficients for agriculture, industry, and transport and communication now turn negative. This suggests that, prior to crises, lending systematically shifts away from these sectors and toward households, construction, and the nontradable sector.

Overall, these preliminary empirical results are a first indication of a systematic pattern of credit allocation around banking crises. However, I urge readers to interpret these with caution. For one, financial crises are notoriously hard to date, and it is unlikely that the same types of debt matter to the same degree across countries. We discuss these sources of heterogeneity in more detail in Müller and Verner (2019). Most importantly, the results here do not imply that credit growth or changes in credit allocation to particular sectors are necessarily good *forecasting* variables for banking crises. Instead, the findings should be read as in-sample correlations that describe broad patterns in credit allocation around crises.

Lessons for Policy Makers

Interpreted jointly with the existing literature, the empirical evidence discussed above seems to suggest a relatively clear pattern: financial crises are often "credit booms gone bust," and there is a predictable shift in credit growth toward particular sectors preceding them. In particular, it seems tempting to conclude that leverage in the nontradable and also real estate sectors might play a special role.

It is all too easy to infer from these patterns that macroprudential tools aimed at sectors such as housing should be well-suited to contain financial stability risks. I want to caution that this conclusion may be premature for three reasons.

First, we do not have a good sense of why exactly credit booms in some sectors systematically precede crises and others do not. We have a few candidate

---

3. Note that the inclusion of country-fixed effects means that countries without banking crises drop out of the sample. The results here are almost equivalent without fixed effects.

theories but no strong sense of which ones best describe the empirical patterns. Maybe some sectors are more prone to booms because their assets are easier to collateralize when financing conditions are loose (e.g., Braun and Larrain 2005; Braun 2005). Maybe some sectors are simply more procyclical than others and move closer in tandem with the ups and downs of the business cycle. Maybe some sectors are less likely to have access to alternative sources of financing and are thus particularly reliant on the health of financial institutions. Maybe lending to some sectors is systematically more profitable than others. Without knowing which factors are key, it is difficult to know whether and how to regulate lending to these sectors.

Second, we do not have reliable causal estimates of the elasticity of different types of credit to changes in macroprudential policy on a granular level. This elasticity, however, is a key statistic for policy prescriptions. If the sectors that most clearly expand prior to crises are also the most responsive to policy tools, regulations targeting aggregate credit may be desirable. But if sectors whose lending growth moves little around crises are the most responsive, aggregate tools could lead to serious distortions, which may provide a rationale for targeted sectoral tools.

Third, there is evidence that time-varying financial regulation is subject to powerful political constraints. For the case of macroprudential regulation, I provide evidence elsewhere that these constraints are most binding for tools aimed at household and real estate credit (Müller 2019). More precisely, I show that sectoral macroprudential tools are subject to a predictable electoral cycle across countries, particularly during booms. Figure 11.6 illustrates this point. Of course, these regulations are aimed at exactly the sectors we may be most worried about from a financial stability perspective, particularly housing. This should make us wary of the idea that even the most enlightened policy makers are, in practice, able to enforce countercyclical regulations.

So what, then, should policy makers do? Clearly, more research is needed before giving clear guidance. But maybe it is worthwhile considering simpler alternatives, particularly in light of evidence that even the most complicated regulations often seem to be systematically circumvented by financial institutions (see, e.g., Behn, Haselmann, and Vig 2016).[4] Simple and transparent guidelines may not only be cheaper but also easier to enforce.

If one were to be convinced that regulation should address sectoral risks, one simple approach could be lending restrictions that vary by sector but not

4. In most places, financial regulation is extremely complex. As one indication, the Basel Committee on Banking Supervision has issued a total of more than 16,000 pages of supervisory guidance (Penikas 2015); Basel III alone has more than 600 pages.

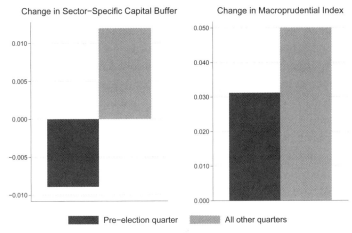

FIGURE 11.6 Macroprudential policy is looser before elections
Note: This figure plots the average change in macroprudential policy (measured by sector-specific capital buffers or an aggregate index). I differentiate between quarters prior to 212 elections, and all other quarters, across fifty-eight countries between 2000 and 2014. See Müller (2019) for more details.

by time. Because the health of large institutions is especially important from a macroeconomic perspective, perhaps one would want to target these institutions. While such regulations are surely also subject to political economy concerns, their time-invariant nature might insulate them at least somewhat from the most short-lived political pressures. It is also worth noting that such restrictions were commonplace in much of the advanced world until the 1980s. In the United States, FDIC regulations limit the maximum exposure of institutions to individual borrowers, which can be thought of as somewhat similar.

Obviously, such regulations introduce inefficiencies that have to be weighed against the benefits from potentially limiting boom-bust patterns. Indeed, we have sound theoretical reasons to think that time-invariant regulations may not be optimal from a welfare perspective (e.g., Bianchi and Mendoza 2018). But I would argue that the conclusions from these models are unlikely to be as clear-cut if we allow for realistic real-time uncertainty in crisis probabilities and political constraints. From a policy perspective, the idea that time-varying sectoral tools will prevent the next systemic banking crisis may be overly optimistic.

Conclusion and Future Work

The main message of this chapter can be summarized as follows. Yes, the sectoral allocation of credit appears to play a role for understanding periods of financial instability. The policy implications, however, are far from clear. This is due to the combination of three factors: a limited understanding of why sectoral debt grows differently prior to crises; a lack of estimates on the elasticity of different credit types to policy tools; and the political economy factors inherent in restricting growth in credit to particular sectors.

I particularly want to highlight the gaps I see in our understanding. Perhaps most importantly, we do not have a good sense of why exactly credit allocation matters. While we have a number of candidate theories, disentangling these in the data is tricky. This makes it difficult for policy makers to draw lessons from the historical record.

We also have surprisingly little direct insight about what actually happens in credit markets during booms on the micro level. The reason for this appears to be that we do not have sufficiently long time series that would allow for detailed insights, so the usual approach is to infer credit outcomes from "real" macroeconomic data. Thus, it is hard to disentangle sectoral allocation from other potentially correlated factors.

Finally, we know very little about what drives fluctuations in credit allocation. While we have a good idea about what predicts the size of credit markets, we do not know much about what drives their structure. The starting point for studying credit allocation clearly has to be more empirical groundwork.

REFERENCES

Adelino, Manuel, Antoinette Schoar, and Felipe Severino. 2012. Credit Supply and House Prices: Evidence from Mortgage Market Segmentation. NBER Working Paper 17832.

Aguiar, Mark, and Gita Gopinath. 2007. Emerging Market Business Cycles: The Cycle Is the Trend. Journal of Political Economy 115: 69–102.

Bahadir, Berrak, and Inci Gumus. 2016. Credit Decomposition and Business Cycles in Emerging Market Economies. Journal of International Economics 103: 250–62.

Barberis, Nicholas, Robin Greenwood, Lawrence Jin, and Andrei Shleifer. 2018. Extrapolation and Bubbles. Journal of Financial Economics 129 (2): 203–27.

Baron, Matthew, Emil Verner, and Wei Xiong. 2021. Banking Crises without Panics. Quarterly Journal of Economics 136 (1): 51–113.

Behn, Markus, Rainer Haselmann, and Vikrant Vig. 2016. The Limits of Model-Based Regulation. Working Paper Series 1928, European Central Bank.

Bernanke, Ben S., Mark Gertler, and Simon Gilchrist. 1999. The Financial Accelerator in a Quantitative Business Cycle Framework. In J. B. Taylor and M. Woodford, eds., Handbook of Macroeconomics, 1: 1341–93. Oxford: Elsevier.

Bianchi, Javier. 2011. Overborrowing and Systemic Externalities in the Business Cycle. American Economic Review 101 (7): 3400–3426.

Bianchi, Javier, and Enrique G. Mendoza. 2018. Optimal Time-Consistent Macroprudential Policy. Journal of Political Economy 126 (2): 588–634.

Bloomberg. 2019. Powell Says Leveraged Lending Isn't Posing a Crash Threat. Available at https://www.bloomberg.com/news/articles/2019-05-20/leveraged-lending-isn-t-posing-crash-threat-fed-chairman-says.

Bordo, Michael, Barry Eichengreen, Daniela Klingebiel, and Maria Soledad Martinez-Peria. 2001. Is the Crisis Problem Growing More Severe? Economic Policy 16 (32): 52–82.

Bordo, Michael D., and Christopher M. Meissner. 2016. Fiscal and Financial Crises. NBER Working Paper 22059.

Borio, Claudio, Enisse Kharroubi, Christian Upper, and Fabrizio Zampolli. 2016. Labour Reallocation and Productivity Dynamics: Financial Causes, Real Consequences. BIS Working Paper 534.

Braun, Matías. 2005. Financial Contractability and Asset Hardness. Available at https://ssrn.com/abstract=2522890.

Braun, Matías, and Borja Larrain. 2005. Finance and the Business Cycle: International, Inter-industry Evidence. Journal of Finance 60 (3): 1097–1128.

Büyükkarabacak, Berrak, and Neven T. Valev. 2010. The Role of Household and Business Credit in Banking Crises. Journal of Banking and Finance 34 (6): 1247–56.

Calvo, Guillermo A., Leonardo Leiderman, and Carmen M. Reinhart. 1996. Inflows of Capital to Developing Countries in the 1990s. Journal of Economic Perspectives 10 (2): 123–39.

Chakraborty, Indraneel, Itay Goldstein, and Andrew MacKinlay. 2018. Housing Price Booms and Crowding-out Effects in Bank Lending. Review of Financial Studies 31 (7): 2806–53.

Chaney, Thomas, David Sraer, and David Thesmar. 2012. The Collateral Channel: How Real Estate Shocks Affect Corporate Investment. American Economic Review 102 (6): 2381–2409.

Charles, Kerwin Kofi, Erik Hurst, and Matthew J. Notowidigdo. 2018. Housing Booms and Busts, Labor Market Opportunities, and College Attendance. American Economic Review 108 (10): 2947–94.

Di Maggio, Marco, and Amir Kermani. 2017. Credit-Induced Boom and Bust. Review of Financial Studies 30 (11): 3711–58.

Doerr, Sebastian. 2018. Collateral, Reallocation, and Aggregate Productivity: Evidence from the U.S. Housing Boom. Available at https://ssrn.com/abstract=3184162.

Eggertsson, Gauti B., and Paul Krugman. 2012. Debt, Deleveraging, and the Liquidity Trap: A Fisher-Minsky-Koo Approach. Quarterly Journal of Economics 127 (3): 1469–1513.

Farhi, Emmanuel, and Iván Werning. 2016. A Theory of Macroprudential Policies in the Presence of Nominal Rigidities. Econometrica 84 (5): 1645–1704.

Favara, Giovanni, and Jean Imbs. 2015. Credit Supply and the Price of Housing. American Economic Review 105 (3): 958–92.

Giovanni, Julian di, Sebnem Kalemli-Ozcan, Mehmet Fatih Ulu, and Yusuf Soner Baskaya. 2017. International Spillovers and Local Credit Cycles. NBER Working Paper 23149.

Gopinath, Gita, Sebnem Kalemli-Özcan, Loukas Karabarbounis, and Carolina Villegas-Sanchez. 2017. Capital Allocation and Productivity in South Europe. Quarterly Journal of Economics 132 (4): 1915–67.

Gorton, Gary, and Guillermo Ordoñez. 2020. Good Booms, Bad Booms. Journal of the European Economic Association 18 (2): 618–65.

Greenwood, Robin, and Samuel G. Hanson. 2013. Issuer Quality and Corporate Bond Returns. Review of Financial Studies 26 (6): 1483–1525.

Guerrieri, Veronica, and Guido Lorenzoni. 2017. Credit Crises, Precautionary Savings, and the Liquidity Trap. Quarterly Journal of Economics 132 (3): 1427–67.

Hsu, Po-Hsuan, Xuan Tian, and Yan Xu. 2014. Financial Development and Innovation: Cross-country Evidence. Journal of Financial Economics 112 (1): 116–35.

Hume, Michael, and Andrew Sentance. 2009. The Global Credit Boom: Challenges for Macroeconomics and Policy. Journal of International Money and Finance 28 (8): 1426–61. The Global Financial Crisis: Causes, Threats and Opportunities.

Jappelli, Tullio, and Marco Pagano. 1994. Saving, Growth, and Liquidity Constraints. The Quarterly Journal of Economics 109 (1): 83–109.

Jeanne, Olivier, and Anton Korinek. 2018. Managing Credit Booms and Busts: A Pigouvian Taxation Approach. Journal of Monetary Economics 107(C): 2–17.

Jones, Callum, Virgiliu Midrigan, and Thomas Philippon. 2018. Household Leverage and the Recession. IMF Working Papers 18/194.

Jordà, Òscar, Moritz Schularick, and Alan M. Taylor. 2015a. Betting the House. Journal of International Economics 96 (S1): 2–18.

———. 2015b. Leveraged Bubbles. Journal of Monetary Economics 76 (S): 1–20.

Justiniano, Alejandro, Giorgio E. Primiceri, and Andrea Tambalotti. 2019. Credit Supply and the Housing Boom. Journal of Political Economy 127 (3): 1317–50.

Kalantzis, Yannick. 2015. Financial Fragility in Small Open Economies: Firm Balance Sheets and the Sectoral Structure. Review of Economic Studies 82 (3): 1194–1222.

Khorrami, Paymon. 2019. The Risk of Risk-Sharing: Diversification and Boom-Bust Cycles. Available at http://papers.paymonkhorrami.com/JMP_twoKmodel_new.pdf.

Kindleberger, C. P. 1978. Manias, Panics, and Crashes: A History of Financial Crises. New York: Basic Books.

Kiyotaki, Nobuhiro, and John Moore. 1997. Credit Cycles. Journal of Political Economy 105 (2): 211–48.

Korinek, Anton, and Alp Simsek. 2016. Liquidity Trap and Excessive Leverage. American Economic Review 106 (3): 699–738.

Krishnamurthy, Arvind, and Tyler Muir. 2017. How Credit Cycles across a Financial Crisis. NBER Working Paper 23850.

Kroszner, Randall S., Luc Laeven, and Daniela Klingebiel. 2007. Banking Crises, Financial Dependence, and Growth. Journal of Financial Economics 84 (1): 187–228.

Laeven, Luc, and Fabian Valencia. 2018. Systemic Banking Crises Revisited. IMF Working Papers 18/206.

Lorenzoni, Guido. 2008. Inefficient Credit Booms. Review of Economic Studies 75 (3): 809–33.

Mendoza, Enrique G. 2002. Credit, Prices, and Crashes: Business Cycles with a Sudden Stop. In Sebastian Edwards and Jeffrey A. Frankel, eds., Preventing Currency Crises in Emerging Markets, 335–92. Chicago: University of Chicago Press.

Mian, Atif, Amir Sufi, and Emil Verner. 2017. Household Debt and Business Cycles Worldwide. Quarterly Journal of Economics 132 (4): 1755–1817.

———. 2020. How Do Credit Supply Shocks Affect the Real Economy? Evidence from the United States in the 1980s. Journal of Finance 75: 949–94.

Müller, Karsten. 2018. Credit Markets Around the World, 1910–2014. Available at https://ssrn.com/abstract=3259636.

———. 2019. Electoral Cycles in Macroprudential Regulation. Available at https://ssrn.com/abstract=3159086.

Müller, Karsten, and Emil Verner. 2020. Credit Allocation and Macroeconomic Fluctuations. Available at https://ssrn.com/abstract=3781981.

Penikas, Henry. 2015. History of Banking Regulation as Developed by the Basel Committee on Banking Supervision 1974–2014 (Brief Overview). Banco De Espana Estabilidad Financiera 28: 9–47.

Radelet, Steven, Jeffrey D. Sachs, Richard N. Cooper, and Barry P. Bosworth. 1998. The East Asian Financial Crisis: Diagnosis, Remedies, Prospects. Brookings Papers on Economic Activity 1: 1–90.

Rajan, Raghuram, and Rodney Ramcharan. 2015. The Anatomy of a Credit Crisis: The Boom and Bust in Farm Land Prices in the United States in the 1920s. American Economic Review 105 (4): 1439–77.

Rajan, Raghuram G., and Luigi Zingales. 1998. Financial Dependence and Growth. American Economic Review 88 (3): 559–86.

Reinhart, Carmen M., and Kenneth S. Rogoff. 2009. This Time Is Different: Eight Centuries of Financial Folly. Princeton, NJ: Princeton University Press.

Reis, Ricardo. 2013. The Portuguese Slump and Crash and the Euro Crisis. NBER Working Paper 19288.

Rognlie, Matthew, Andrei Shleifer, and Alp Simsek. 2018. Investment Hangover and the Great Recession. American Economic Journal: Macroeconomics 10 (2): 113–53.

Schmitt-Grohé, Stephanie, and Martín Uribe. 2016. Downward Nominal Wage Rigidity, Currency Pegs, and Involuntary Unemployment. Journal of Political Economy 124 (5): 1466–1514.

Schneider, Martin, and Aaron Tornell. 2004. Balance Sheet Effects, Bailout Guarantees and Financial Crises. Review of Economic Studies 71 (3): 883–913.

Tornell, Aaron, and Frank Westermann. 2005. Boom-Bust Cycles and Financial Liberalization. Vol. 1. Cambridge, MA: MIT Press.

Wall Street Journal. 2019. SEC Chief Raises Concerns About Risky Lending. April 8, 2019. Available at https://www.wsj.com/articles/sec-chief-raises-concerns-about-risky-lending-11554739726.

Comment by Orsola Costantini

PREDICTION OR PREVENTION?
WHEN THE BEST IS THE ENEMY OF THE GOOD

The idea that instability in certain sectors has broad repercussions on the rest of the economy is not new, and business cycle theorists have often identified the construction sector as of particular interest (Hansen 1941). That was reflected in policy early on: the American New Deal reform of the housing and mortgage sectors was intended to solve a grave social problem but also to reduce instability. As Alvin Hansen wrote, "if the Federal Housing Administration (with the reforms it has instituted in the house mortgage field) had been in the picture [in the 1920s], the housing boom and collapse would certainly have been less violent" (Hansen 1946, 69). Those measures were an integral

Orsola Costantini is economic affairs officer at the United Nations Conference on Trade and Development (UNCTAD). The opinions expressed here are her own.

part of a larger package that deeply reconfigured the financial environment, protecting deposits and limiting the risk that systemically relevant institutions could take on.

But when it came to eroding financial controls, the United States again led the pack, from the 1970s onward (Sherman 2009). In the long aftermath of the greatest financial crisis since 1929, support for seriously binding regulation has not been able to command sustained political majorities; in fact the subsequent administrations have repeatedly weakened the already soft Dodd-Frank Wall Street Reform and Consumer Protection Act of 2010 (Kane 2012; Ferguson et al. 2017).

Academia, of course, reflects society, and the very term "financial regulation" sounds too much like "financial repression" for most scholars to argue in its favor without extreme caution.[1] Karsten Müller deals with that caution. But his conclusions, by his own admission, are not reassuring.

His chapter searches for a solution to the difficult trade-off between efficiency of a regulation (in terms of cost and enforceability) and the desire to keep under tight control only what is strictly necessary, when it is necessary. The problem can be summarized as follows. The creation of new liquidity through credit is the condition for an economy to grow and, eventually, to reduce any outstanding debt previously created. Accordingly, financial repression would fail at accommodating the necessities of a growing economy. However, credit expansion can bear some dangers, especially in a globalized context. In order to prevent or reduce the risk of crisis and at the same time allow finance to unleash all its positive powers, argues Müller, it is useful to understand what characteristics or thresholds of debt can be a reliable warning sign and whether we can condition public action to those triggers.

If the total amount of credit is too vague a variable, there is an ocean of distinctions that we can use to segment it: quality of the borrowers, quality of the lenders (profitability, quality of the assets), types of credit (bonds, loans, mortgages, stock lending), fixed or flexible interest payments, maturity, and so forth.

But, as Müller points out, for policy purposes we also need to find an efficient minimum degree of disaggregation that allows us to find the right balance between discipline and elasticity (Mehrling 2010, 2016). In fact, complex and lengthy regulations are costly and easy to circumvent. In addition, Müller maintains, we need to consider the possibility that the political process itself is not fully transparent or objective.

---

1. Exceptions of course exist, as plenty of research commissioned by the Institute for New Economic Thinking testifies.

Müller asks whether credit expansion in specific sectors, relative to others, might help predict financial crises. He presents evidence drawn from a new, more comprehensive international data set, which confirms that credit growth in construction and, more broadly, the nontradable sectors is strongly associated with financial crises. In addition, he shows that the allocation of credit matters independently of the leverage. That is, *keeping the leverage constant*, he finds a significant association between crises and the increase in the *share* of debt allocated to nontradables, especially when at the expense of manufacturing. This he often styles a "reallocation" of credit, a point to which I will come back later.

The author himself cautions against concluding that "credit growth or changes in credit allocation to particular sectors are good forecasting variables for banking crises" (Müller 2019, 16). The same prudence, in his view, should also apply to other indicators, such as the publicly available real-time warning indicators of banking crises issued by the Bank for International Settlements.

The temptation to overstate our predictive capacity might arise due to recent scientific support given to the idea that time-varying regulation (particularly debt taxes) might be closer to optimal than the simpler time-invariant version. This idea seems problematic to Müller, who suggests that time-varying policies might be especially subject to political interference. He provides evidence that macroprudential policies targeting specific sectors are subject to electoral cycles across countries. In conclusion, he argues that, while sectoral allocation of credit seems to provide useful insights about financial fragility, it is still far too difficult to assess risks in real time and have a clear understanding of the economic and political forces at play.

Müller's chapter addresses a very important research question in an original way and crucially includes considerations about the political aspects of regulatory architectures.

However, one problem needs to be mentioned right away: we need to be careful when we use the term "reallocation" of credit, which alludes to a loanable funds approach in which savings are given before the production process begins and can be allocated in the capital market (Rogers 1989). "Allocation" better describes the empirical problem under discussion, which is perfectly compatible with an endogenous money approach.

The matter is not just semantic or purely pertaining to abstract theory: the correct definition is preconditional to understanding the role and behavior of the main actors in the system, the credit and financial institutions. It is also indispensable, among other reasons, in order to distinguish between long-term debt accumulation and speculative credit cycles. In fact, if credit availability is given, as in the loanable funds approach, its allocation to one sector tends to crowd out other uses. Hence, for instance, a reallocation of credit toward households would crowd out more productive uses. A similar reasoning would apply to employment, if we assume it is full in equilibrium (Mian et al. 2017).

On the contrary, from an endogenous money perspective, it is always possible for firms and capitalists, and even more so for the government, to make an autonomous investment decision that can support growth and reduce the leverage (see, e.g., the contributions in Deleplace and Nell 1996). It is only when job-creating enterprises are not initiated, particularly in a context of tight public budgets and wage repression, that debt accumulates in domestic or foreign sectors and becomes the condition for the others to accumulate wealth. Whether the resulting savings at each time are invested or hoarded (or taxed as in Mian 2019), the amount of credit that banks can issue remains independent of those savings. Hence the problem of the long-term accumulation of debt, rather than depending on credit allocation, excess savings, or financial regulation, becomes one of employment, welfare, and industrial policy (including trade), that is, one of sustainable growth. This might be relevant to Müller's finding that there has been "a secular shift within corporate credit towards real estate and service industries" (Müller 2019, 12).

These situations of imbalance can last a long time, depending on institutional conditions, as we can grasp from two examples: household debt in the United States (Cynamon and Fazzari 2008; Jordà et al. 2016) and the intra-Eurozone imbalances between Germany and the southern countries (O'Connor 2015; Celi et al. 2018).

In fact, the issue must be kept separate from that of speculative credit cycles. Credit booms, as we know, can emerge regardless of the underlying income distribution. Their severity depends mostly on the type of regulation in place which can create a phenomenon recently defined as excess elasticity or banking glut (Borio and Disyatat 2011; Shin 2011). That concerns international gross capital flows which are unrelated to the countries' current account imbalances and instead depend on the leverage cycle of global banks. In this context, speculation does not per se prevent productive firms to rise, but it drags them down when the more highly leveraged ones fall (Minsky 1992).

Of course, the two problems are interconnected: speculative credit flows are especially disruptive in economies with a small financial sector and an underdeveloped industrial sector: the "*big fish, small pond*" problem (Haldane 2011). Speculation finds opportunities in heavily imbalanced economies and, more generally, tends to discourage more long-term productive investment as less profitable (Akyüz 1993; Lazonick and O'Sullivan 2000; Griffith-Jones 2000; Seccareccia 2012). However, recognizing the distinction can help discriminate between national economic policy challenges and those related to the global financial system.

A second point concerns the policy discussion. First, I agree that we should avoid relying too much on discretionary interventions or, for that matter, on automatic temporary reactions based on technical assessments. Those are usually opaque and biased. For instance, market risk is not even among the priorities spelled out by the banking supervision authority of the European Central Bank in its annual reports, which reflects how the stress tests are built (Giacché 2017; Kane 2017). Indeed, not only are economists incapable of predicting crises (Eichengreen 1999; Grabel 2003), but they themselves are subject to conflicts of interest and ideological bias (Carrick-Hagenbarth and Epstein 2012; Javdani and Chang 2018).

In fact, the political problem does not only pertain to the electoral cycle; it also involves lobbying, legal corruption (such as "revolving doors"), and illegal corruption (Blanis i Vidal et al. 2012; Ferguson and Johnson 2013). Indeed, if we do not need to tax the wealthy to reduce the indebtedness of the economy, it would certainly help to do so if we want to reduce their political influence through money (though that alone cannot solve the problem). All this adds to the difficulty of enforcing global harmonization.

Let me also mention that it seems hard to give too much credit to the cited theoretical proof that simple time-invariant rules are suboptimal based on Dynamic Stochastic General Equilibrium (DSGE) models where banks do not even appear, and which focus on one specific type of regulation (cited in Müller 2019). Those models have been widely and convincingly criticized for their identification problems and, more generally, for their treatment of banking and finance (Romer 2016; Rogers 2018).

Second, concentrating on single markets is an interesting option, but it has some limitations, especially on a world scale. To mention an example made in the chapter, the German housing market is tightly regulated and in fact, in the 2000s, house prices followed the international cycle hardly at all (Celi et al. 2018). However, this did not save Germany from the international banking crisis entirely, since its banks were exposed and contributed to the bubbles elsewhere. German banks had to be rescued repeatedly, and they still represent a risk for global stability (Kane 2017). On the other hand, the fact that the housing sector was protected limited the deflationary consequences of the crisis domestically. The U.S. savings and loans institutions make another good example: subject to many limitations to the advantage of the loan takers, they did not survive the unstable financial conditions and monetary policy shock of the late 1970s and early 1980s (Black et al. 1995).

Hence, if a focus on particularly vulnerable and economically and socially relevant sectors such as housing or social security and pensions is important (Baker and Weisbrot 2002; Ghilarducci 2013), the approach to financial stability and to sustainability should be broader, reflecting the distinctions between long-term debt accumulation and speculation made above. The Great Depression was overcome by massive public deficit spending (sadly, mostly during World War II): from that we should learn that regulation must be accompanied by other economic policies that reduce the sources of uncertainty that make the economy fragile and prone to economic, not only financial, crises (Seccareccia 2011; Dow 2015). This means also that the international financial architecture should protect the space for these stabilizing and growth-friendly domestic policies and, more generally, for the accountability of economic policies by the political body.

REFERENCES

Akyüz, Yilmaz. 1993. Financial Liberalization: The Key Issues. United Nations Conference on Trade and Development Discussion Papers 56. Available at https://www.southcentre.int /wp-content/uploads/2013/08/REP1_FInancial-Liberalization_EN.pdf.

Baker, Dean, and Mark Weisbrot. 2002. The Role of Social Security Privatization in Argentina's Economic Crisis. Center for Economic and Policy Research (CEPR) publications. Available at https://www.cepr.net/documents/publications/argentina_2002_04.pdf.

Black, K. William, Kitty Calavita, and Henry N. Pontell. 1995. The Savings and Loan Debacle of the 1980s: White-Collar Crime or Risky Business? Law and Politics 17 (1): 23–55. https://doi .org/10.1111/j.1467-9930.1995.tb00138.x

Blanes i Vidal, Jordi, Mirko Draca, and Christian Fons-Rosen. 2012. Revolving Door Lobbyists. American Economic Review 102 (7): 3731–48. https://doi.org/10.1257/aer.102.7.3731.

Borio, Claudio, and Piti Disyatat. 2011. Global Imbalances and the Financial Crisis: Link or No Link? Bank for International Settlements Working Papers 346. Available at https://www.bis .org/publ/work346.pdf.

Carrick-Hagenbarth, Jessica, and Gerald A. Epstein. 2012. Dangerous Interconnectedness: Economists' Conflicts of Interest, Ideology and Financial Crisis. Cambridge Journal of Economics 36 (1): 43–63. https://doi.org/10.1093/cje/ber036.

Celi, Giuseppe, Andrea Ginzburg, Dario Guarascio, and Annamaria Simonazzi. 2018. Crisis in the European Monetary Union: A Core-Periphery Perspective. London: Routledge.

Cynamon, Barry Z., and Steven M. Fazzari. 2008. Household Debt in the Consumer Age: Source of Growth/Risk of Collapse. Capitalism and Society 3 (3): article 3. https//doi.org /10.2202/1932-0213.1037. Available at http://citeseerx.ist.psu.edu/viewdoc/download?doi =10.1.1.1076.4657&rep=rep1&type=pdf.

Deleplace, Ghislain, and Nell Edward. 1996. Money in Motion. London: Palgrave Macmillan.

Dow, Sheila C. 2015. Addressing Uncertainty in Economics and the Economy. Cambridge Journal of Economics 39 (1): 33–47. http://doi.org/10.1093/cje/beu022.

Eichengreen, Barry. 1999. Toward a New International Financial Architecture: A Practical Post-Asia Agenda. Washington, DC: Institute for International Economics.

Ferguson, Thomas, and Robert Johnson. 2013. When Wolves Cry "Wolf": Systemic Financial Crises and the Myth of the Danaid Jar. In Louis-Philippe Rochon and Mario Seccareccia, eds., Monetary Economies of Production Banking and Financial Circuits and the Role of the State, 73–98. Cheltenham, UK: Edward Elgar Publishing.

Ferguson, Thomas, Paul Jorgensen, and Jie Chen. 2017. Fifty Shades of Green: High Finance, Political Money, and the U.S. Congress. Working Paper at the Roosevelt Institute.

Ghilarducci, Teresa. 2013. Pension Policies to Minimize Future Economic Crises. In Martin H. Wolfson and Gerald A. Epstein, eds., Handbook of the Political Economy of Financial Crises, 677–95. Oxford: Oxford University Press.

Giacché, Vladimiro. 2017. The Real Cause of the Italian Bank Bailouts and Euro Banking Troubles. Available at https://www.ineteconomics.org/perspectives/blog/the-real-cause-of-the-italian -bank-bailouts-and-euro-banking-troubles.

Grabel, Ilene. 2003. Averting Crisis? Assessing Measures to Manage Financial Integration in Emerging Economies. Cambridge Journal of Economics 27 (3): 317–36. https://doi.org/10 .1093/cje/27.3.317.

Griffith-Jones, Stephany. 2000. International Capital Flows to Latin America. Serie Reformas Ecó- nomicas, Naciones Unidas Comisión Económica para América Latina y el Caribe (CEPAL) 55.

Haldane, Andy G. 2011. The Big Fish, Small Pond Problem. Paper presented at the Institute for New Economic Thinking Annual Conference, Bretton Woods, New Hampshire, April 9.

Hansen, Alvin H. 1941. Fiscal Policy and Business Cycles. New York: W. W. Norton. Available at https://archive.org/details/in.ernet.dli.2015.499543/page/n3.

———. 1946. Notes on Mints' Paper on Monetary Policy. Review of Economics and Statistics 28 (2): 69–74. https://doi.org/10.2307/1927351.

Javdani, Mohsen, and Ha-Joon Chang. 2019. Who Said or What Said? Estimating Ideological Bias in Views among Economists. Available at https://ssrn.com/abstract=3356309.

Jordà, Òscar, Moritz Schularick, and Alan M. Taylor. 2016. The Great Mortgaging: Housing Fi- nance, Crises and Business Cycles. Economic Policy 31 (85): 107–52. https://doi.org/10.1093 /epolic/eiv017.

Kane, Edward. 2012. Missing Elements in US Financial Reform: A Kübler-Ross Interpretation of the Inadequacy of the Dodd-Frank Act. Journal of Banking and Finance 36 (3): 654–61. https://doi.org/10.1016/j.jbankfin.2011.05.020.

———. 2017. Europe's Zombie Megabanks and the Differential Regulatory Arrangements That Keep Them in Play. Institute for New Economic Thinking Working Paper Series, no. 64.

Lazonick, William, and Mary O'Sullivan. 2000. Maximizing Shareholder Value: A New Ide- ology for Corporate Governance. Economy and Society 29 (1): 13–35. https://doi.org/10 .1080/030851400360541.

Mehrling, Perry. 2010. The New Lombard Street: How the Fed Became the Dealer of Last Resort. Princeton, NJ: Princeton University Press.

———. 2015. Elasticity and Discipline in the Global Swap Network. International Journal of Political Economy 44 (4): 311–24. https://doi.org/10.1080/08911916.2015.1129848.

Mian, Atif. 2019. How to Think about Finance? Paper presented at the 2019 NEXTGEN Confer- ence in New York.

Mian, Atif, Amir Sufi, and Emil Verner. 2017. How Do Credit Supply Shocks Affect the Real Economy? Evidence from the United States in the 1980s. NBER Working Paper 23802.

Minsky, Hyman. 1982. The Financial Instability Hypothesis. Jerome Levy Economics Institute Working Paper 74.

Müller, Karsten. 2019. Does Sectoral Allocation of Credit Matter for Financial Stability Risks? Paper presented at 2019 NEXTGEN Conference in New York.

O'Connell, Arturo. 2015. European Crisis: A New Tale of Center-Periphery Relations in the World of Financial Liberalization/Globalization? International Journal of Political Economy 44 (3): 174–95. https://doi.org/10.1080/08911916.2015.1035986.

Rogers, Colin. 1989. Money, Interest and Capital: A Study in the Foundations of Monetary Theory. Cambridge: Cambridge University Press.

———. 2018. The Conceptual Flaw in the Microeconomic Foundations of Dynamic Stochastic General Equilibrium Models. Review of Political Economy 30 (1): 1–12. https://doi.org/10.1080/09538259.2018.1442894.

Romer, Paul. 2016. The Trouble with Macroeconomics. Commons Memorial Lecture of the Omicron Delta Epsilon Society. Available at https://paulromer.net/the-trouble-with-macro/WP-Trouble.pdf.

Seccareccia, Mario. 2011. The Role of Public Investment as Principal Macroeconomic Tool to Promote Long-Term Growth: Keynes's Legacy. International Journal of Political Economy 40 (4): 62–82. https://doi.org/10.2753/IJP0891-1916400403.

Sherman, Matthew. 2009. A Short History of Financial Deregulation in the United States. Center for Economic and Policy Research paper. Available at https://cepr.net/documents/publications/dereg-timeline-2009-07.pdf.

Shin, Hyun S. 2012. Global Banking Glut and Loan Risk Premium. Mundell-Fleming Lecture, presented at the 2011 IMF Annual Research Conference, November 10–11, 2011, and Princeton University, January 2012.

Index

306